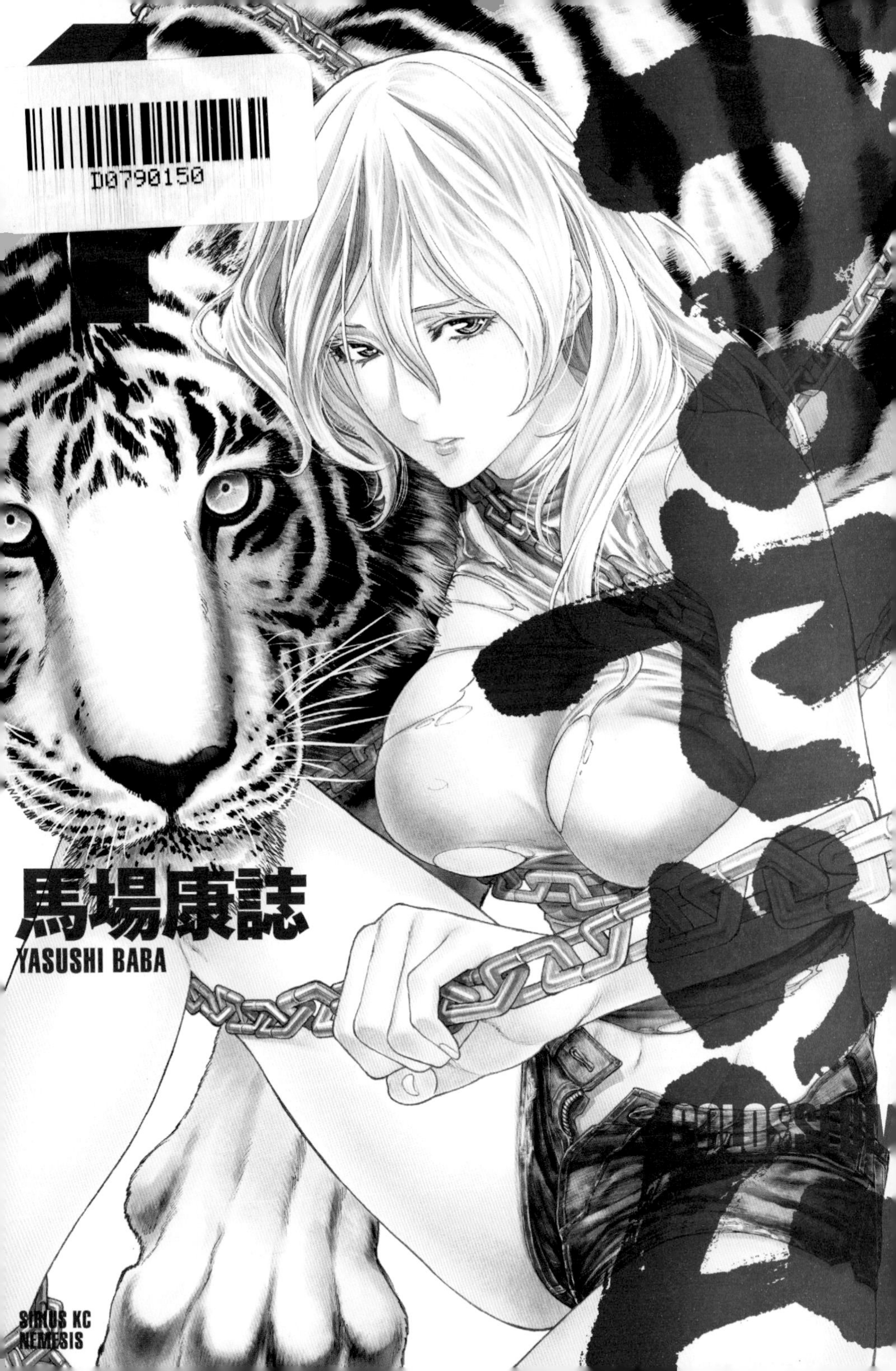
馬場康誌
YASUSHI BABA
SIRIUS KC
NEMESIS

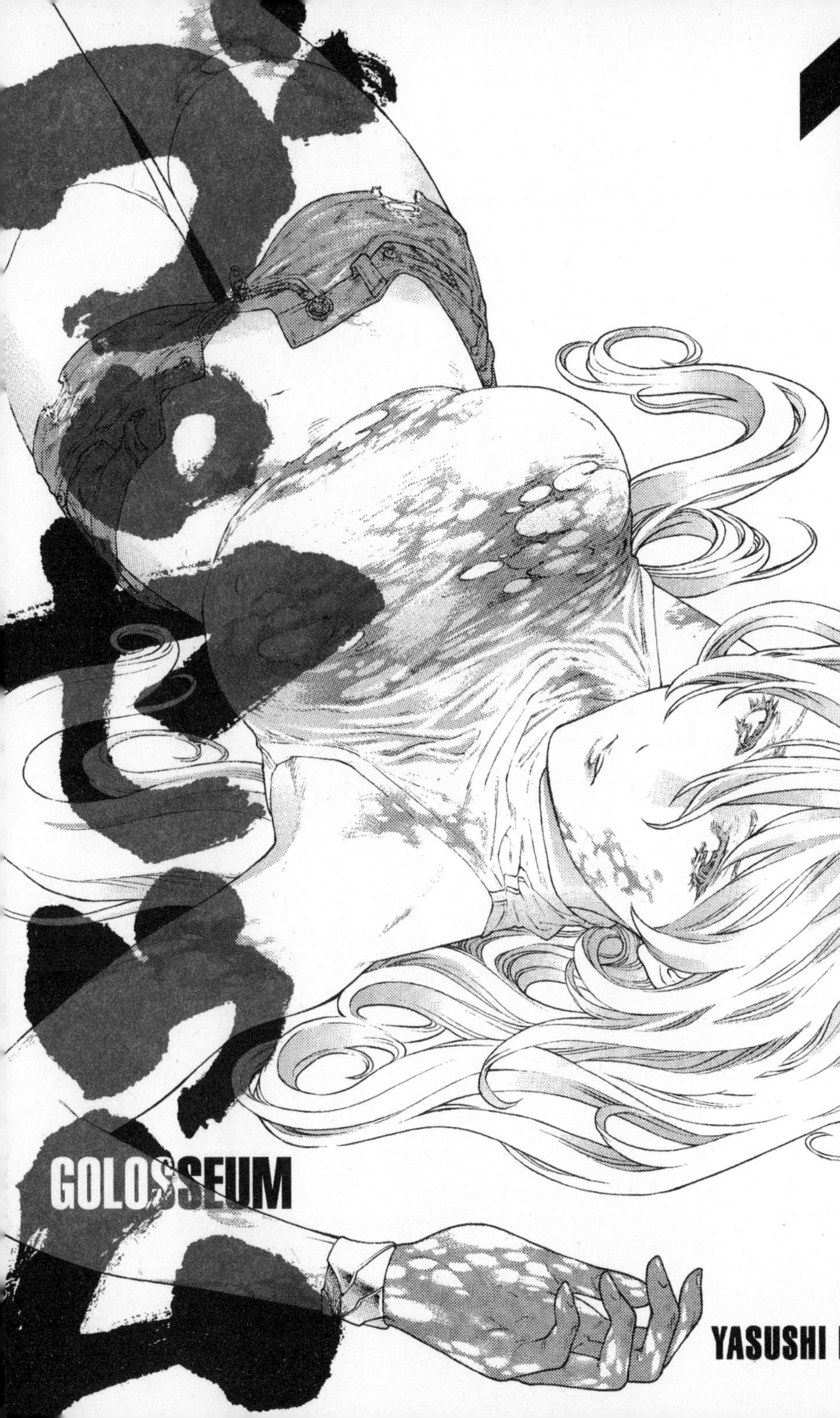
GOLOSSEUM

1

YASUSHI BABA

BANNER: Makoto (sincerity)

The year: 1869.

BOOM

BOOM

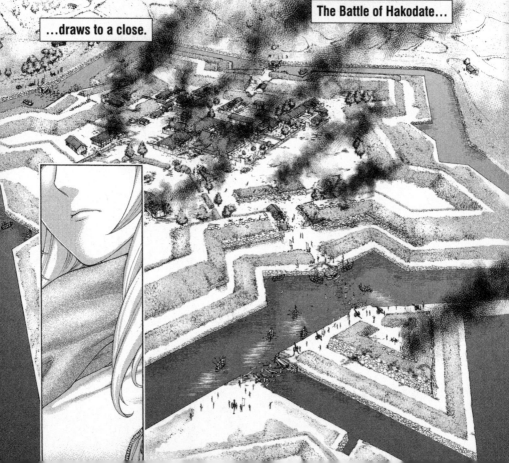

The Battle of Hakodate...

...draws to a close.

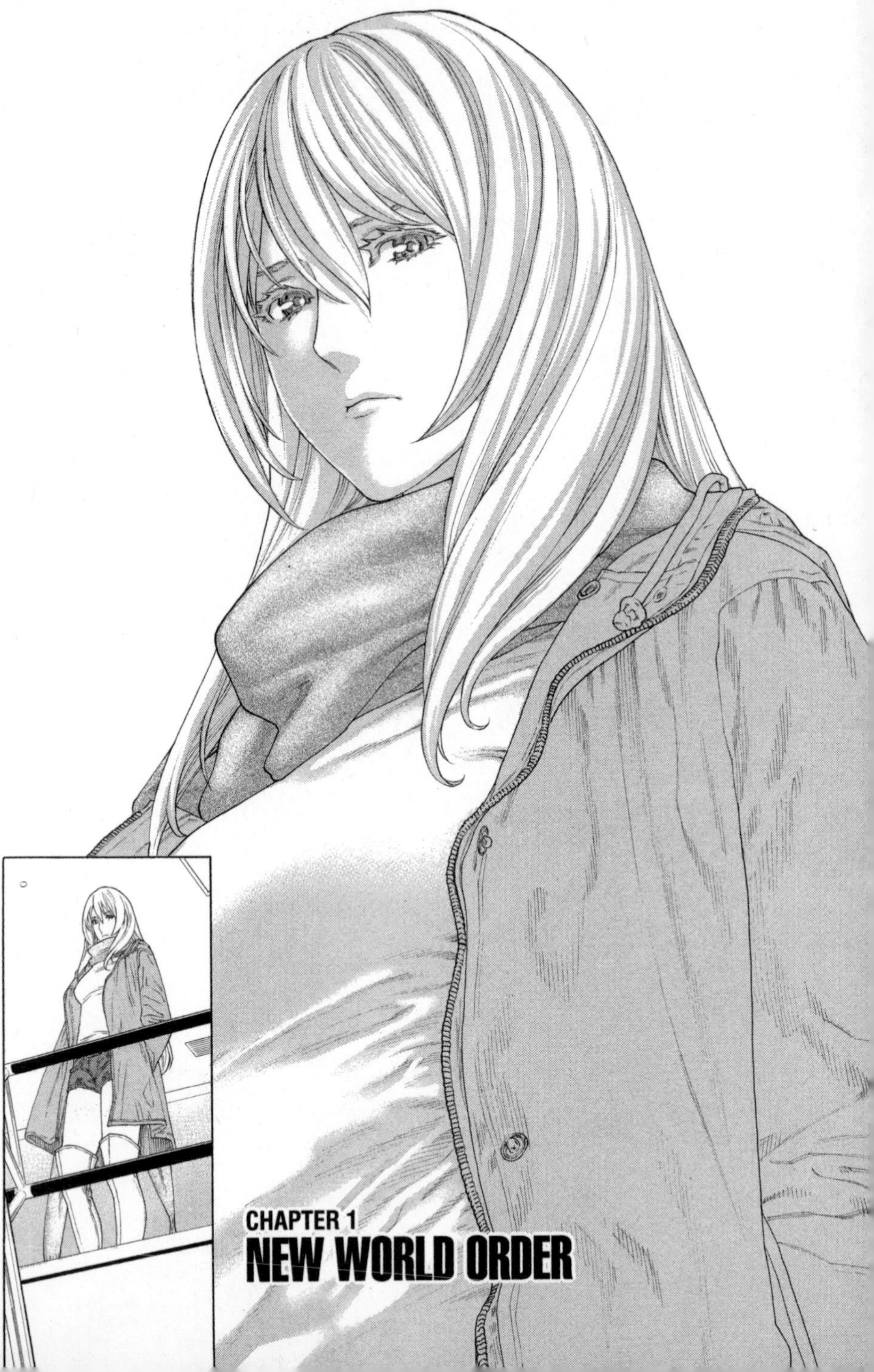
CHAPTER 1
NEW WORLD ORDER

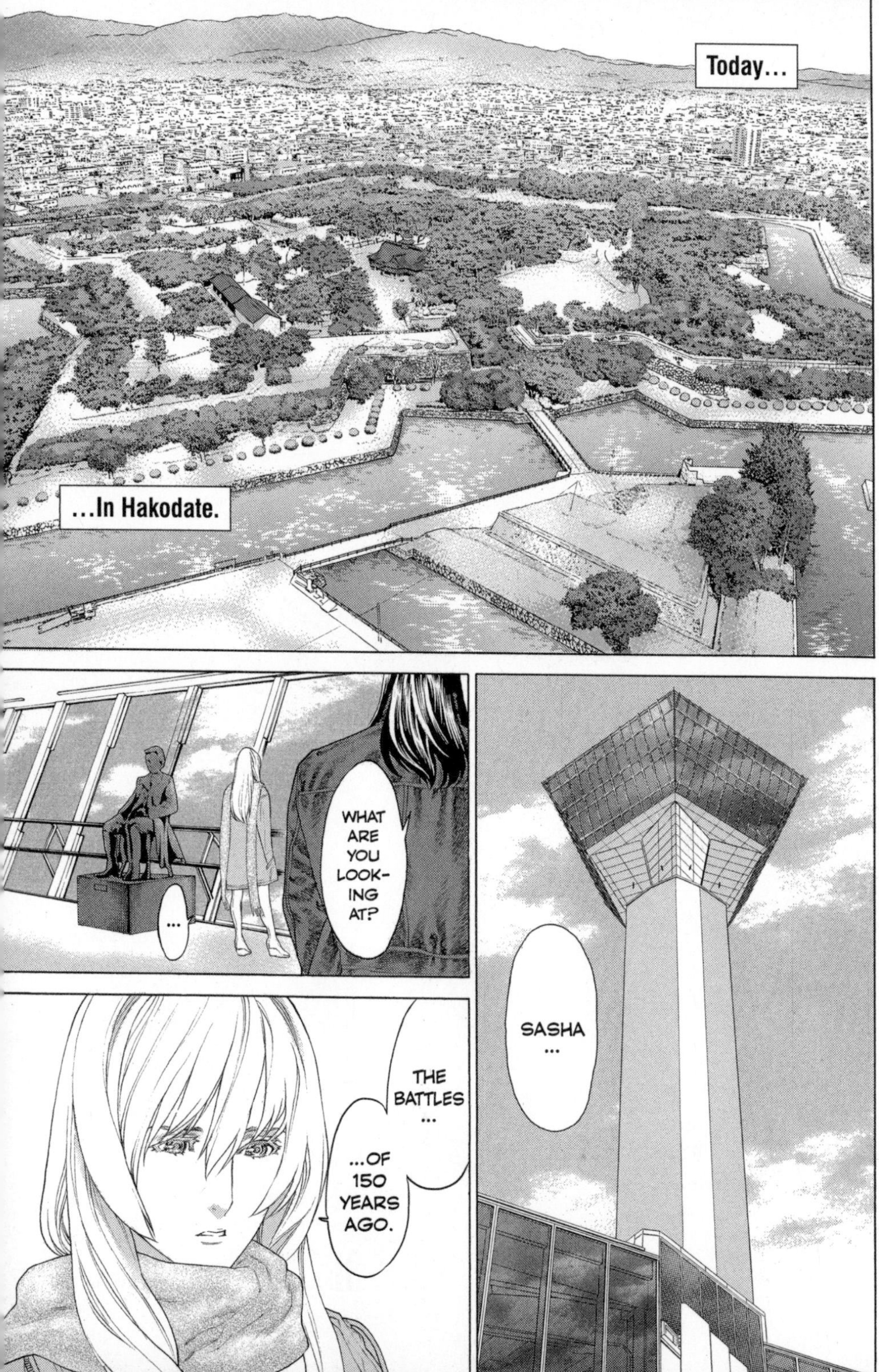
Today…
…In Hakodate.
SASHA …
WHAT ARE YOU LOOKING AT?
…
THE BATTLES …
…OF 150 YEARS AGO.

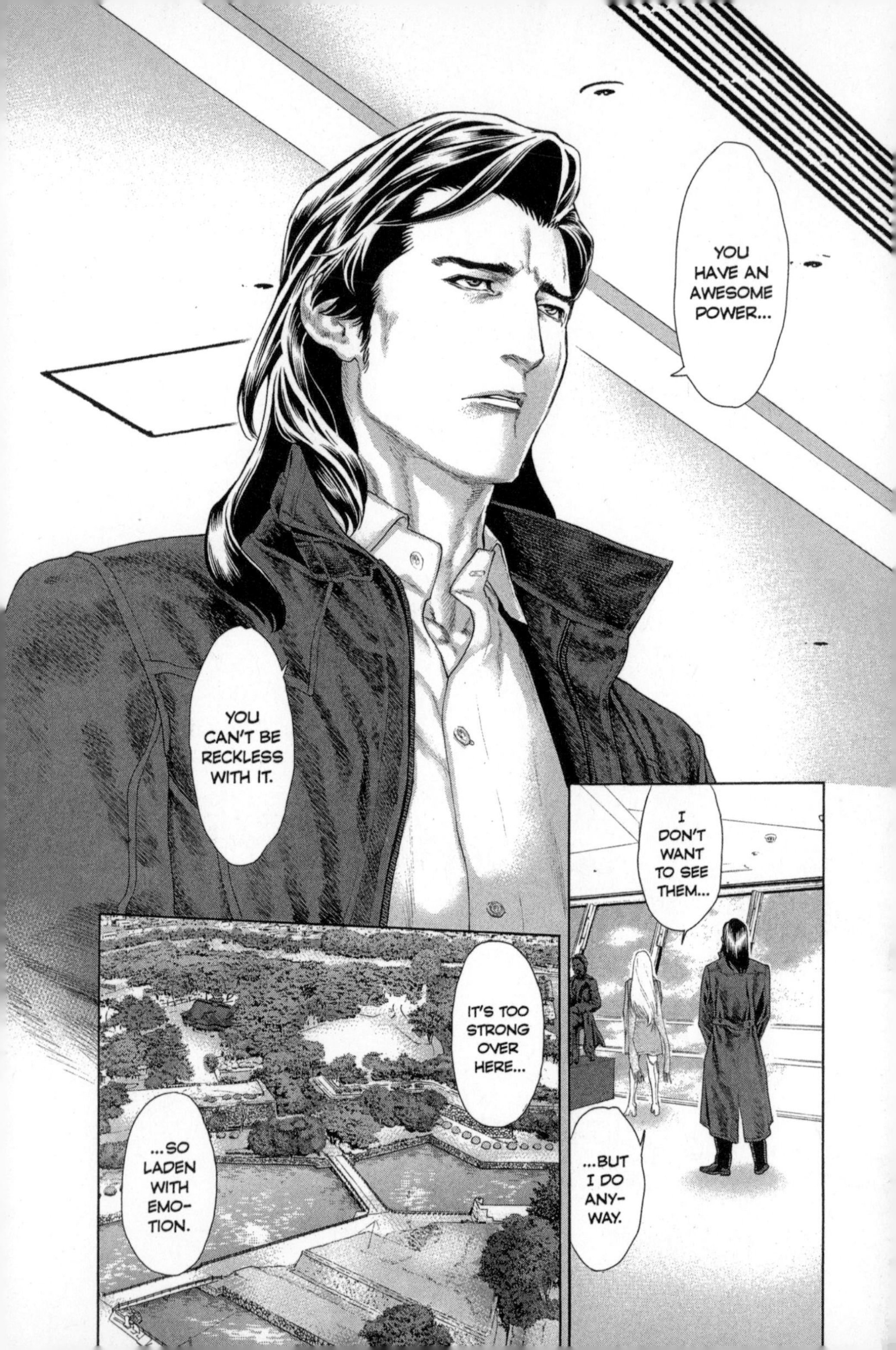
YOU HAVE AN AWESOME POWER...
YOU CAN'T BE RECKLESS WITH IT.
I DON'T WANT TO SEE THEM...
...BUT I DO ANY-WAY.
IT'S TOO STRONG OVER HERE...
...SO LADEN WITH EMO-TION.

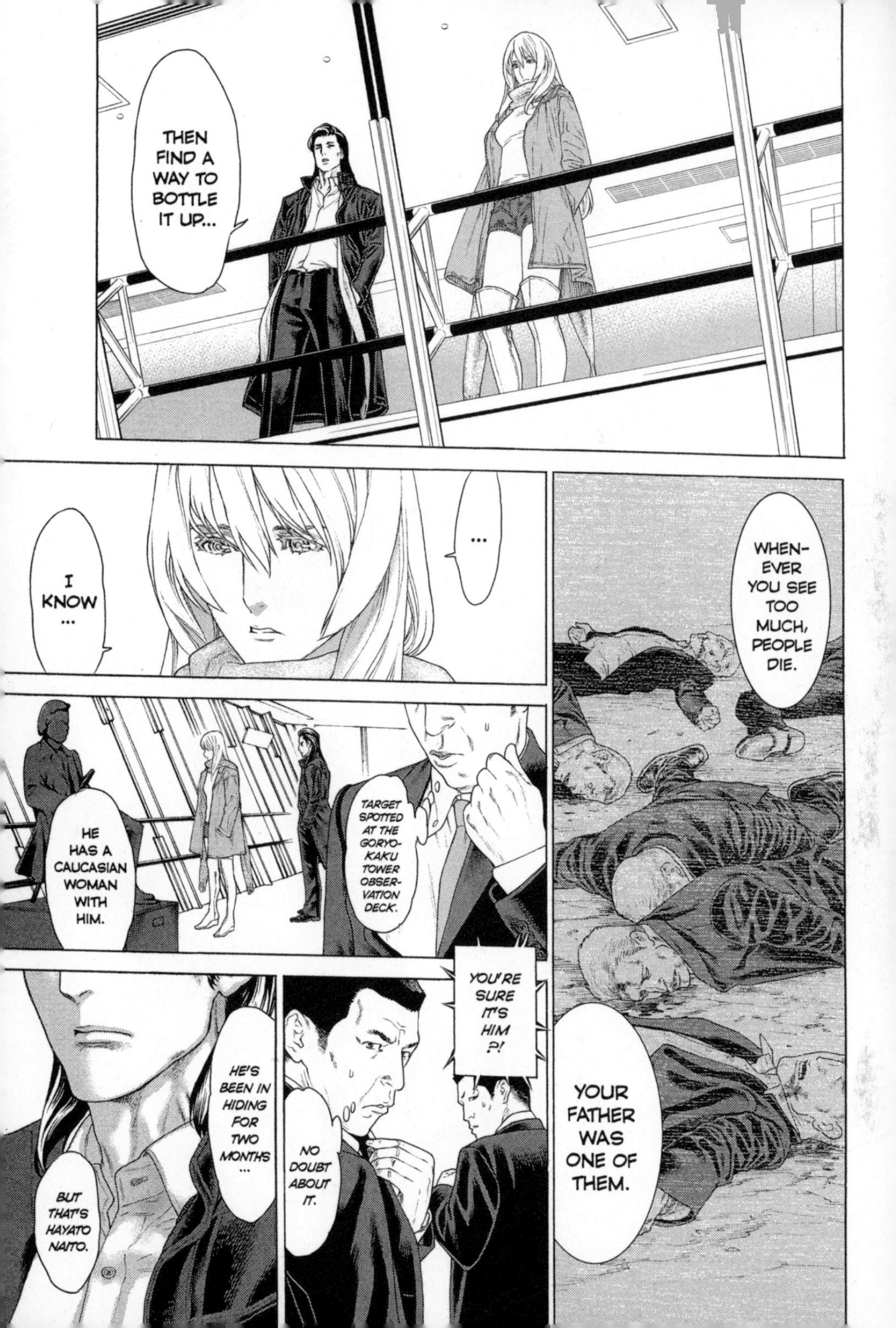
THEN FIND A WAY TO BOTTLE IT UP...
WHENEVER YOU SEE TOO MUCH, PEOPLE DIE.
YOUR FATHER WAS ONE OF THEM.
...
I KNOW ...
TARGET SPOTTED AT THE GORYOKAKU TOWER OBSERVATION DECK.
HE HAS A CAUCASIAN WOMAN WITH HIM.
YOU'RE SURE IT'S HIM ?!
NO DOUBT ABOUT IT.
HE'S BEEN IN HIDING FOR TWO MONTHS ...
BUT THAT'S HAYATO NAITO.

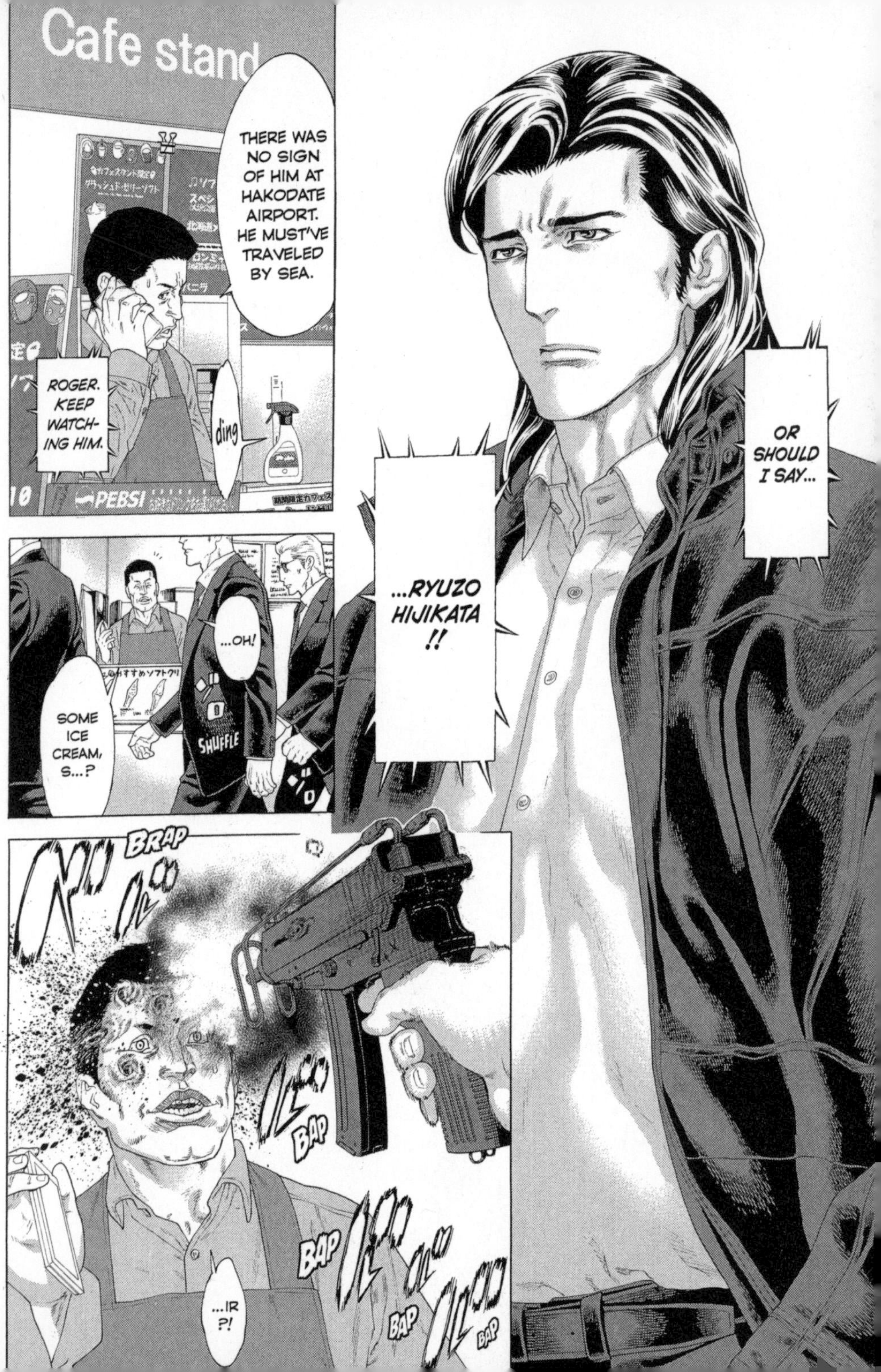
OR SHOULD I SAY...
...RYUZO HIJIKATA !!
Cafe stand
THERE WAS NO SIGN OF HIM AT HAKODATE AIRPORT. HE MUST'VE TRAVELED BY SEA.
ding
ROGER. KEEP WATCHING HIM.
PEBSI
...OH!
SHUFFLE
SOME ICE CREAM, S...?
BRAP
BAP
BAP
...IR ?!
BAP
BAP

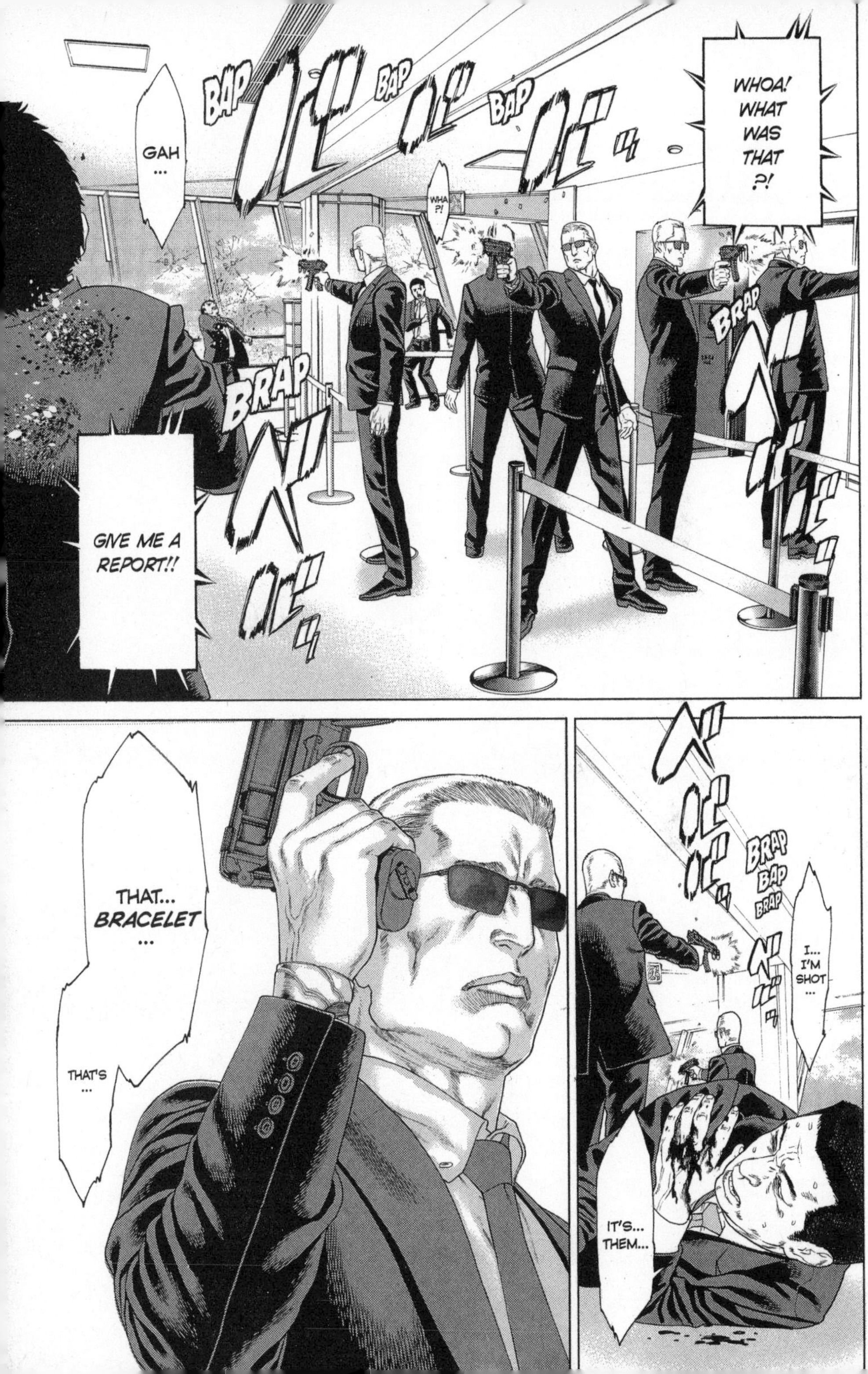
WHOA! WHAT WAS THAT?!
BRAP
BAP
BAP
BAP
WHA?!
GAH...
BRAP
GIVE ME A REPORT!!
BRAP
BAP
BRAP
I... I'M SHOT...
IT'S... THEM...
THAT... BRACELET...
THAT'S...

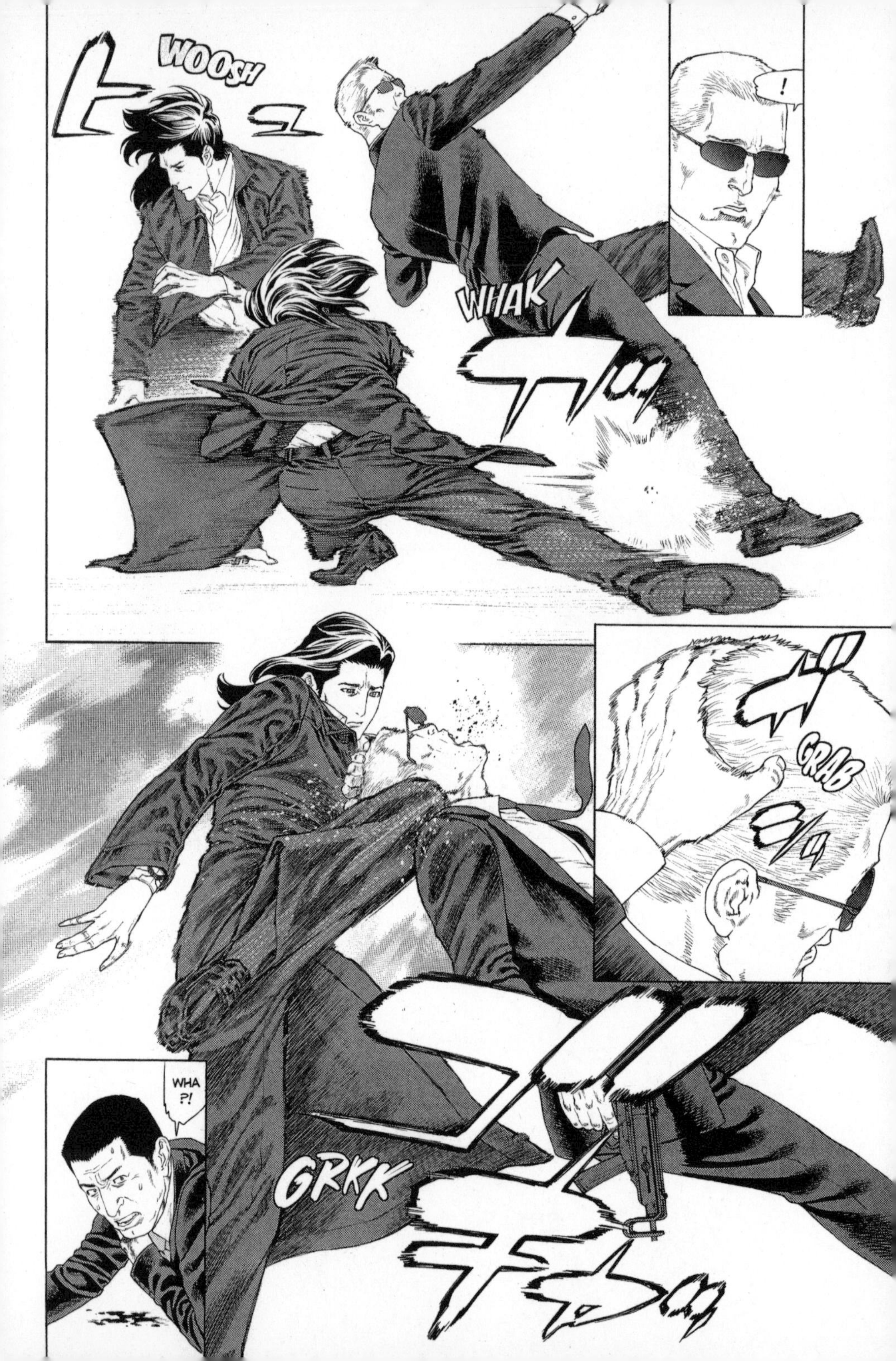
!
WOOSH
WHAK
GRAB
GRKK
WHA ?!

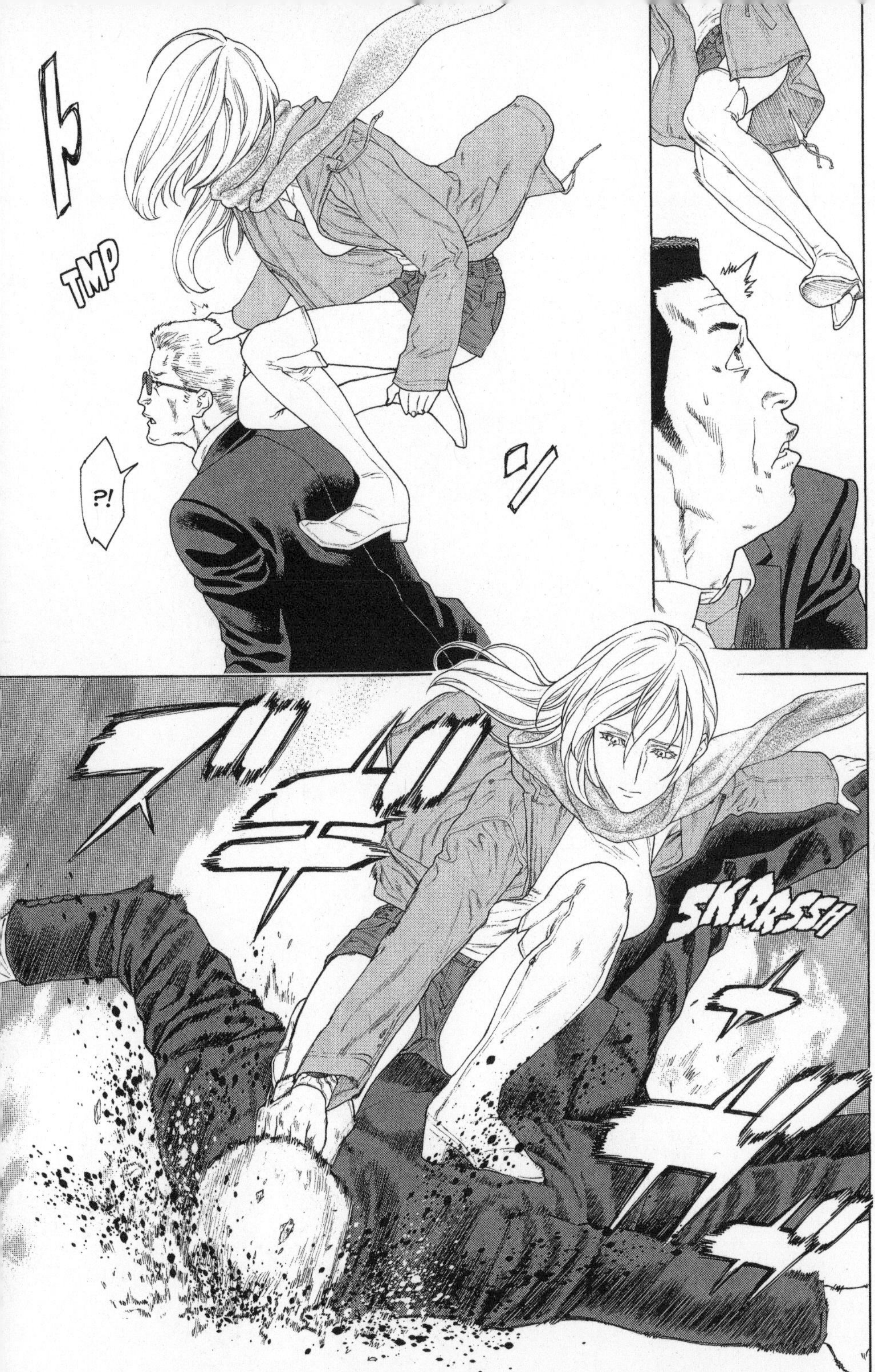
TMP
?!
SKRRSSH

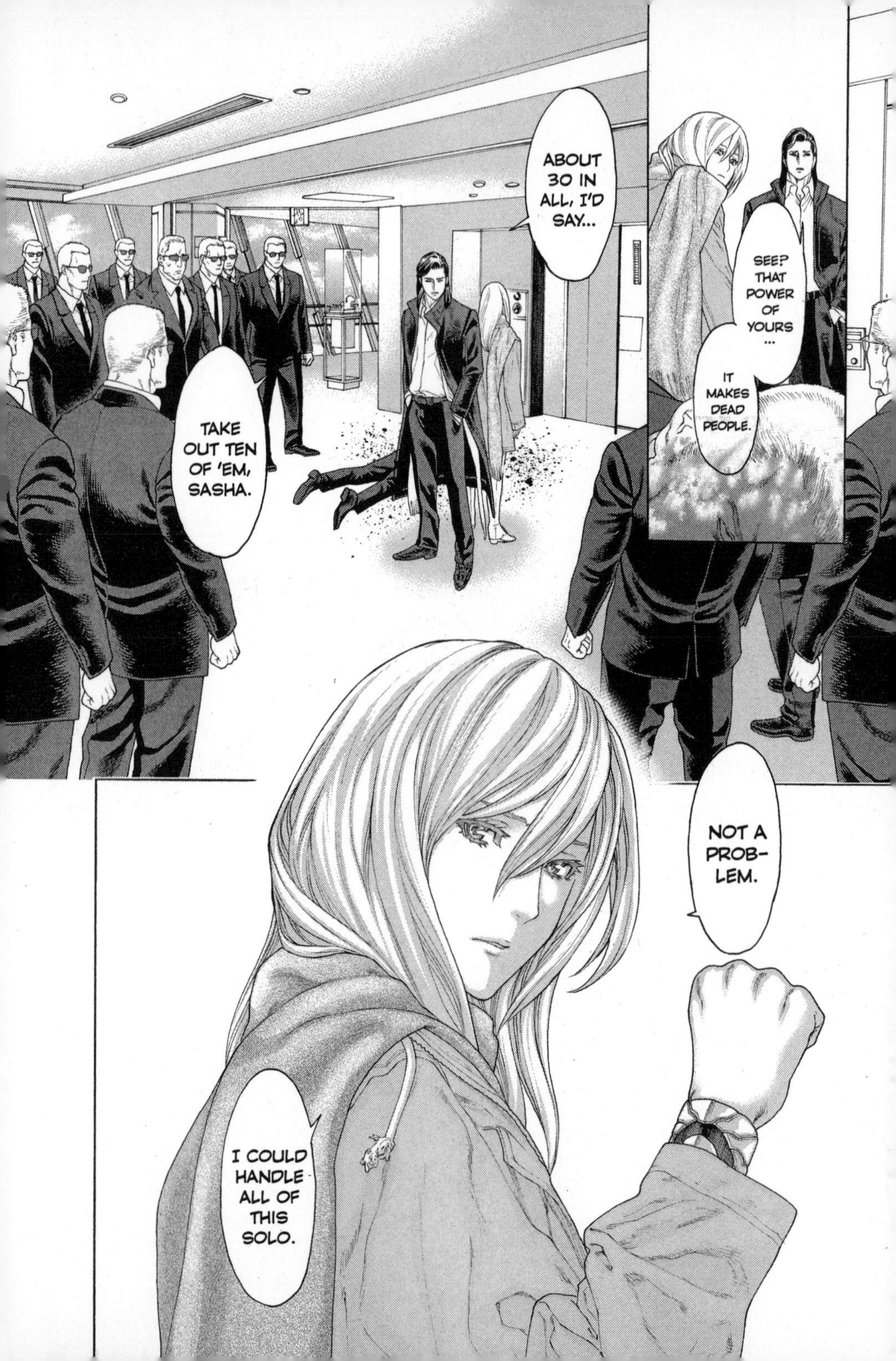
SEE? THAT POWER OF YOURS ...
IT MAKES DEAD PEOPLE.
ABOUT 30 IN ALL, I'D SAY...
TAKE OUT TEN OF 'EM, SASHA.
NOT A PROB-LEM.
I COULD HANDLE ALL OF THIS SOLO.

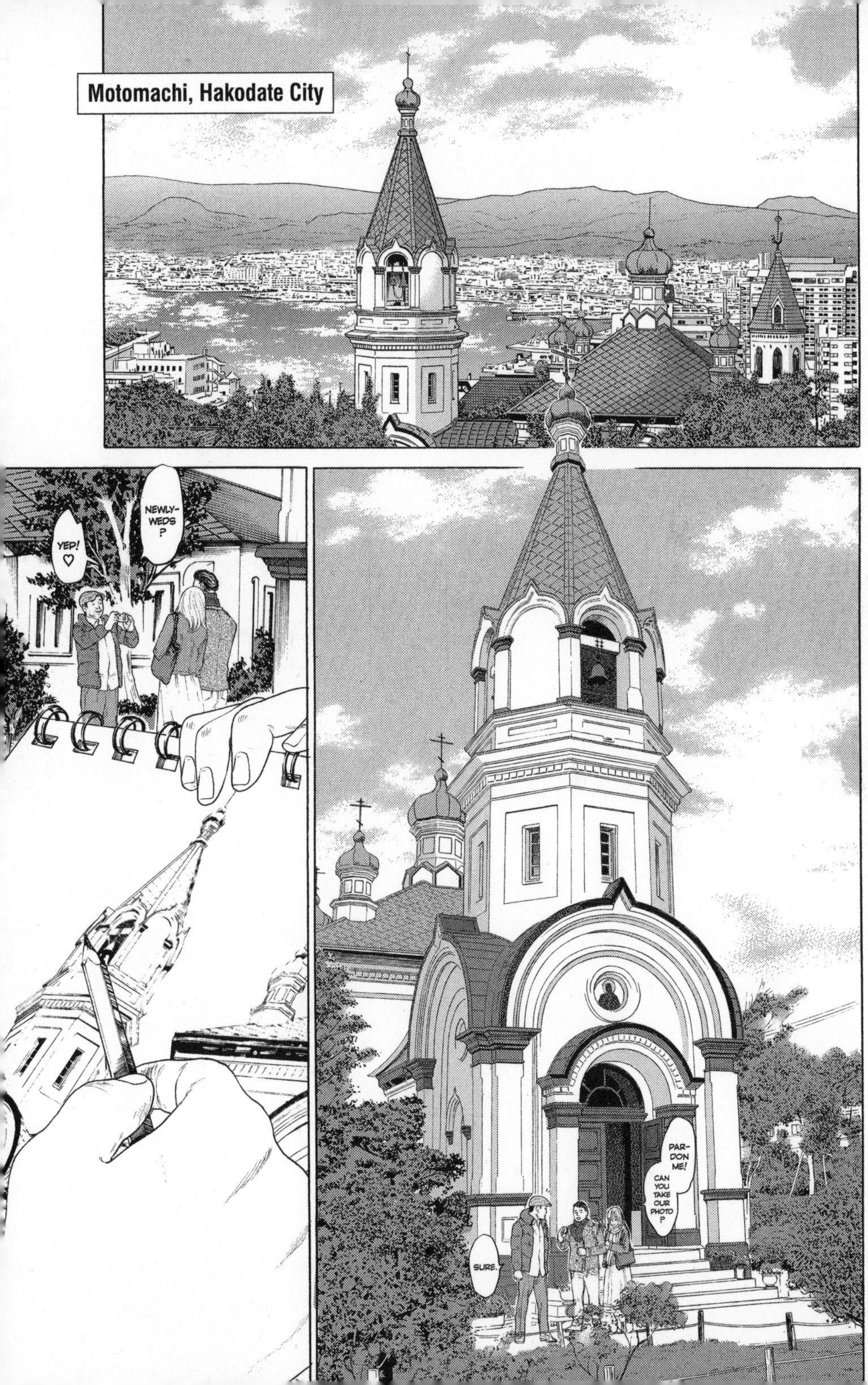
Motomachi, Hakodate City
PARDON ME!
CAN YOU TAKE OUR PHOTO?
SURE.
NEWLY-WEDS?
YEP! ♥

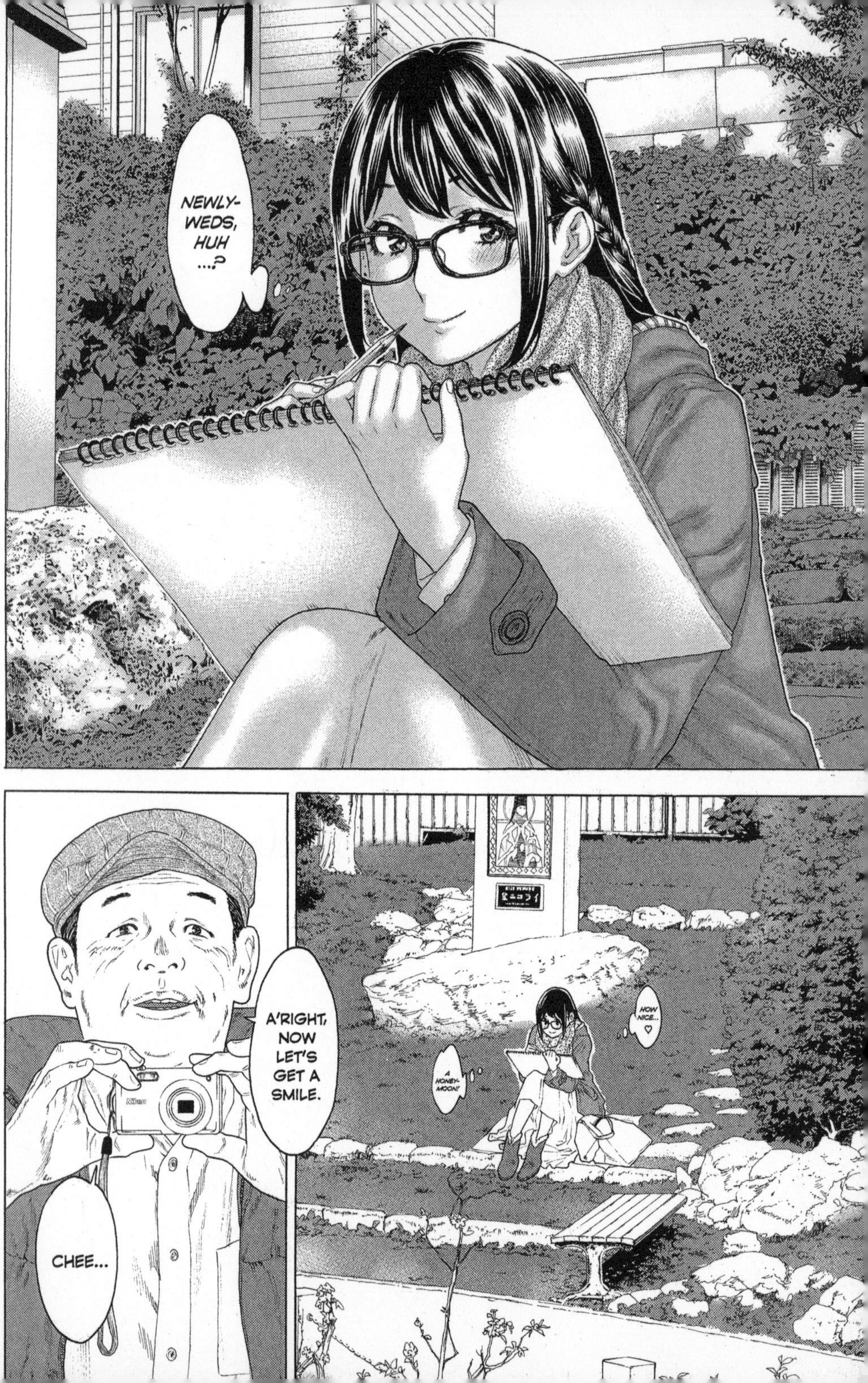
NEWLY-WEDS, HUH ...?
HOW NICE... ♡
A HONEY-MOON!
A'RIGHT, NOW LET'S GET A SMILE.
CHEE...

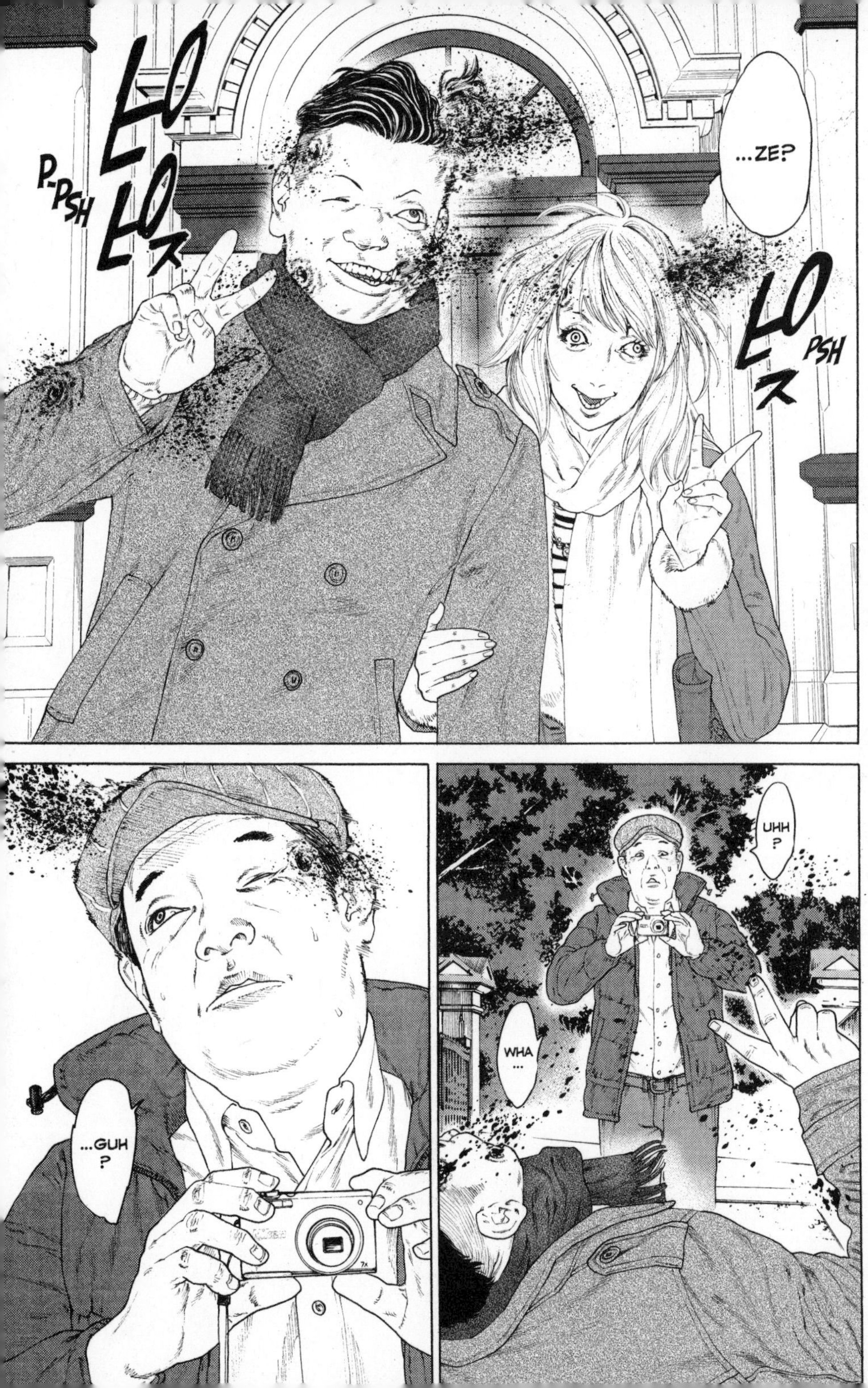
...ZE?
PSH
P-PSH
UHH ?
WHA ...
...GUH ?

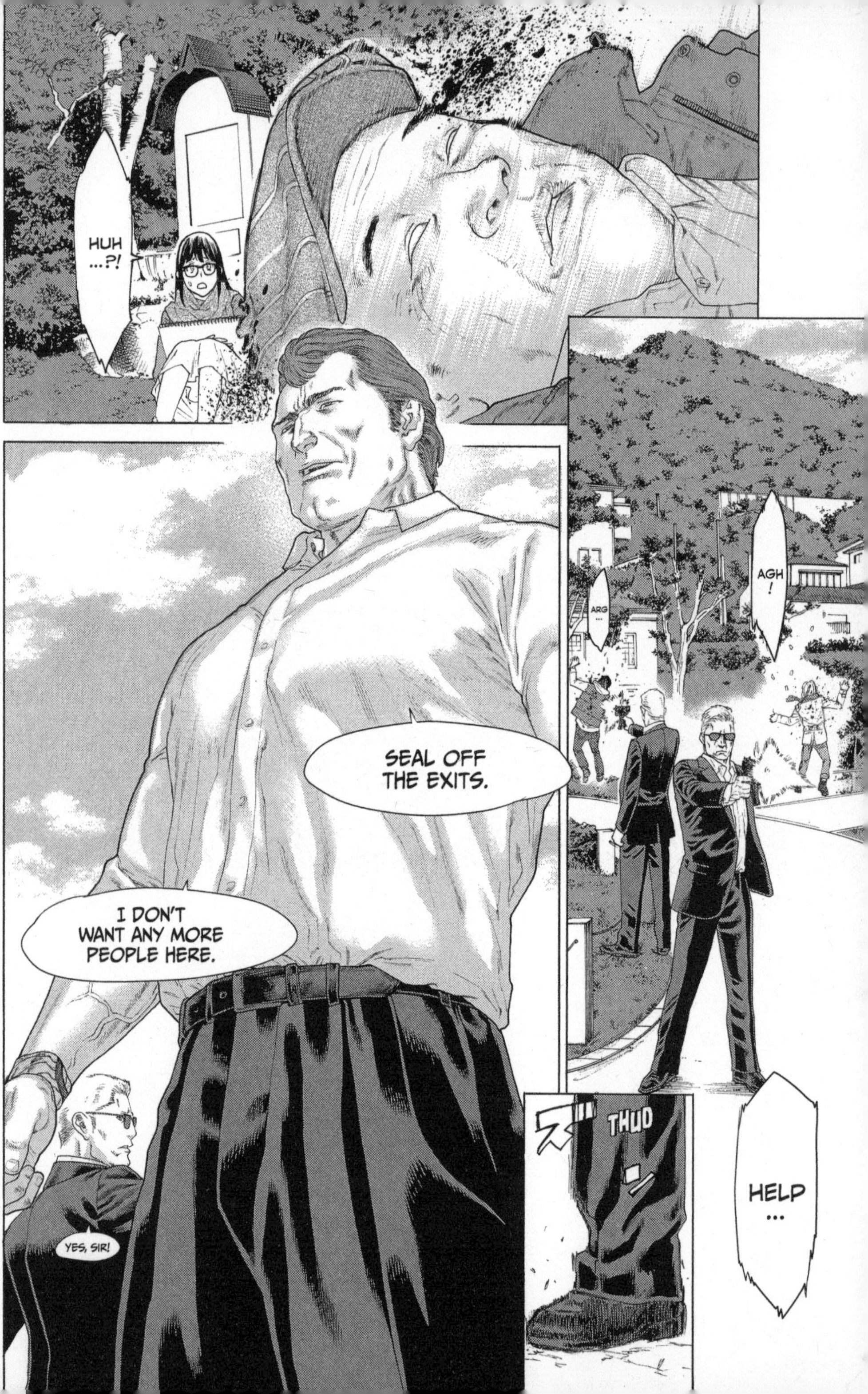
HUH ...?!
AGH!
ARG...
THUD
HELP...
SEAL OFF THE EXITS.
I DON'T WANT ANY MORE PEOPLE HERE.
YES, SIR!

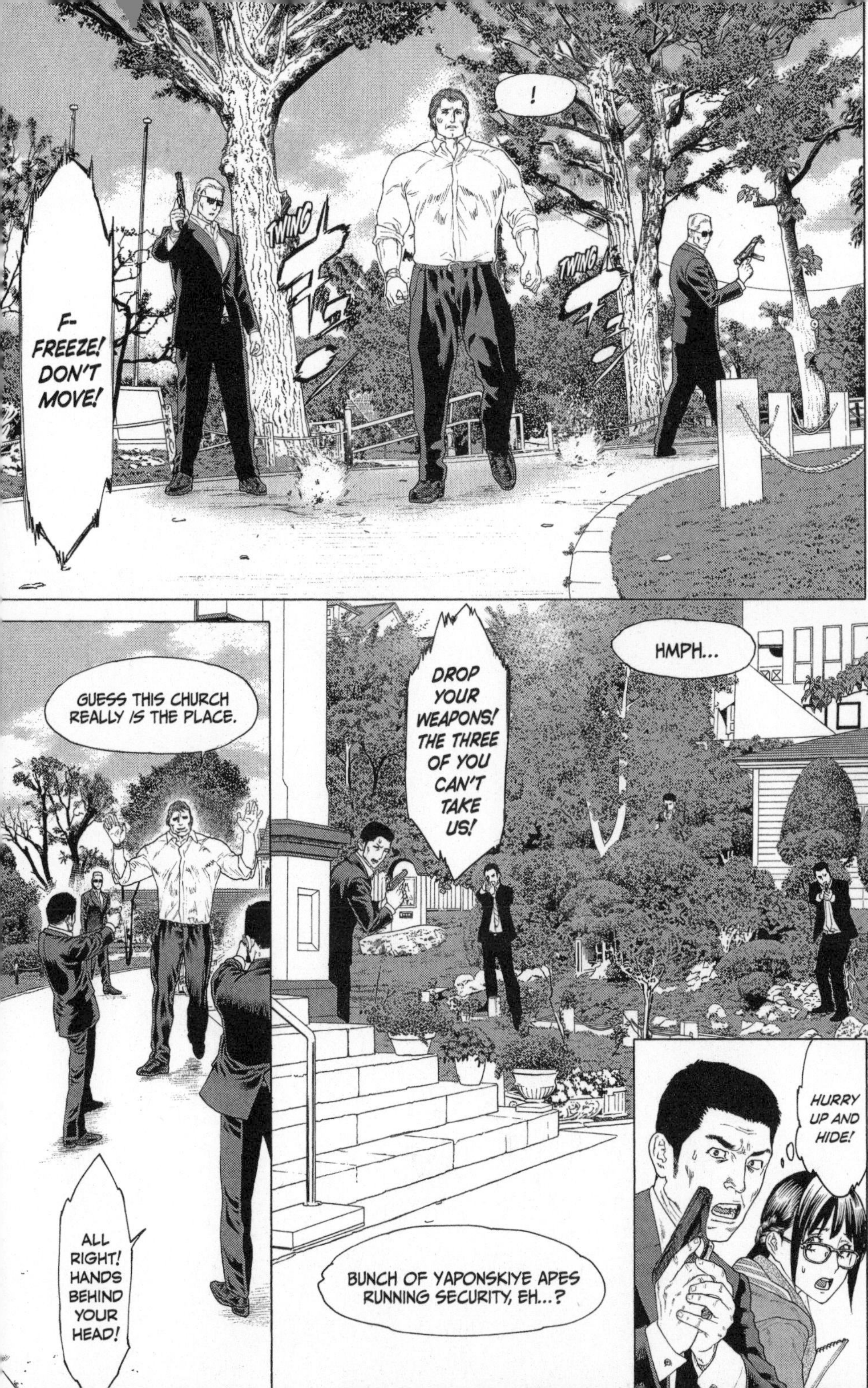
!
TWING
TWING
F-FREEZE! DON'T MOVE!
HMPH...
DROP YOUR WEAPONS! THE THREE OF YOU CAN'T TAKE US!
HURRY UP AND HIDE!
BUNCH OF YAPONSKIYE APES RUNNING SECURITY, EH...?
GUESS THIS CHURCH REALLY IS THE PLACE.
ALL RIGHT! HANDS BEHIND YOUR HEAD!

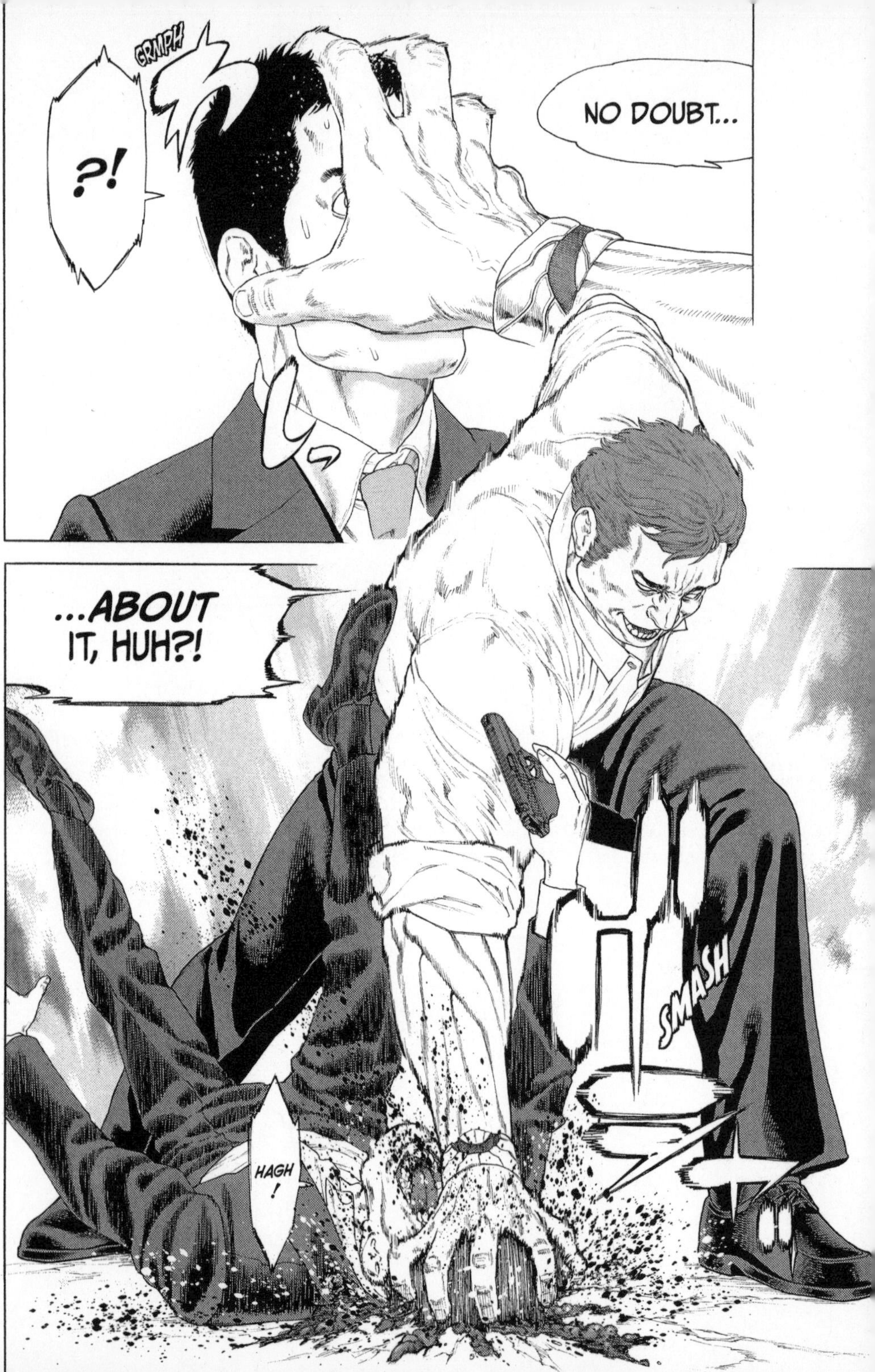
NO DOUBT...
GRMPH
?!
...ABOUT IT, HUH?!
SMASH
HAGH!

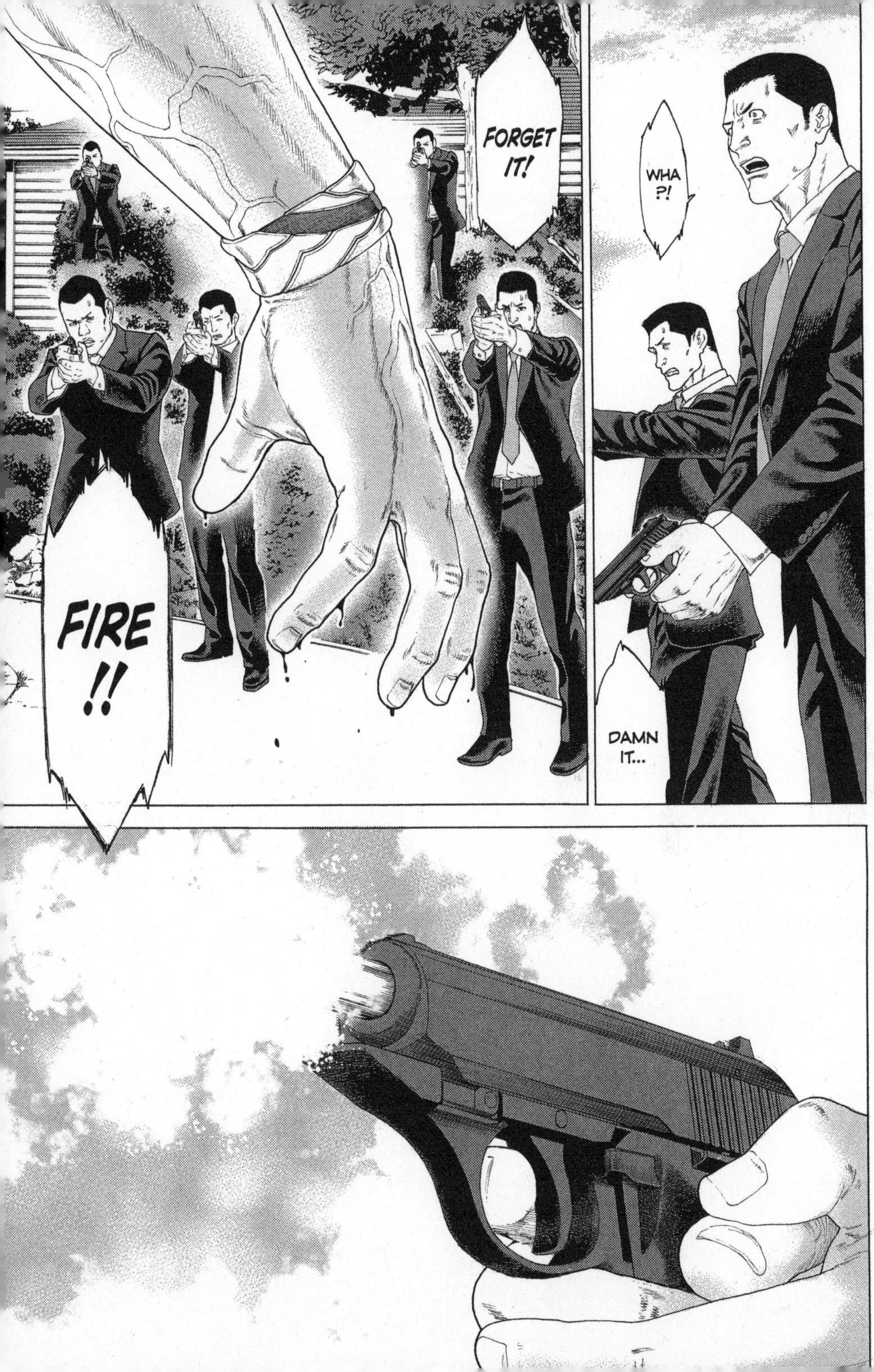
WHA?!
DAMN IT...
FORGET IT!
FIRE!!

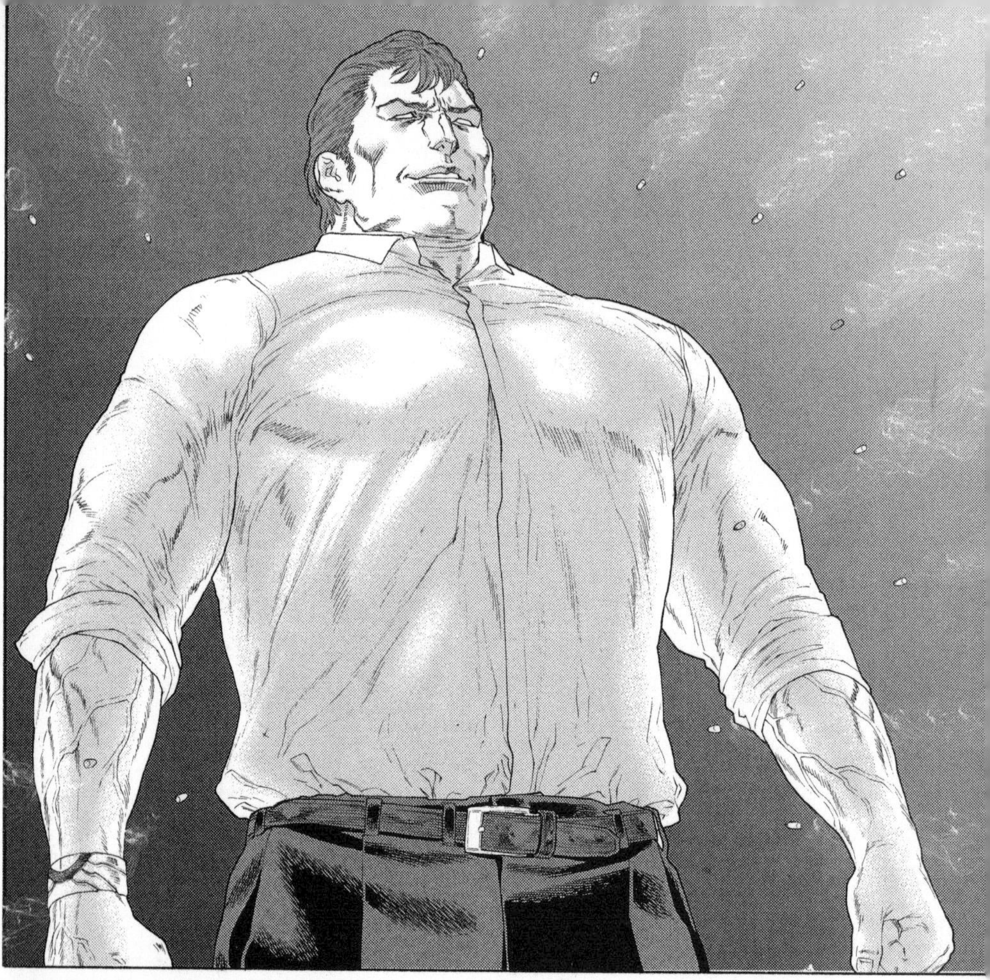
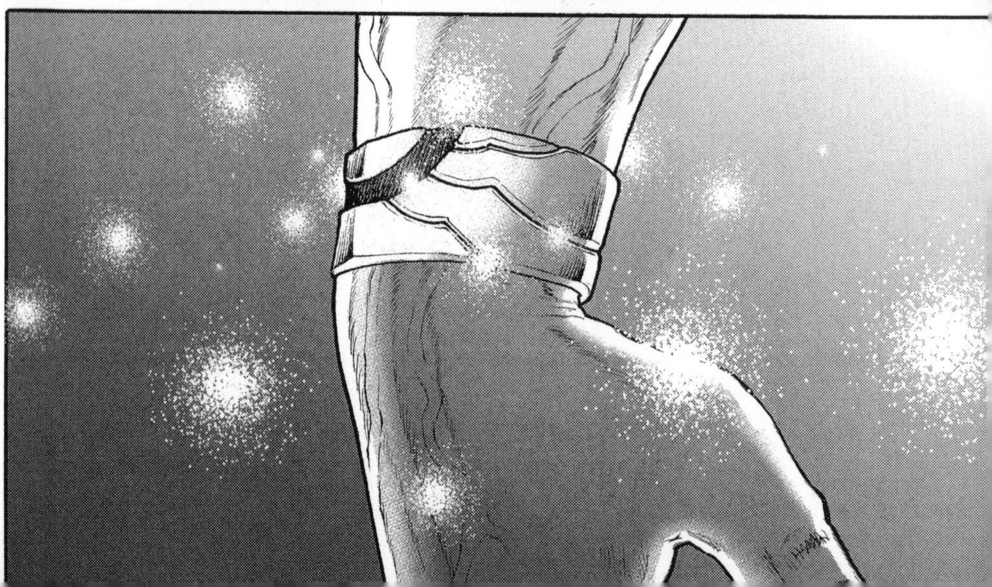

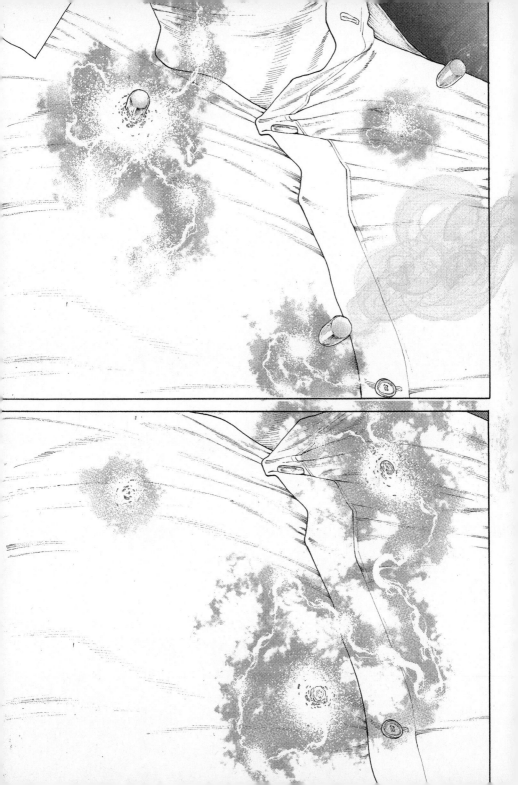

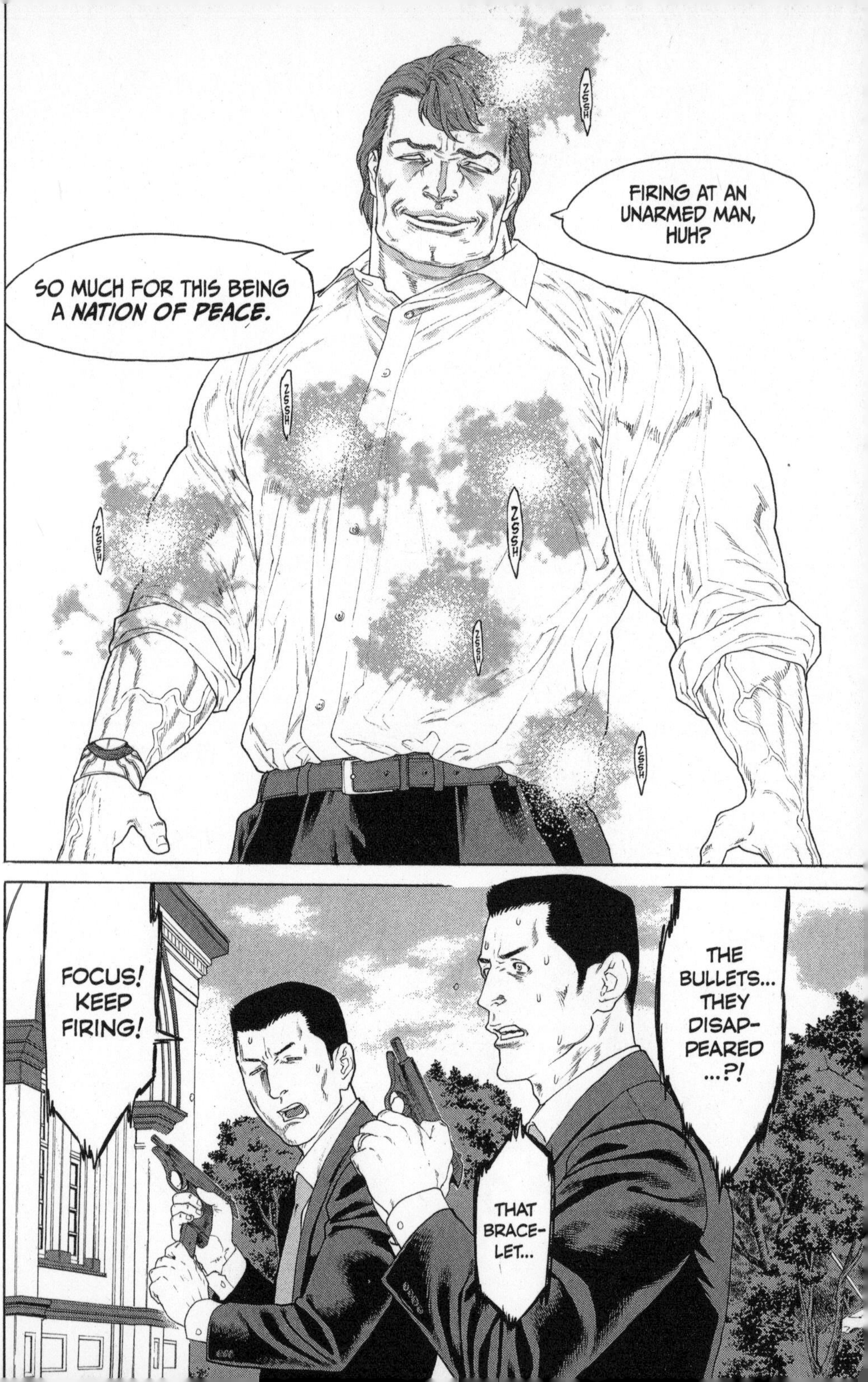
ZSSH
FIRING AT AN UNARMED MAN, HUH?
SO MUCH FOR THIS BEING A *NATION OF PEACE.*
ZSSH
ZSSH
ZSSH
ZSSH
ZSSH
THE BULLETS... THEY DISAPPEARED ...?!
THAT BRACELET...
FOCUS! KEEP FIRING!

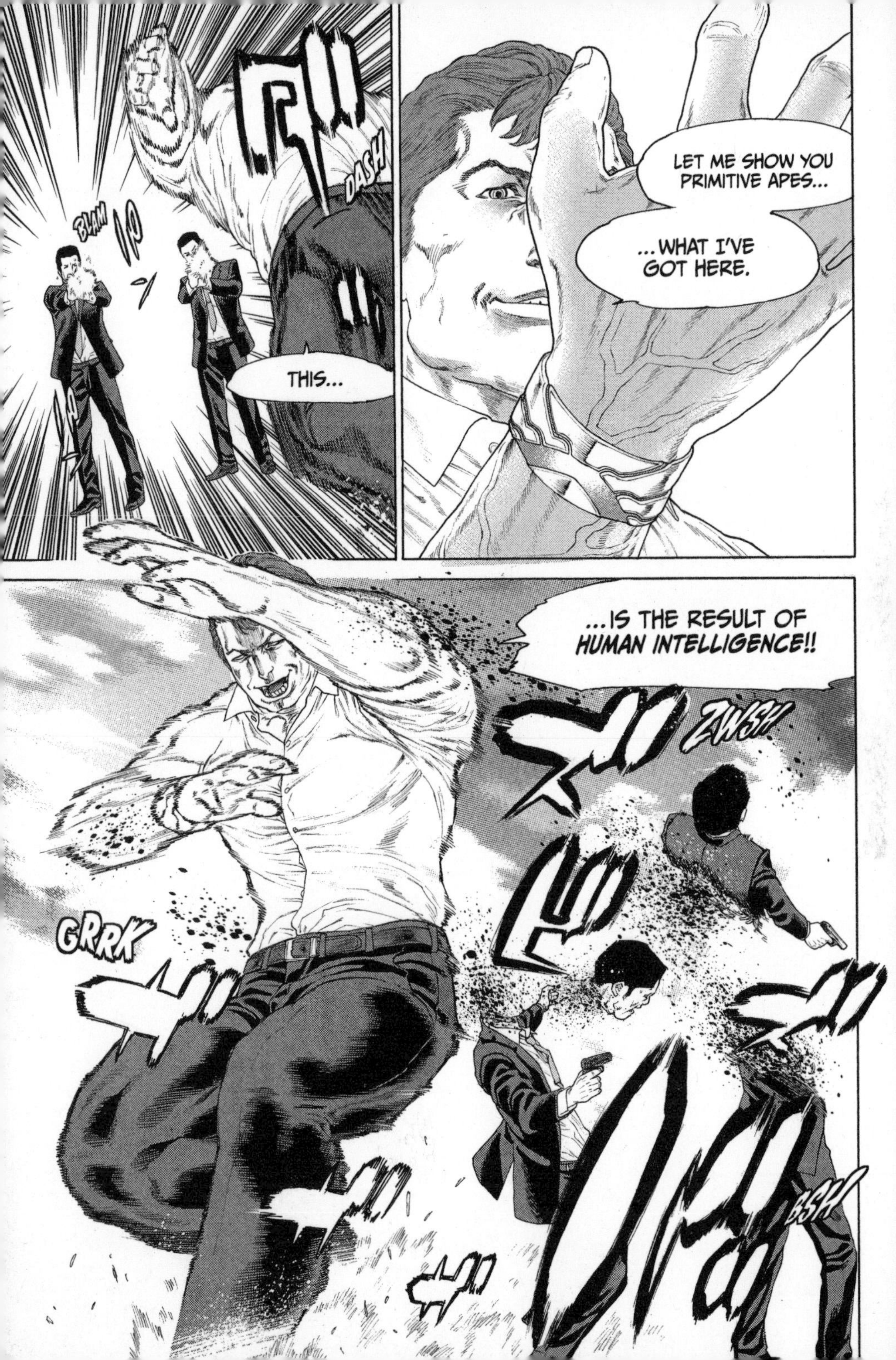
LET ME SHOW YOU PRIMITIVE APES...
...WHAT I'VE GOT HERE.
DASH
BLAM
THIS...
...IS THE RESULT OF HUMAN INTELLIGENCE!!
ZWSH
BSH
GRRK

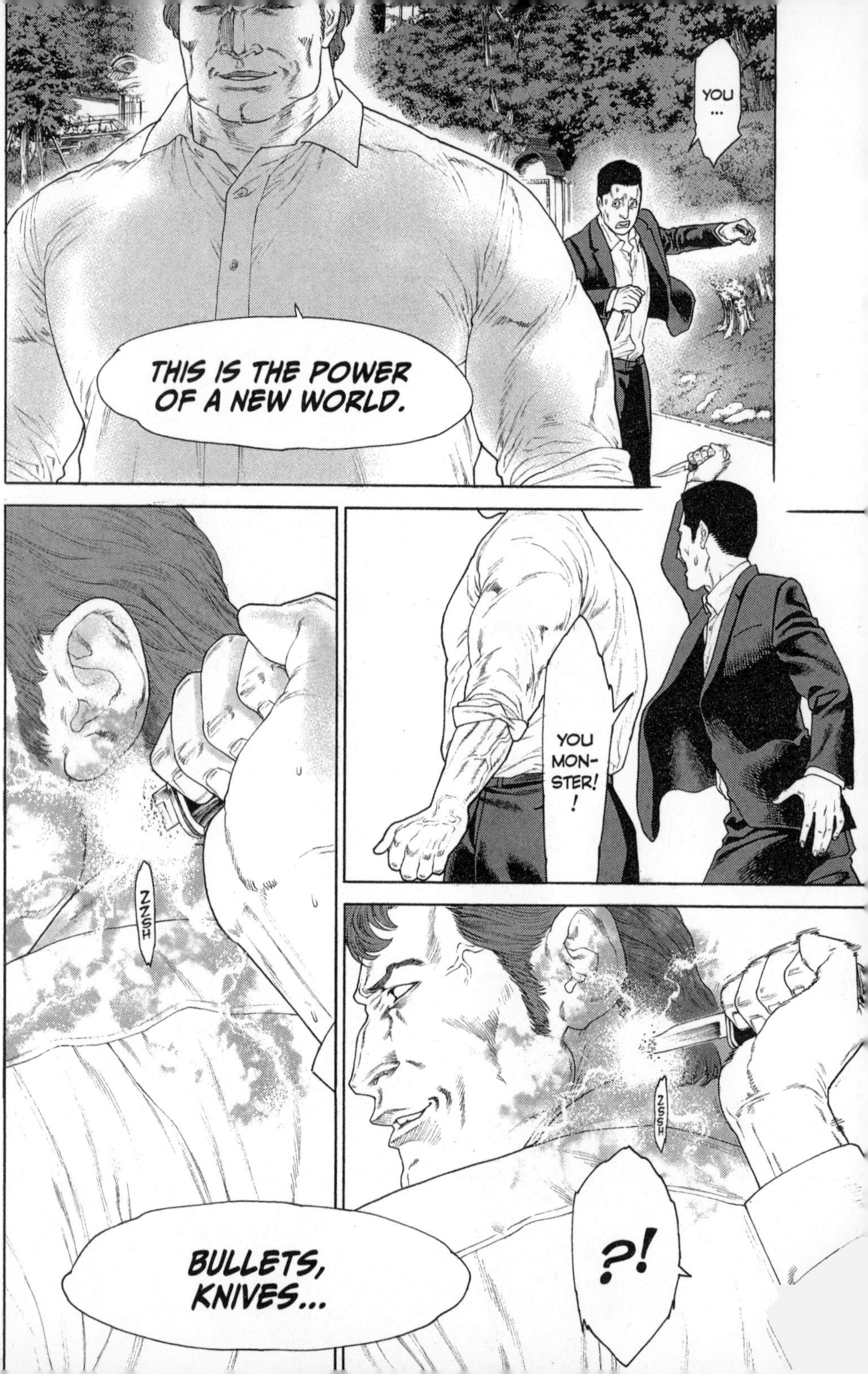
YOU ...
THIS IS THE POWER OF A NEW WORLD.
YOU MONSTER!!
ZSSH
?!
ZZSH
BULLETS, KNIVES...

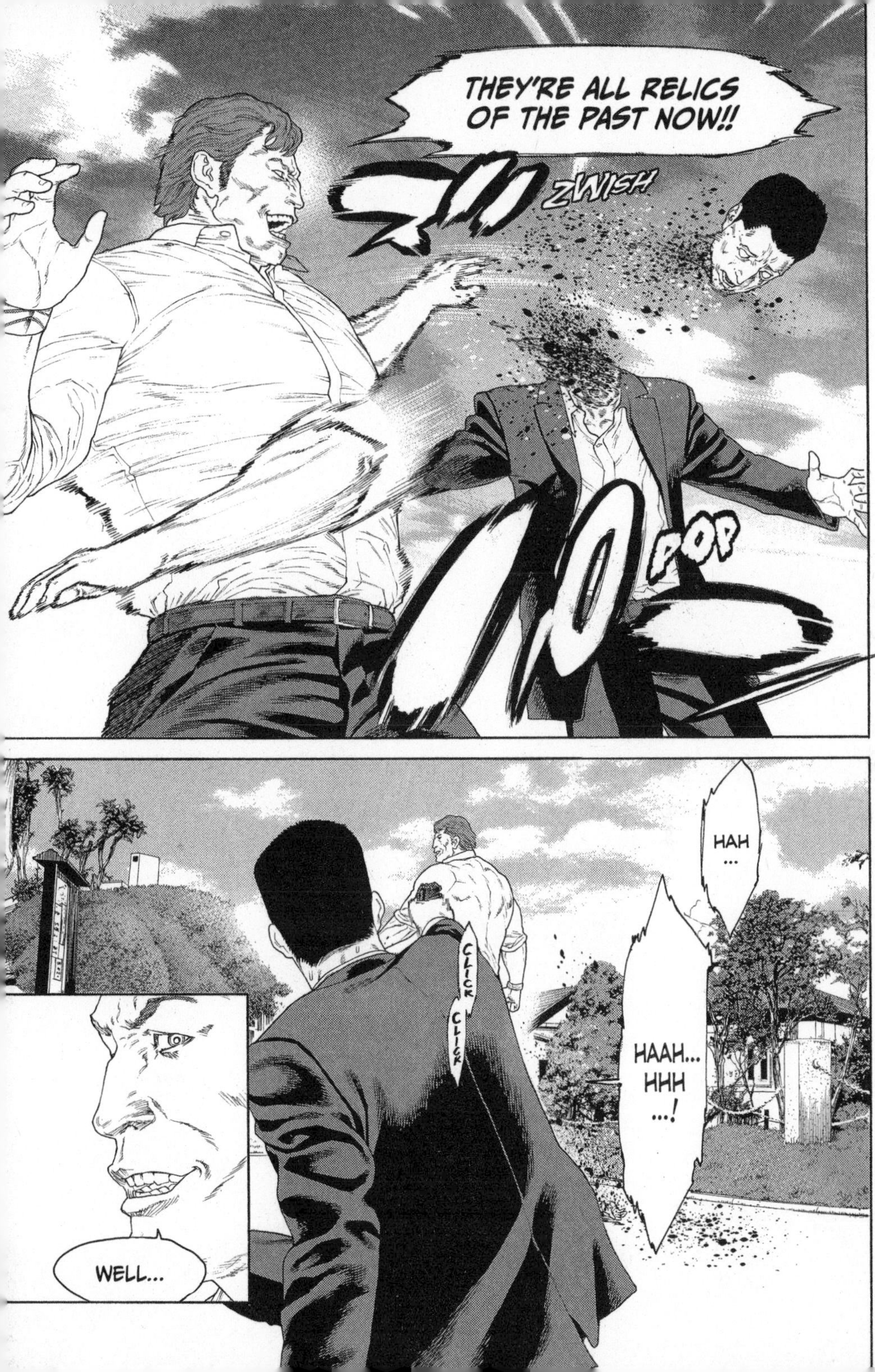
THEY'RE ALL RELICS OF THE PAST NOW!!
ZWISH
POP
HAH...
HAAAH... HHH ...!
CLICK CLICK
WELL...

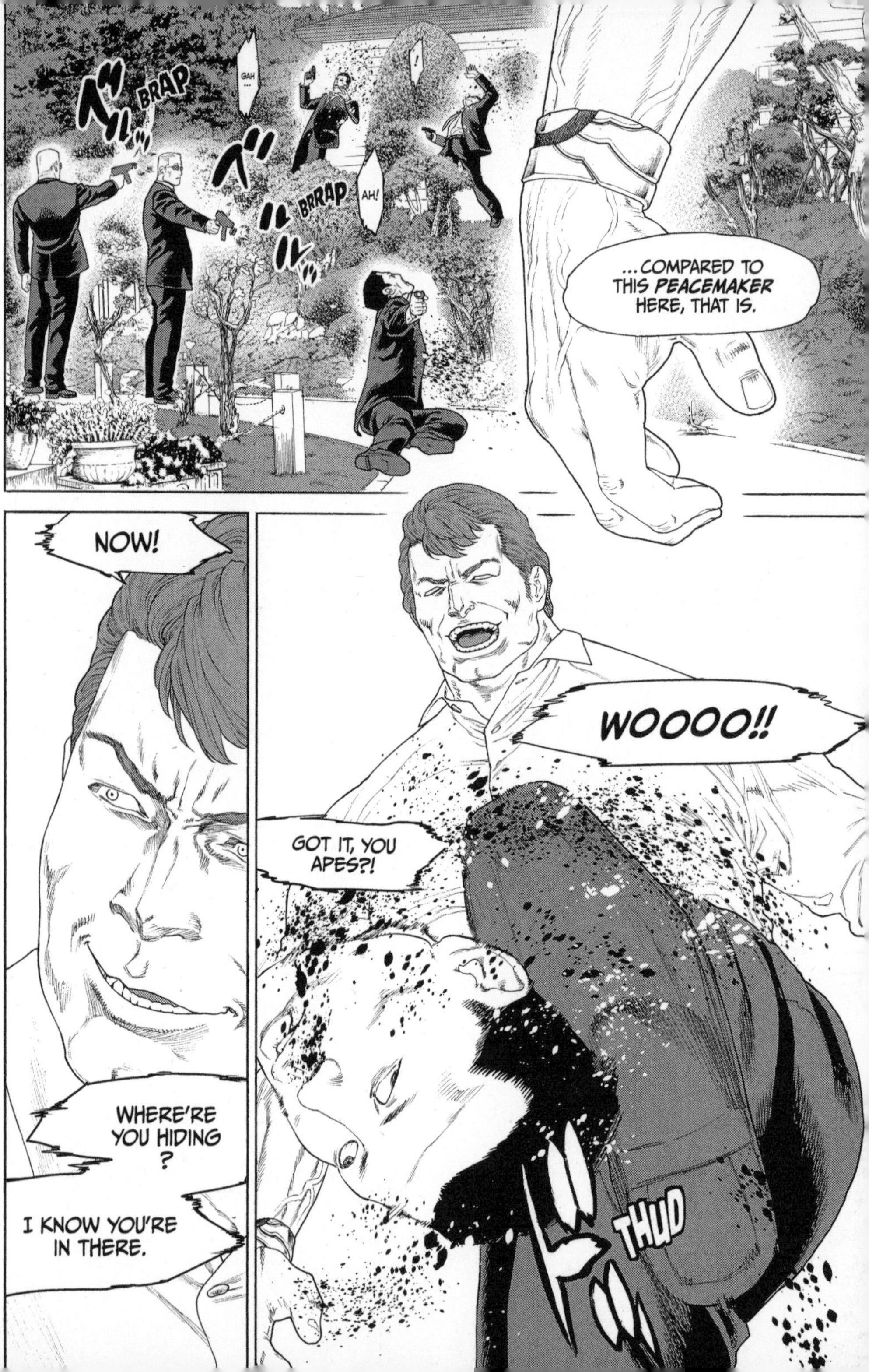
...COMPARED TO THIS *PEACEMAKER* HERE, THAT IS.
!
GAH ...
BRAP
AH!
BRRAP
WOOOO!!
GOT IT, YOU APES?!
THUD
NOW!
WHERE'RE YOU HIDING ?
I KNOW YOU'RE IN THERE.

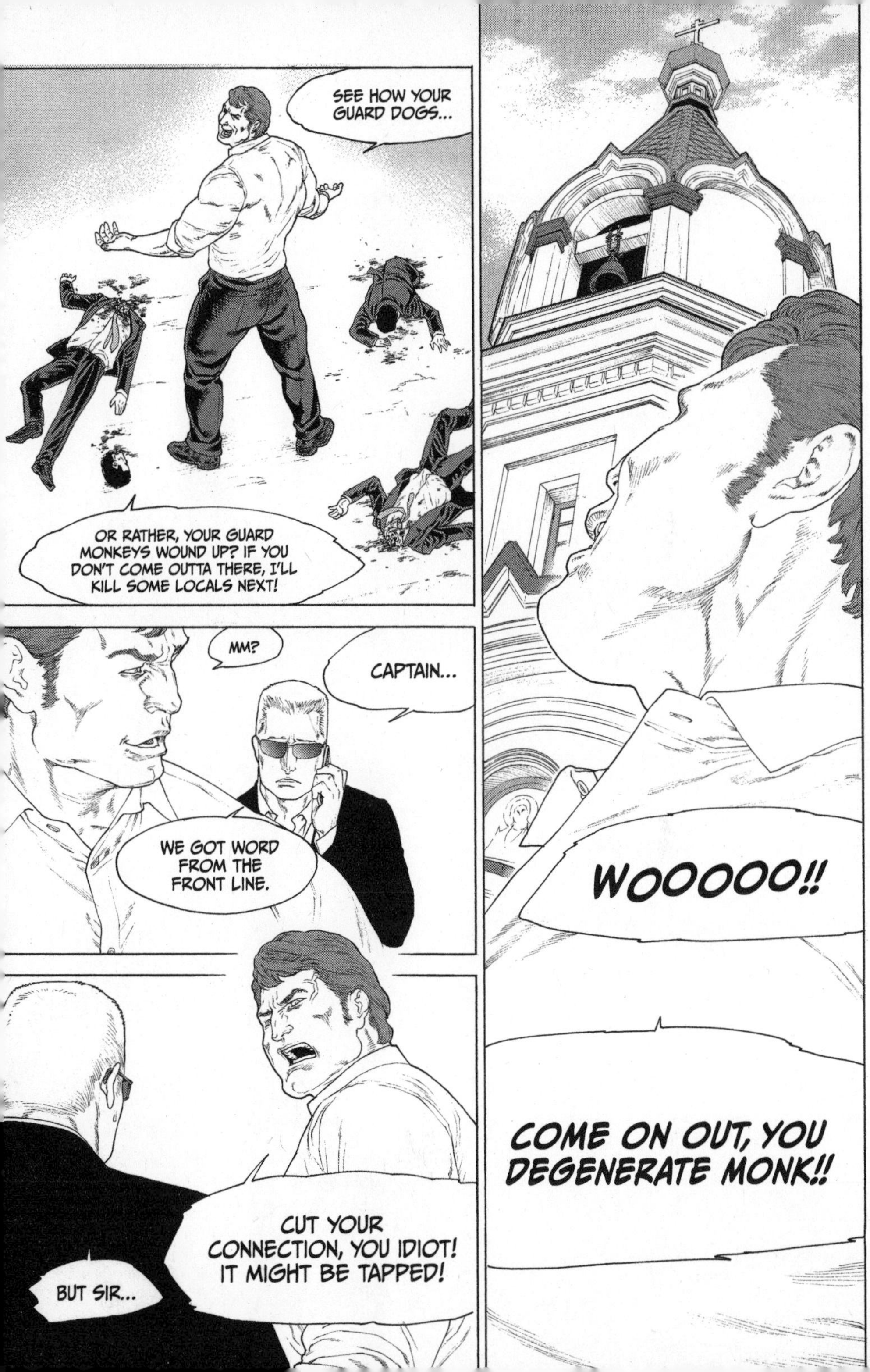
WOOOOO!!
COME ON OUT, YOU DEGENERATE MONK!!
SEE HOW YOUR GUARD DOGS...
OR RATHER, YOUR GUARD MONKEYS WOUND UP? IF YOU DON'T COME OUTTA THERE, I'LL KILL SOME LOCALS NEXT!
CAPTAIN...
MM?
WE GOT WORD FROM THE FRONT LINE.
CUT YOUR CONNECTION, YOU IDIOT! IT MIGHT BE TAPPED!
BUT SIR...

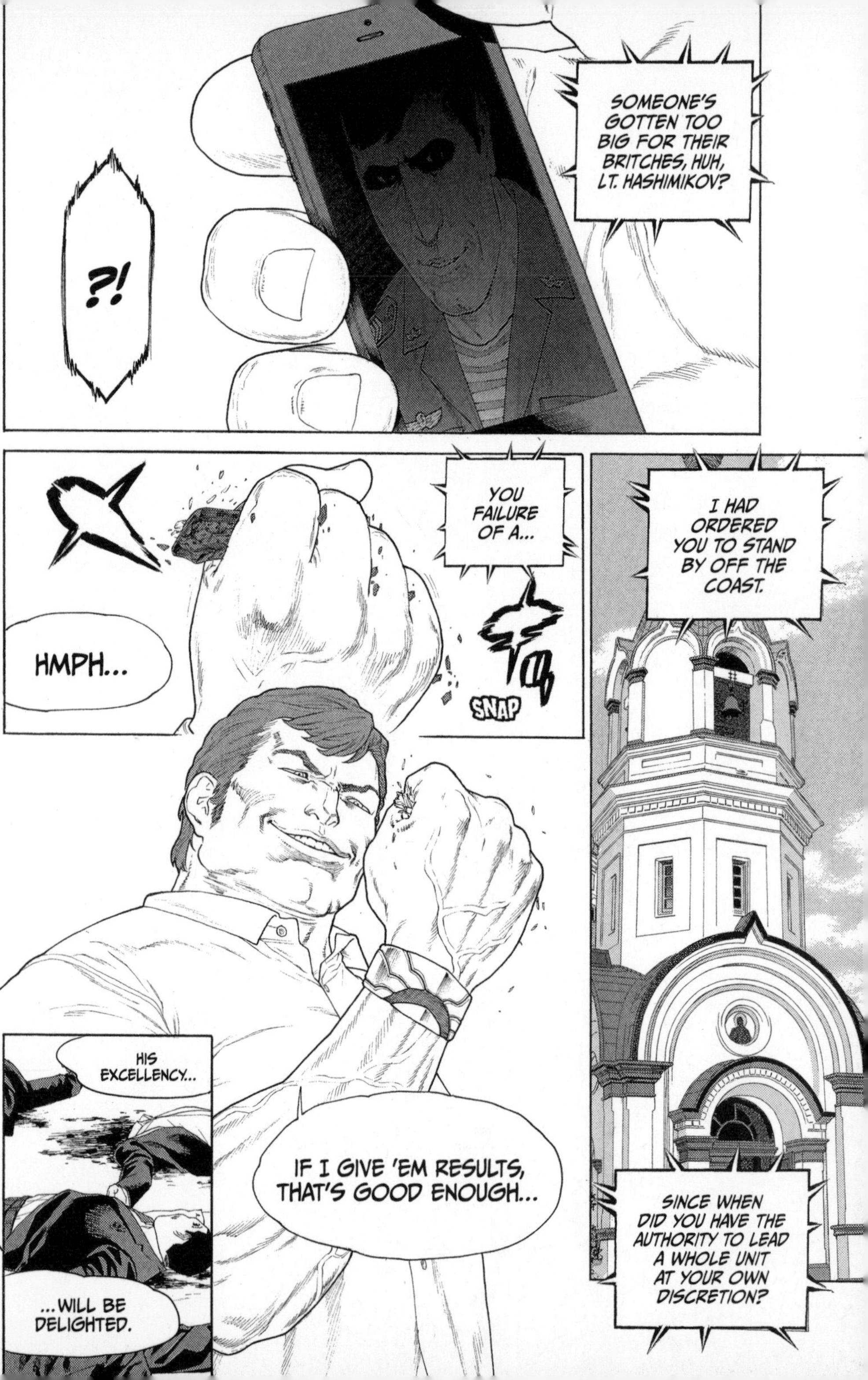
SOMEONE'S GOTTEN TOO BIG FOR THEIR BRITCHES, HUH, LT. HASHIMIKOV?
?!
I HAD ORDERED YOU TO STAND BY OFF THE COAST.
SINCE WHEN DID YOU HAVE THE AUTHORITY TO LEAD A WHOLE UNIT AT YOUR OWN DISCRETION?
YOU FAILURE OF A...
SNAP
HMPH...
IF I GIVE 'EM RESULTS, THAT'S GOOD ENOUGH...
HIS EXCELLENCY...
...WILL BE DELIGHTED.

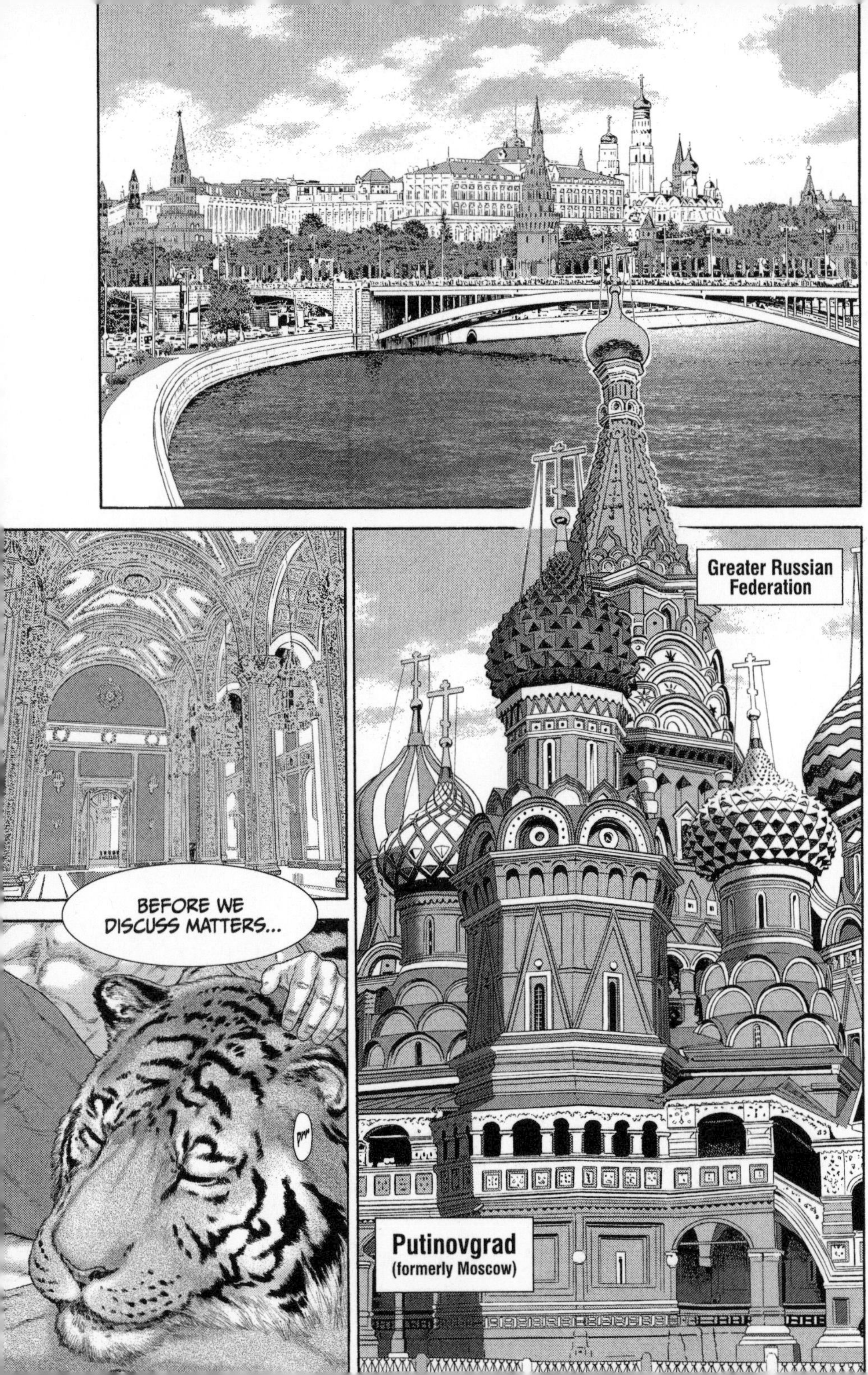
Greater Russian Federation
Putinovgrad (formerly Moscow)
BEFORE WE DISCUSS MATTERS...

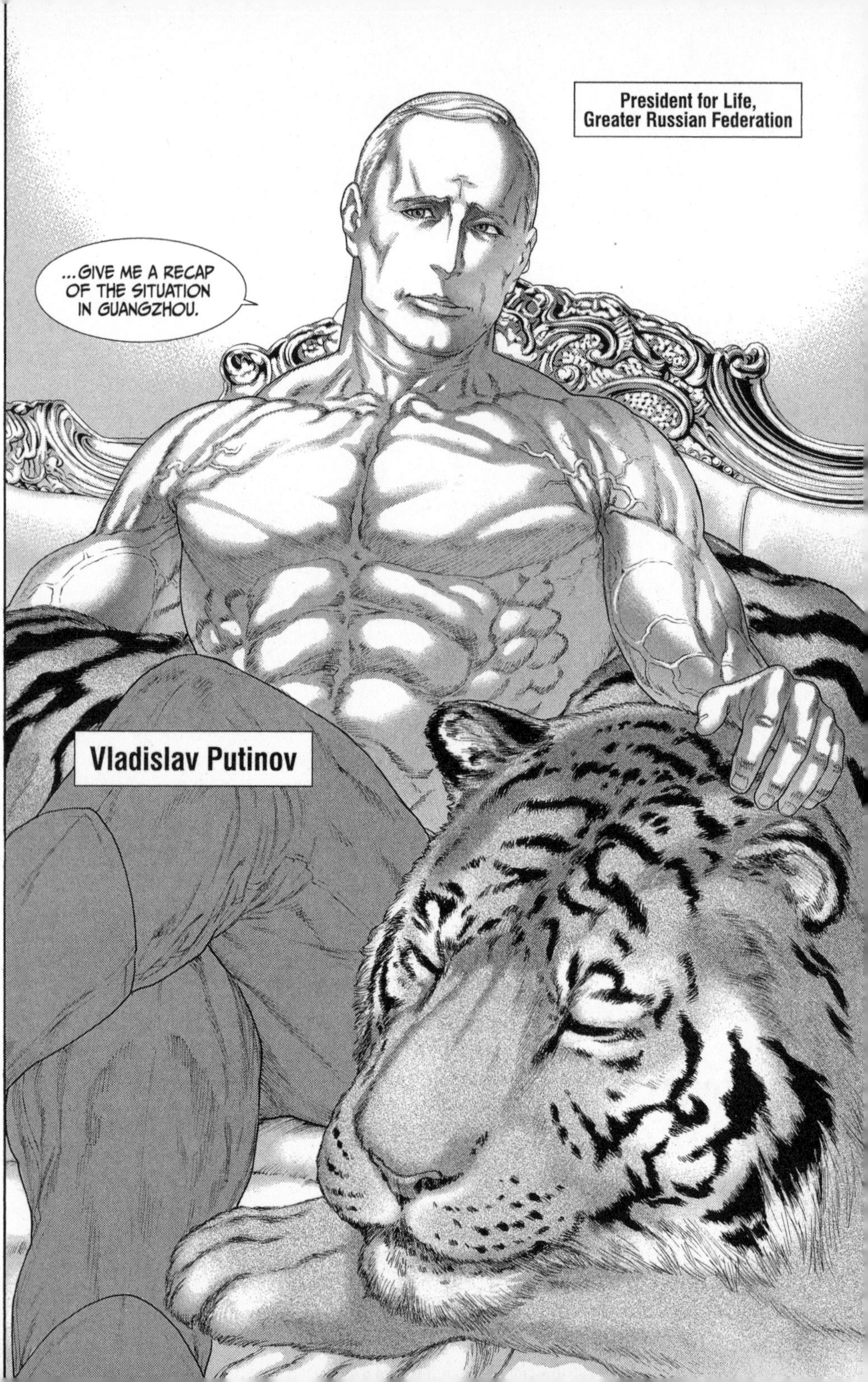
President for Life,
Greater Russian Federation
...GIVE ME A RECAP OF THE SITUATION IN GUANGZHOU.
Vladislav Putinov

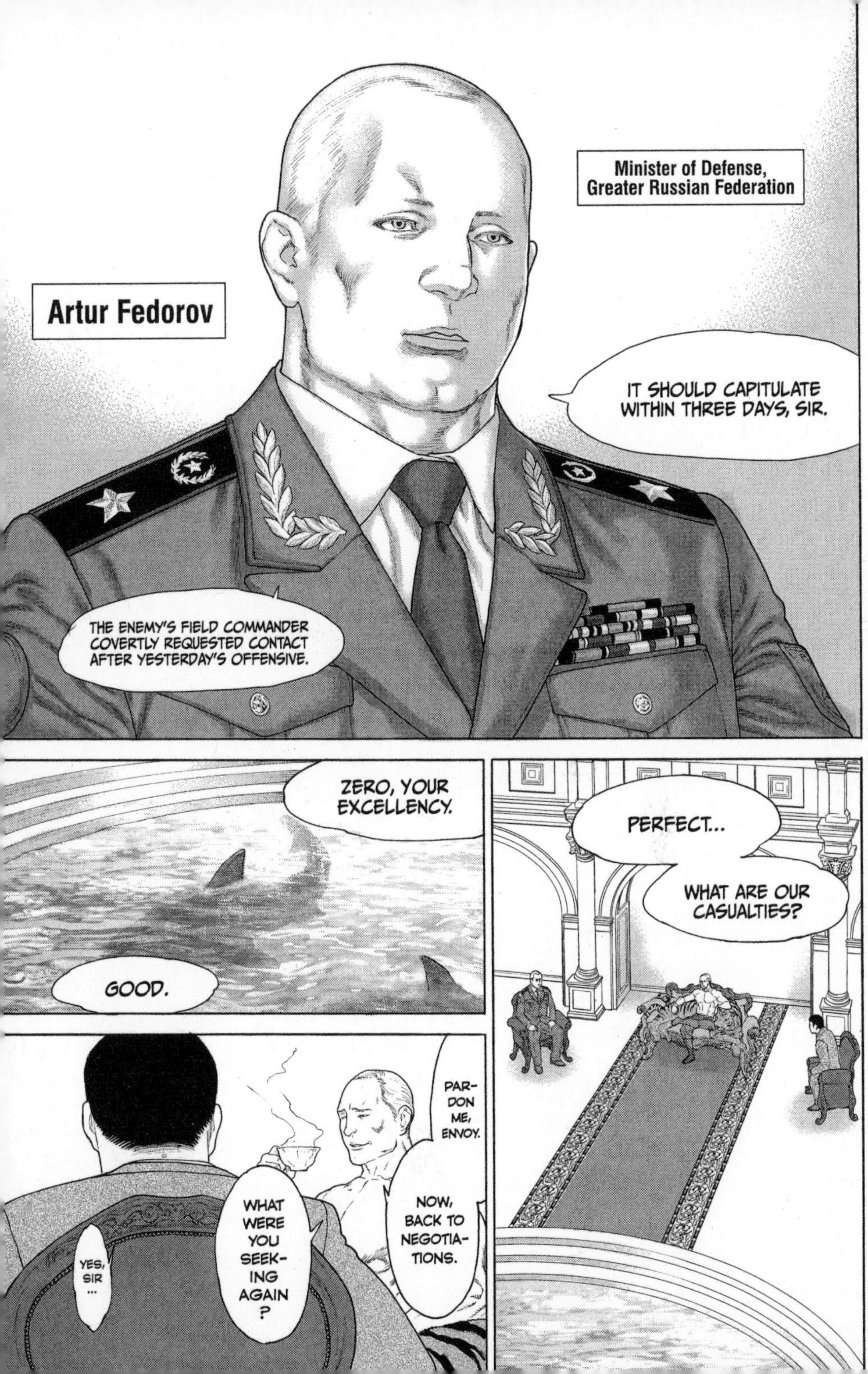
Minister of Defense, Greater Russian Federation
Artur Fedorov
IT SHOULD CAPITULATE WITHIN THREE DAYS, SIR.
THE ENEMY'S FIELD COMMANDER COVERTLY REQUESTED CONTACT AFTER YESTERDAY'S OFFENSIVE.
PERFECT...
WHAT ARE OUR CASUALTIES?
ZERO, YOUR EXCELLENCY.
GOOD.
PARDON ME, ENVOY.
NOW, BACK TO NEGOTIATIONS.
WHAT WERE YOU SEEKING AGAIN?
YES, SIR...

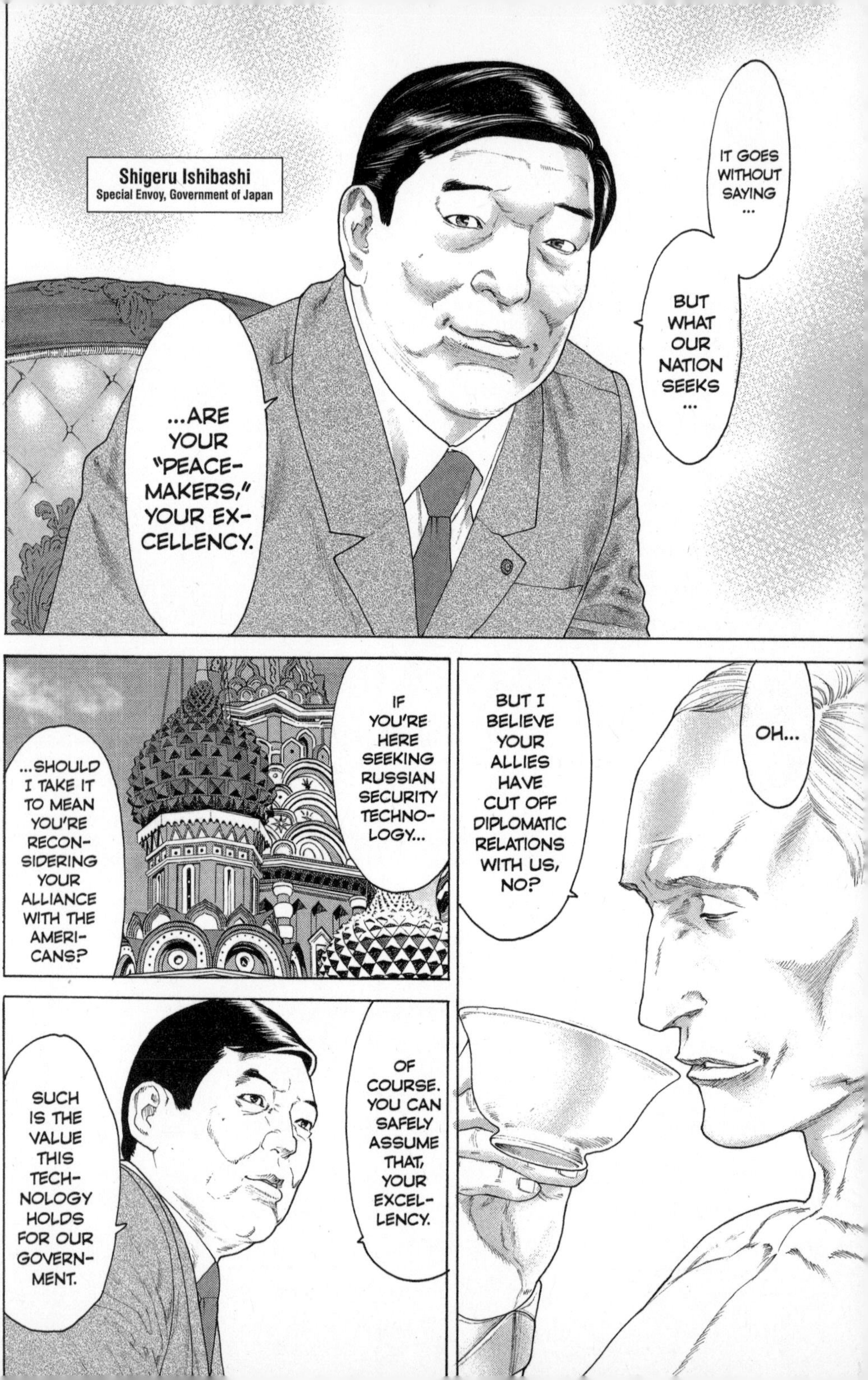

Shigeru Ishibashi
Special Envoy, Government of Japan
IT GOES WITHOUT SAYING ...
BUT WHAT OUR NATION SEEKS ...
...ARE YOUR "PEACE-MAKERS," YOUR EX-CELLENCY.
OH...
BUT I BELIEVE YOUR ALLIES HAVE CUT OFF DIPLOMATIC RELATIONS WITH US, NO?
IF YOU'RE HERE SEEKING RUSSIAN SECURITY TECHNO-LOGY...
...SHOULD I TAKE IT TO MEAN YOU'RE RECON-SIDERING YOUR ALLIANCE WITH THE AMERI-CANS?
OF COURSE. YOU CAN SAFELY ASSUME THAT, YOUR EXCEL-LENCY.
SUCH IS THE VALUE THIS TECH-NOLOGY HOLDS FOR OUR GOVERN-MENT.

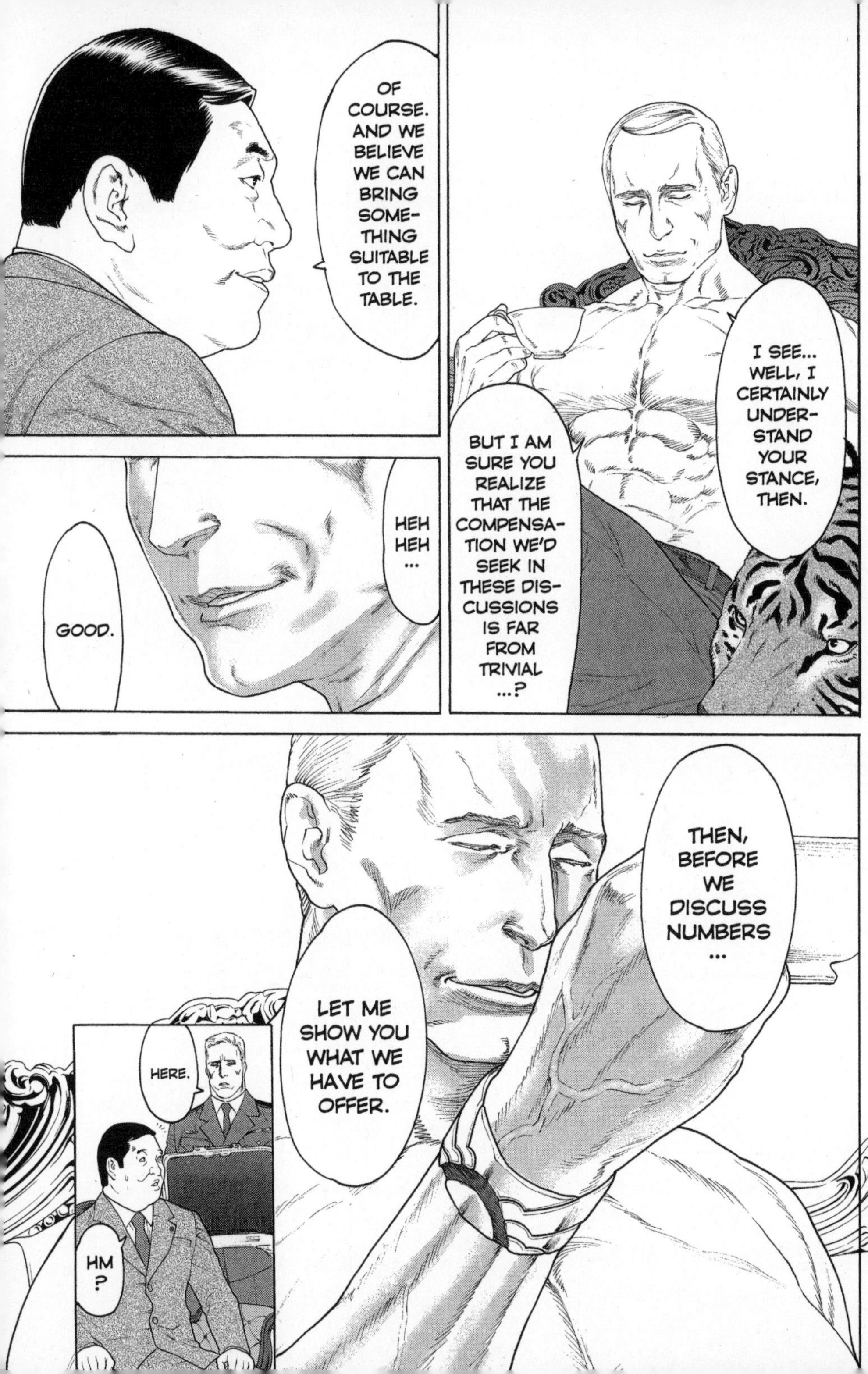
I SEE... WELL, I CERTAINLY UNDERSTAND YOUR STANCE, THEN.
BUT I AM SURE YOU REALIZE THAT THE COMPENSATION WE'D SEEK IN THESE DISCUSSIONS IS FAR FROM TRIVIAL ...?
OF COURSE. AND WE BELIEVE WE CAN BRING SOMETHING SUITABLE TO THE TABLE.
HEH HEH ...
GOOD.
THEN, BEFORE WE DISCUSS NUMBERS ...
LET ME SHOW YOU WHAT WE HAVE TO OFFER.
HERE.
HM ?

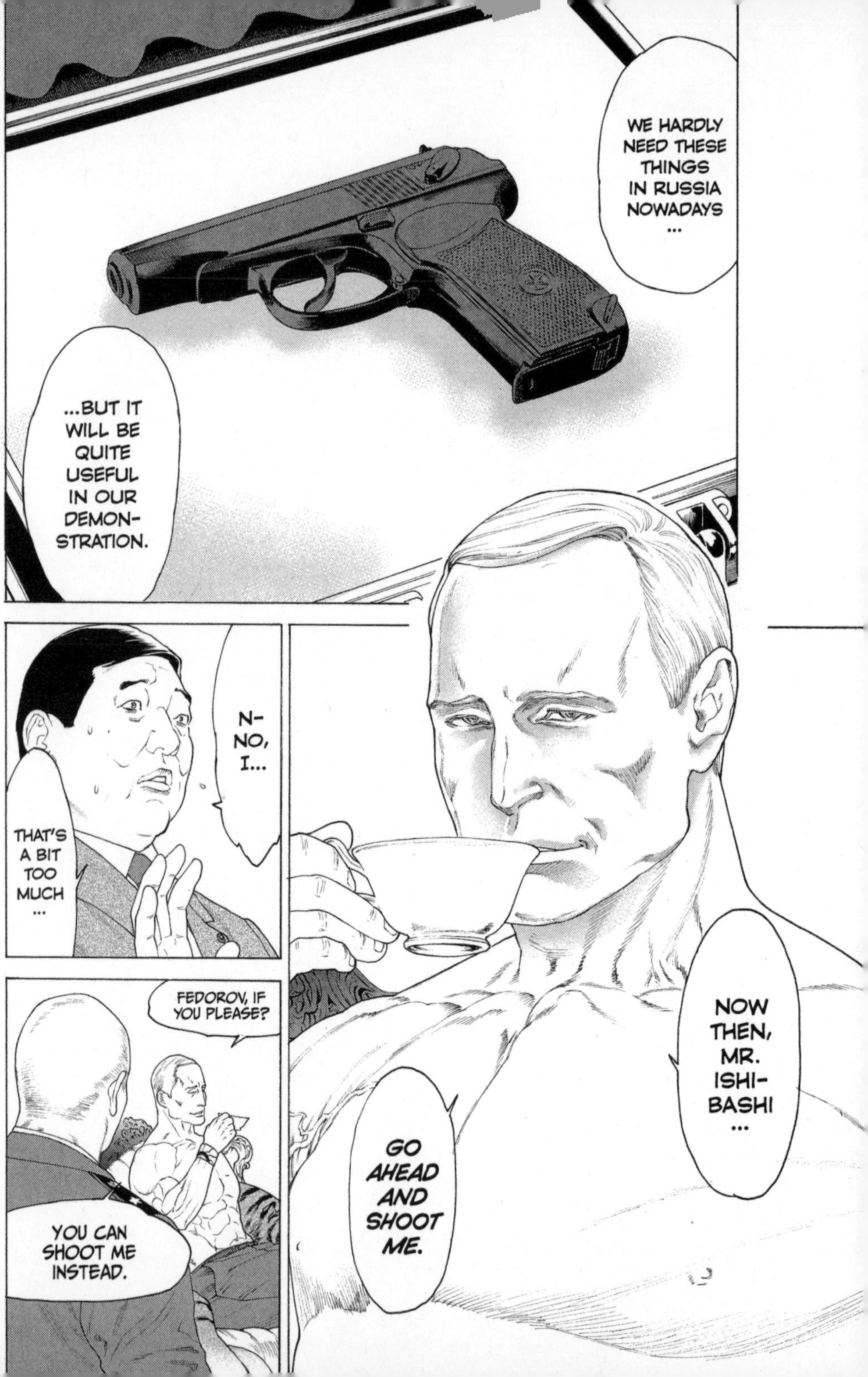
WE HARDLY NEED THESE THINGS IN RUSSIA NOWADAYS ...
...BUT IT WILL BE QUITE USEFUL IN OUR DEMON-STRATION.
NOW THEN, MR. ISHI-BASHI ...
GO AHEAD AND SHOOT ME.
N-NO, I...
THAT'S A BIT TOO MUCH ...
FEDOROV, IF YOU PLEASE?
YOU CAN SHOOT ME INSTEAD.

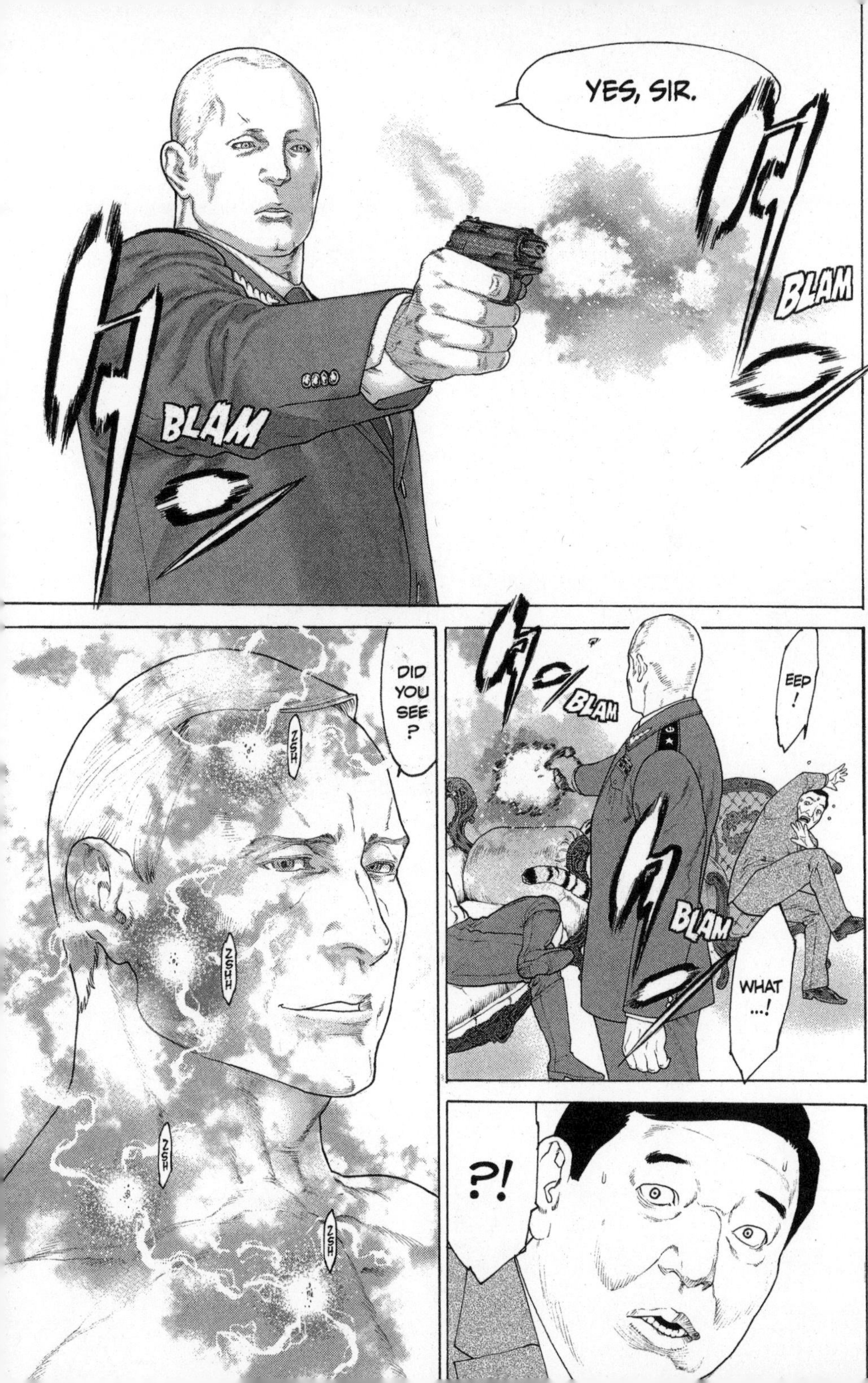
YES, SIR.
BLAM
BLAM
EEP!
BLAM
BLAM
WHAT...!
?!
DID YOU SEE?
ZSH
ZSHH
ZSH
ZSH

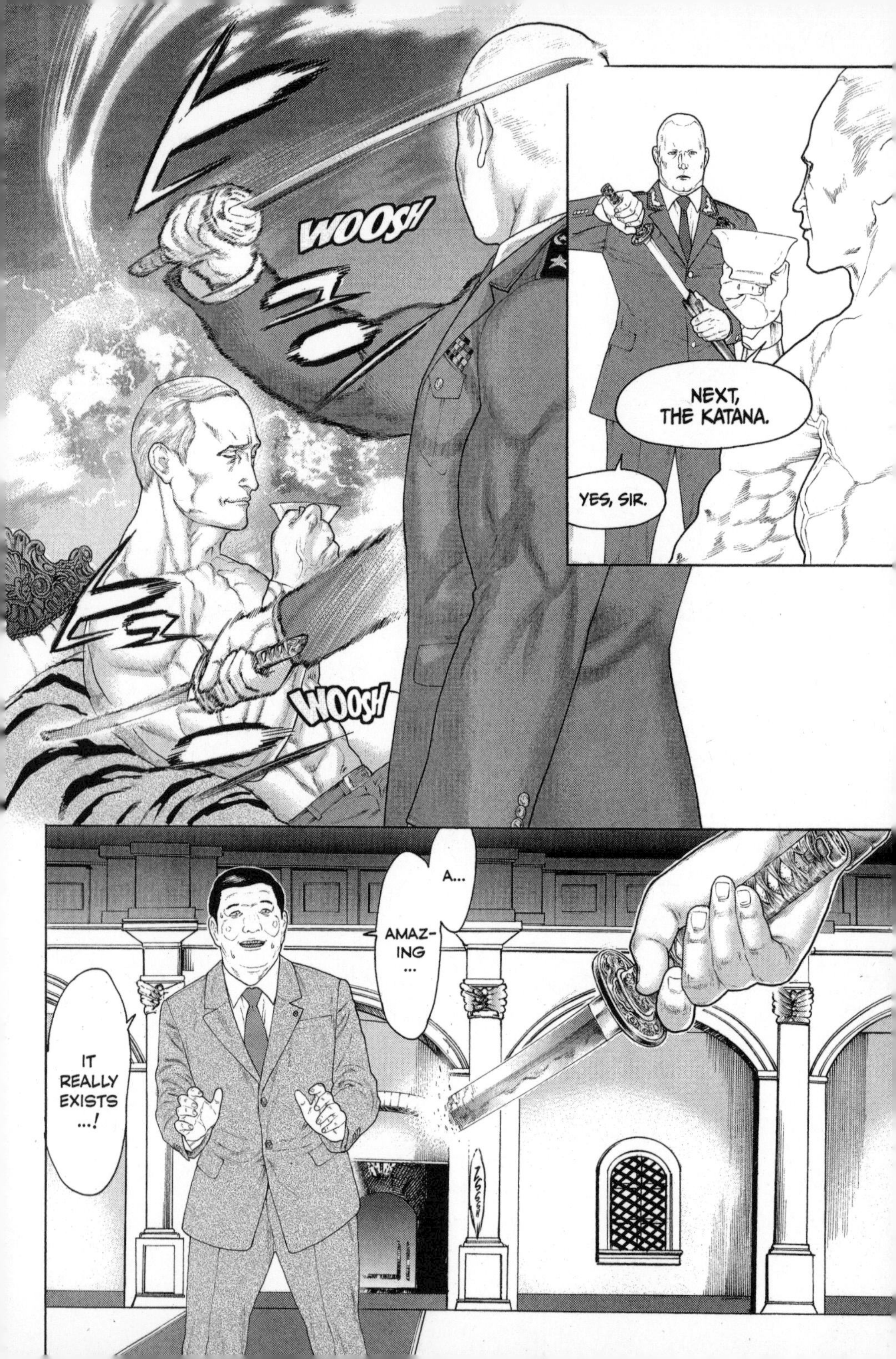
NEXT, THE KATANA.
YES, SIR.
WOOSH
WOOSH
A...
AMAZ-ING ...
IT REALLY EXISTS ...!

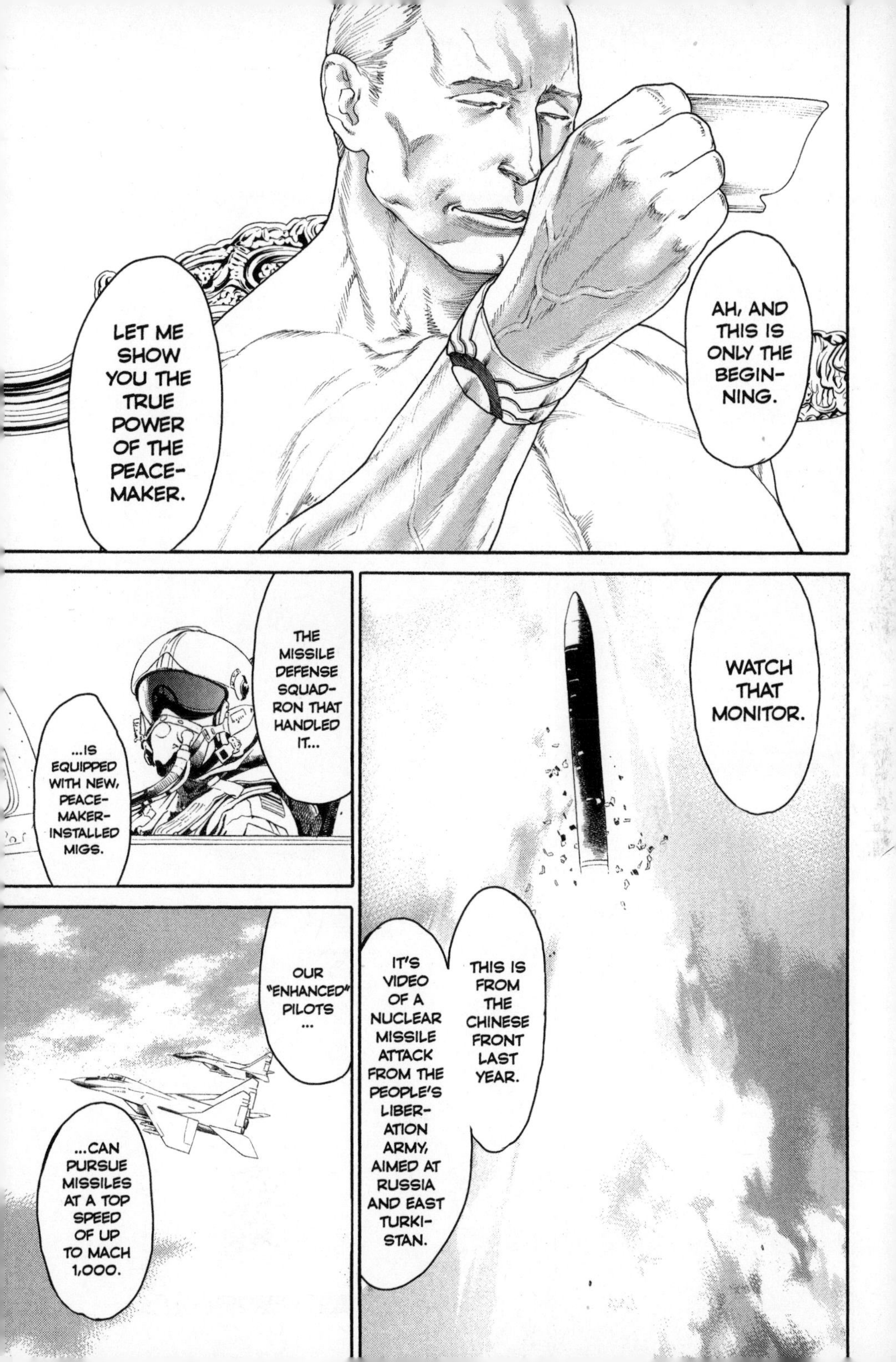
AH, AND THIS IS ONLY THE BEGIN- NING.
LET ME SHOW YOU THE TRUE POWER OF THE PEACE- MAKER.
WATCH THAT MONITOR.
THIS IS FROM THE CHINESE FRONT LAST YEAR.
IT'S VIDEO OF A NUCLEAR MISSILE ATTACK FROM THE PEOPLE'S LIBER- ATION ARMY, AIMED AT RUSSIA AND EAST TURKI- STAN.
THE MISSILE DEFENSE SQUAD- RON THAT HANDLED IT...
...IS EQUIPPED WITH NEW, PEACE- MAKER- INSTALLED MIGS.
OUR "ENHANCED" PILOTS ...
...CAN PURSUE MISSILES AT A TOP SPEED OF UP TO MACH 1,000.

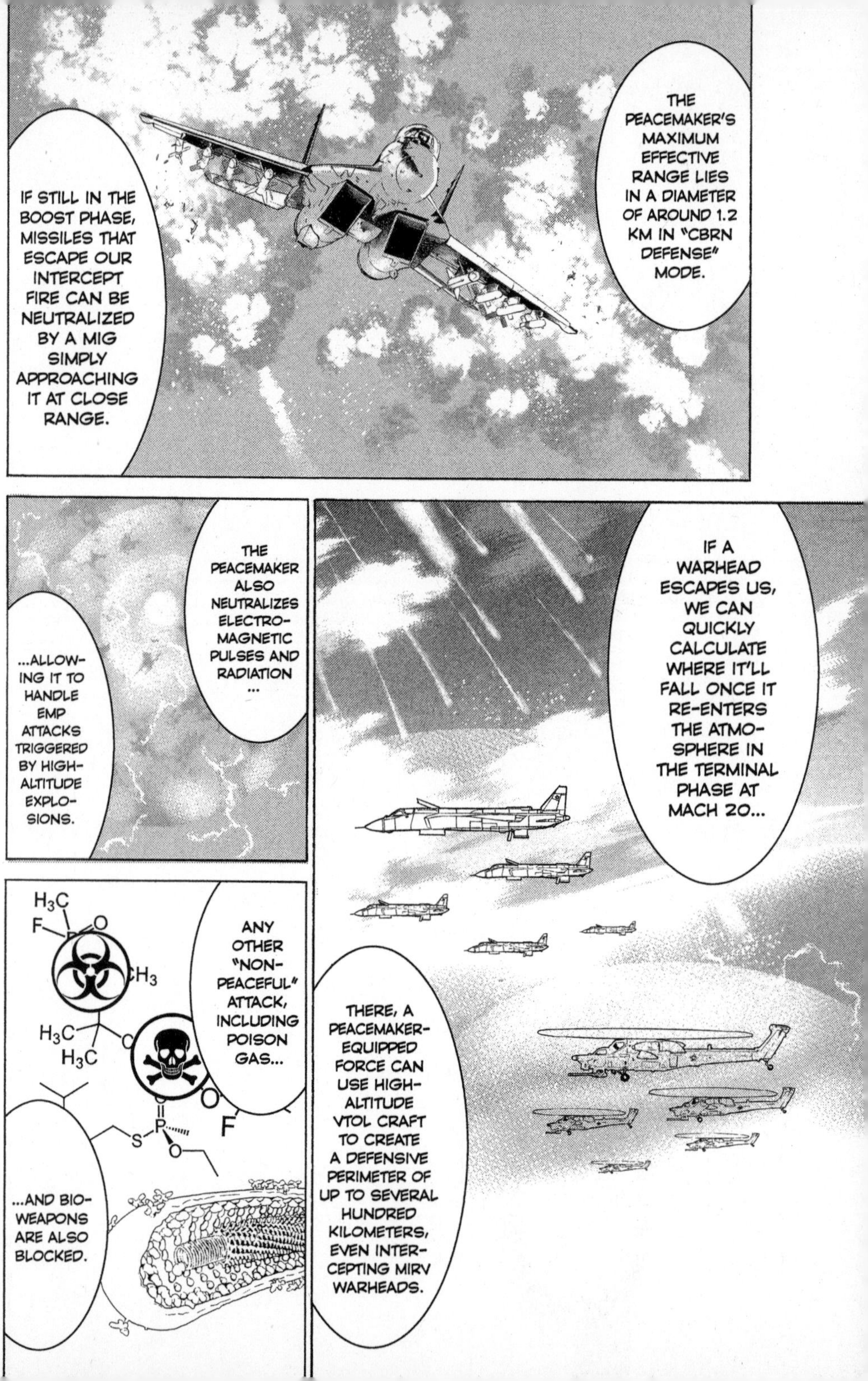
THE PEACEMAKER'S MAXIMUM EFFECTIVE RANGE LIES IN A DIAMETER OF AROUND 1.2 KM IN "CBRN DEFENSE" MODE.
IF STILL IN THE BOOST PHASE, MISSILES THAT ESCAPE OUR INTERCEPT FIRE CAN BE NEUTRALIZED BY A MIG SIMPLY APPROACHING IT AT CLOSE RANGE.
IF A WARHEAD ESCAPES US, WE CAN QUICKLY CALCULATE WHERE IT'LL FALL ONCE IT RE-ENTERS THE ATMOSPHERE IN THE TERMINAL PHASE AT MACH 20...
THERE, A PEACEMAKER-EQUIPPED FORCE CAN USE HIGH-ALTITUDE VTOL CRAFT TO CREATE A DEFENSIVE PERIMETER OF UP TO SEVERAL HUNDRED KILOMETERS, EVEN INTERCEPTING MIRV WARHEADS.
THE PEACEMAKER ALSO NEUTRALIZES ELECTRO-MAGNETIC PULSES AND RADIATION...
...ALLOWING IT TO HANDLE EMP ATTACKS TRIGGERED BY HIGH-ALTITUDE EXPLOSIONS.
ANY OTHER "NON-PEACEFUL" ATTACK, INCLUDING POISON GAS...
...AND BIO-WEAPONS ARE ALSO BLOCKED.

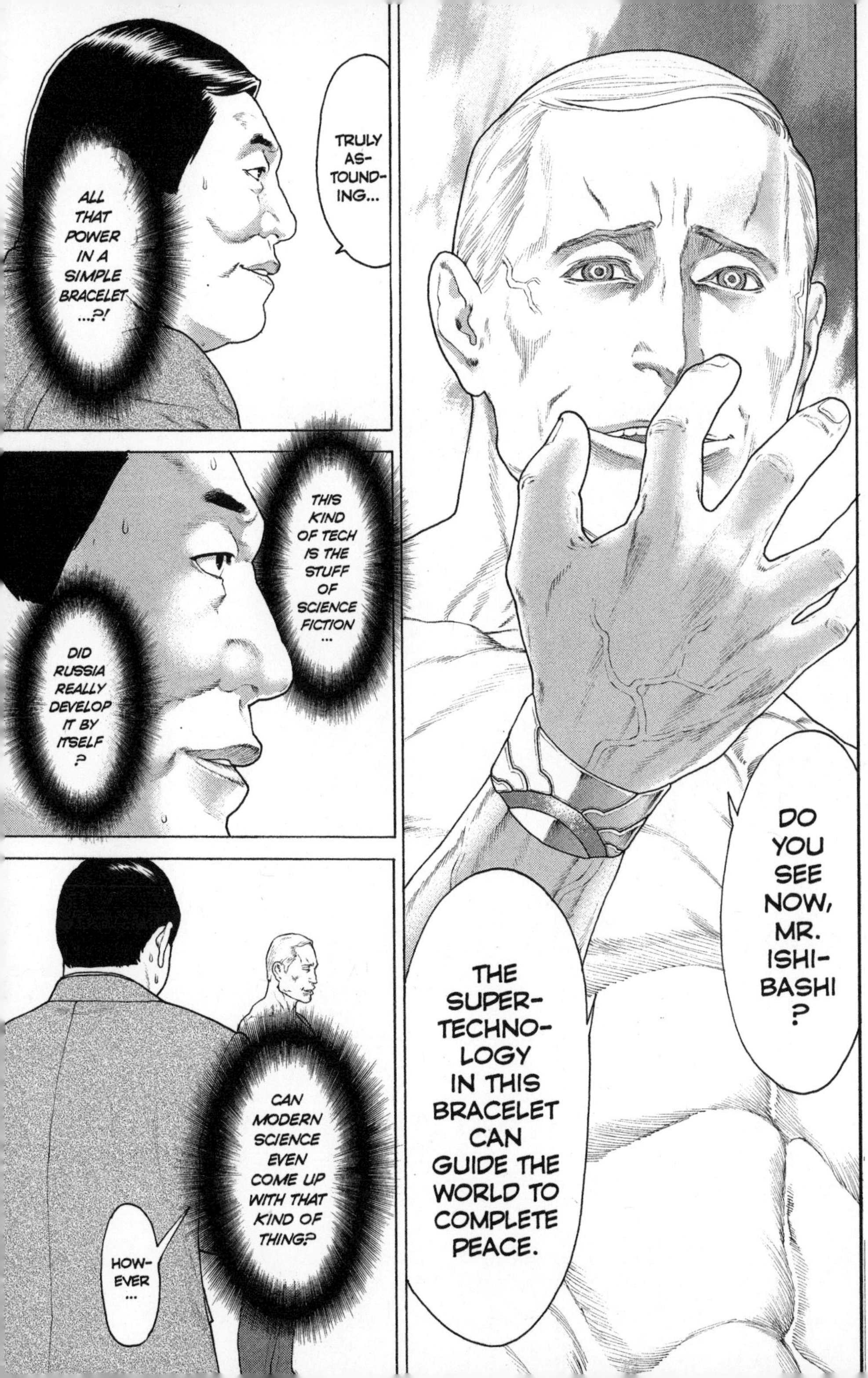
DO YOU SEE NOW, MR. ISHI-BASHI?
THE SUPER-TECHNOLOGY IN THIS BRACELET CAN GUIDE THE WORLD TO COMPLETE PEACE.
TRULY AS-TOUND-ING...
ALL THAT POWER IN A SIMPLE BRACELET ...?!
THIS KIND OF TECH IS THE STUFF OF SCIENCE FICTION ...
DID RUSSIA REALLY DEVELOP IT BY ITSELF?
CAN MODERN SCIENCE EVEN COME UP WITH THAT KIND OF THING?
HOW-EVER ...

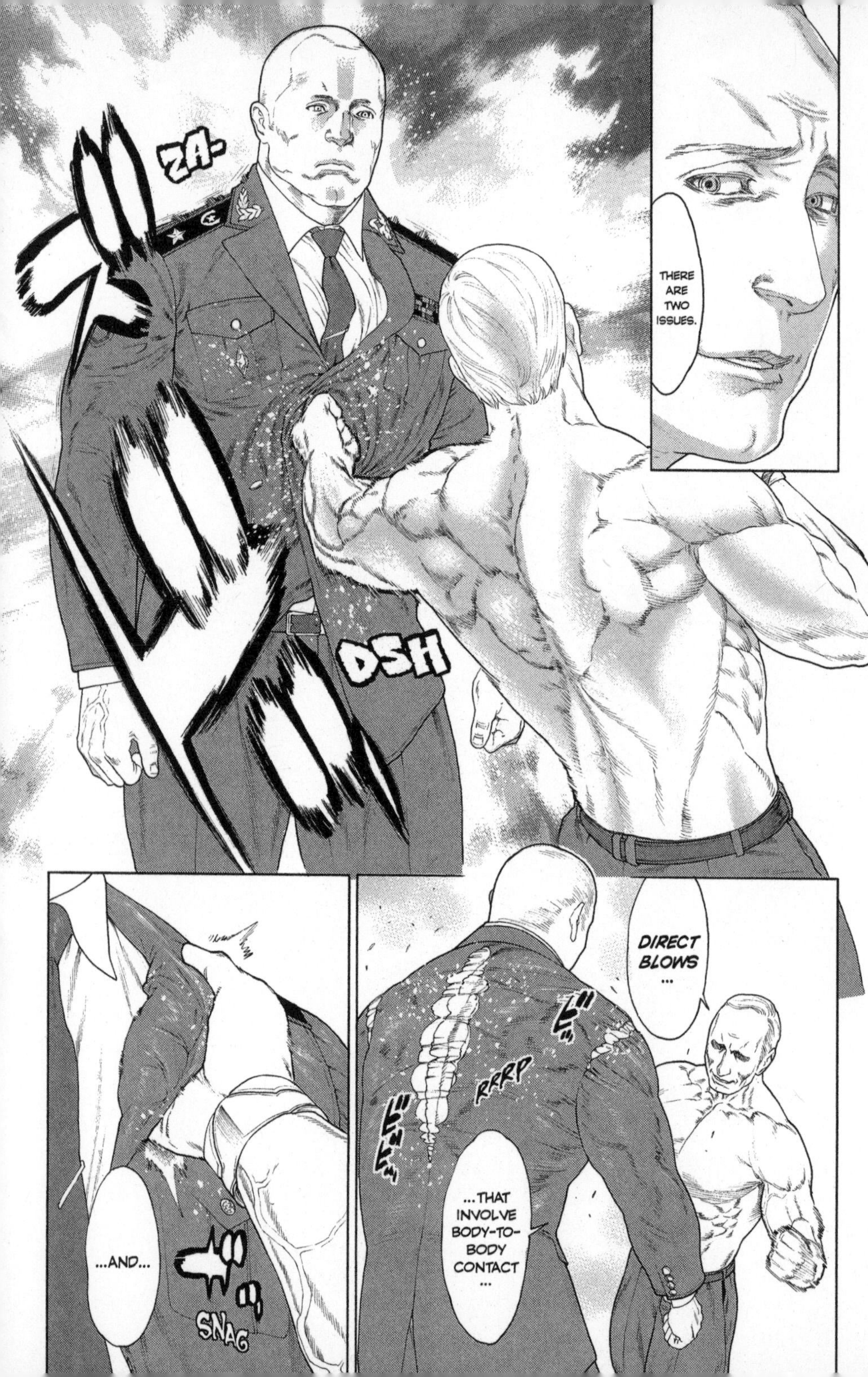
THERE ARE TWO ISSUES.
ZA-
DSH
DIRECT BLOWS ...
RRRP
...THAT INVOLVE BODY-TO-BODY CONTACT ...
...AND...
SNAG

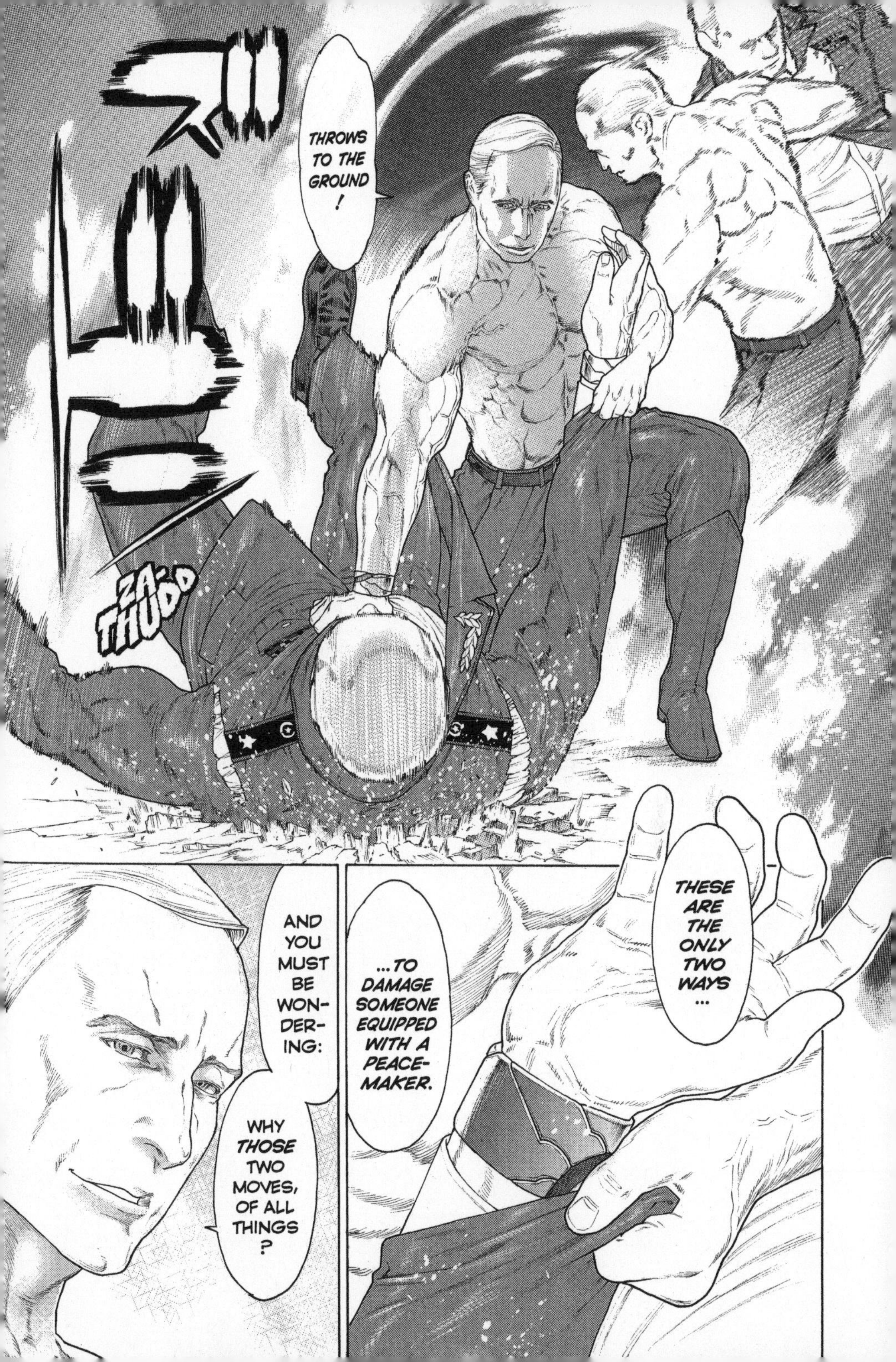
THROWS TO THE GROUND!
ZA-THUDD
THESE ARE THE ONLY TWO WAYS...
...TO DAMAGE SOMEONE EQUIPPED WITH A PEACE-MAKER.
AND YOU MUST BE WON-DER-ING:
WHY *THOSE* TWO MOVES, OF ALL THINGS?

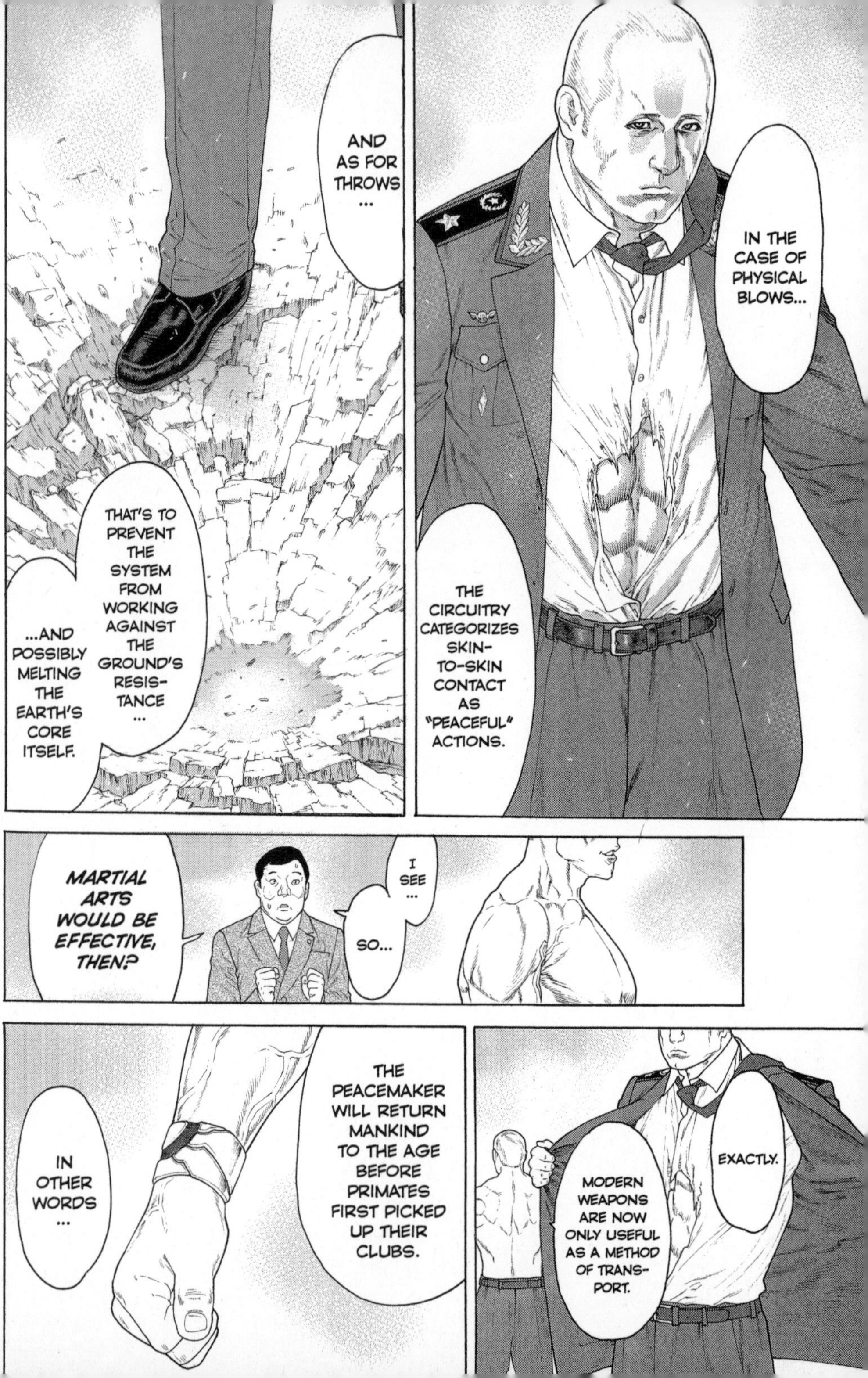
IN THE CASE OF PHYSICAL BLOWS...
THE CIRCUITRY CATEGORIZES SKIN-TO-SKIN CONTACT AS "PEACEFUL" ACTIONS.
AND AS FOR THROWS ...
THAT'S TO PREVENT THE SYSTEM FROM WORKING AGAINST THE GROUND'S RESISTANCE ...
...AND POSSIBLY MELTING THE EARTH'S CORE ITSELF.
I SEE ...
SO...
MARTIAL ARTS WOULD BE EFFECTIVE, THEN?
EXACTLY.
MODERN WEAPONS ARE NOW ONLY USEFUL AS A METHOD OF TRANS-PORT.
IN OTHER WORDS ...
THE PEACEMAKER WILL RETURN MANKIND TO THE AGE BEFORE PRIMATES FIRST PICKED UP THEIR CLUBS.

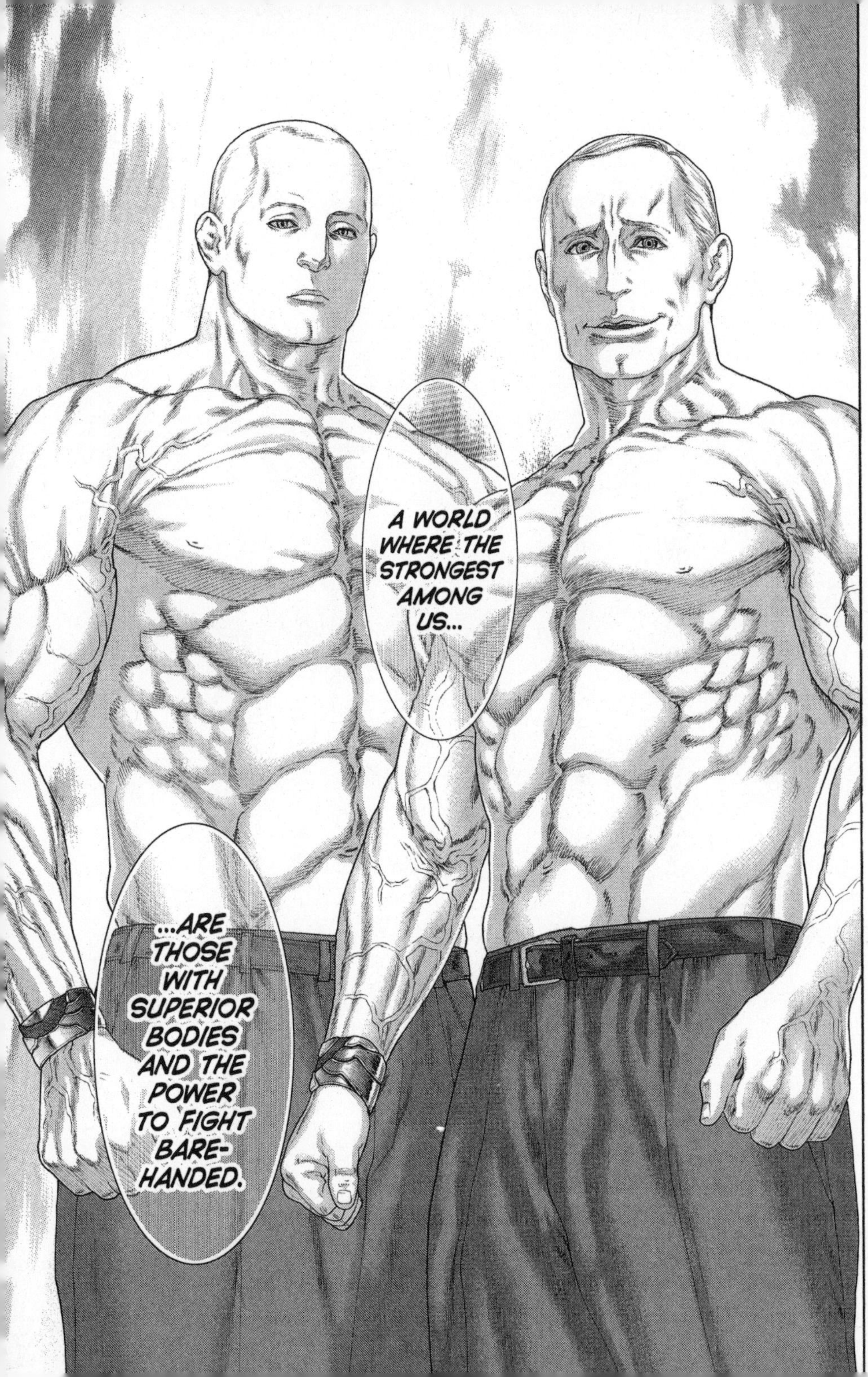
A WORLD WHERE THE STRONGEST AMONG US...
...ARE THOSE WITH SUPERIOR BODIES AND THE POWER TO FIGHT BARE-HANDED.

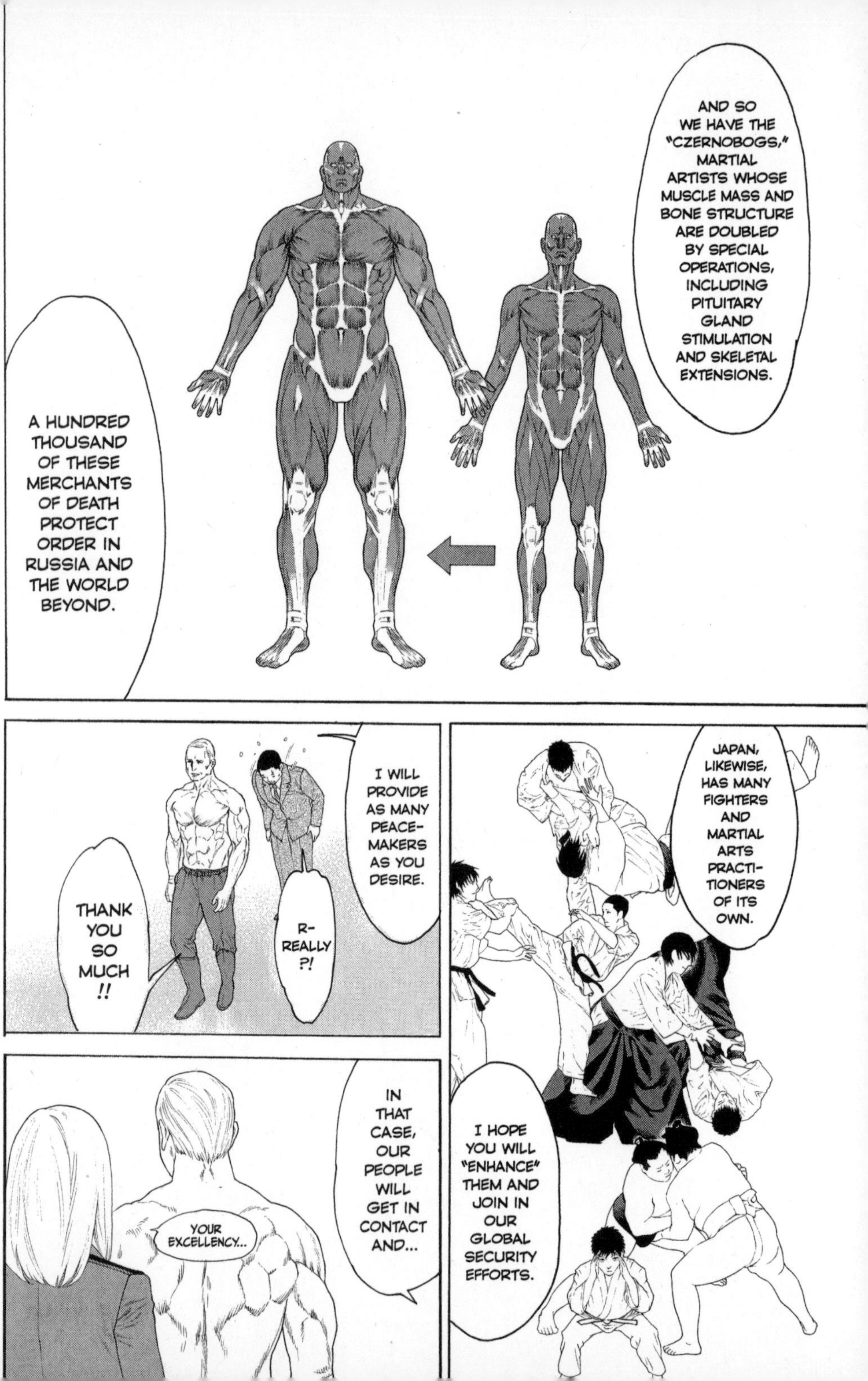
AND SO WE HAVE THE "CZERNOBOGS," MARTIAL ARTISTS WHOSE MUSCLE MASS AND BONE STRUCTURE ARE DOUBLED BY SPECIAL OPERATIONS, INCLUDING PITUITARY GLAND STIMULATION AND SKELETAL EXTENSIONS.
A HUNDRED THOUSAND OF THESE MERCHANTS OF DEATH PROTECT ORDER IN RUSSIA AND THE WORLD BEYOND.
JAPAN, LIKEWISE, HAS MANY FIGHTERS AND MARTIAL ARTS PRACTITIONERS OF ITS OWN.
I HOPE YOU WILL "ENHANCE" THEM AND JOIN IN OUR GLOBAL SECURITY EFFORTS.
I WILL PROVIDE AS MANY PEACE-MAKERS AS YOU DESIRE.
R-REALLY?!
THANK YOU SO MUCH!!
IN THAT CASE, OUR PEOPLE WILL GET IN CONTACT AND...
YOUR EXCELLENCY...

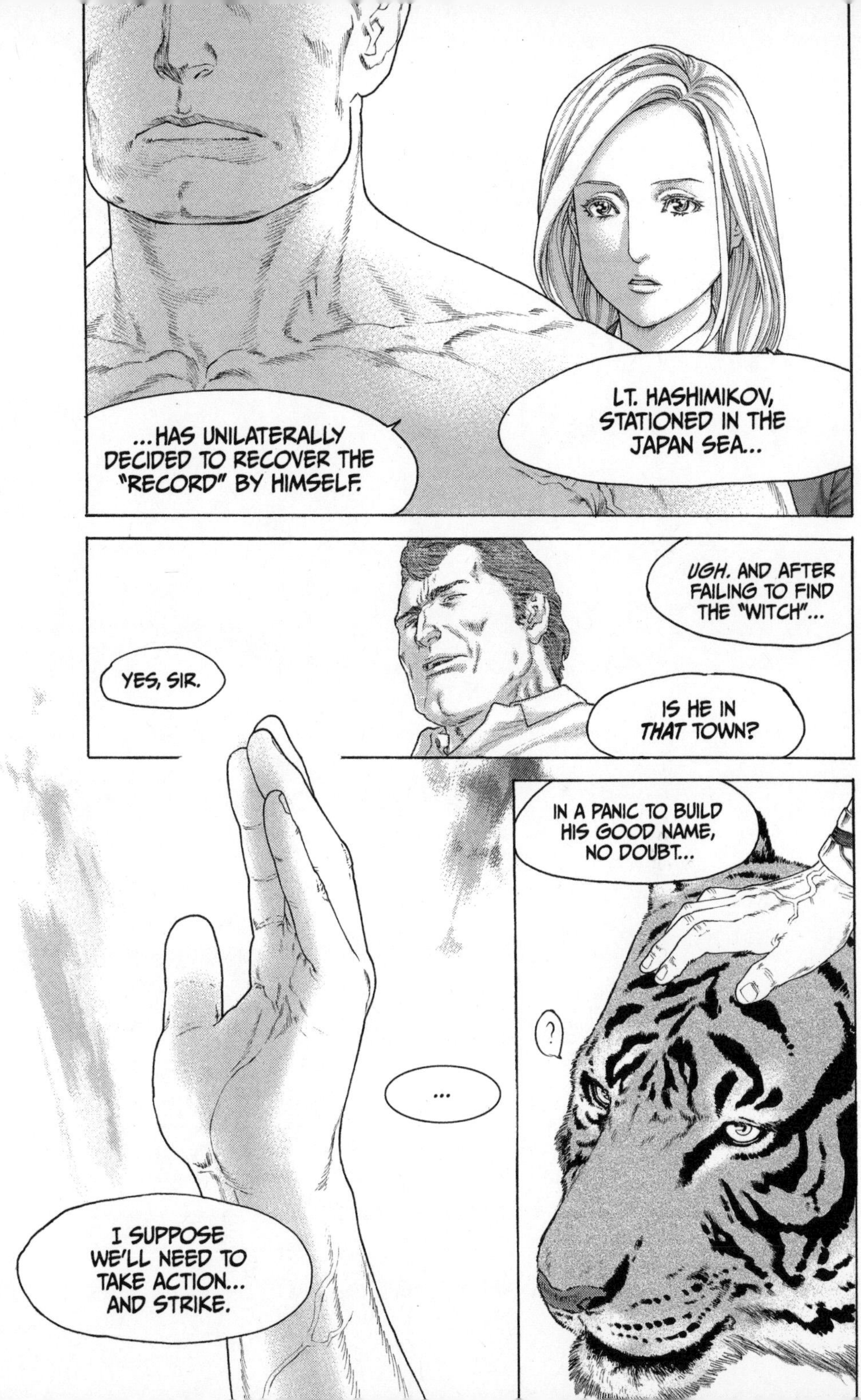
LT. HASHIMIKOV, STATIONED IN THE JAPAN SEA...
...HAS UNILATERALLY DECIDED TO RECOVER THE "RECORD" BY HIMSELF.
UGH. AND AFTER FAILING TO FIND THE "WITCH"...
IS HE IN *THAT* TOWN?
YES, SIR.
IN A PANIC TO BUILD HIS GOOD NAME, NO DOUBT...
?
...
I SUPPOSE WE'LL NEED TO TAKE ACTION... AND STRIKE.

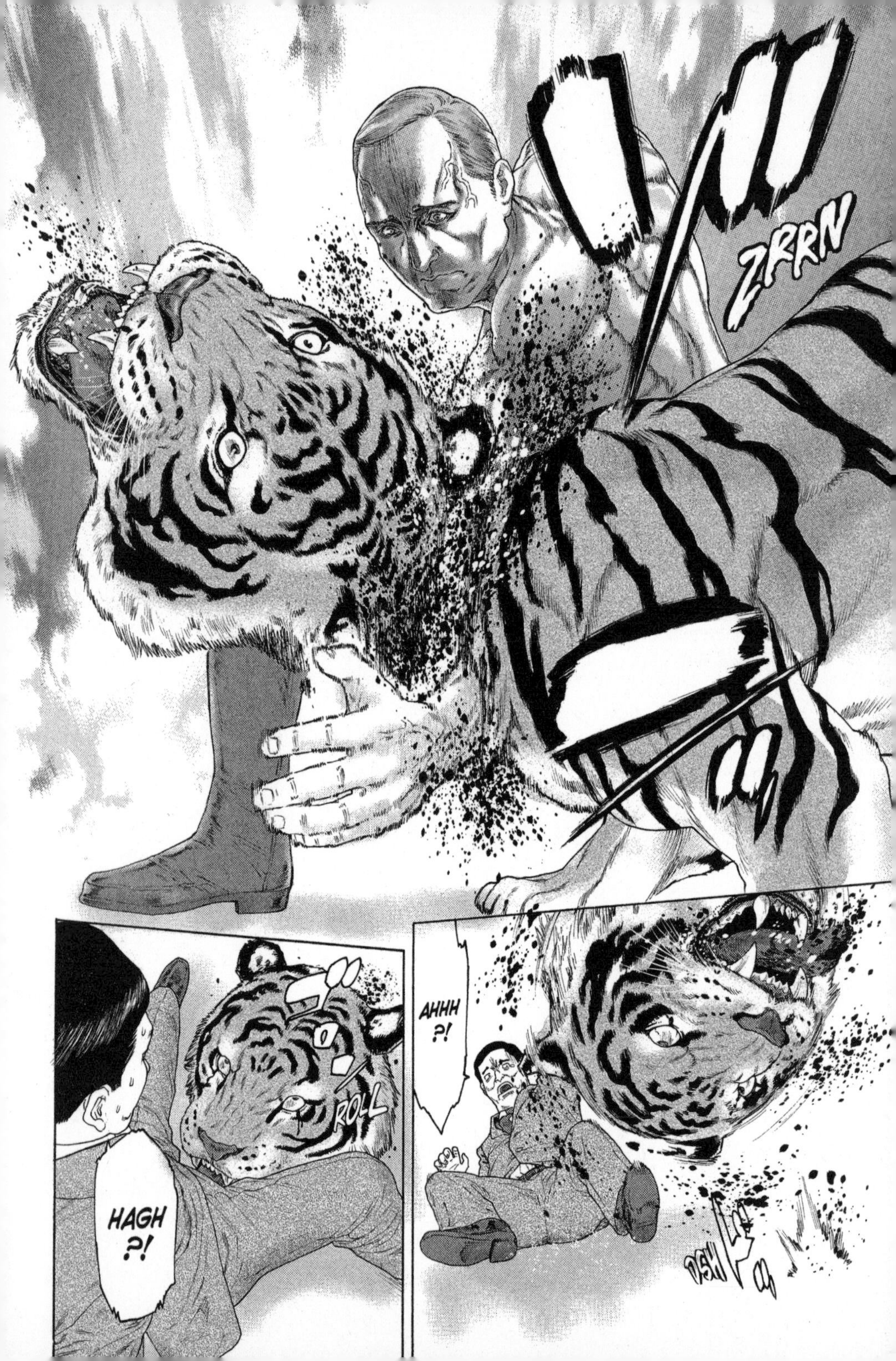
ZRRN
AHHH ?!
ROLL
HAGH ?!

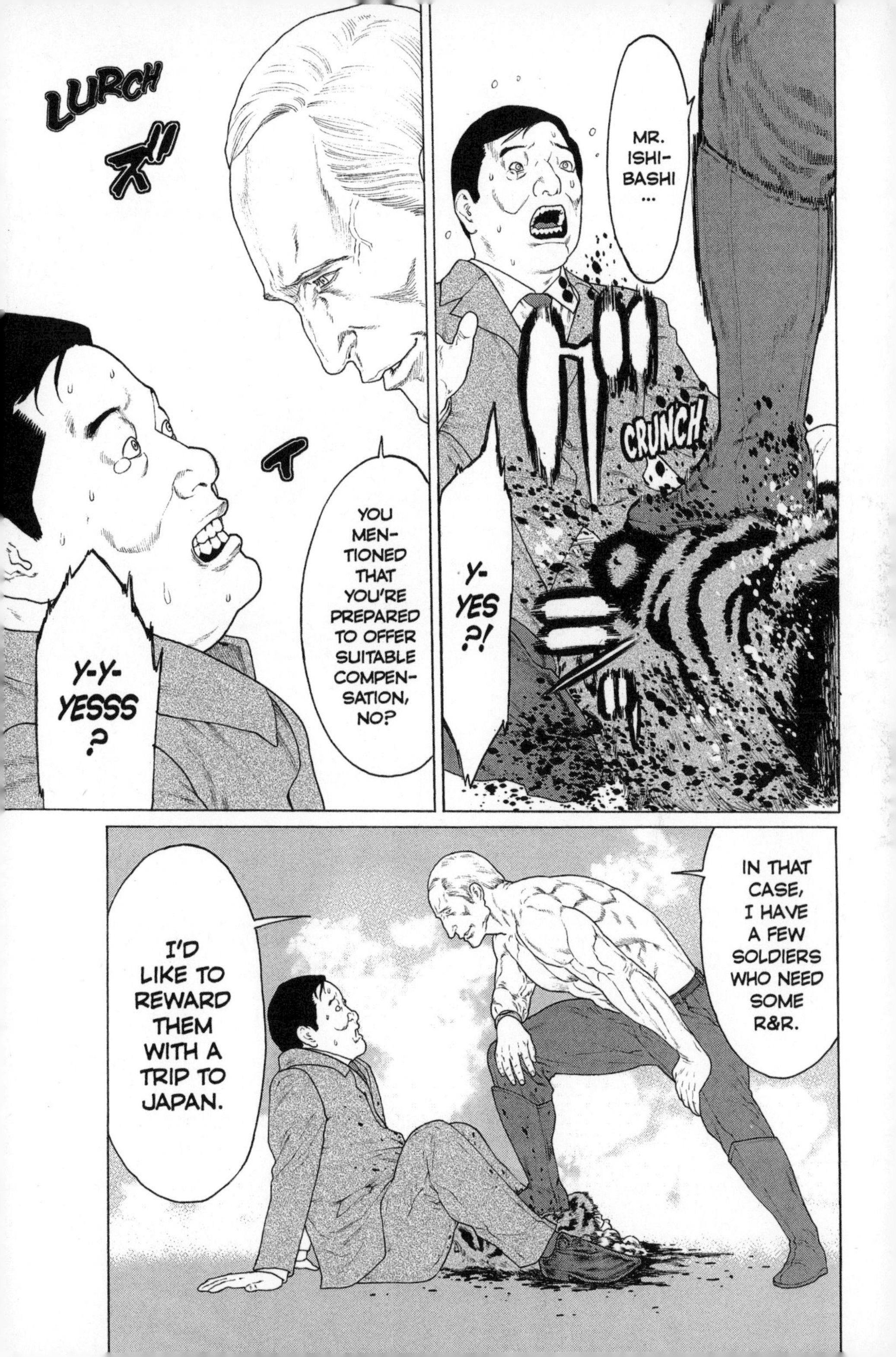
MR. ISHI-BASHI...
CRUNCH
Y-YES?!
LURCH
YOU MEN-TIONED THAT YOU'RE PREPARED TO OFFER SUITABLE COMPEN-SATION, NO?
Y-Y-YESSS?
IN THAT CASE, I HAVE A FEW SOLDIERS WHO NEED SOME R&R.
I'D LIKE TO REWARD THEM WITH A TRIP TO JAPAN.

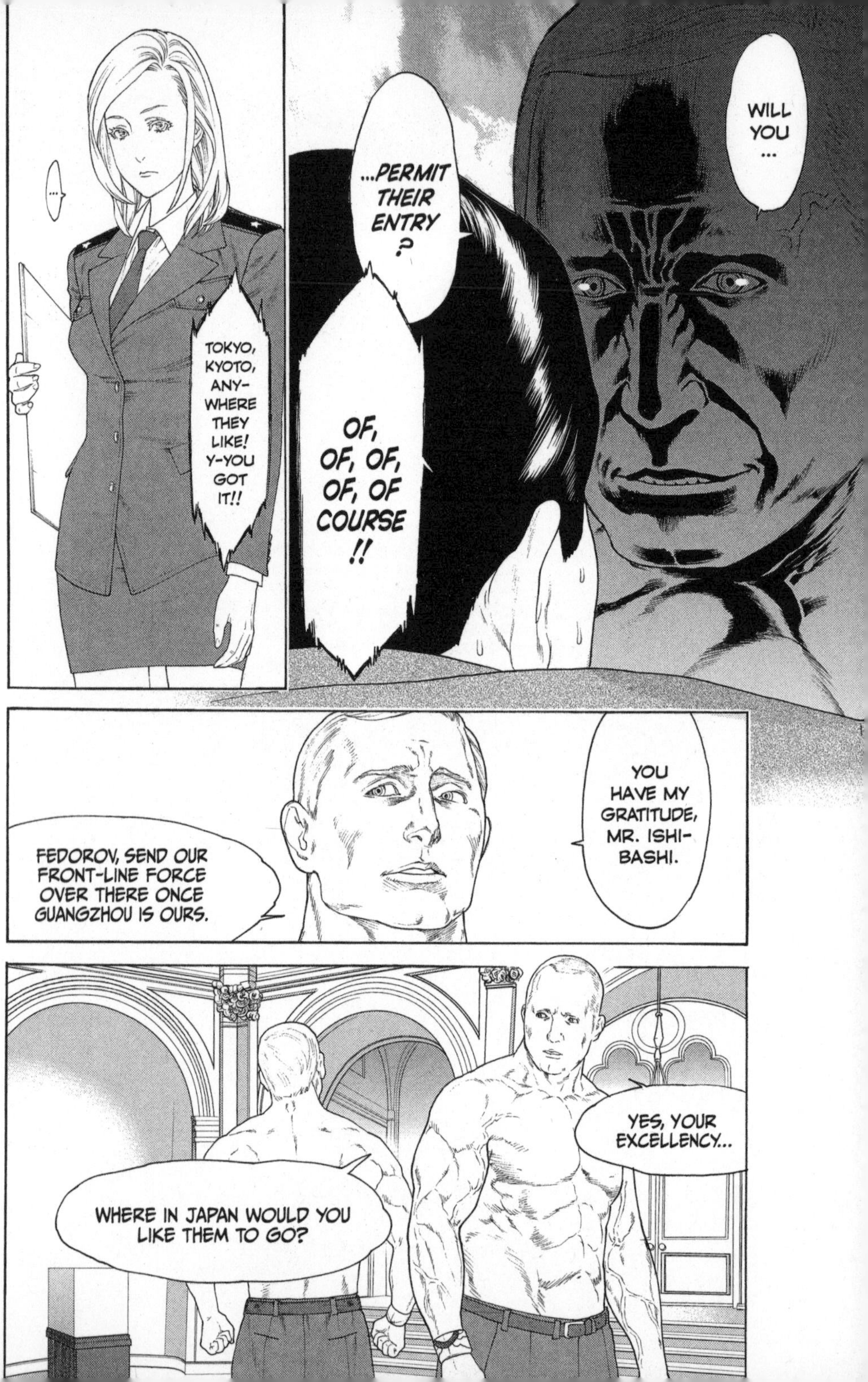
WILL YOU ...
...PERMIT THEIR ENTRY?
OF, OF, OF, OF, OF COURSE!!
...
TOKYO, KYOTO, ANY-WHERE THEY LIKE! Y-YOU GOT IT!!
YOU HAVE MY GRATITUDE, MR. ISHI-BASHI.
FEDOROV, SEND OUR FRONT-LINE FORCE OVER THERE ONCE GUANGZHOU IS OURS.
YES, YOUR EXCELLENCY...
WHERE IN JAPAN WOULD YOU LIKE THEM TO GO?

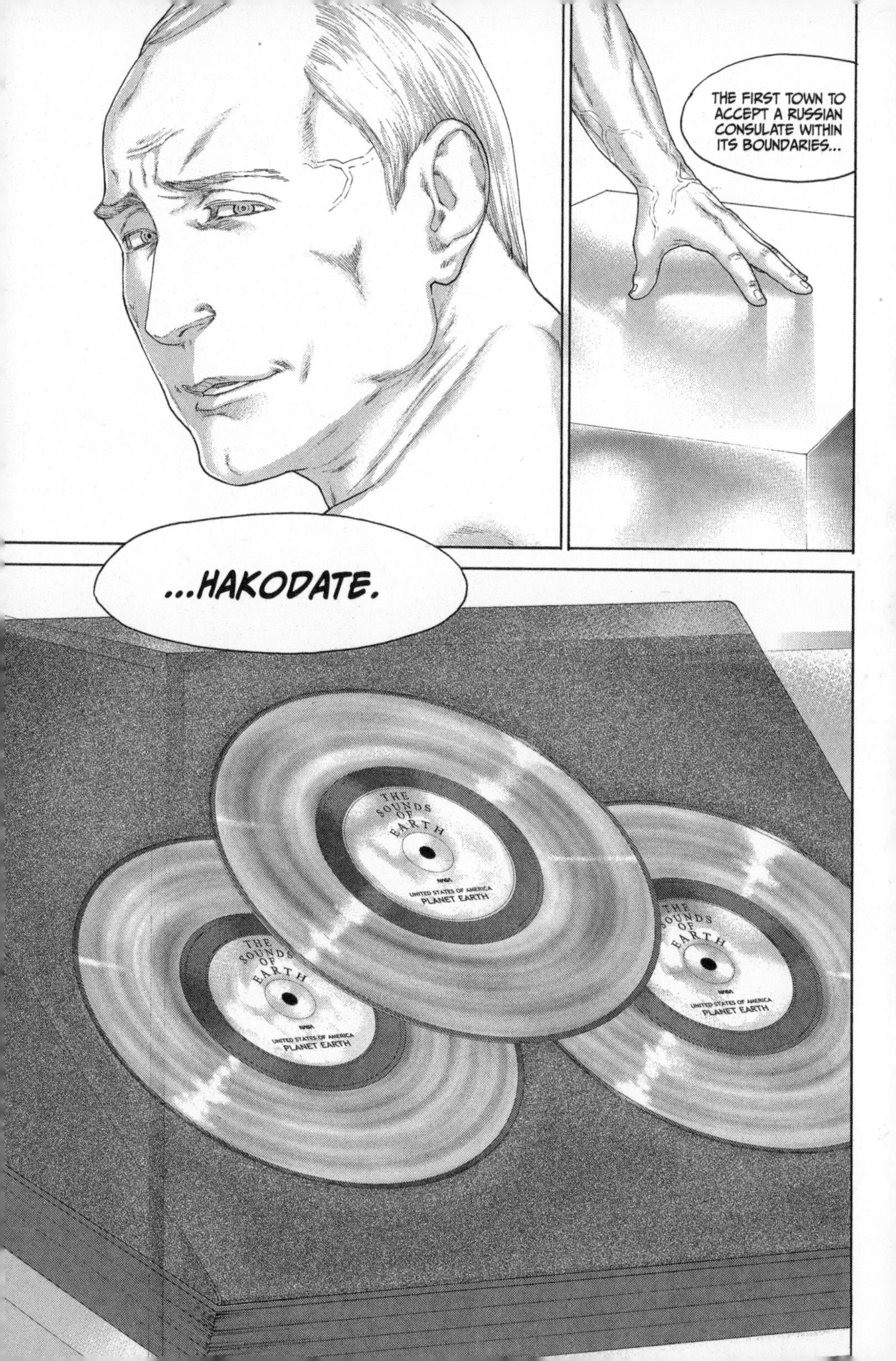
THE FIRST TOWN TO ACCEPT A RUSSIAN CONSULATE WITHIN ITS BOUNDARIES...
...HAKODATE.
THE SOUNDS OF EARTH
NASA
UNITED STATES OF AMERICA
PLANET EARTH

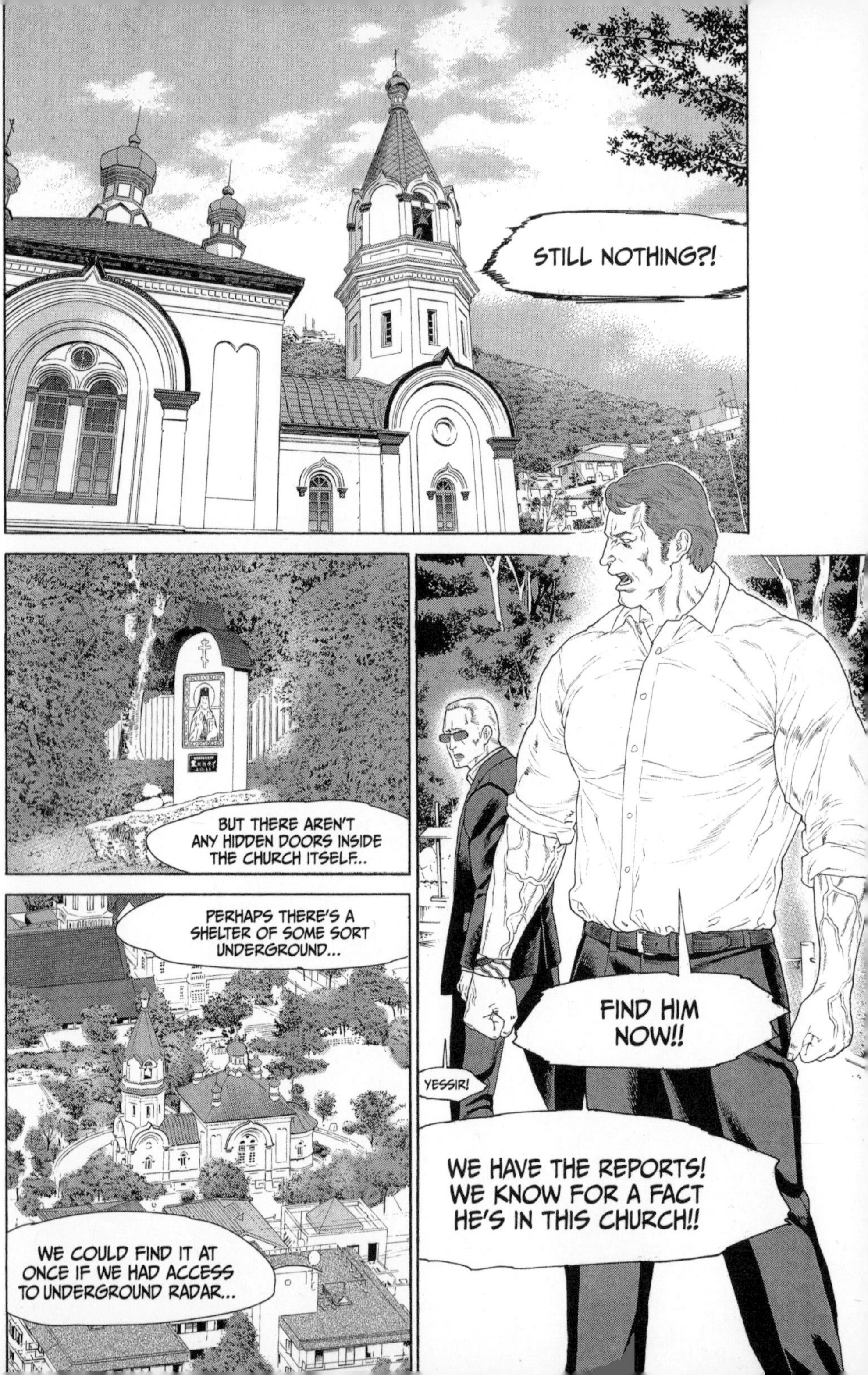
STILL NOTHING?!
FIND HIM NOW!!
YESSIR!
WE HAVE THE REPORTS! WE KNOW FOR A FACT HE'S IN THIS CHURCH!!
BUT THERE AREN'T ANY HIDDEN DOORS INSIDE THE CHURCH ITSELF...
PERHAPS THERE'S A SHELTER OF SOME SORT UNDERGROUND...
WE COULD FIND IT AT ONCE IF WE HAD ACCESS TO UNDERGROUND RADAR...

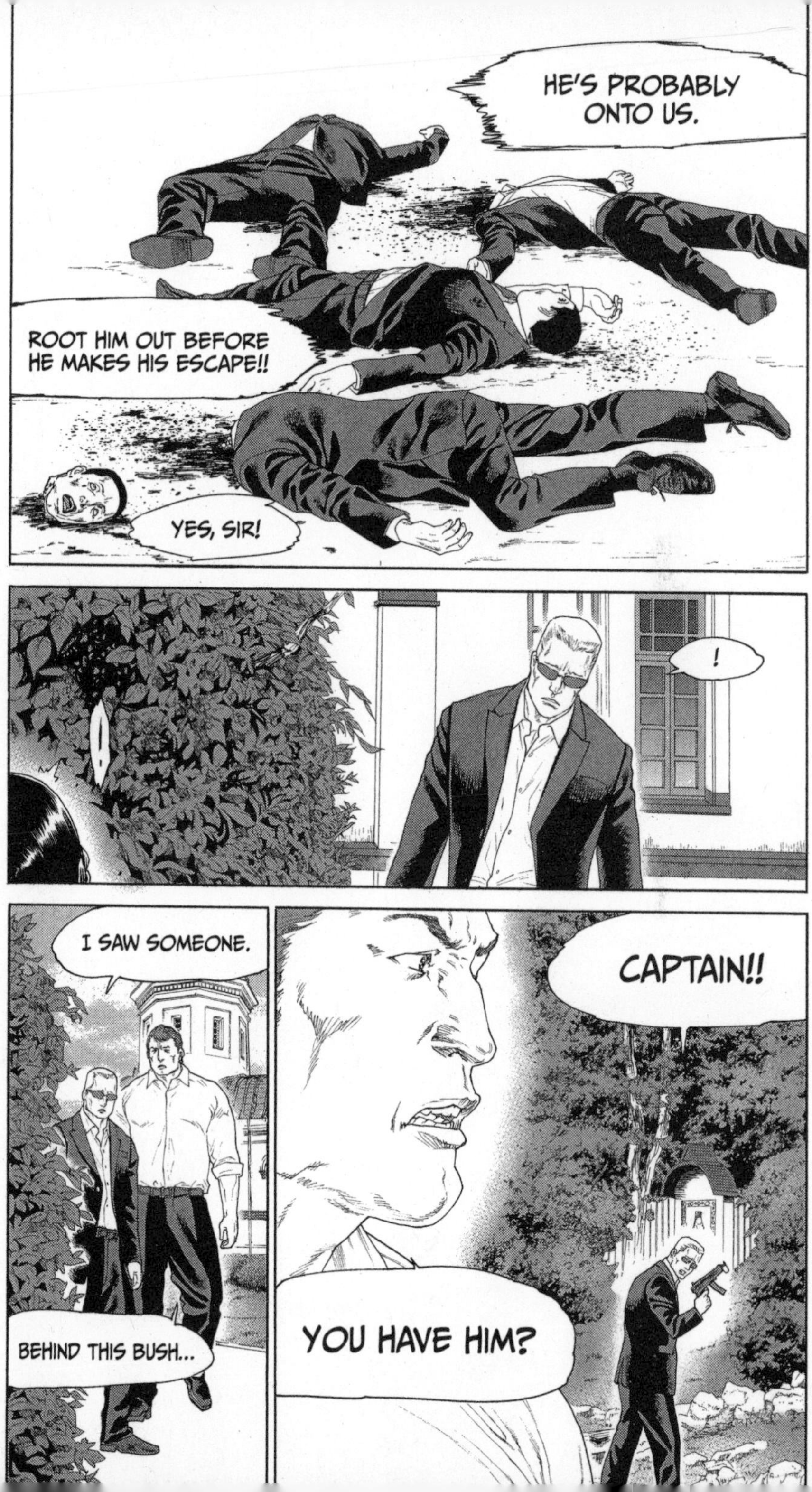
HE'S PROBABLY ONTO US.
ROOT HIM OUT BEFORE HE MAKES HIS ESCAPE!!
YES, SIR!
!
!
CAPTAIN!!
YOU HAVE HIM?
I SAW SOMEONE.
BEHIND THIS BUSH...

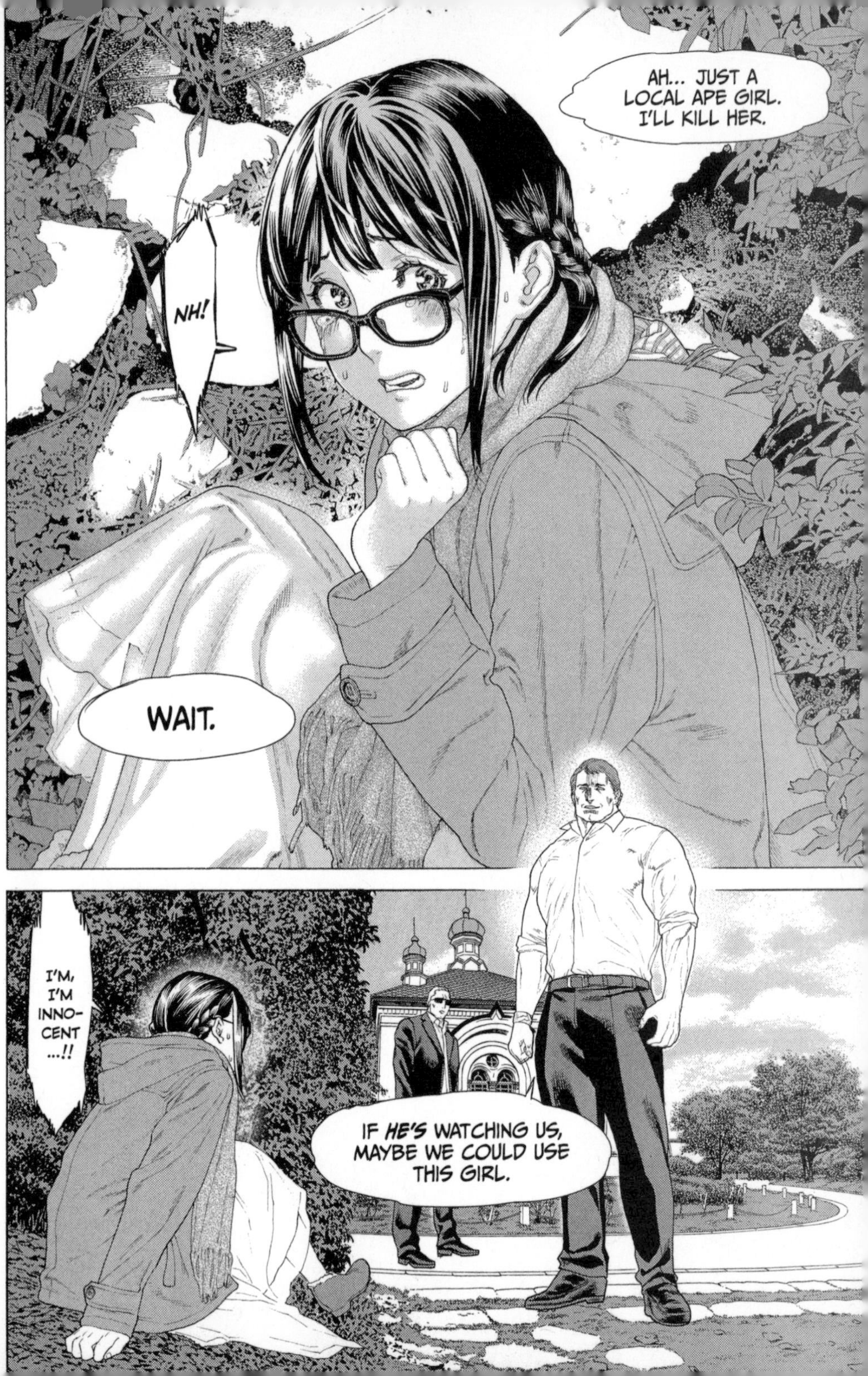
AH... JUST A LOCAL APE GIRL. I'LL KILL HER.
NH!
WAIT.
IF *HE'S* WATCHING US, MAYBE WE COULD USE THIS GIRL.
I'M, I'M INNO-CENT ...!!

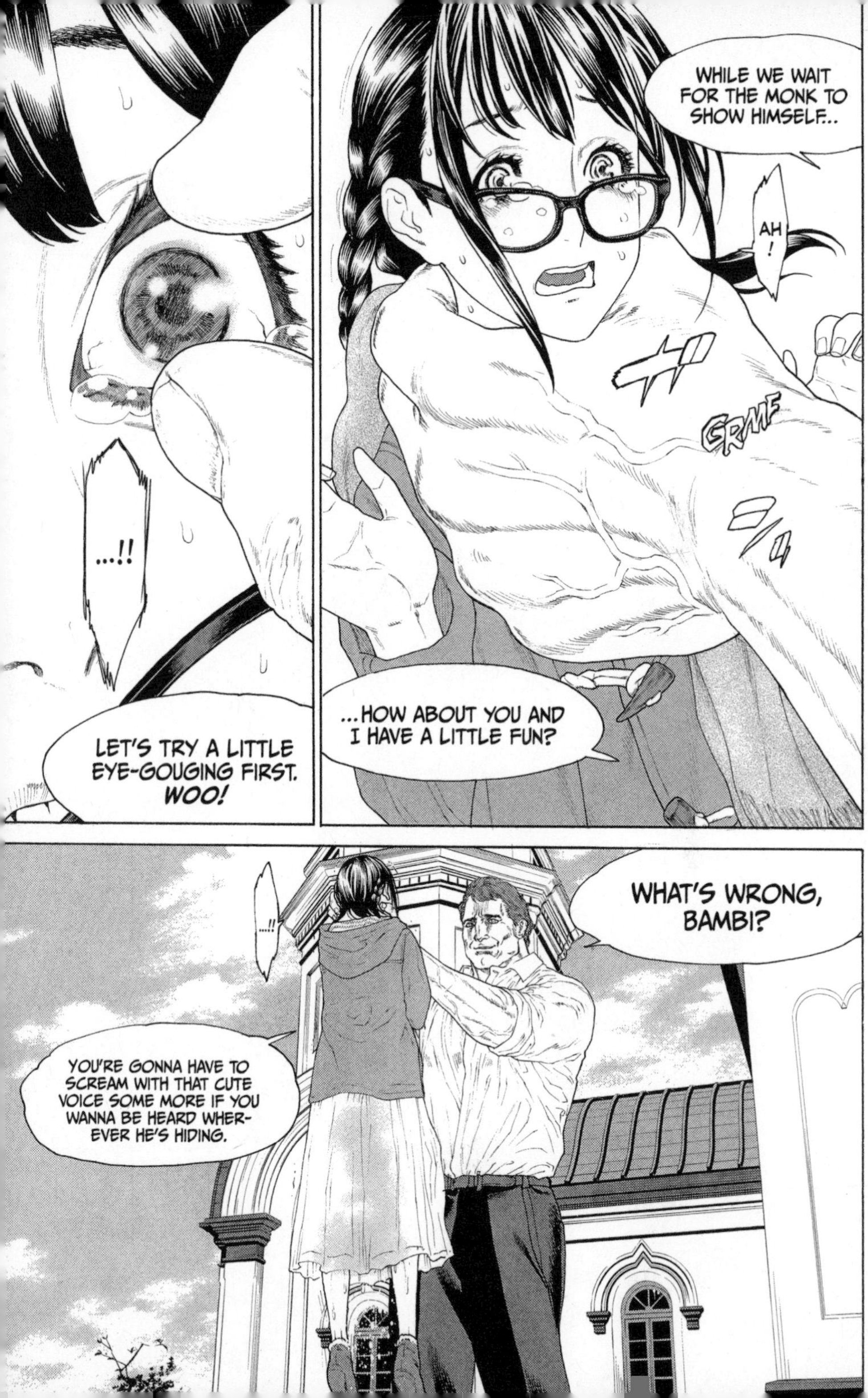
WHILE WE WAIT FOR THE MONK TO SHOW HIMSELF...
AH!
GRMF
...HOW ABOUT YOU AND I HAVE A LITTLE FUN?
...!!
LET'S TRY A LITTLE EYE-GOUGING FIRST. WOO!
WHAT'S WRONG, BAMBI?
...!!
YOU'RE GONNA HAVE TO SCREAM WITH THAT CUTE VOICE SOME MORE IF YOU WANNA BE HEARD WHEREVER HE'S HIDING.

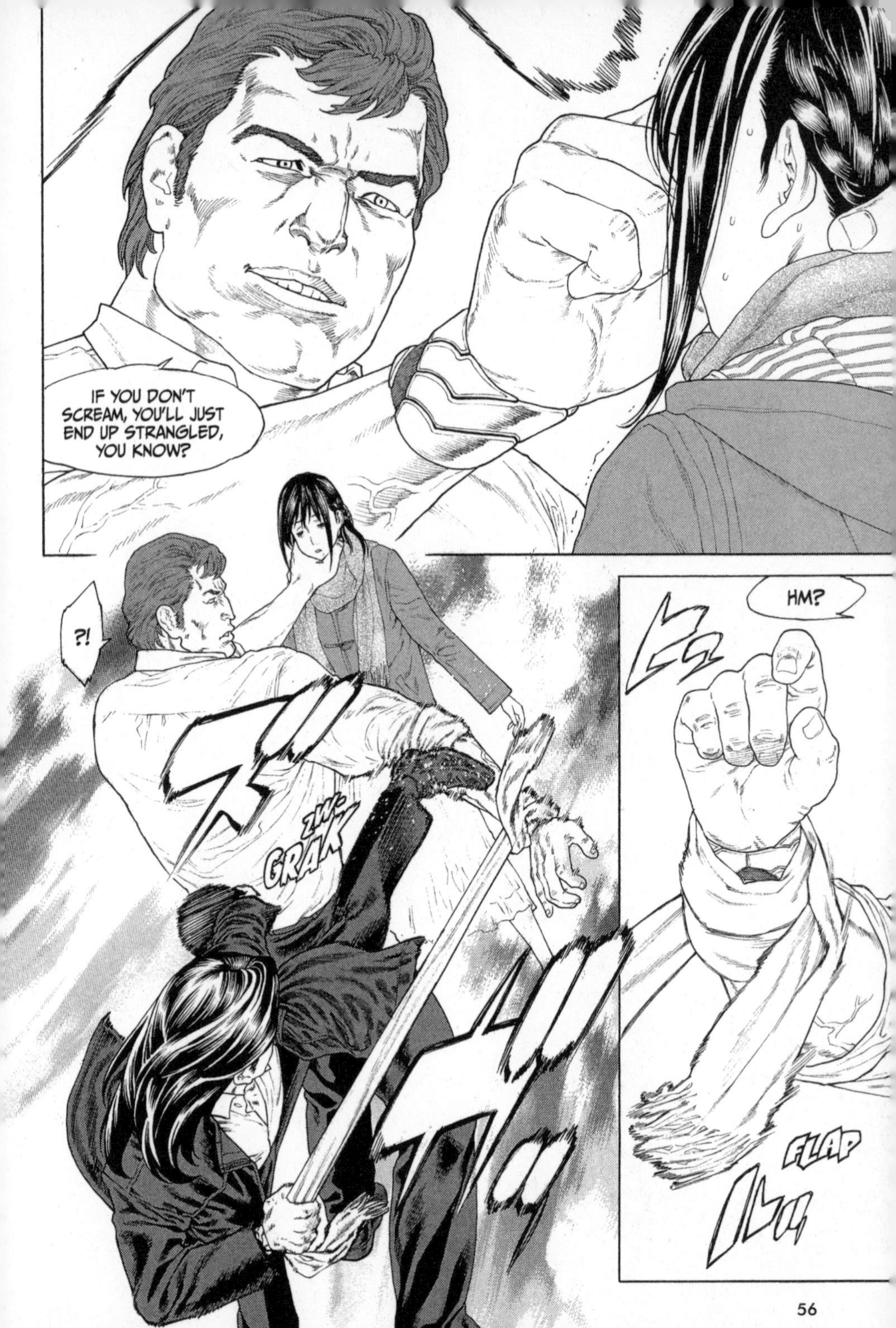
IF YOU DON'T SCREAM, YOU'LL JUST END UP STRANGLED, YOU KNOW?
HM?
FLAP
?!
ZW-GRAK

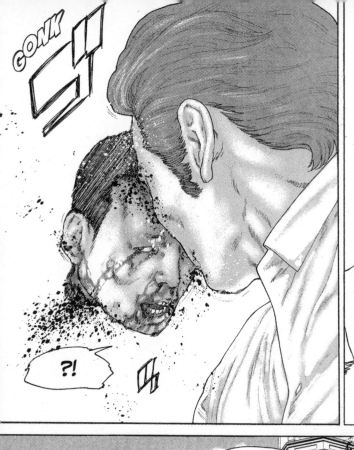

GONK

?!

HUHH?!

NGH...!

ZSSH

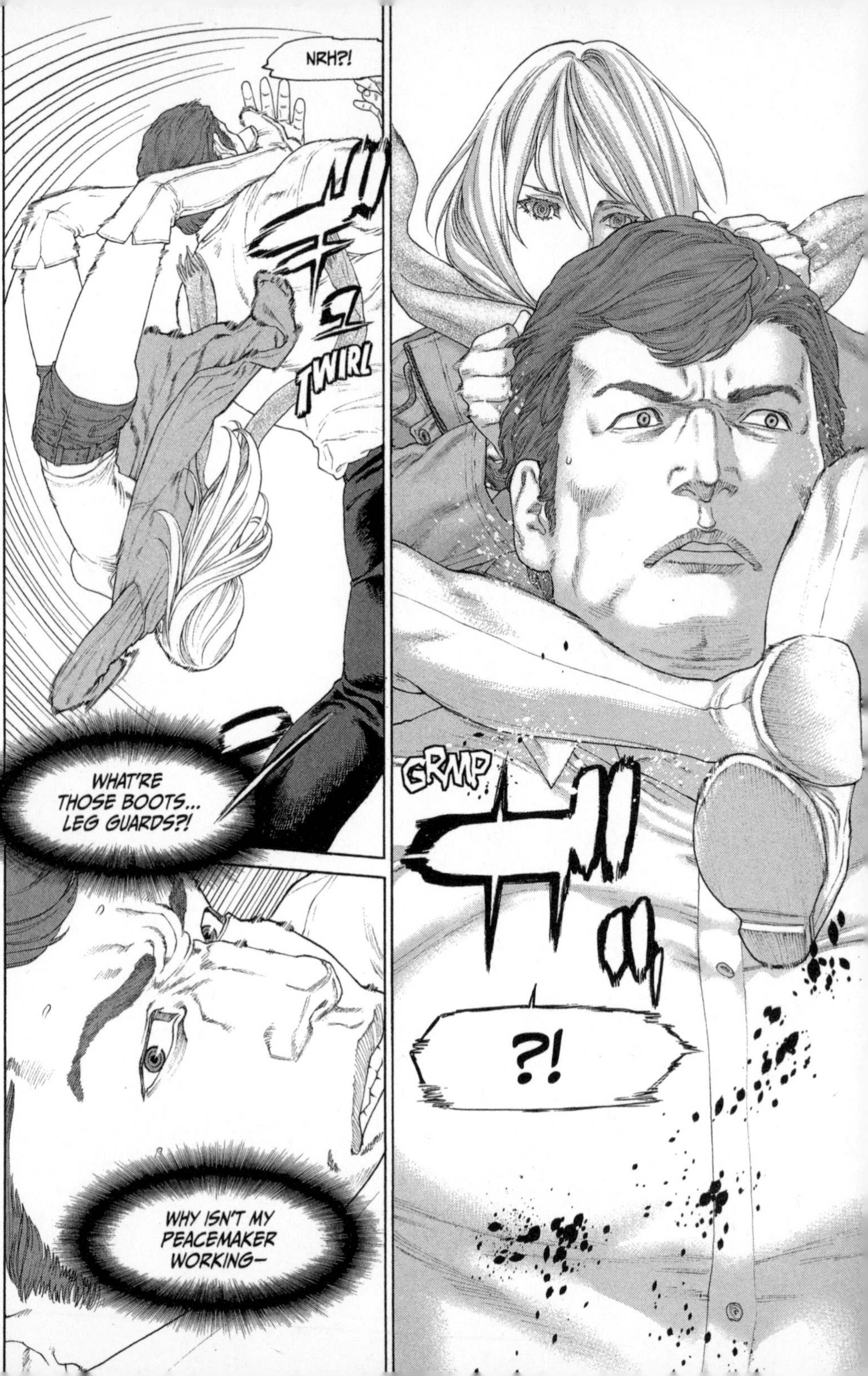
CRMP
?!
NRH?!
TWIRL
WHAT'RE THOSE BOOTS... LEG GUARDS?!
WHY ISN'T MY PEACEMAKER WORKING—

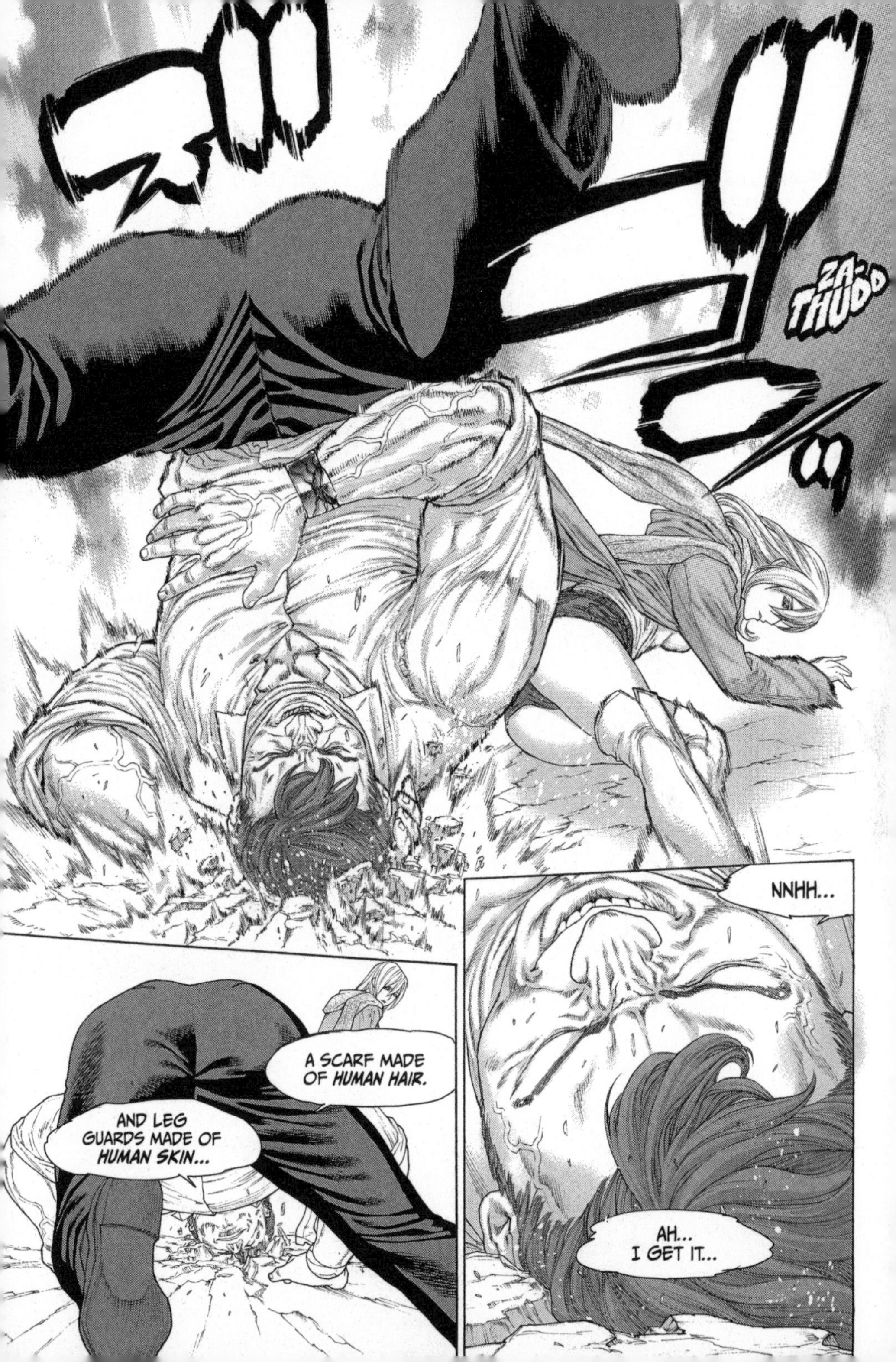
ZA-THUDD
NNHH...
AH... I GET IT...
A SCARF MADE OF HUMAN HAIR.
AND LEG GUARDS MADE OF HUMAN SKIN...

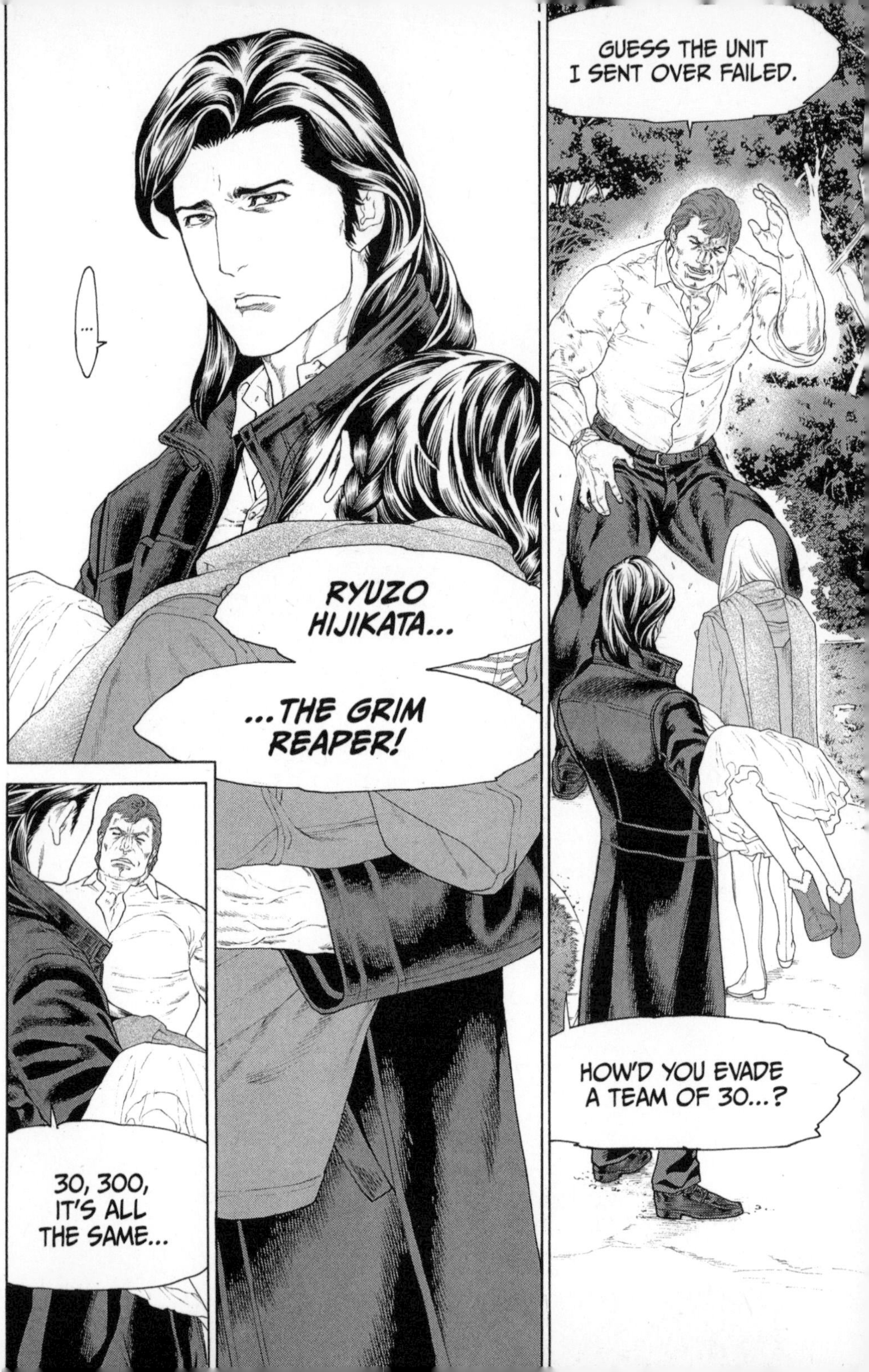
GUESS THE UNIT I SENT OVER FAILED.
HOW'D YOU EVADE A TEAM OF 30...?
...
RYUZO HIJIKATA...
...THE GRIM REAPER!
30, 300, IT'S ALL THE SAME...

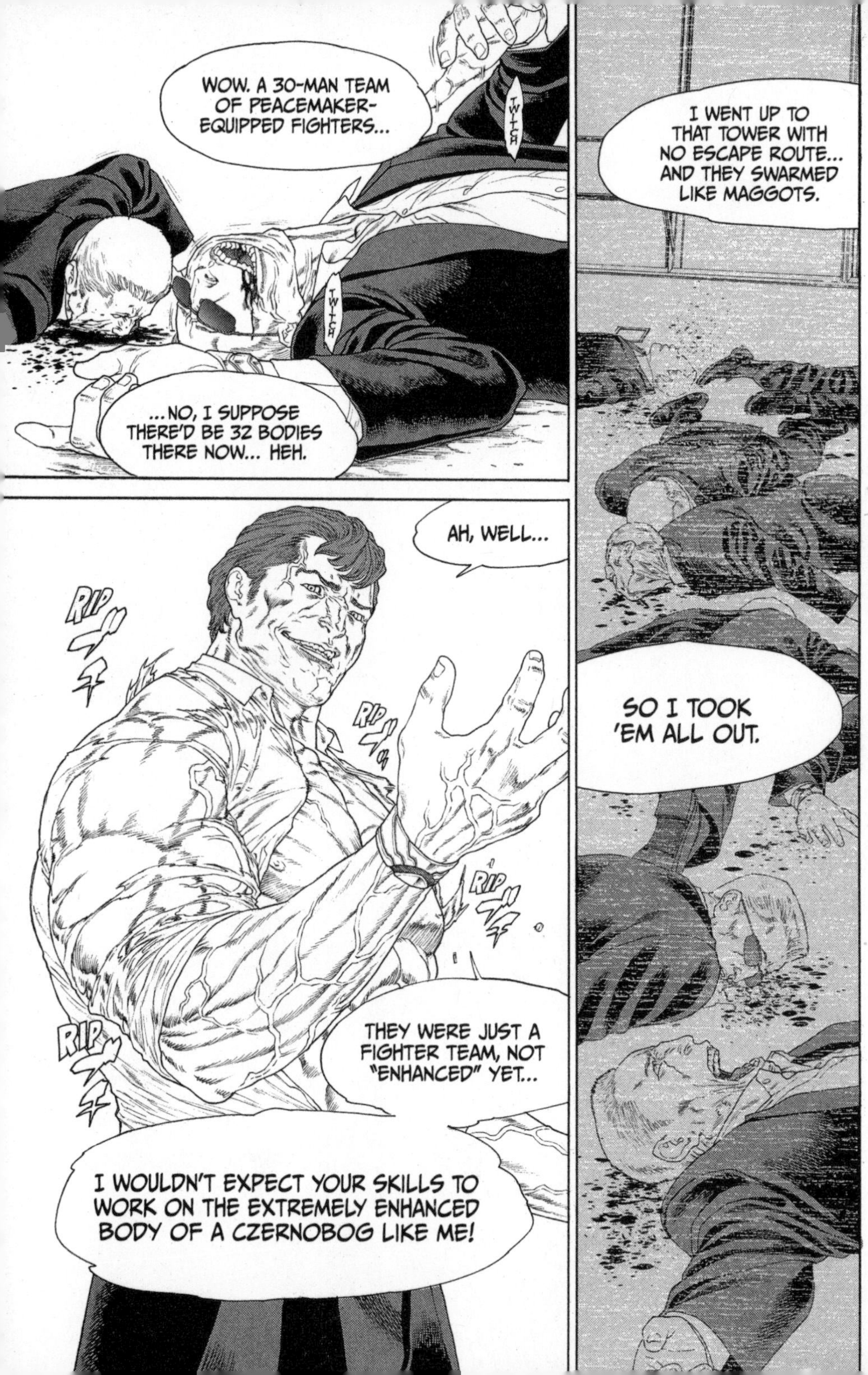
I WENT UP TO THAT TOWER WITH NO ESCAPE ROUTE... AND THEY SWARMED LIKE MAGGOTS.
SO I TOOK 'EM ALL OUT.
WOW. A 30-MAN TEAM OF PEACEMAKER-EQUIPPED FIGHTERS...
TWITCH
TWITCH
...NO, I SUPPOSE THERE'D BE 32 BODIES THERE NOW... HEH.
AH, WELL...
RIP
RIP
RIP
RIP
THEY WERE JUST A FIGHTER TEAM, NOT "ENHANCED" YET...
I WOULDN'T EXPECT YOUR SKILLS TO WORK ON THE EXTREMELY ENHANCED BODY OF A CZERNOBOG LIKE ME!

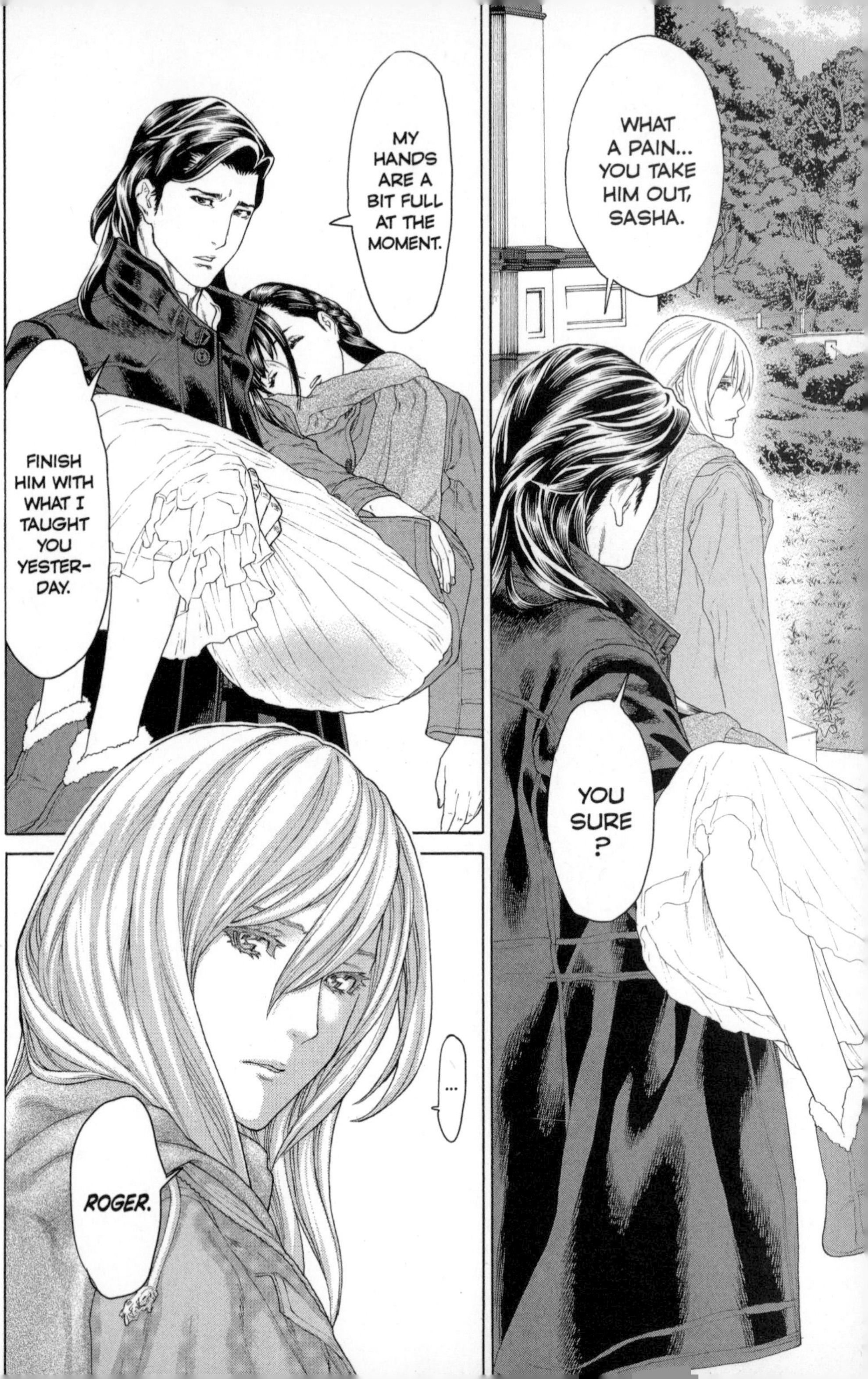
WHAT A PAIN... YOU TAKE HIM OUT, SASHA.
YOU SURE?
MY HANDS ARE A BIT FULL AT THE MOMENT.
FINISH HIM WITH WHAT I TAUGHT YOU YESTER-DAY.
...
ROGER.

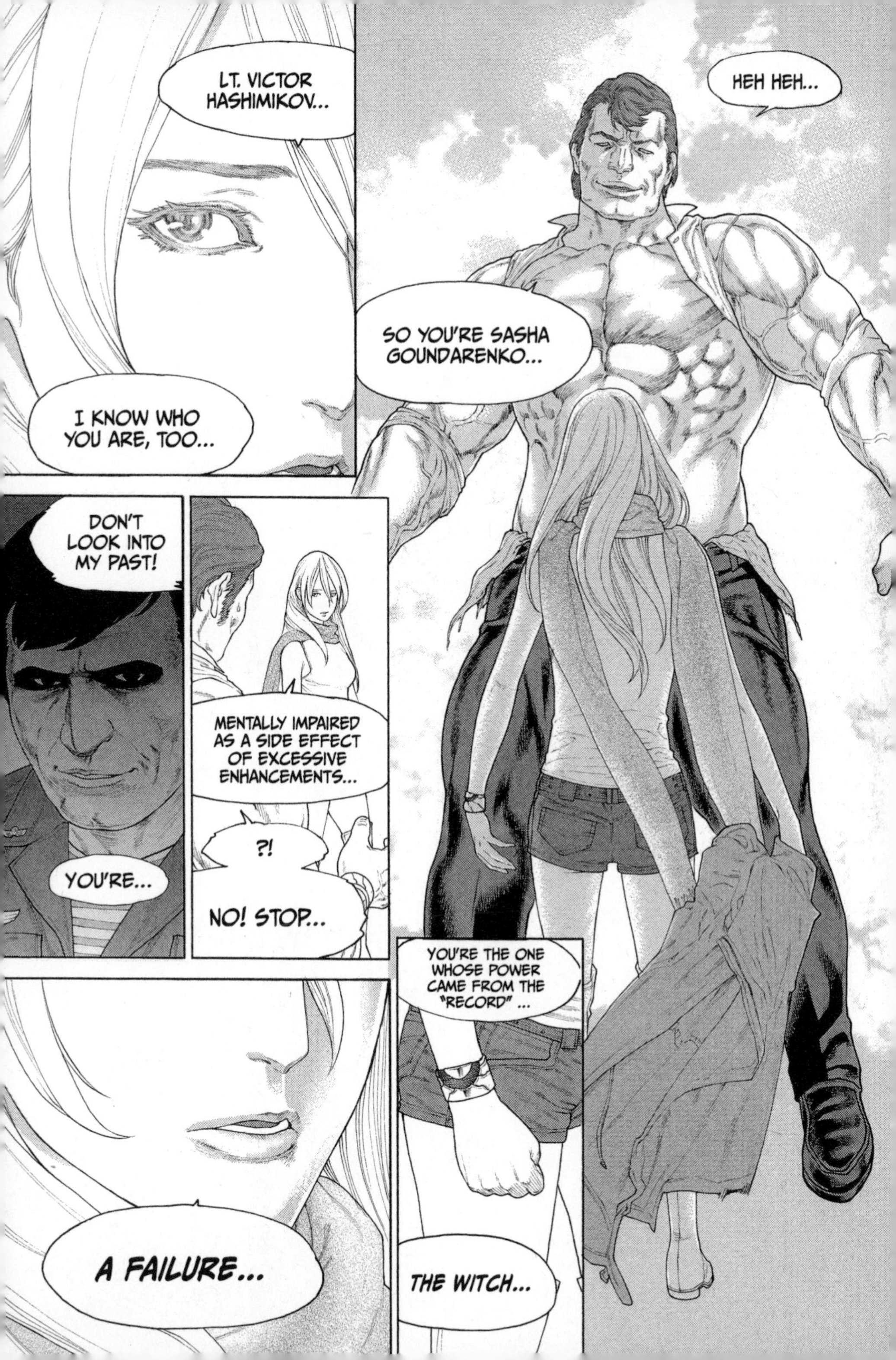
HEH HEH...
SO YOU'RE SASHA GOUNDARENKO...
LT. VICTOR HASHIMIKOV...
I KNOW WHO YOU ARE, TOO...
MENTALLY IMPAIRED AS A SIDE EFFECT OF EXCESSIVE ENHANCEMENTS...
?!
NO! STOP...
DON'T LOOK INTO MY PAST!
YOU'RE...
YOU'RE THE ONE WHOSE POWER CAME FROM THE "RECORD" ...
THE WITCH...
A FAILURE...

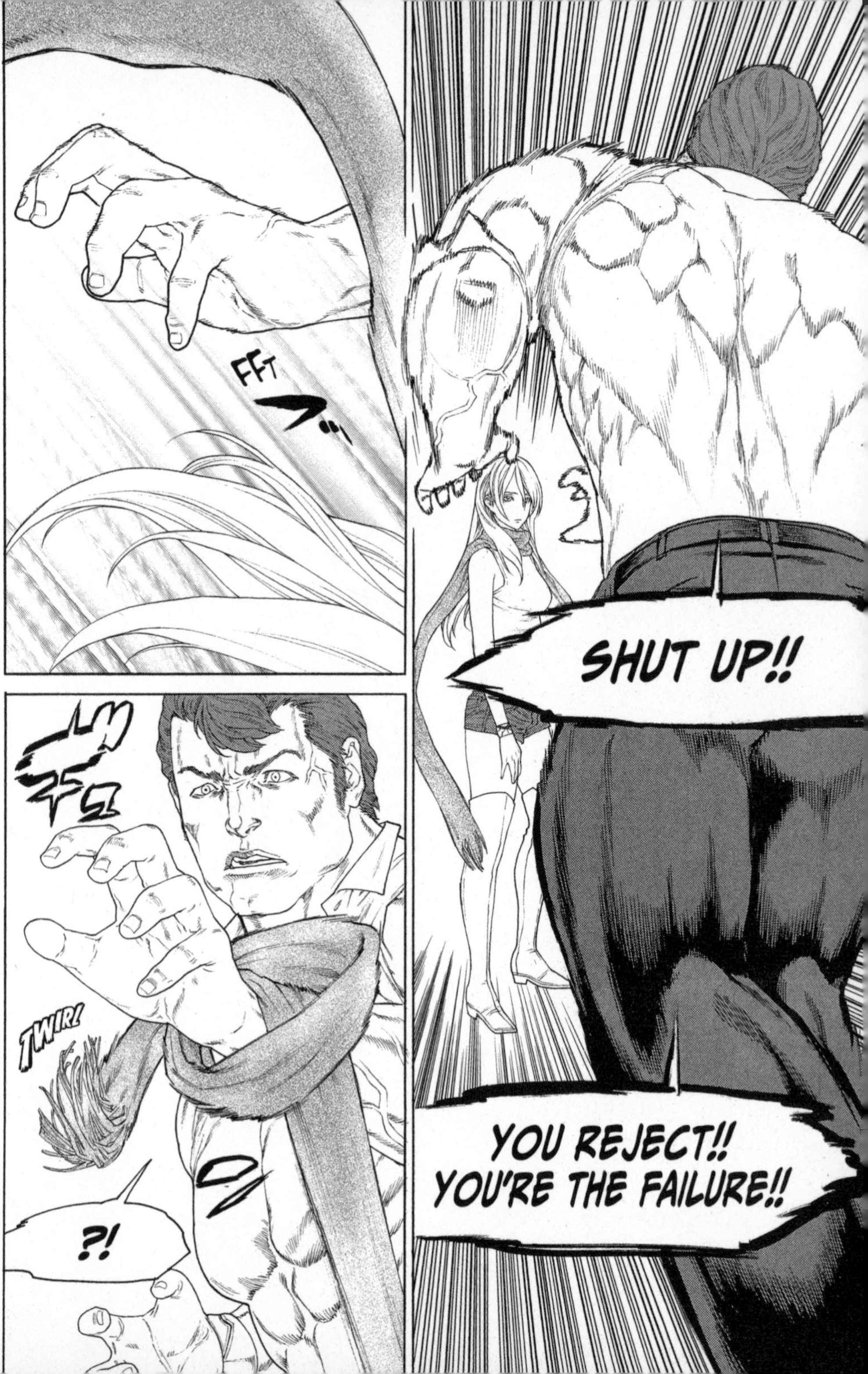
SHUT UP!!
YOU REJECT!! YOU'RE THE FAILURE!!
FFT
TWIRL
?!

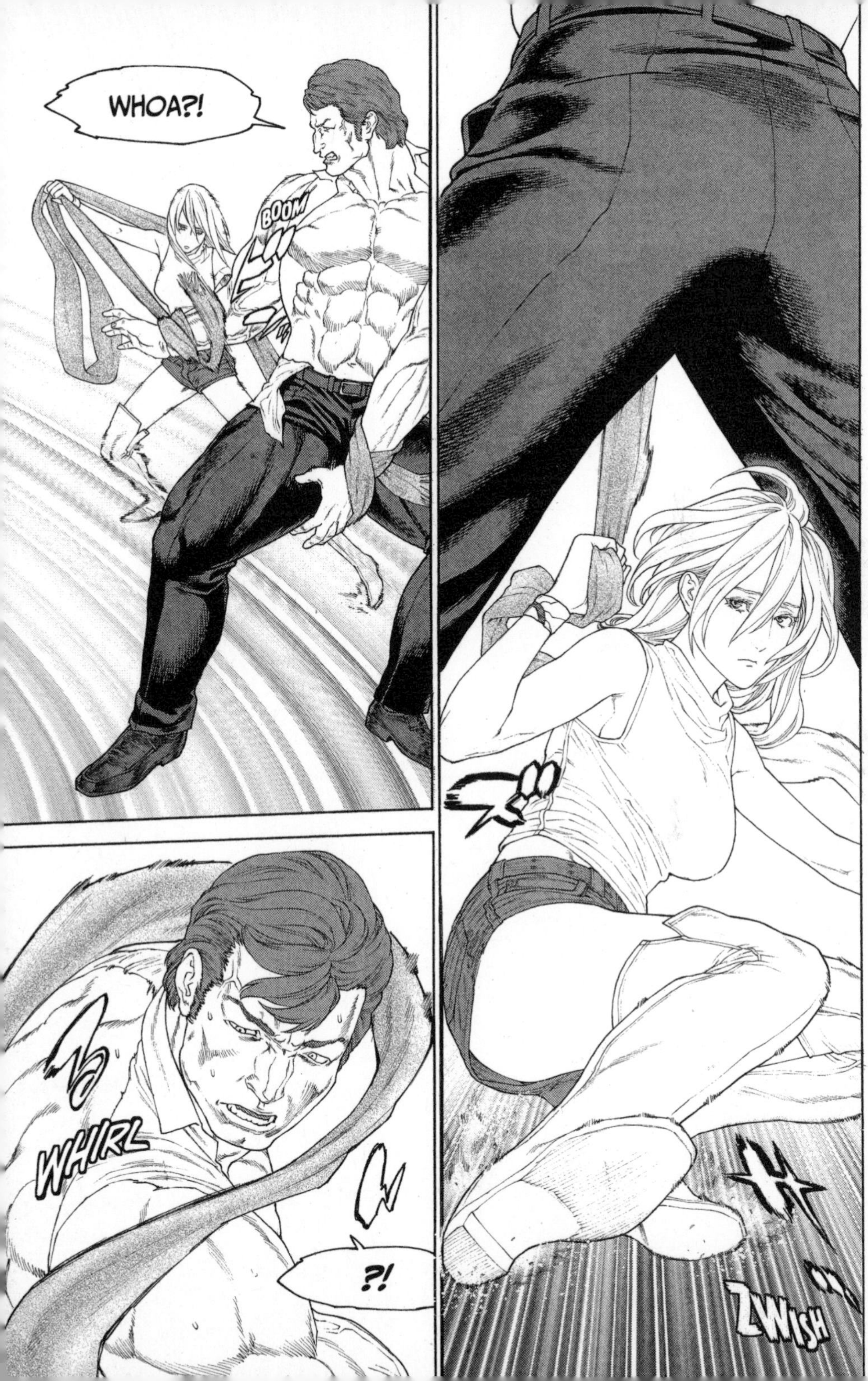
ZWISH
WHOA?!
BOOM
WHIRL
?!

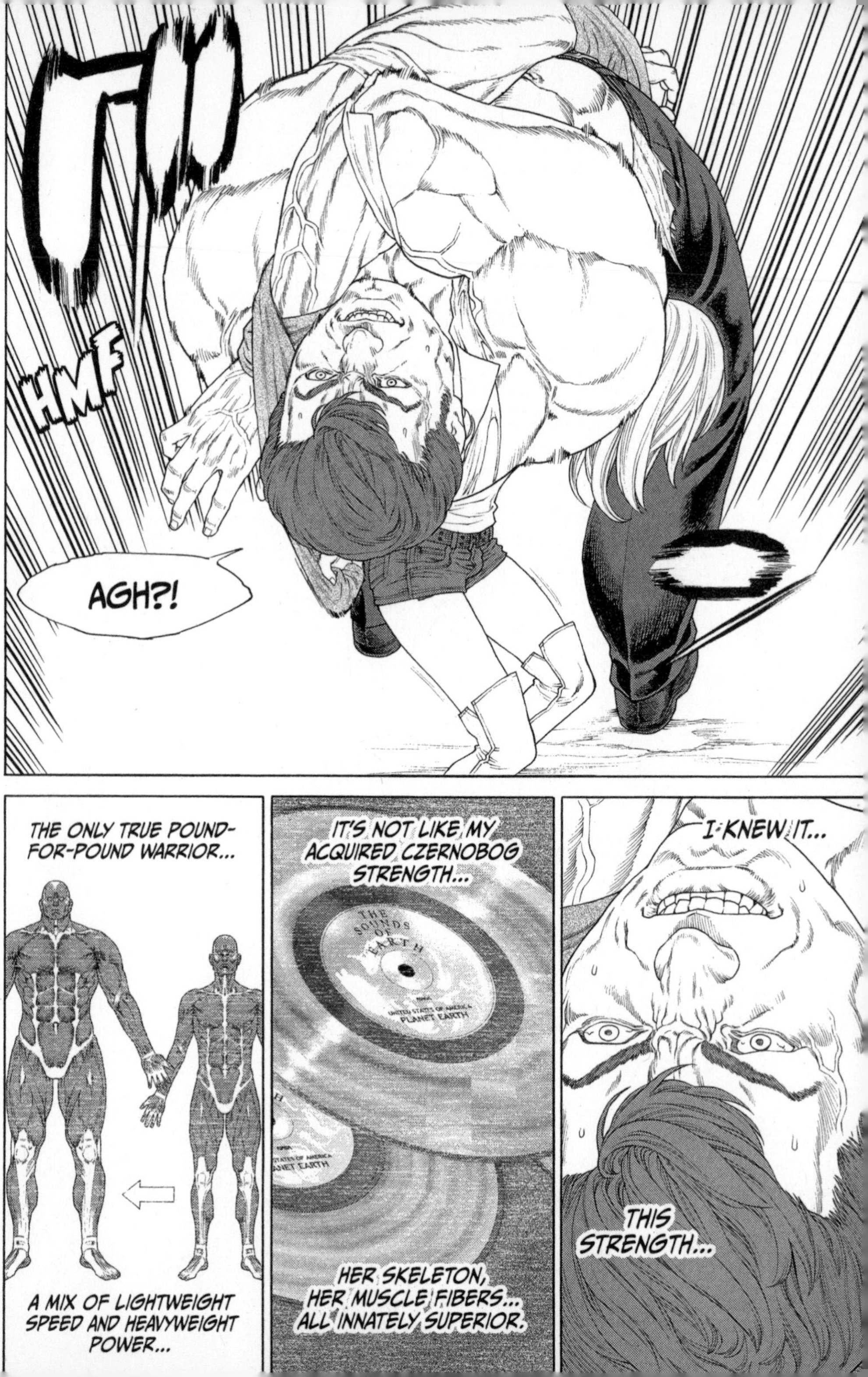
HMF
AGH?!
I KNEW IT...
THIS STRENGTH...
IT'S NOT LIKE MY ACQUIRED CZERNOBOG STRENGTH...
THE SOUNDS OF EARTH
UNITED STATES OF AMERICA
PLANET EARTH
HER SKELETON, HER MUSCLE FIBERS... ALL INNATELY SUPERIOR.
THE ONLY TRUE POUND-FOR-POUND WARRIOR...
A MIX OF LIGHTWEIGHT SPEED AND HEAVYWEIGHT POWER...

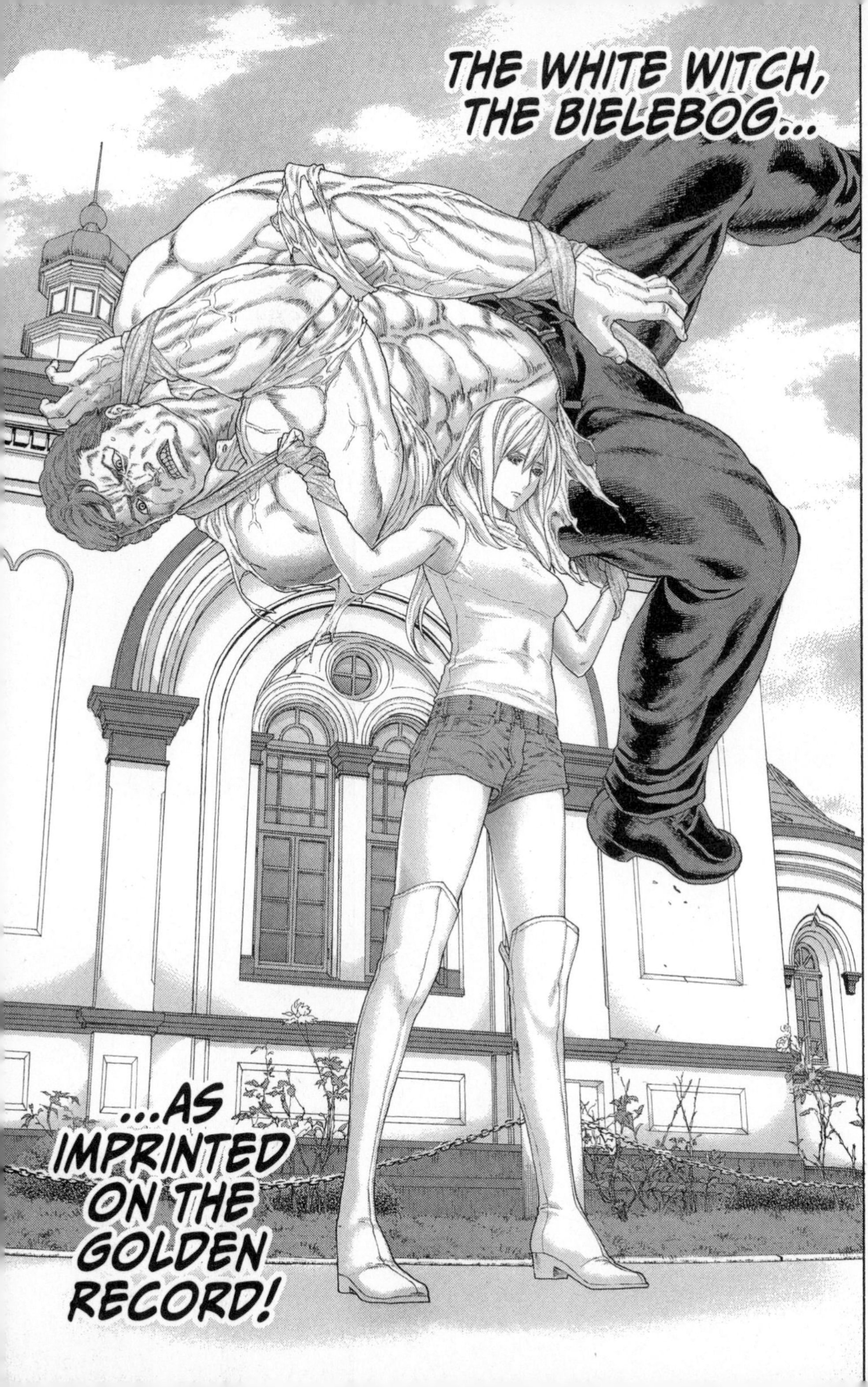
THE WHITE WITCH, THE BIELEBOG...
...AS IMPRINTED ON THE GOLDEN RECORD!

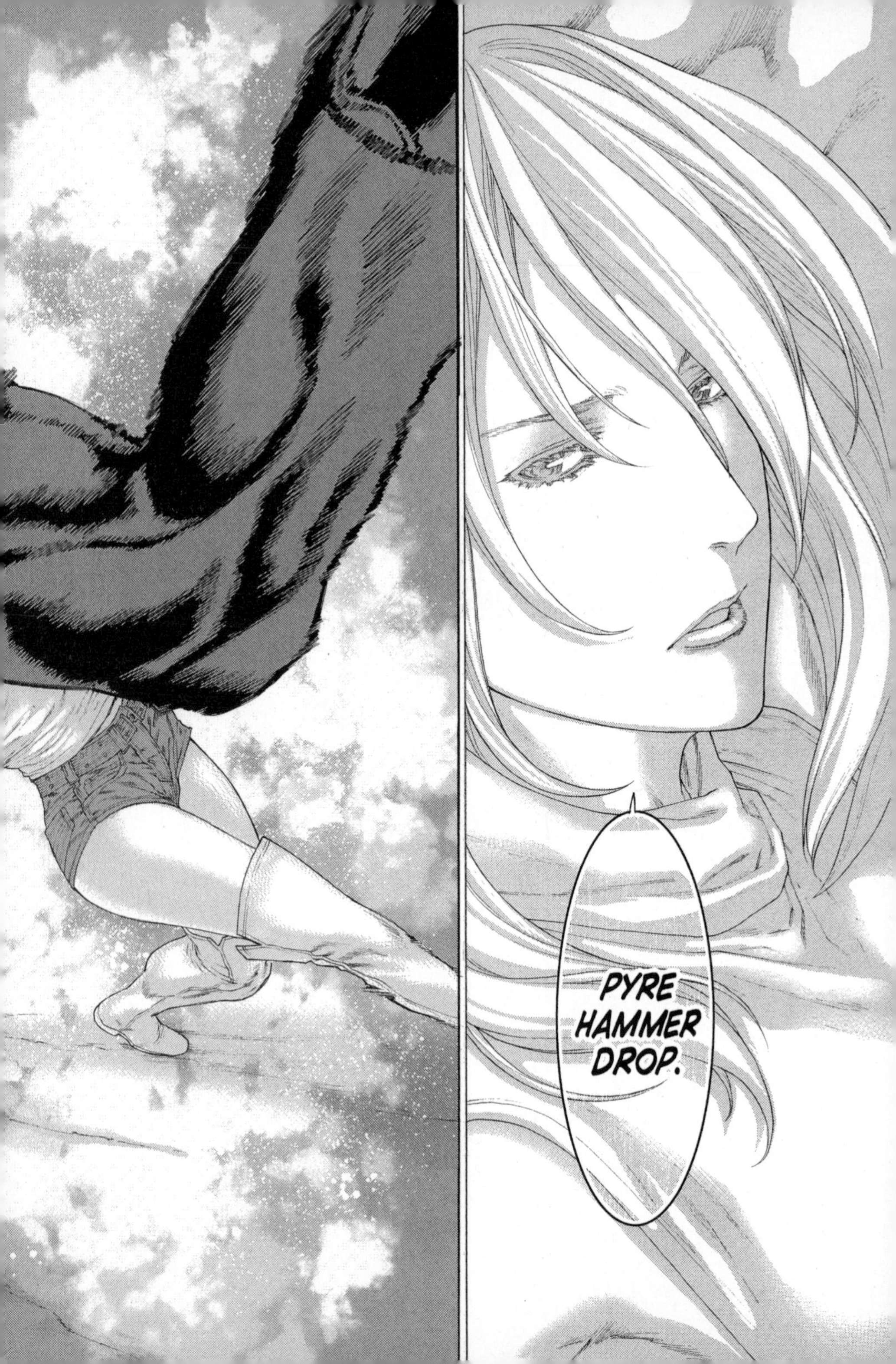
PYRE HAMMER DROP.

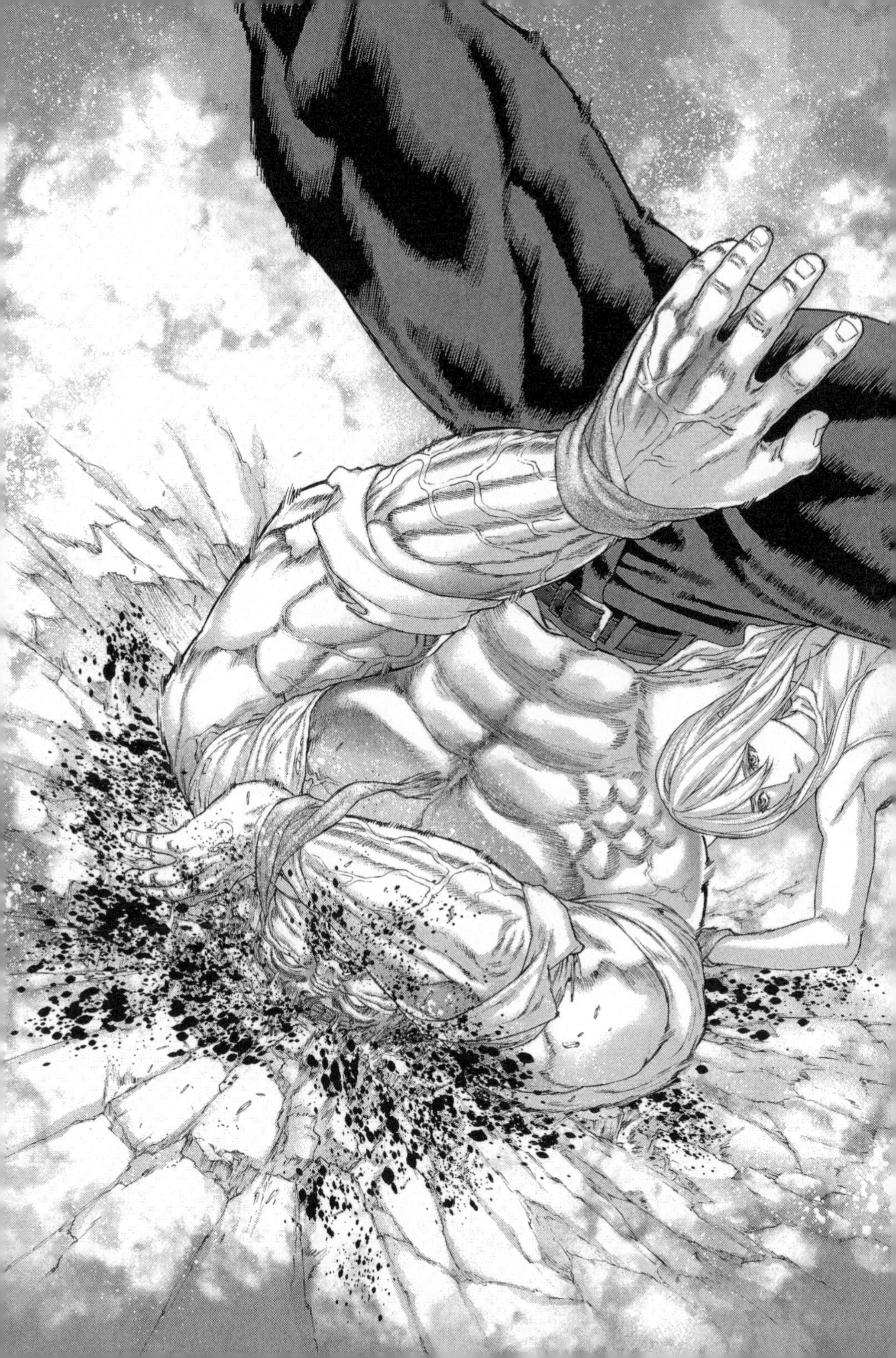

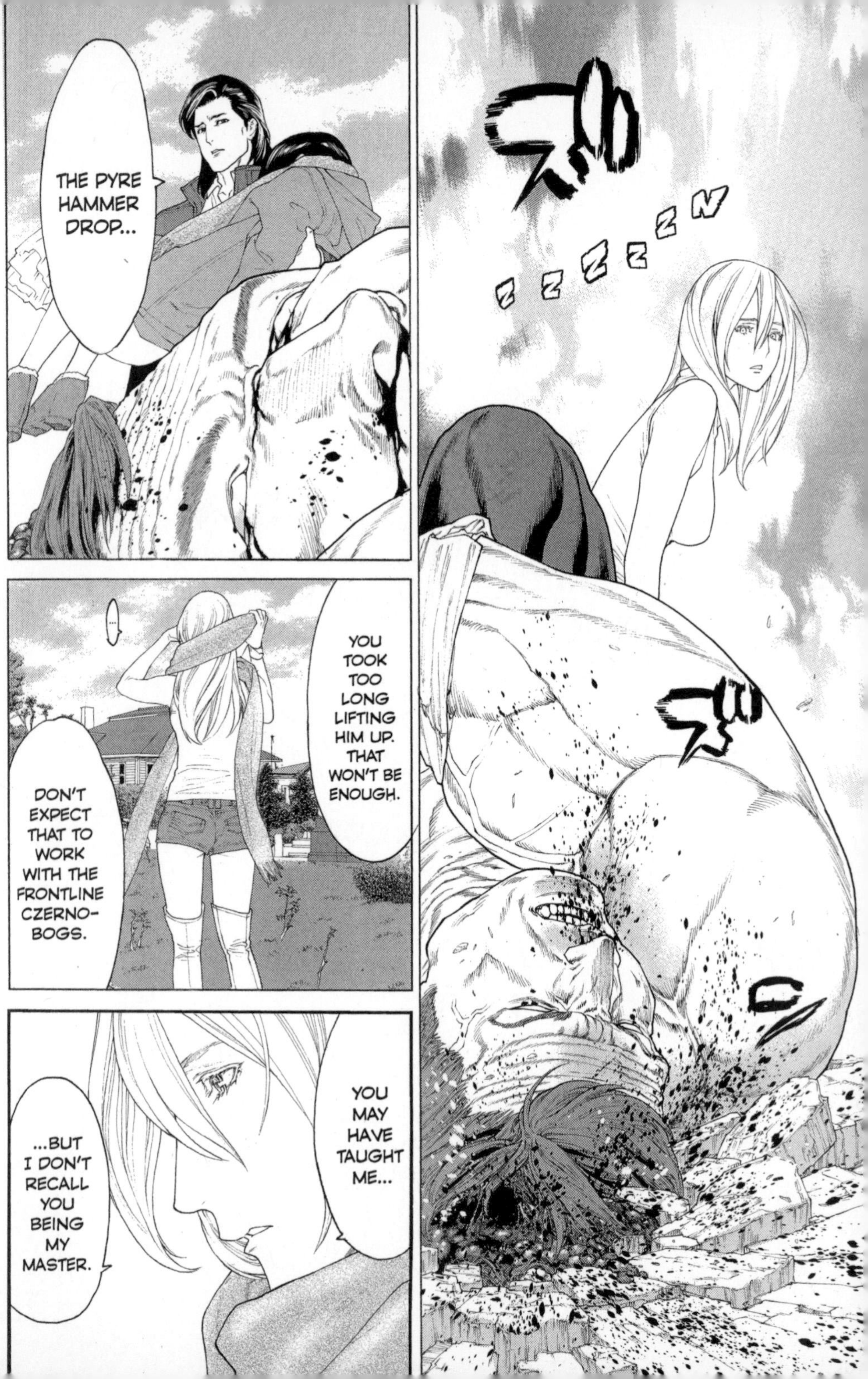
ZZZZZN
THE PYRE HAMMER DROP...
YOU TOOK TOO LONG LIFTING HIM UP. THAT WON'T BE ENOUGH.
...
DON'T EXPECT THAT TO WORK WITH THE FRONTLINE CZERNO-BOGS.
YOU MAY HAVE TAUGHT ME...
...BUT I DON'T RECALL YOU BEING MY MASTER.

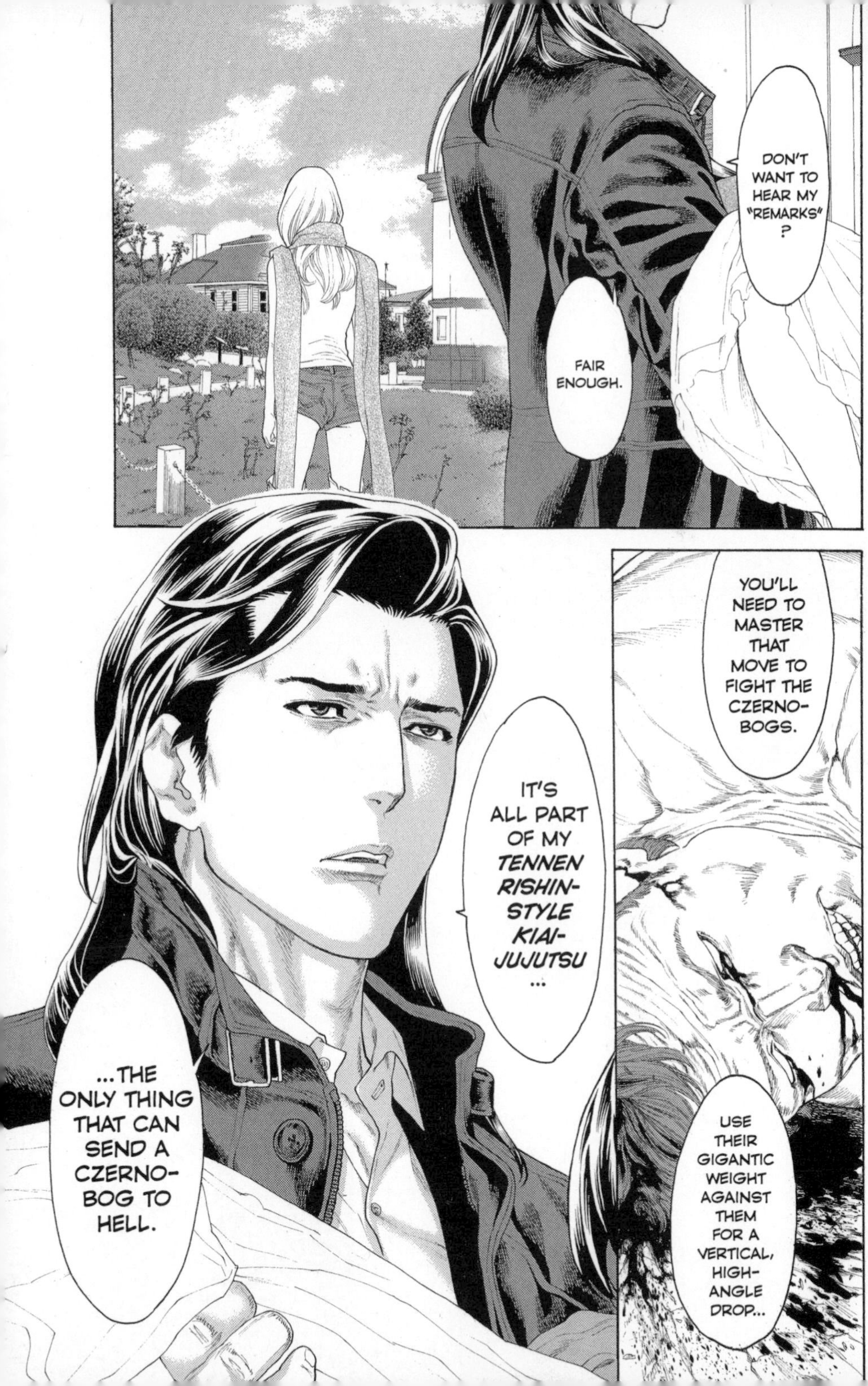
DON'T WANT TO HEAR MY "REMARKS" ?
FAIR ENOUGH.
YOU'LL NEED TO MASTER THAT MOVE TO FIGHT THE CZERNO-BOGS.
USE THEIR GIGANTIC WEIGHT AGAINST THEM FOR A VERTICAL, HIGH-ANGLE DROP...
IT'S ALL PART OF MY *TENNEN RISHIN-STYLE KIAI-JUJUTSU* ...
...THE ONLY THING THAT CAN SEND A CZERNO-BOG TO HELL.

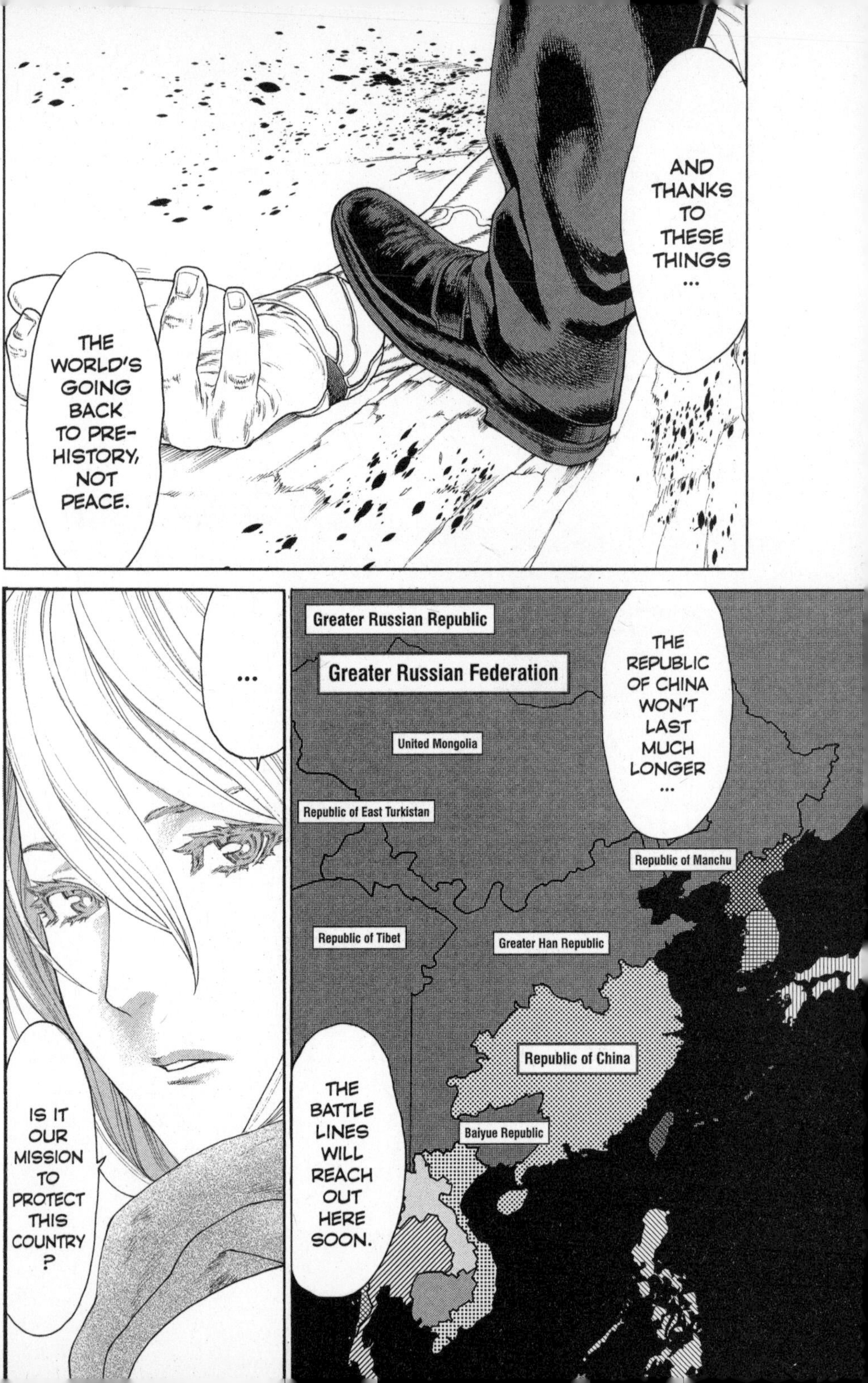

AND THANKS TO THESE THINGS...
THE WORLD'S GOING BACK TO PRE-HISTORY, NOT PEACE.
THE REPUBLIC OF CHINA WON'T LAST MUCH LONGER...
Greater Russian Republic
Greater Russian Federation
United Mongolia
Republic of East Turkistan
Republic of Manchu
Republic of Tibet
Greater Han Republic
Republic of China
Baiyue Republic
THE BATTLE LINES WILL REACH OUT HERE SOON.
...
IS IT OUR MISSION TO PROTECT THIS COUNTRY?

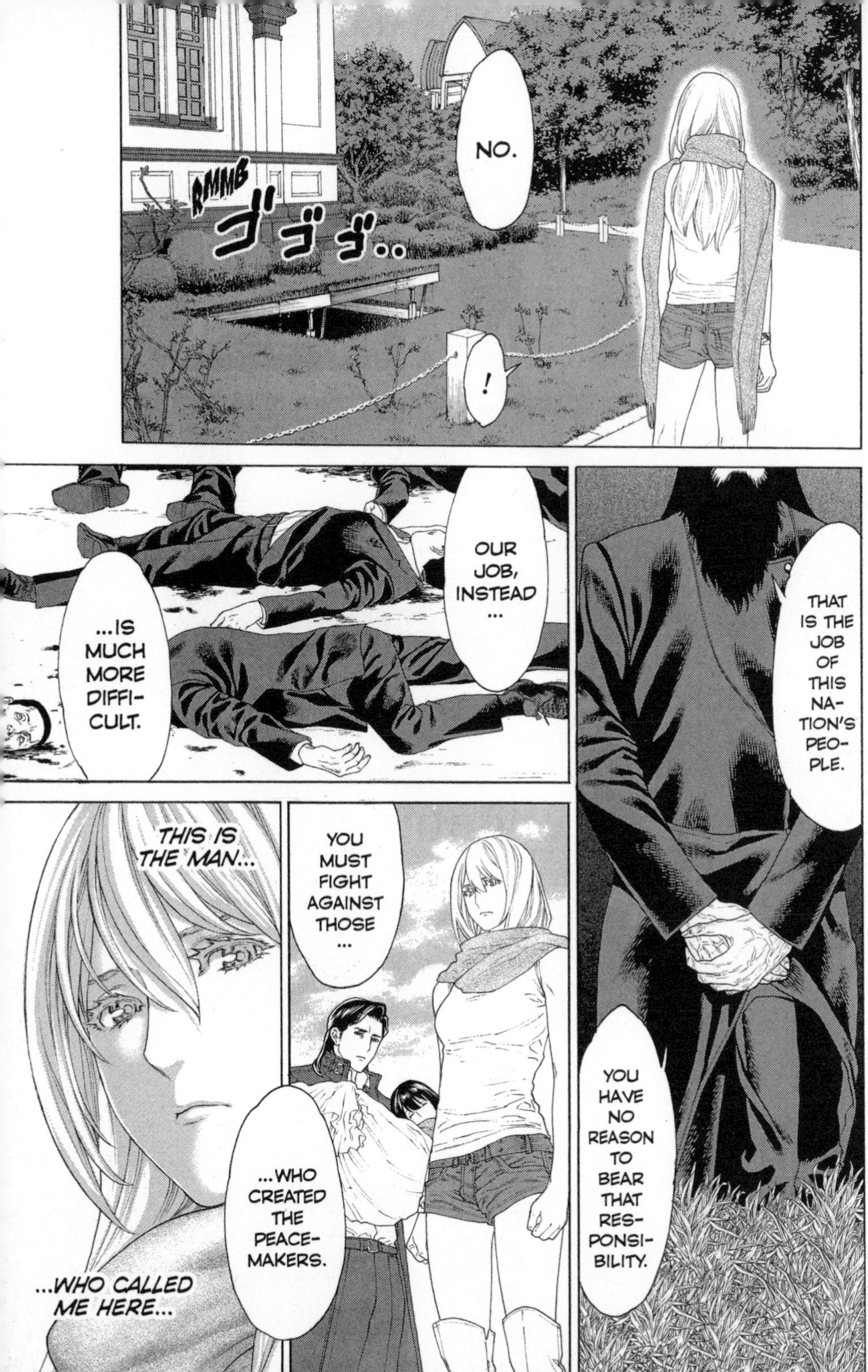
NO.
RMMB
ゴゴゴ..
!
THAT IS THE JOB OF THIS NATION'S PEOPLE.
YOU HAVE NO REASON TO BEAR THAT RESPONSIBILITY.
OUR JOB, INSTEAD...
...IS MUCH MORE DIFFICULT.
YOU MUST FIGHT AGAINST THOSE...
...WHO CREATED THE PEACE-MAKERS.
THIS IS THE MAN...
...WHO CALLED ME HERE...

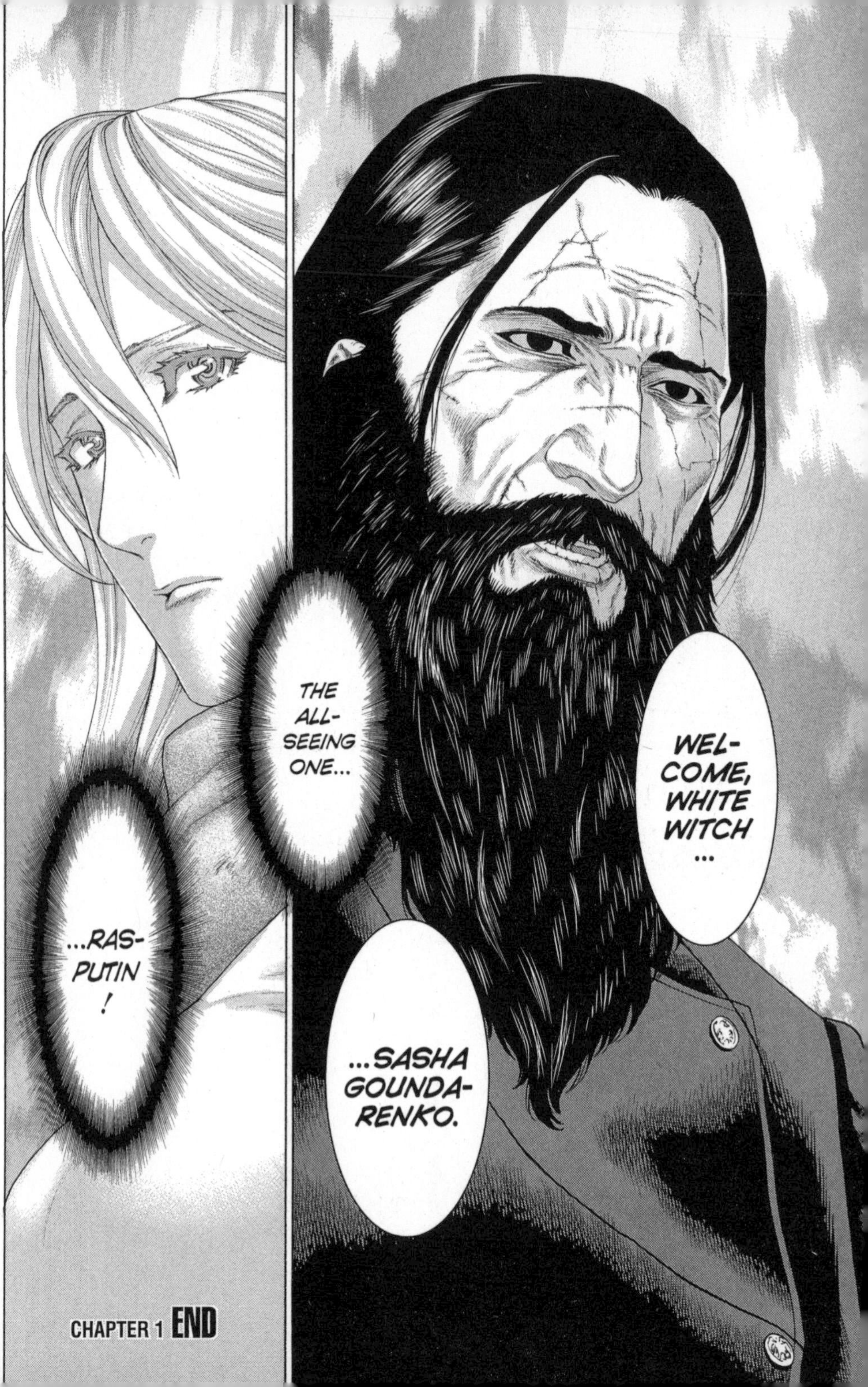
WEL-COME, WHITE WITCH...
...SASHA GOUNDA-RENKO.
THE ALL-SEEING ONE...
...RAS-PUTIN!
CHAPTER 1 END

ごろせうむ

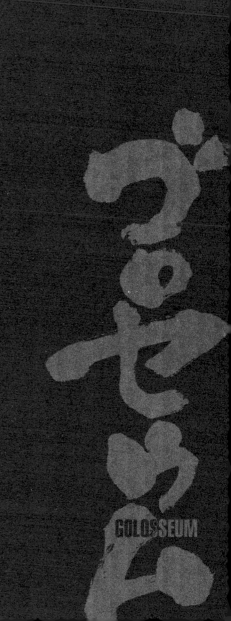

GOLOSSEUM

CHAPTER 2
DIVINE REVELATIONS

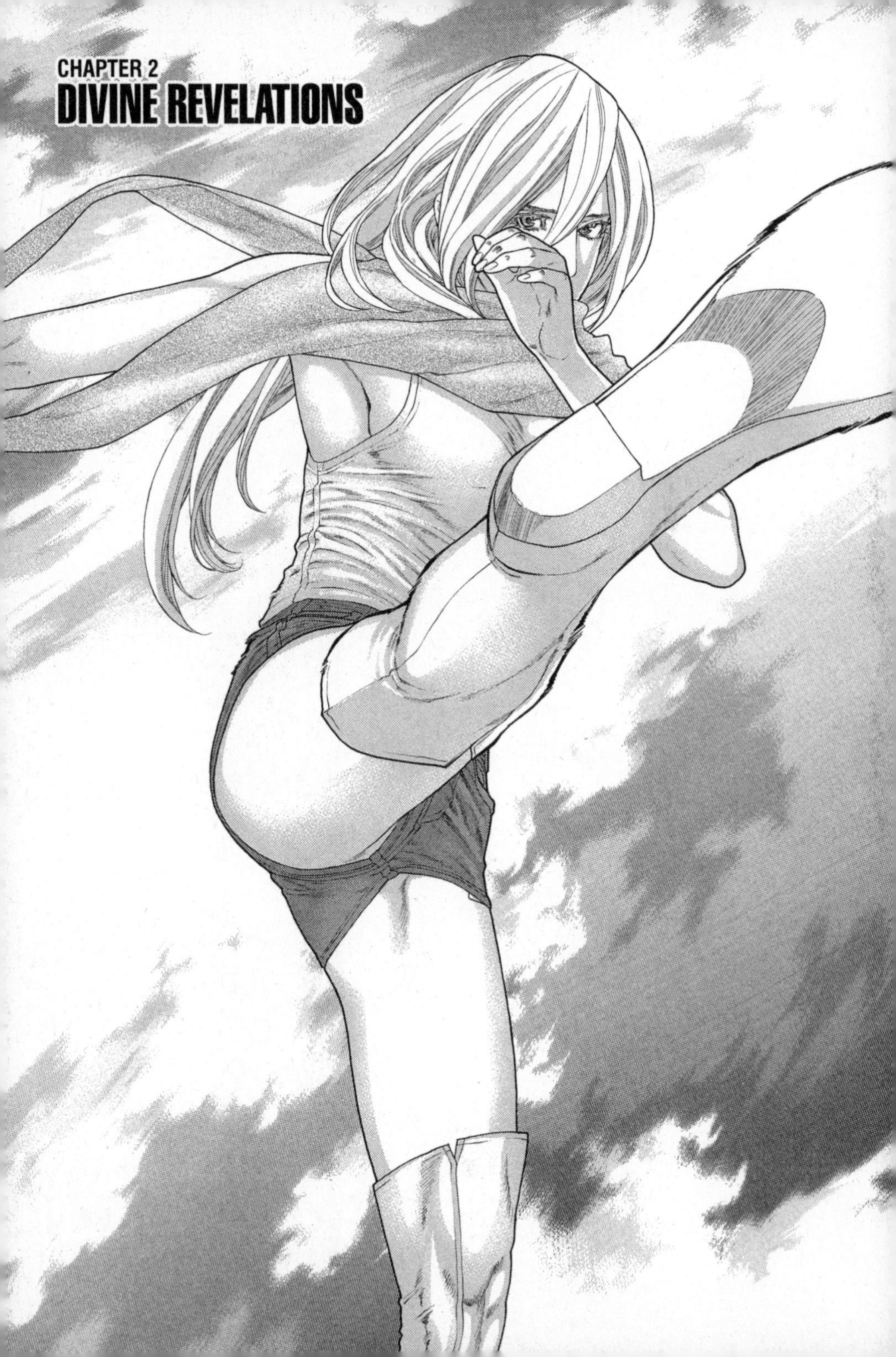

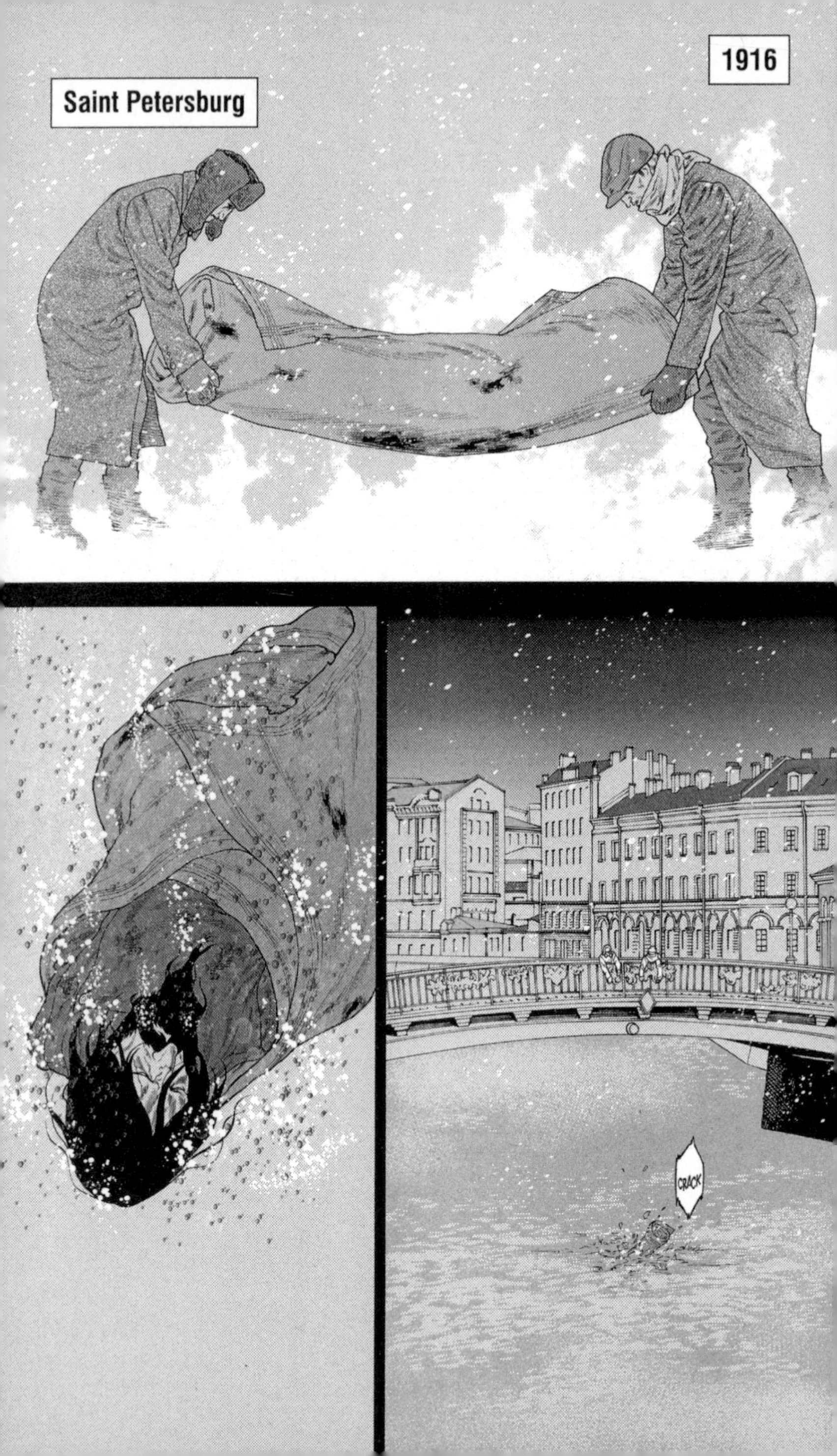
1916
Saint Petersburg
CRACK

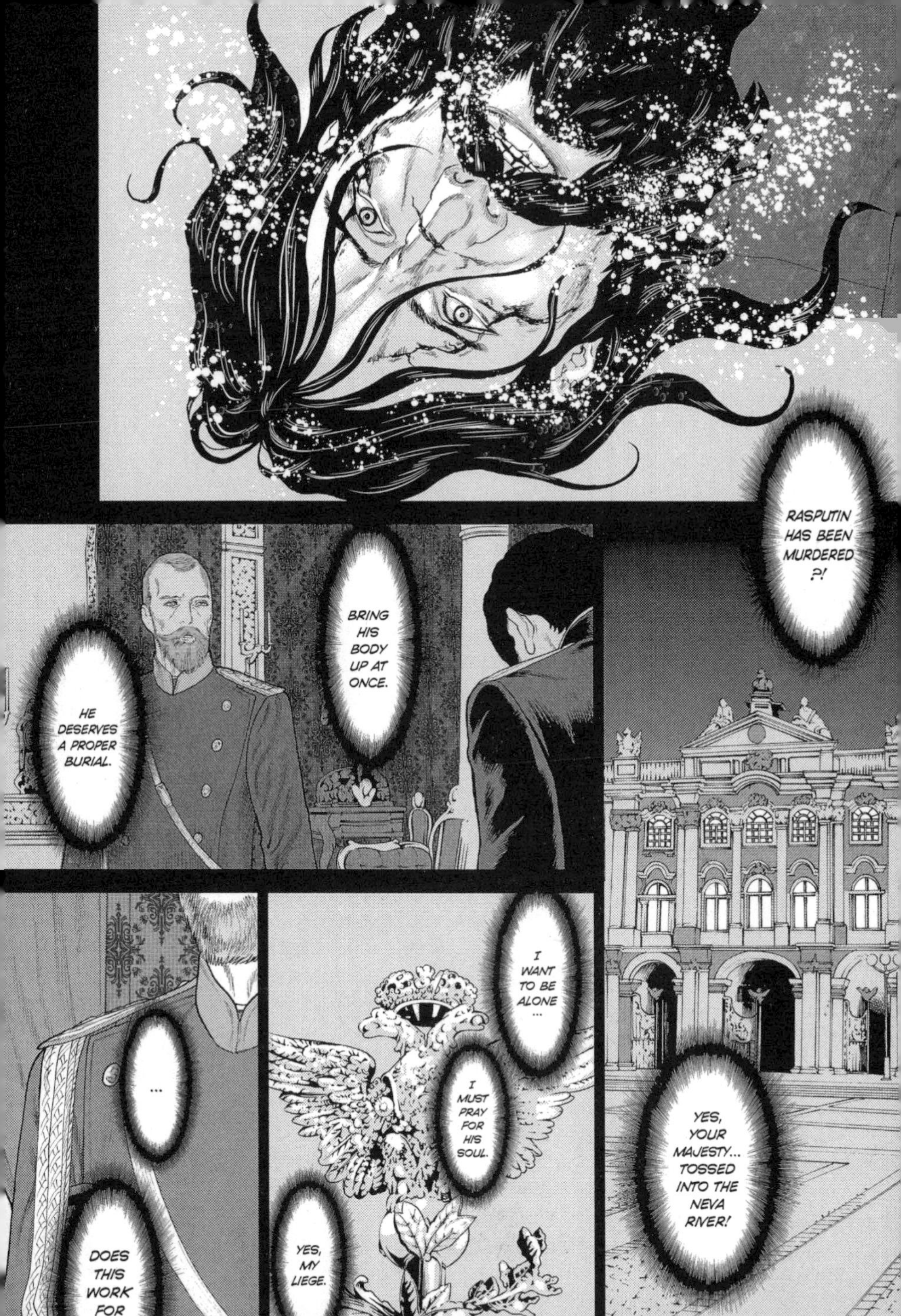
RASPUTIN HAS BEEN MURDERED ?!
YES, YOUR MAJESTY... TOSSED INTO THE NEVA RIVER!
BRING HIS BODY UP AT ONCE.
HE DESERVES A PROPER BURIAL.
I WANT TO BE ALONE ...
I MUST PRAY FOR HIS SOUL.
YES, MY LIEGE.
...
DOES THIS WORK FOR YOU ?

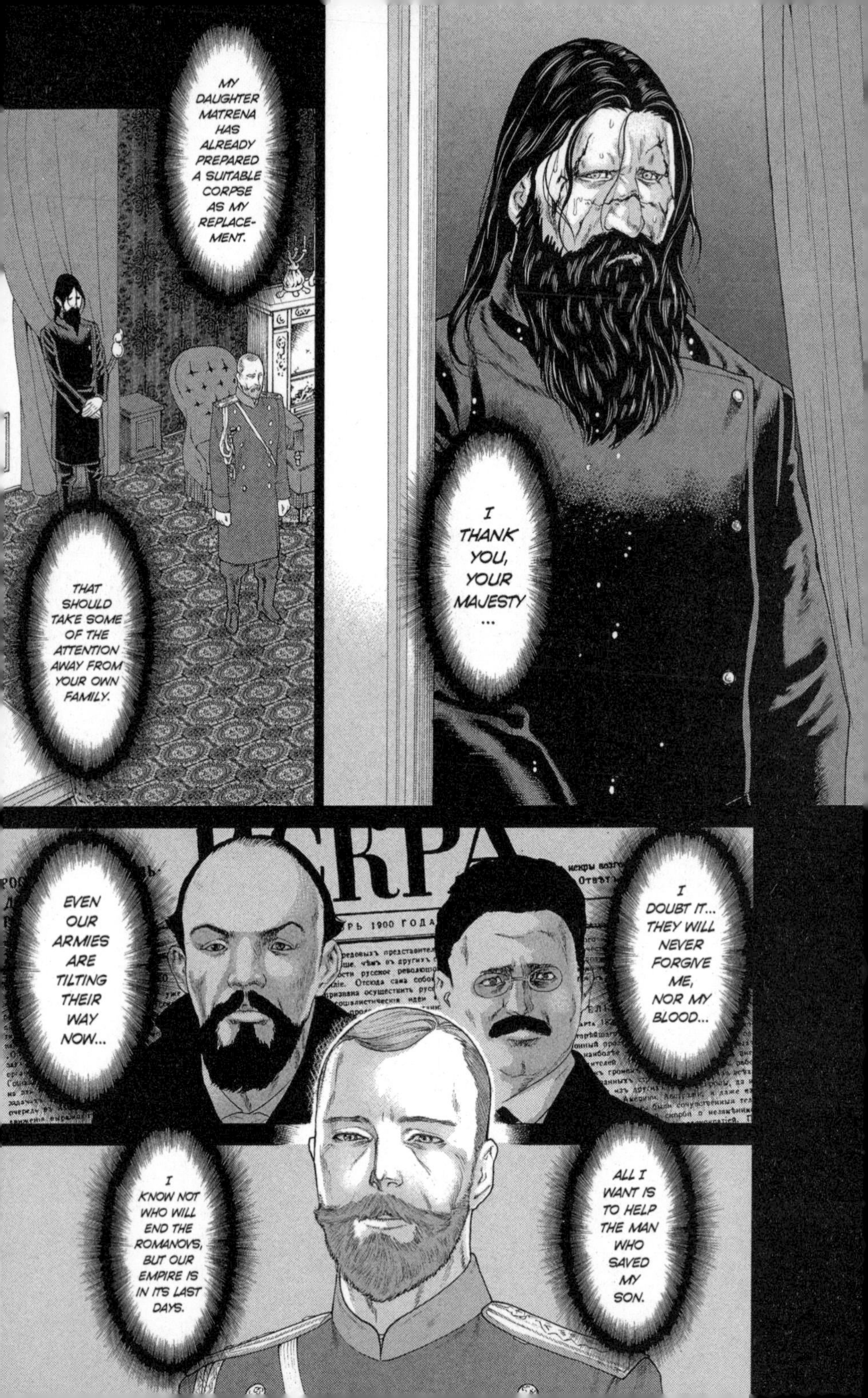
I THANK YOU, YOUR MAJESTY...
MY DAUGHTER MATRENA HAS ALREADY PREPARED A SUITABLE CORPSE AS MY REPLACEMENT.
THAT SHOULD TAKE SOME OF THE ATTENTION AWAY FROM YOUR OWN FAMILY.
I DOUBT IT... THEY WILL NEVER FORGIVE ME, NOR MY BLOOD...
EVEN OUR ARMIES ARE TILTING THEIR WAY NOW...
ALL I WANT IS TO HELP THE MAN WHO SAVED MY SON.
I KNOW NOT WHO WILL END THE ROMANOVS, BUT OUR EMPIRE IS IN ITS LAST DAYS.

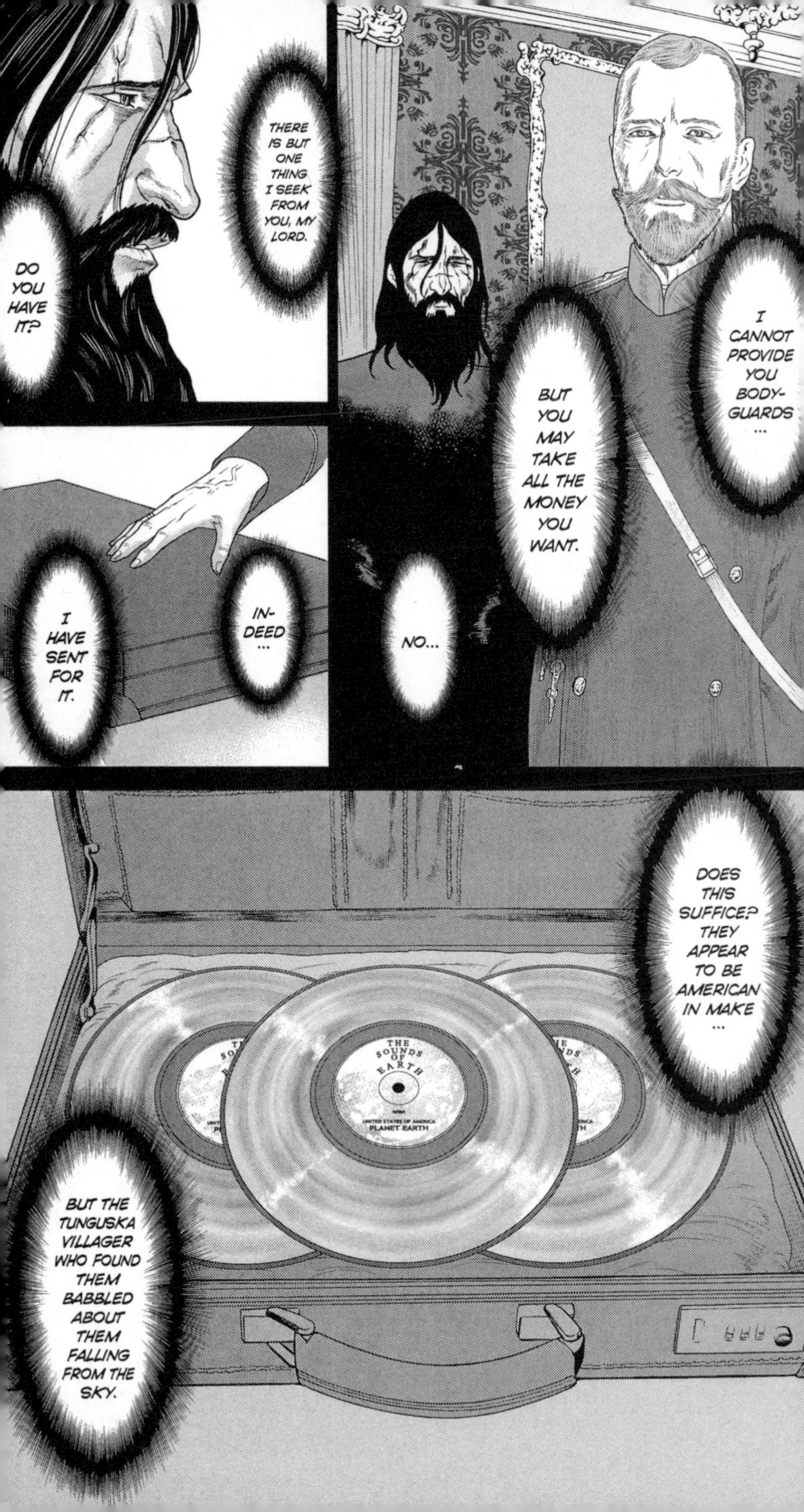
I CANNOT PROVIDE YOU BODYGUARDS...
BUT YOU MAY TAKE ALL THE MONEY YOU WANT.
NO...
THERE IS BUT ONE THING I SEEK FROM YOU, MY LORD.
DO YOU HAVE IT?
INDEED...
I HAVE SENT FOR IT.
DOES THIS SUFFICE? THEY APPEAR TO BE AMERICAN IN MAKE...
THE SOUNDS OF EARTH
UNITED STATES OF AMERICA
PLANET EARTH
BUT THE TUNGUSKA VILLAGER WHO FOUND THEM BABBLED ABOUT THEM FALLING FROM THE SKY.

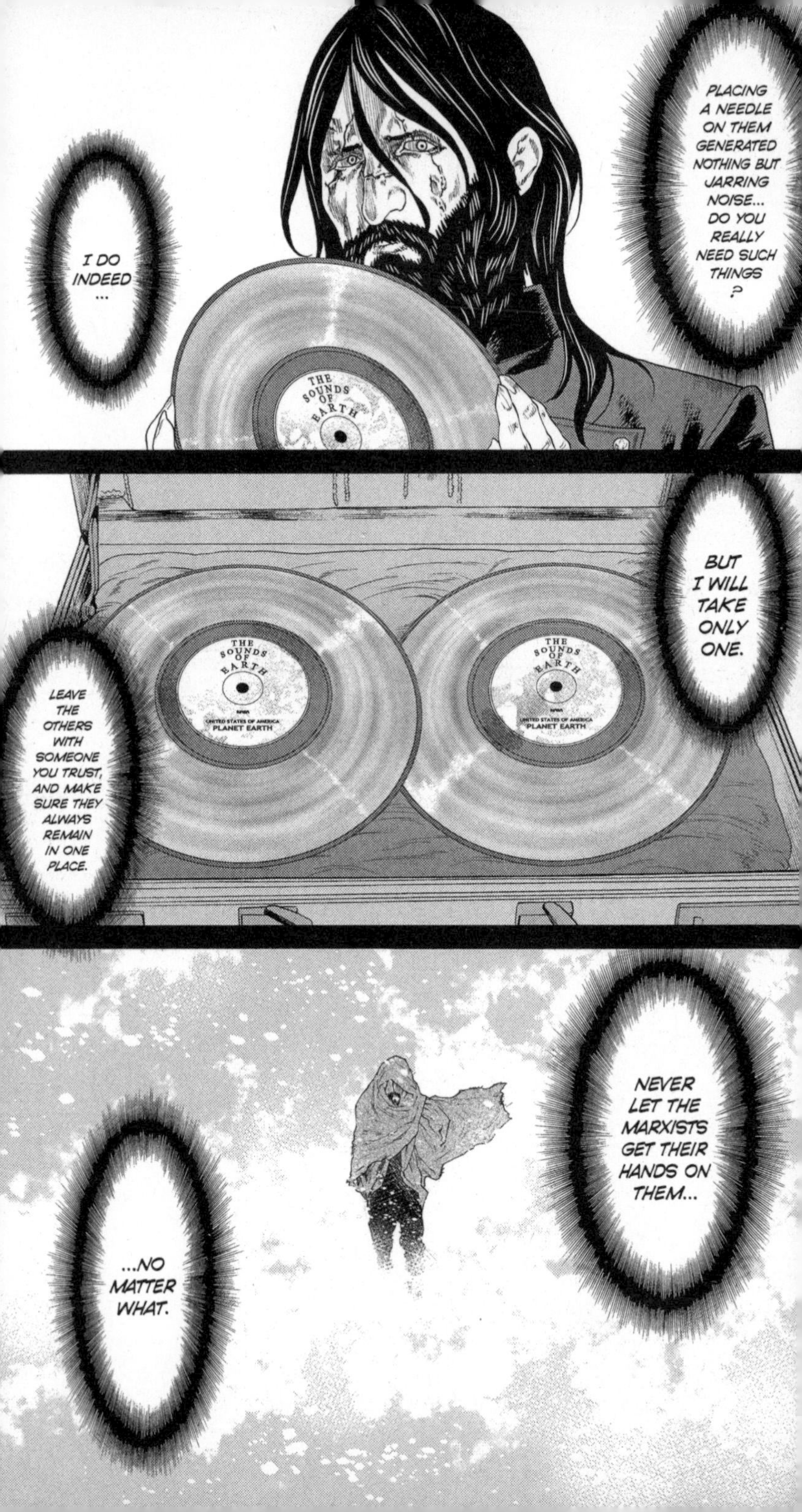
PLACING A NEEDLE ON THEM GENERATED NOTHING BUT JARRING NOISE... DO YOU REALLY NEED SUCH THINGS ?
I DO INDEED ...
THE SOUNDS OF EARTH
BUT I WILL TAKE ONLY ONE.
THE SOUNDS OF EARTH
UNITED STATES OF AMERICA
PLANET EARTH
THE SOUNDS OF EARTH
UNITED STATES OF AMERICA
PLANET EARTH
LEAVE THE OTHERS WITH SOMEONE YOU TRUST, AND MAKE SURE THEY ALWAYS REMAIN IN ONE PLACE.
NEVER LET THE MARXISTS GET THEIR HANDS ON THEM...
...NO MATTER WHAT.

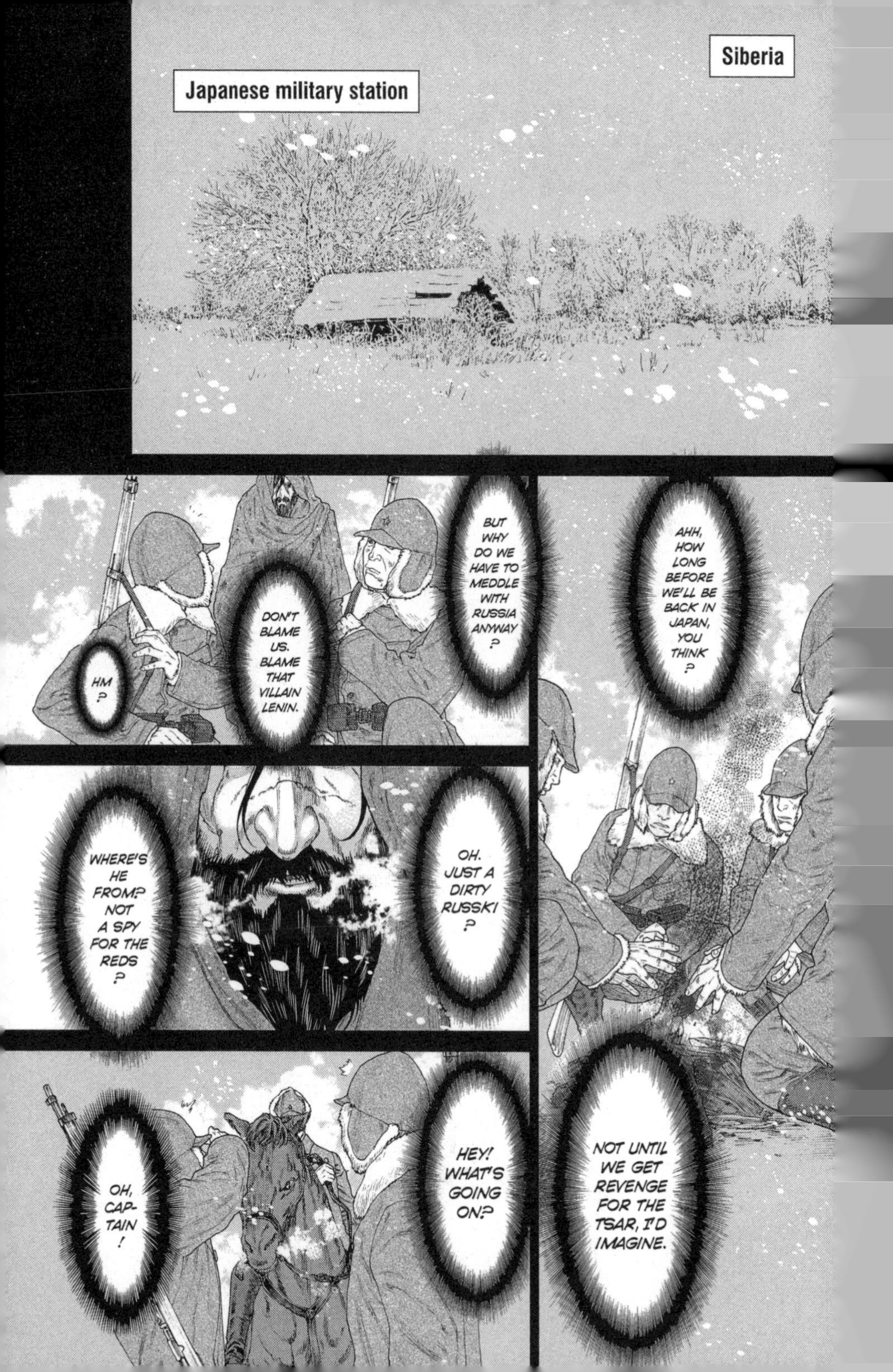
Siberia
Japanese military station
AHH, HOW LONG BEFORE WE'LL BE BACK IN JAPAN, YOU THINK?
NOT UNTIL WE GET REVENGE FOR THE TSAR, I'D IMAGINE.
BUT WHY DO WE HAVE TO MEDDLE WITH RUSSIA ANYWAY?
DON'T BLAME US. BLAME THAT VILLAIN LENIN.
HM?
OH. JUST A DIRTY RUSSKI?
WHERE'S HE FROM? NOT A SPY FOR THE REDS?
HEY! WHAT'S GOING ON?
OH, CAP-TAIN!

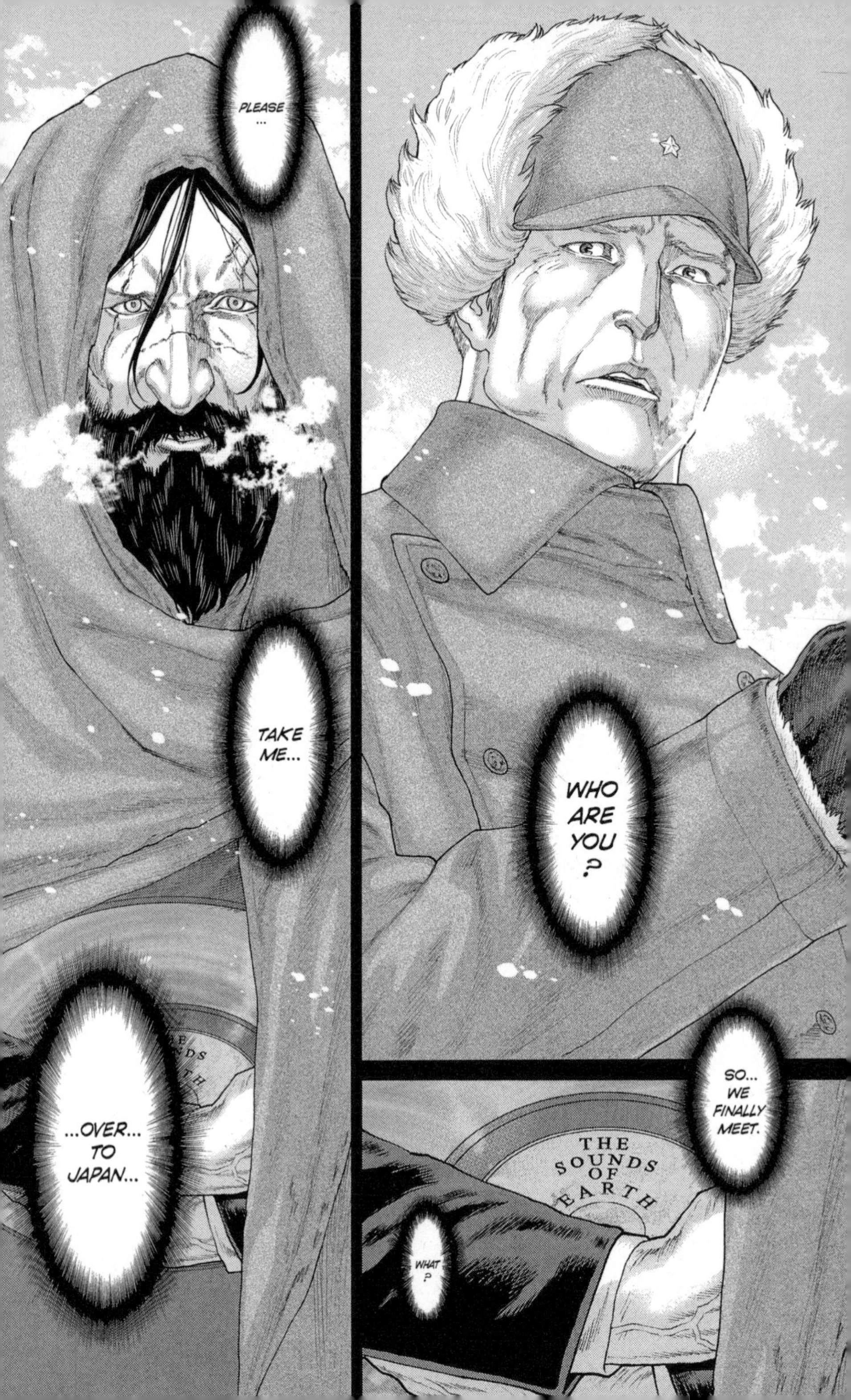
WHO ARE YOU?
SO... WE FINALLY MEET.
THE SOUNDS OF EARTH
WHAT?
PLEASE...
TAKE ME...
...OVER... TO JAPAN...

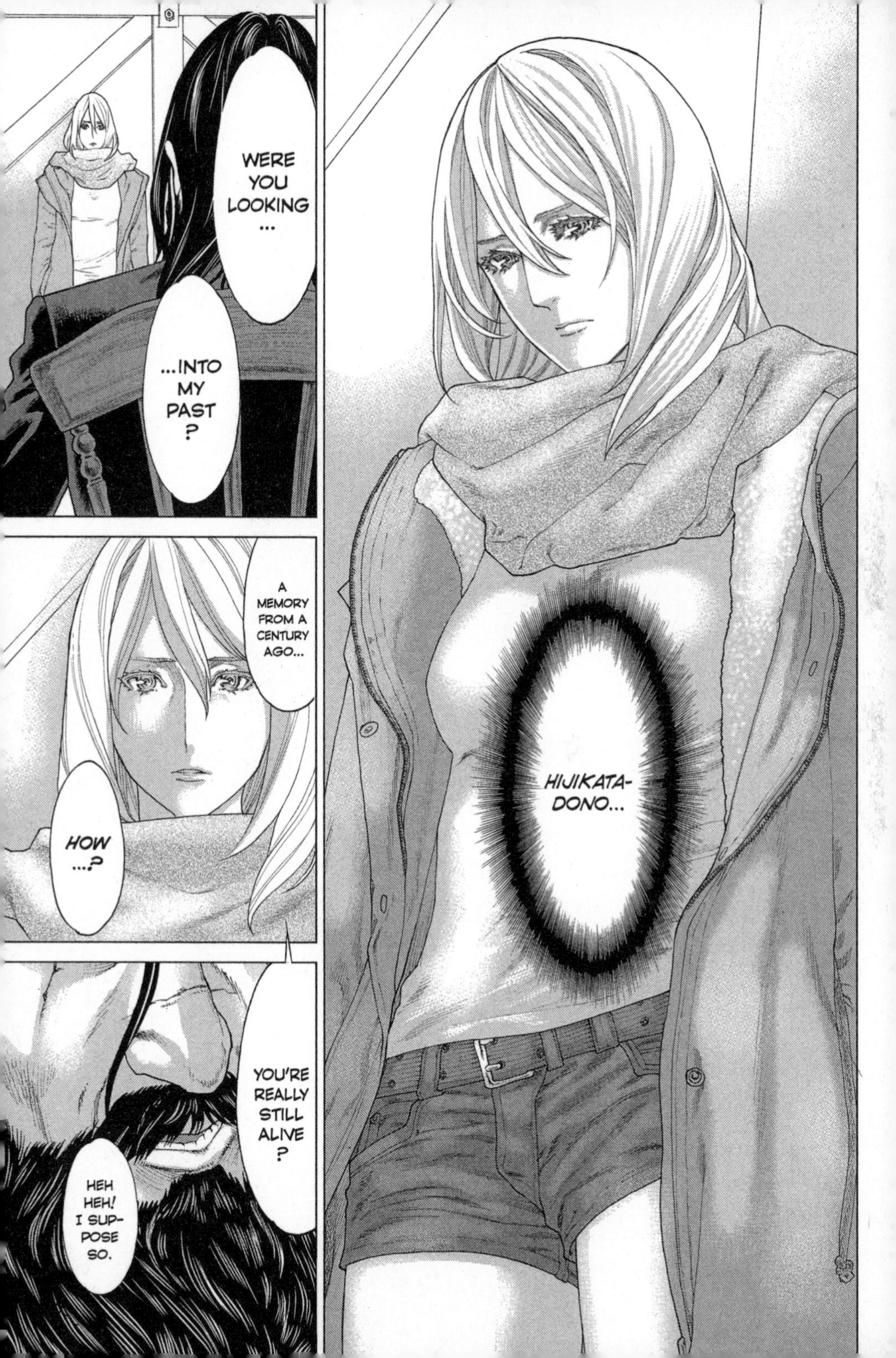
HIJIKATA-DONO...
WERE YOU LOOKING ...
...INTO MY PAST ?
A MEMORY FROM A CENTURY AGO...
HOW ...?
YOU'RE REALLY STILL ALIVE ?
HEH HEH! I SUP-POSE SO.

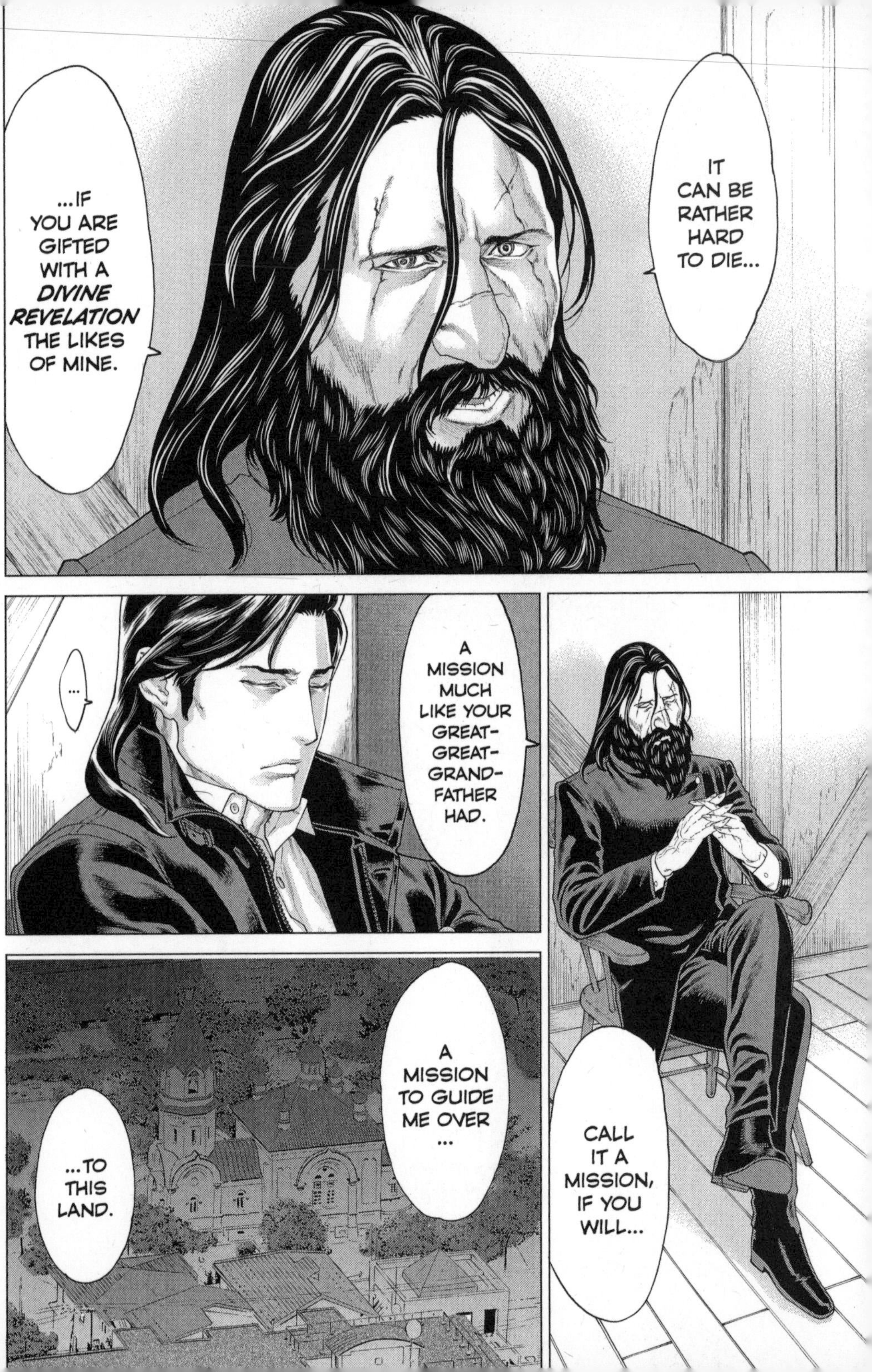
IT CAN BE RATHER HARD TO DIE...
...IF YOU ARE GIFTED WITH A *DIVINE REVELATION* THE LIKES OF MINE.
CALL IT A MISSION, IF YOU WILL...
A MISSION MUCH LIKE YOUR GREAT-GREAT-GRANDFATHER HAD.
...
A MISSION TO GUIDE ME OVER ...
...TO THIS LAND.

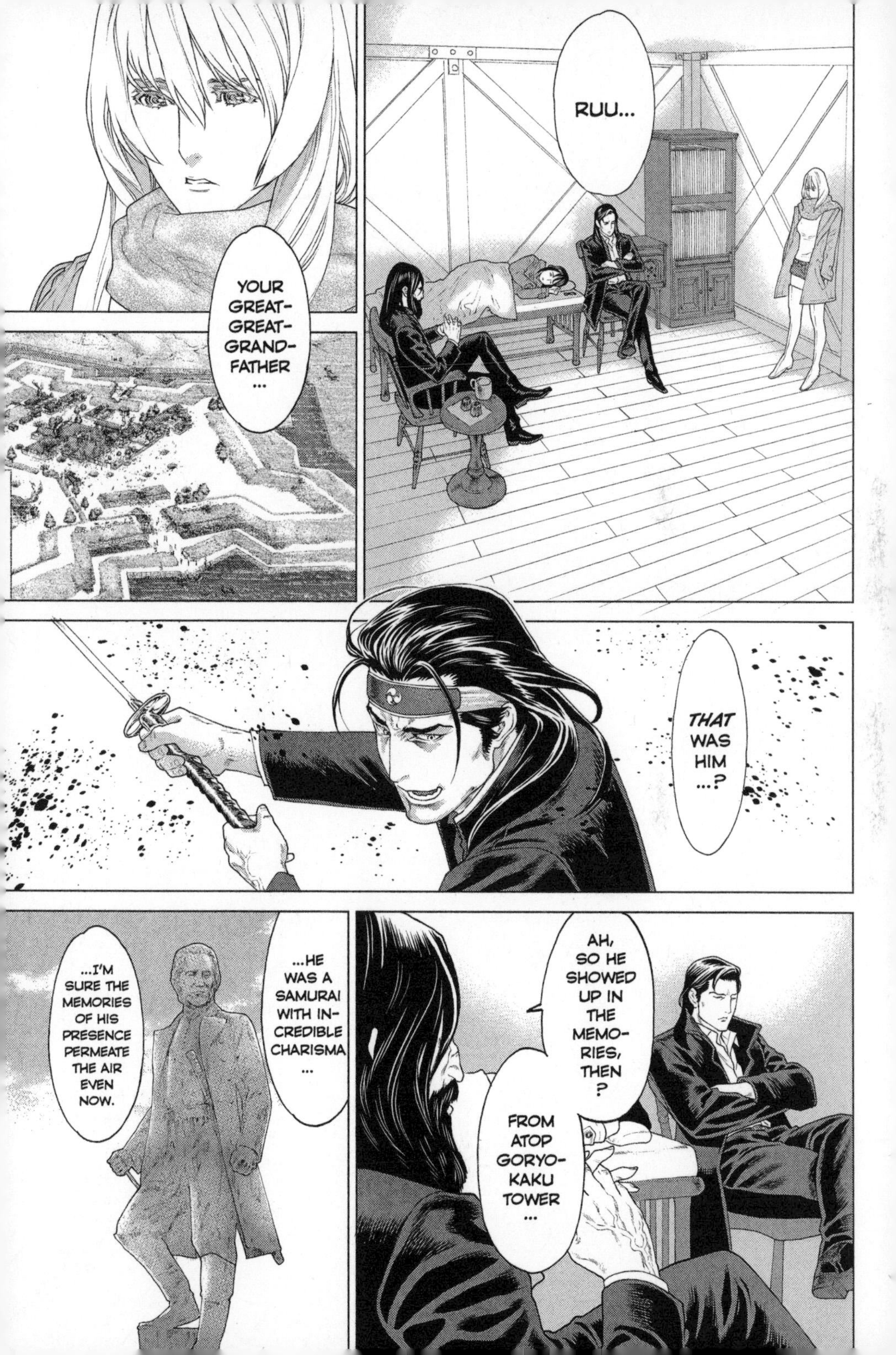
RUU...
YOUR GREAT-GREAT-GRANDFATHER...
THAT WAS HIM ...?
AH, SO HE SHOWED UP IN THE MEMORIES, THEN?
FROM ATOP GORYOKAKU TOWER...
...HE WAS A SAMURAI WITH INCREDIBLE CHARISMA...
...I'M SURE THE MEMORIES OF HIS PRESENCE PERMEATE THE AIR EVEN NOW.

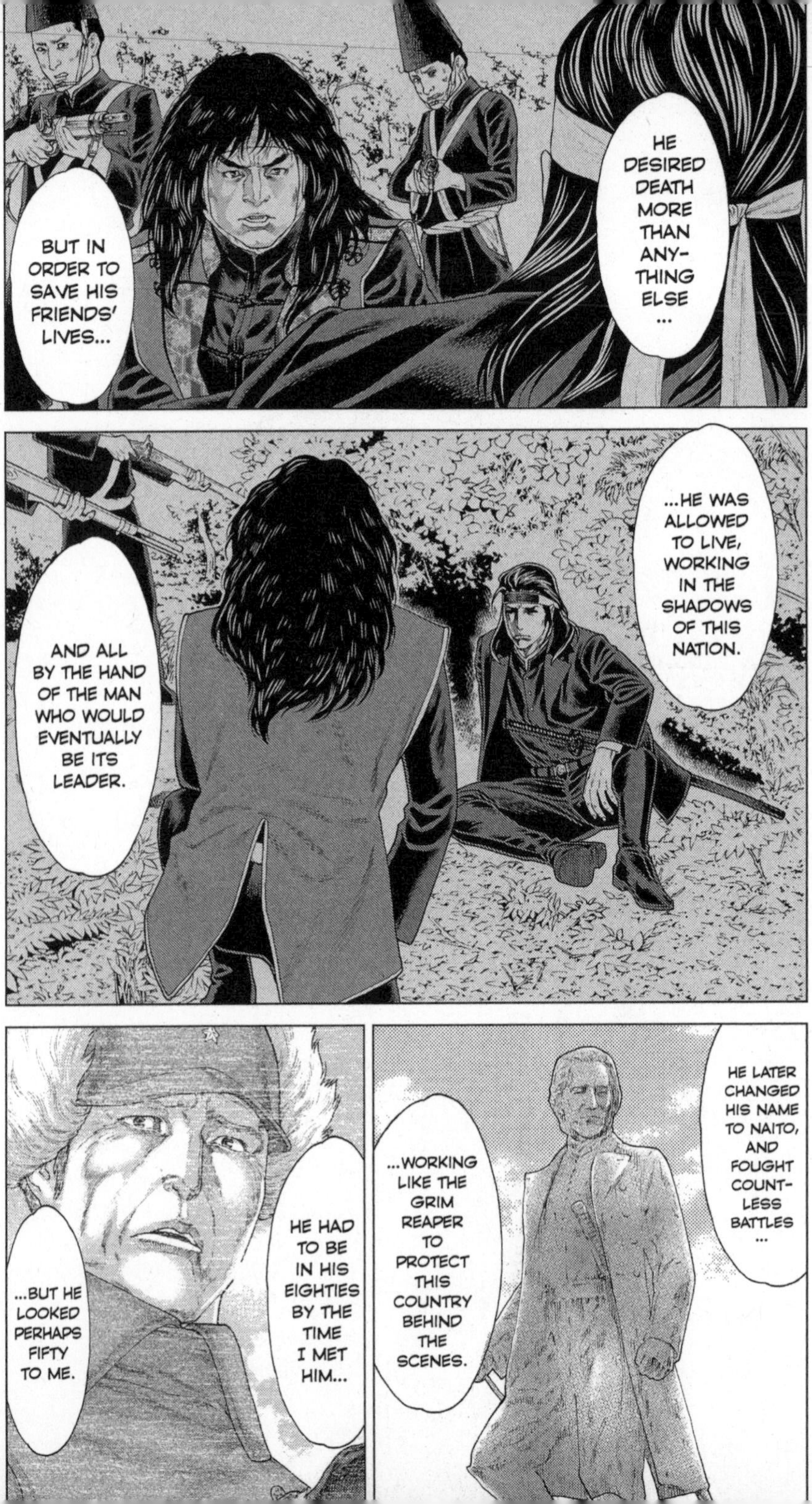
HE DESIRED DEATH MORE THAN ANYTHING ELSE...
BUT IN ORDER TO SAVE HIS FRIENDS' LIVES...
...HE WAS ALLOWED TO LIVE, WORKING IN THE SHADOWS OF THIS NATION.
AND ALL BY THE HAND OF THE MAN WHO WOULD EVENTUALLY BE ITS LEADER.
HE LATER CHANGED HIS NAME TO NAITO, AND FOUGHT COUNTLESS BATTLES...
...WORKING LIKE THE GRIM REAPER TO PROTECT THIS COUNTRY BEHIND THE SCENES.
HE HAD TO BE IN HIS EIGHTIES BY THE TIME I MET HIM...
...BUT HE LOOKED PERHAPS FIFTY TO ME.

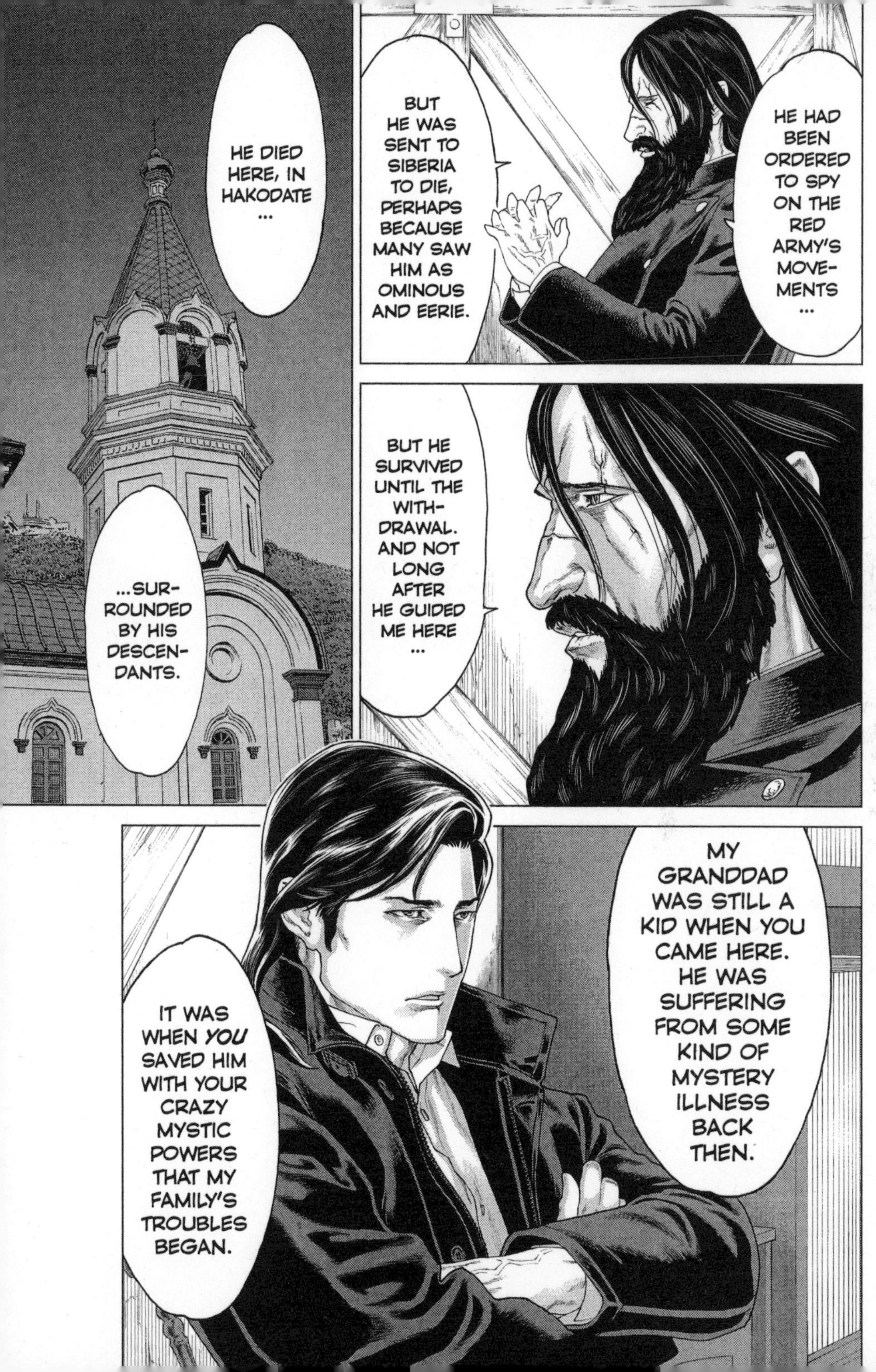
HE HAD BEEN ORDERED TO SPY ON THE RED ARMY'S MOVE-MENTS ...
BUT HE WAS SENT TO SIBERIA TO DIE, PERHAPS BECAUSE MANY SAW HIM AS OMINOUS AND EERIE.
BUT HE SURVIVED UNTIL THE WITH-DRAWAL. AND NOT LONG AFTER HE GUIDED ME HERE ...
HE DIED HERE, IN HAKODATE ...
...SUR-ROUNDED BY HIS DESCEN-DANTS.
MY GRANDDAD WAS STILL A KID WHEN YOU CAME HERE. HE WAS SUFFERING FROM SOME KIND OF MYSTERY ILLNESS BACK THEN.
IT WAS WHEN *YOU* SAVED HIM WITH YOUR CRAZY MYSTIC POWERS THAT MY FAMILY'S TROUBLES BEGAN.

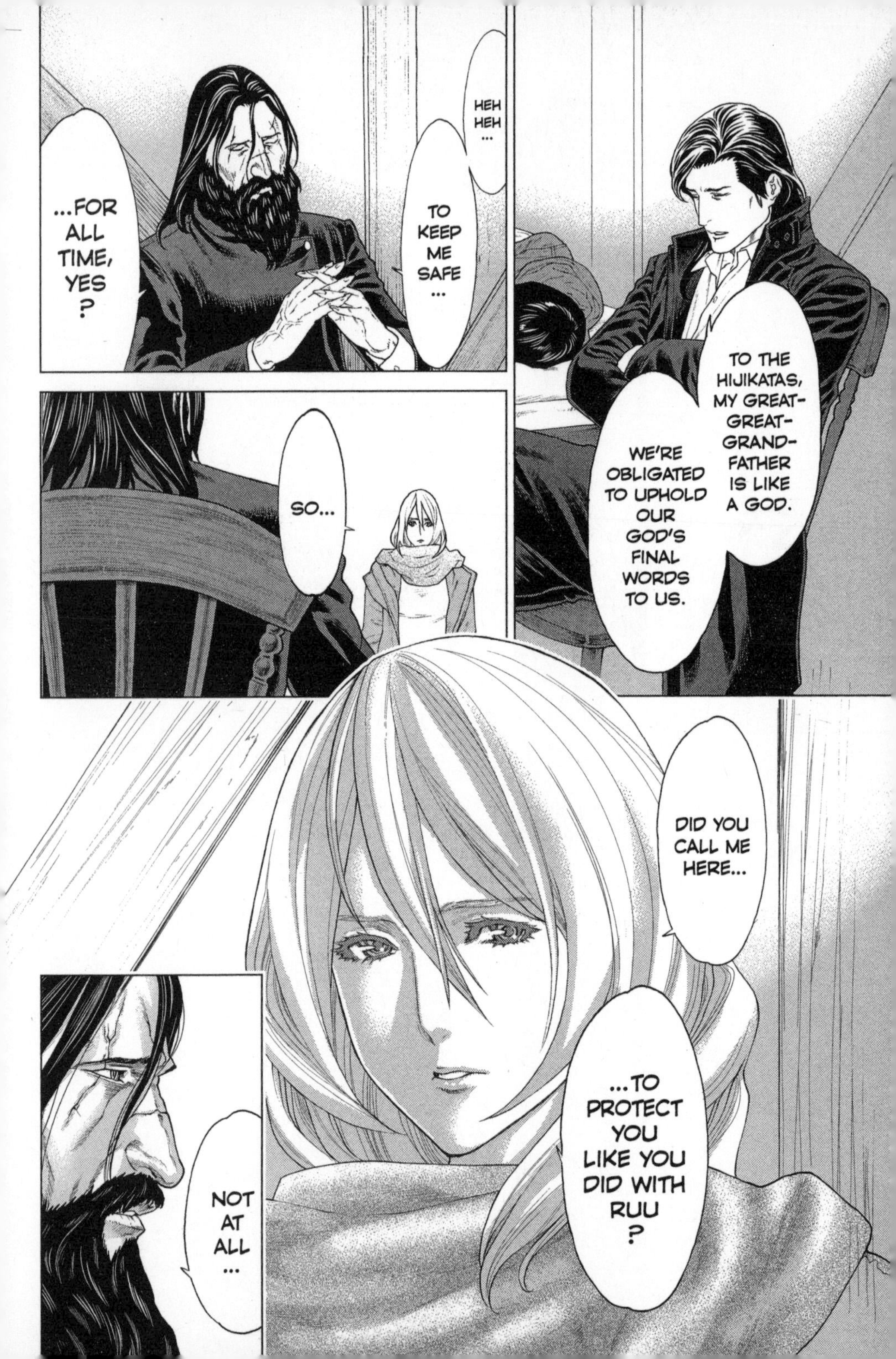
TO THE HIJIKATAS, MY GREAT-GREAT-GRANDFATHER IS LIKE A GOD.
WE'RE OBLIGATED TO UPHOLD OUR GOD'S FINAL WORDS TO US.
HEH HEH ...
TO KEEP ME SAFE ...
...FOR ALL TIME, YES ?
SO...
DID YOU CALL ME HERE...
...TO PROTECT YOU LIKE YOU DID WITH RUU ?
NOT AT ALL ...

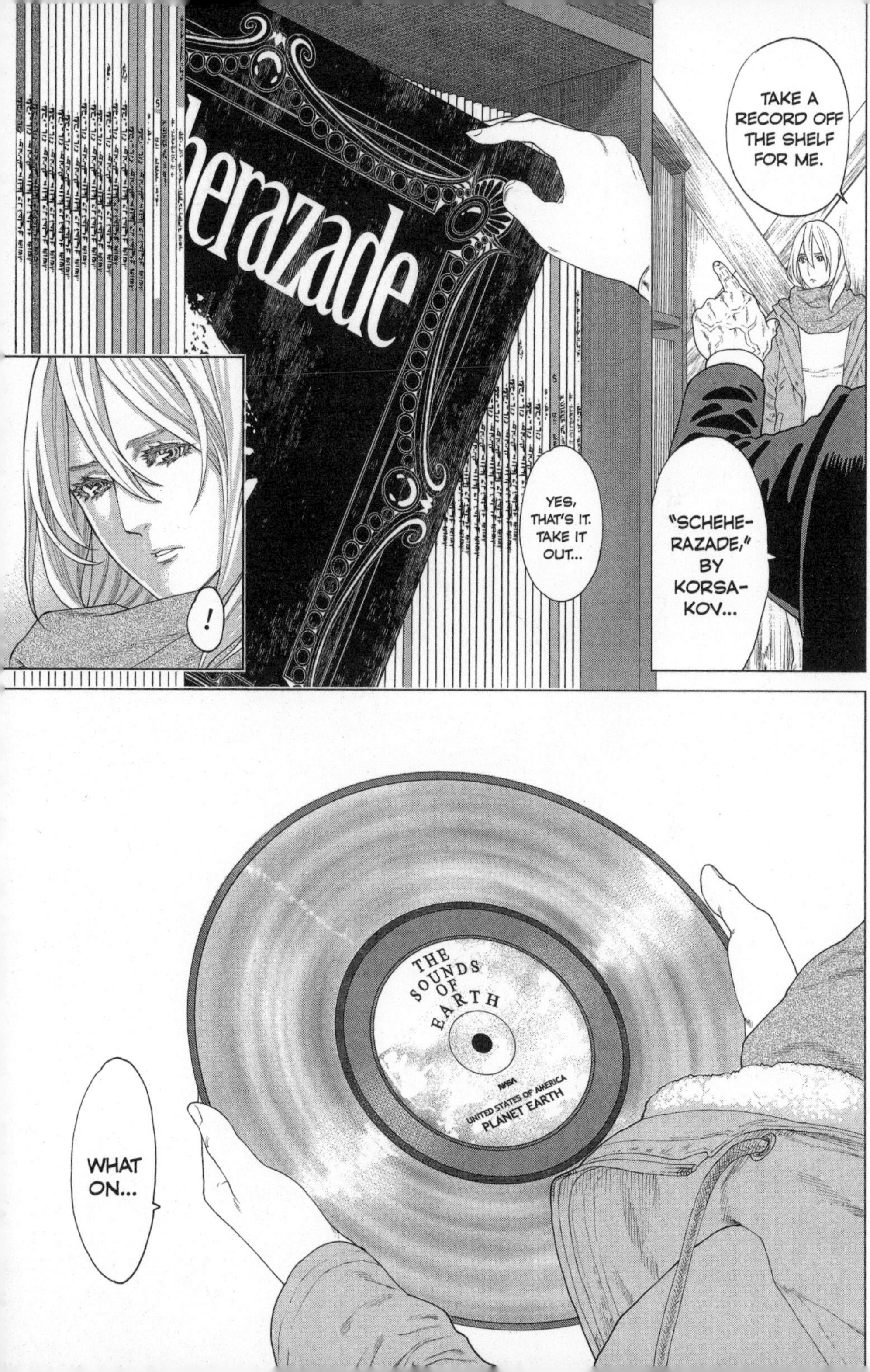
TAKE A RECORD OFF THE SHELF FOR ME.
"SCHEHE-RAZADE," BY KORSA-KOV...
herazade
YES, THAT'S IT. TAKE IT OUT...
!
THE SOUNDS OF EARTH
NASA
UNITED STATES OF AMERICA
PLANET EARTH
WHAT ON...

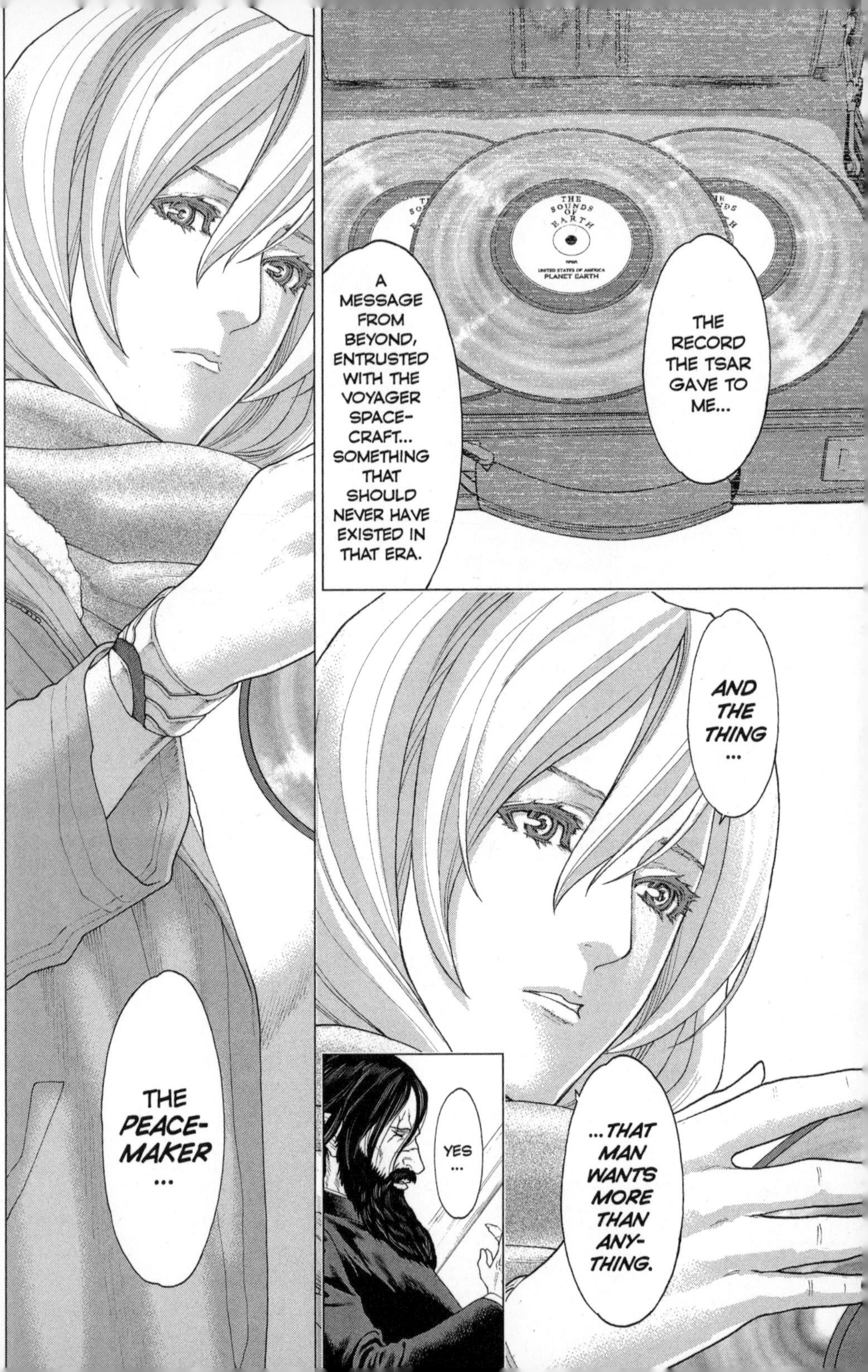
THE SOUNDS OF EARTH
UNITED STATES OF AMERICA
PLANET EARTH
THE RECORD THE TSAR GAVE TO ME...
A MESSAGE FROM BEYOND, ENTRUSTED WITH THE VOYAGER SPACECRAFT... SOMETHING THAT SHOULD NEVER HAVE EXISTED IN THAT ERA.
AND THE THING...
...THAT MAN WANTS MORE THAN ANYTHING.
YES...
THE *PEACEMAKER*...

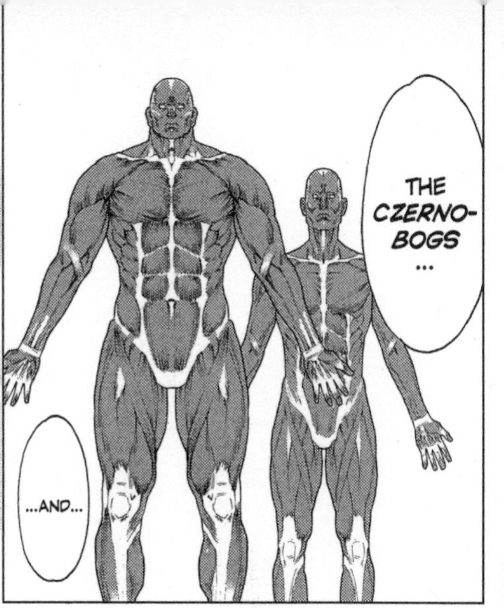
THE CZERNO-BOGS ...
...AND...
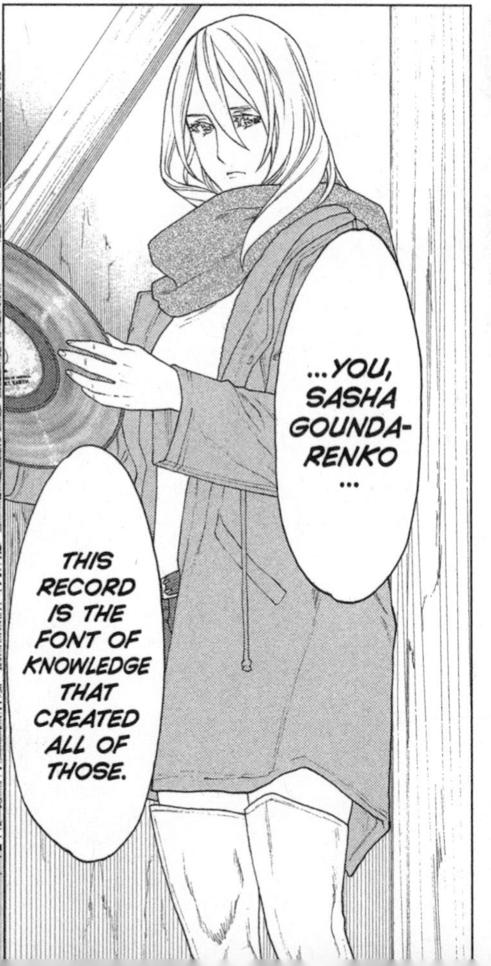
...YOU, SASHA GOUNDA-RENKO ...
THIS RECORD IS THE FONT OF KNOWLEDGE THAT CREATED ALL OF THOSE.
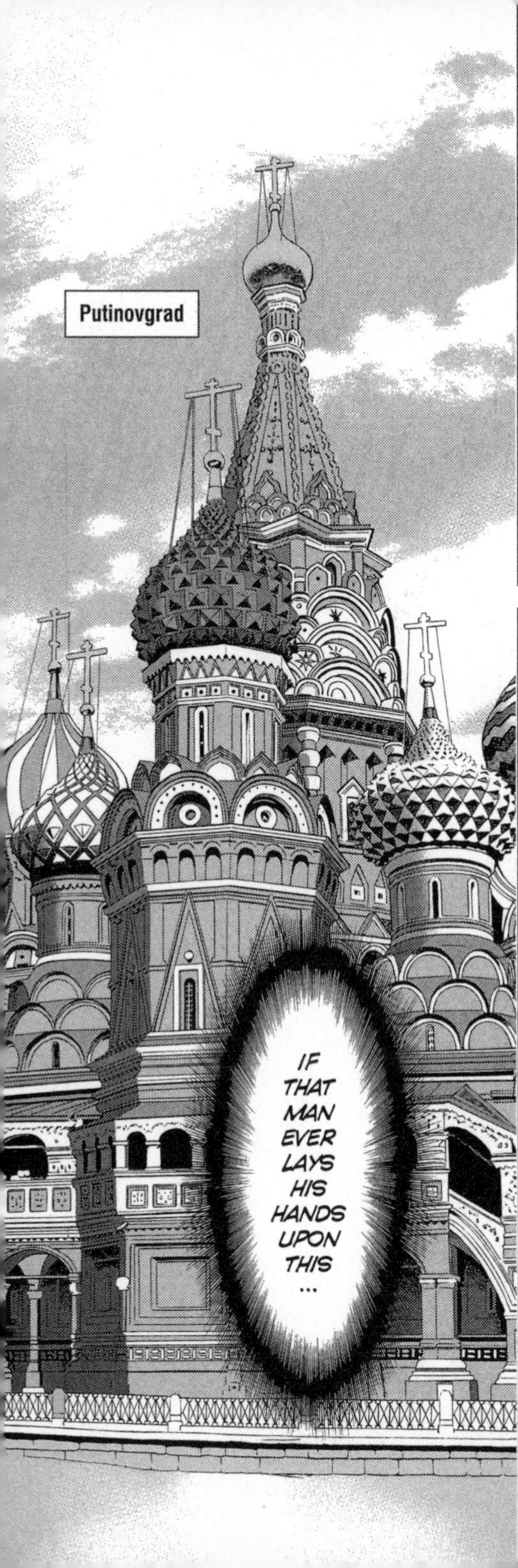
Putinovgrad
IF THAT MAN EVER LAYS HIS HANDS UPON THIS ...

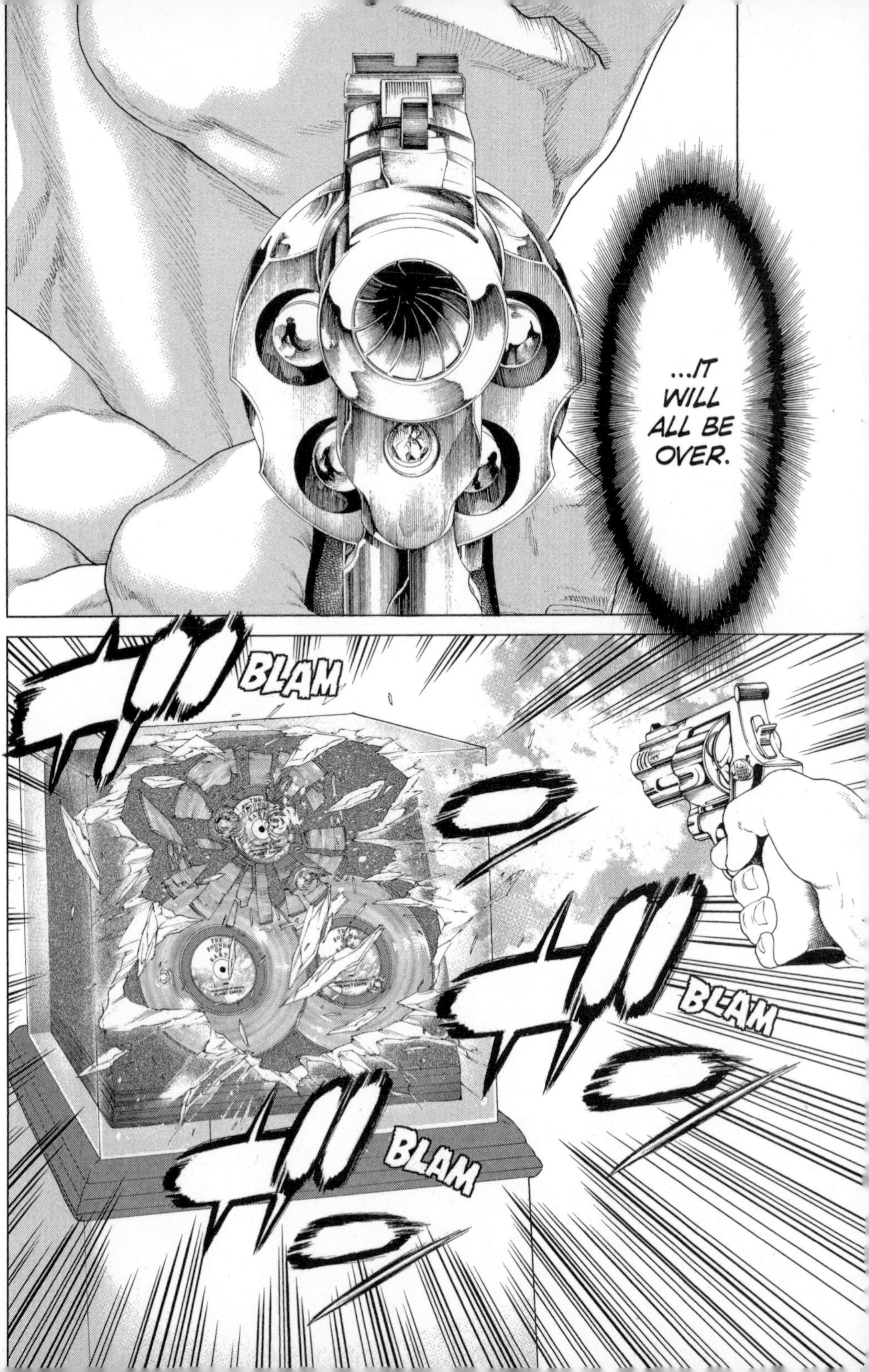
...IT WILL ALL BE OVER.
BLAM
BLAM
BLAM

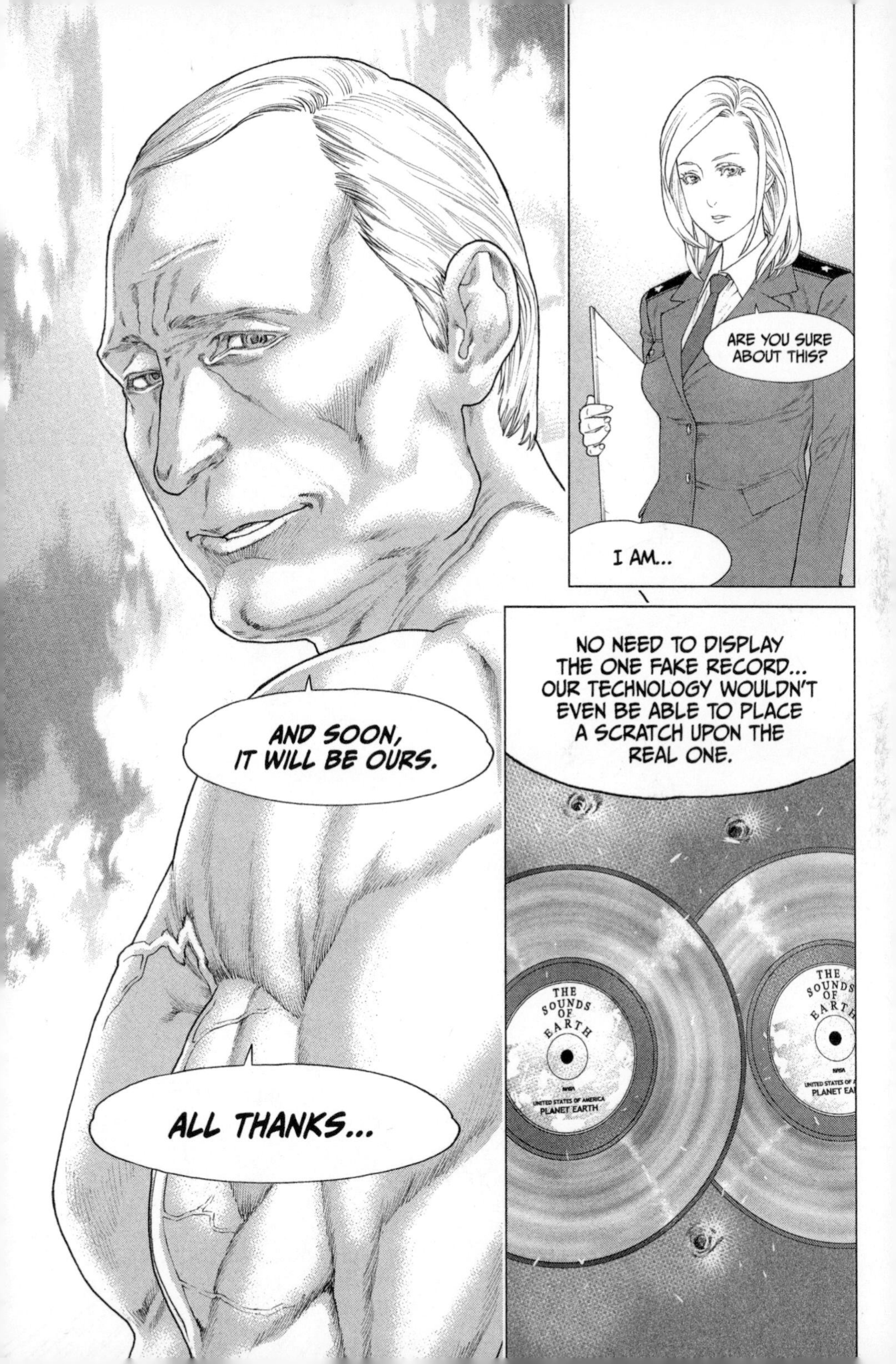
ARE YOU SURE ABOUT THIS?
I AM...
NO NEED TO DISPLAY THE ONE FAKE RECORD... OUR TECHNOLOGY WOULDN'T EVEN BE ABLE TO PLACE A SCRATCH UPON THE REAL ONE.
THE SOUNDS OF EARTH
NASA
UNITED STATES OF AMERICA
PLANET EARTH
AND SOON, IT WILL BE OURS.
ALL THANKS...

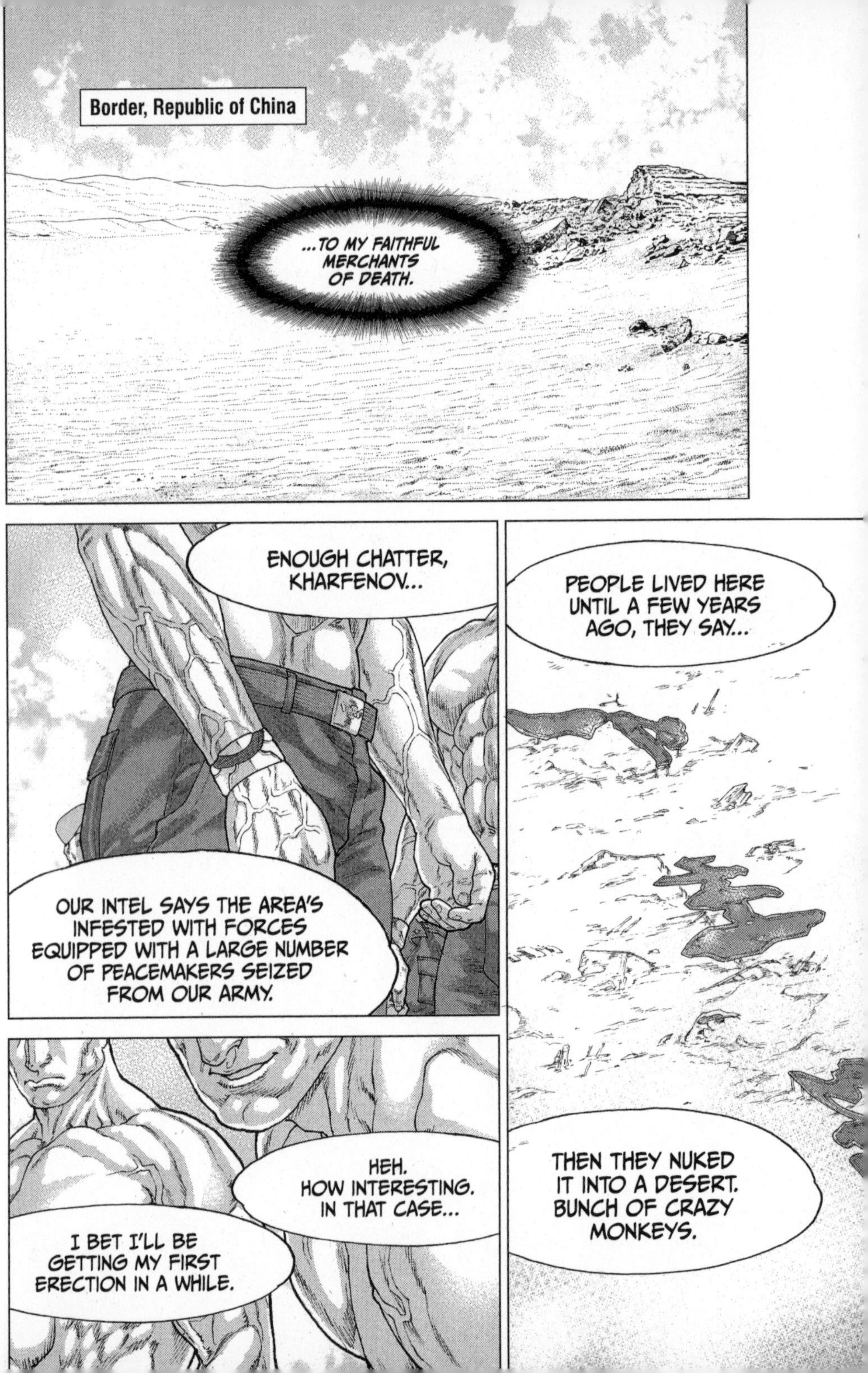
Border, Republic of China
...TO MY FAITHFUL MERCHANTS OF DEATH.
PEOPLE LIVED HERE UNTIL A FEW YEARS AGO, THEY SAY...
THEN THEY NUKED IT INTO A DESERT. BUNCH OF CRAZY MONKEYS.
ENOUGH CHATTER, KHARFENOV...
OUR INTEL SAYS THE AREA'S INFESTED WITH FORCES EQUIPPED WITH A LARGE NUMBER OF PEACEMAKERS SEIZED FROM OUR ARMY.
HEH. HOW INTERESTING. IN THAT CASE...
I BET I'LL BE GETTING MY FIRST ERECTION IN A WHILE.

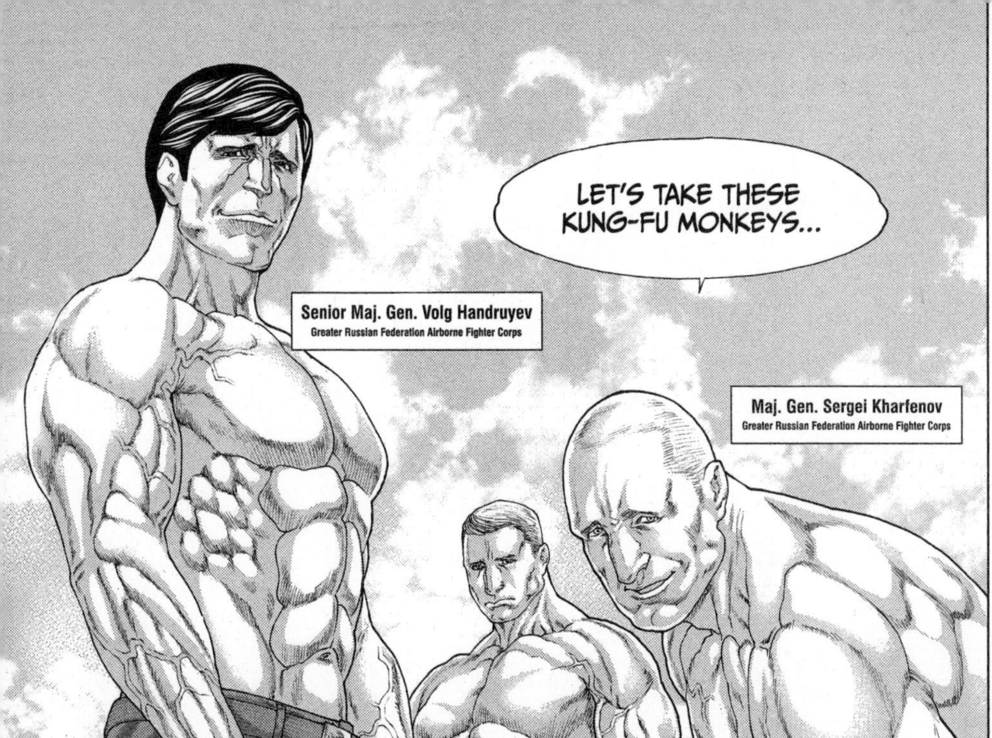
LET'S TAKE THESE KUNG-FU MONKEYS...
Senior Maj. Gen. Volg Handruyev
Greater Russian Federation Airborne Fighter Corps
Maj. Gen. Sergei Kharfenov
Greater Russian Federation Airborne Fighter Corps
Maj. Gen. Viktor Kulichenko
Greater Russian Federation Airborne Fighter Corps
...AND SHOW THEM THE LIGHT.
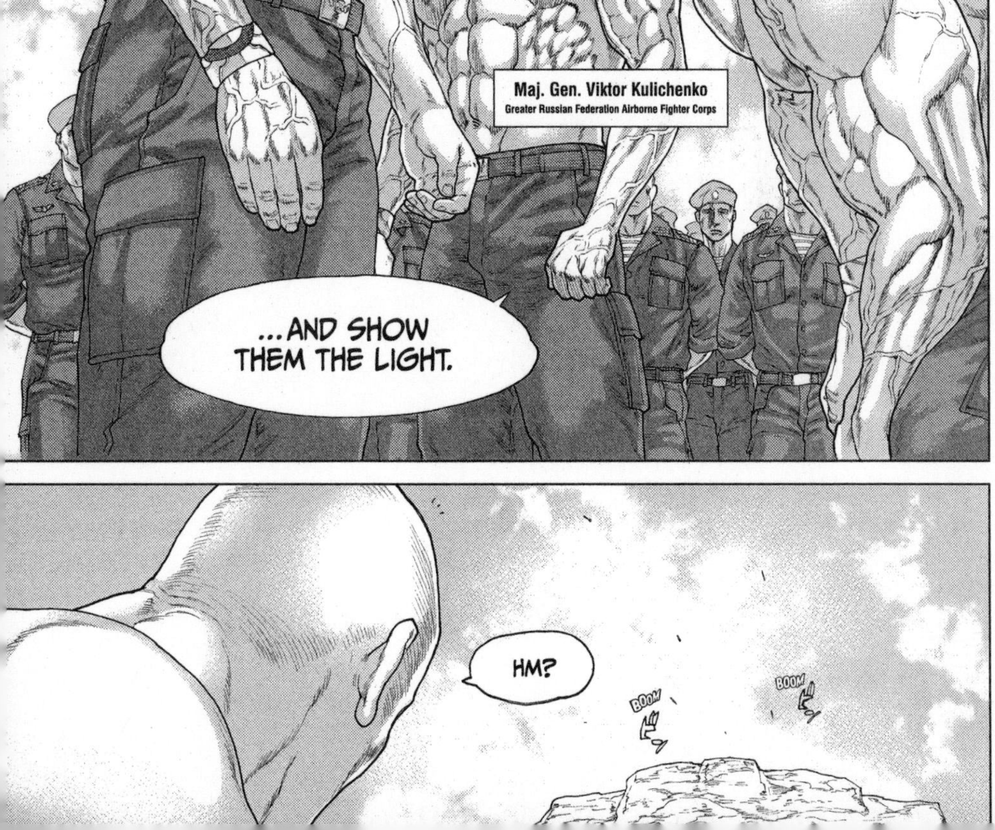
HM?
BOOM
BOOM

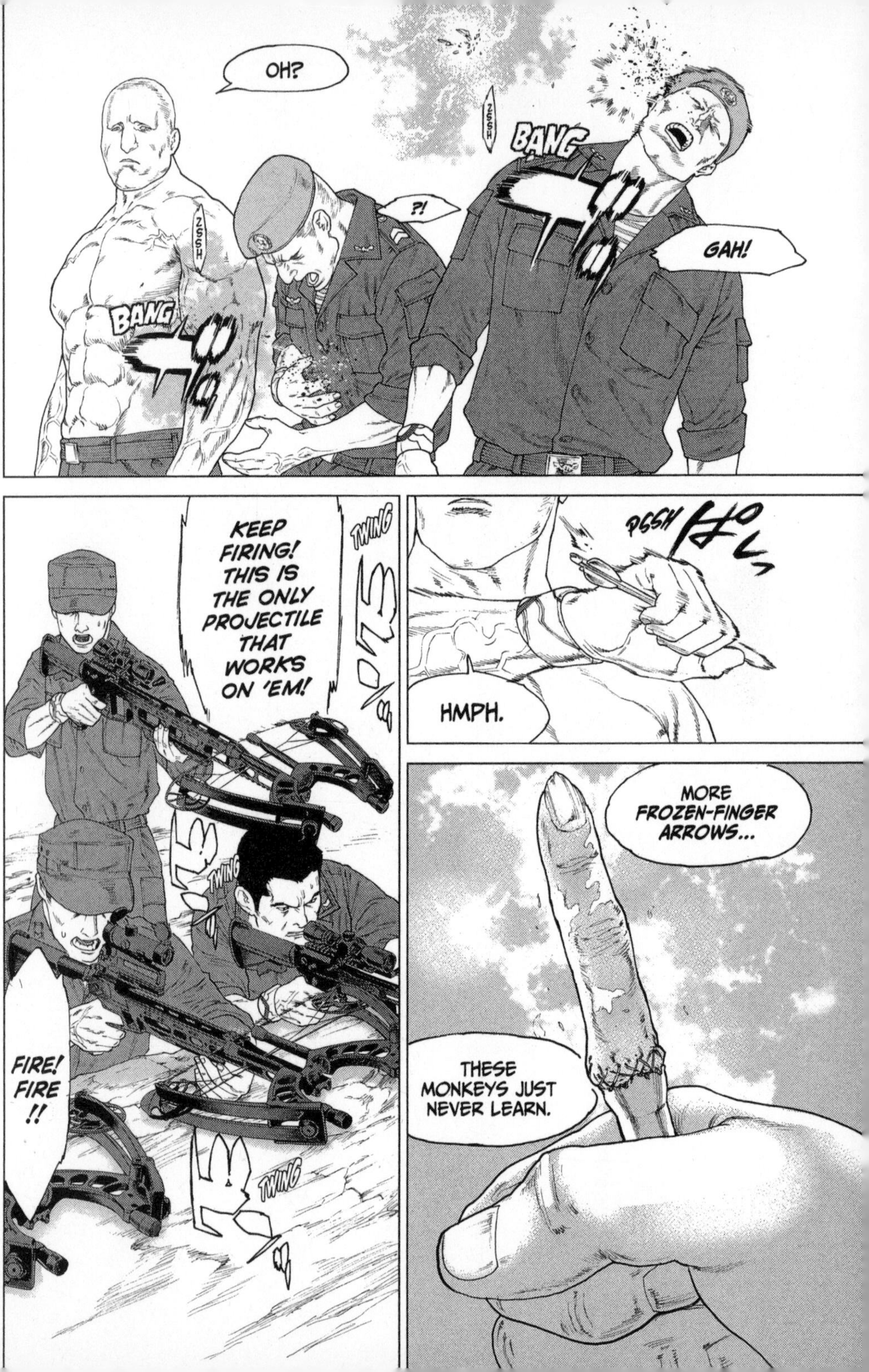
BANG
ZSSH
OH?
?!
GAH!
ZSSH
BANG
PSSH
ぱしっ
HMPH.
MORE FROZEN-FINGER ARROWS...
THESE MONKEYS JUST NEVER LEARN.
TWING
KEEP FIRING! THIS IS THE ONLY PROJECTILE THAT WORKS ON 'EM!
TWING
FIRE! FIRE !!
TWING

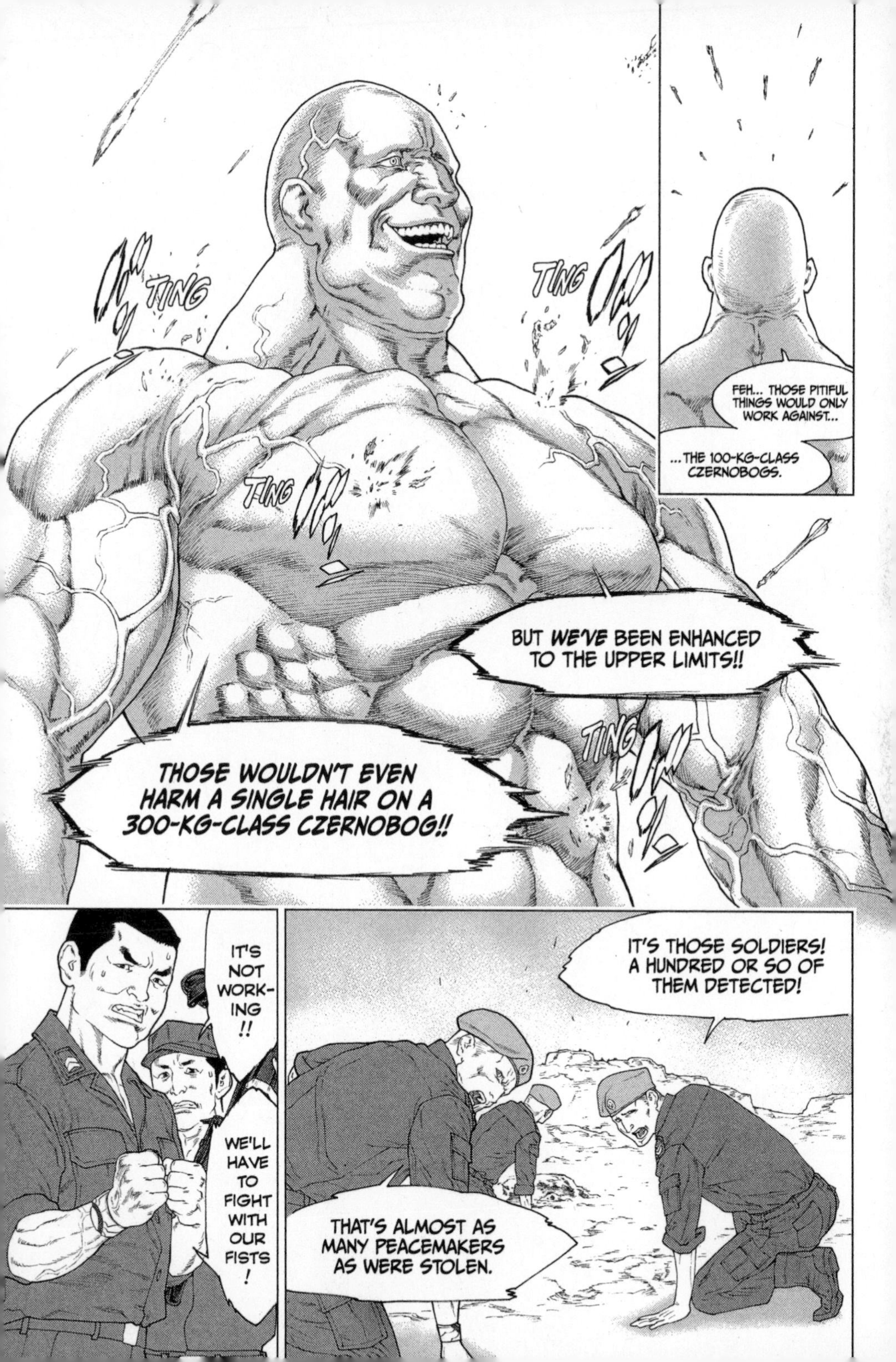
FEH... THOSE PITIFUL THINGS WOULD ONLY WORK AGAINST...
...THE 100-KG-CLASS CZERNOBOGS.
TING
TING
TING
BUT WE'VE BEEN ENHANCED TO THE UPPER LIMITS!!
TING
THOSE WOULDN'T EVEN HARM A SINGLE HAIR ON A 300-KG-CLASS CZERNOBOG!!
IT'S THOSE SOLDIERS! A HUNDRED OR SO OF THEM DETECTED!
THAT'S ALMOST AS MANY PEACEMAKERS AS WERE STOLEN.
IT'S NOT WORKING!!
WE'LL HAVE TO FIGHT WITH OUR FISTS!

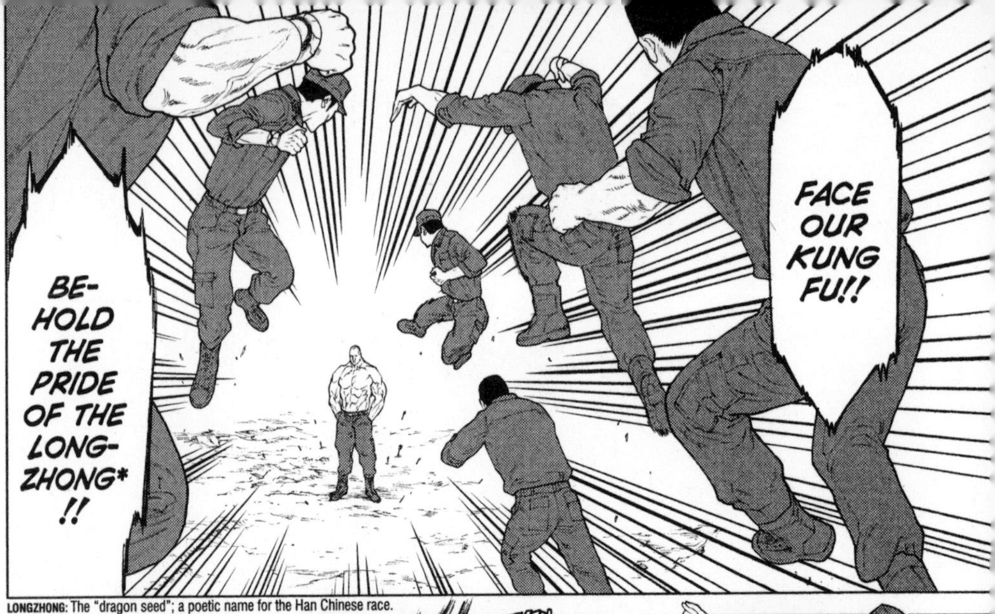
FACE OUR KUNG FU!!
BE-HOLD THE PRIDE OF THE LONG-ZHONG* !!

LONGZHONG: The "dragon seed"; a poetic name for the Han Chinese race.

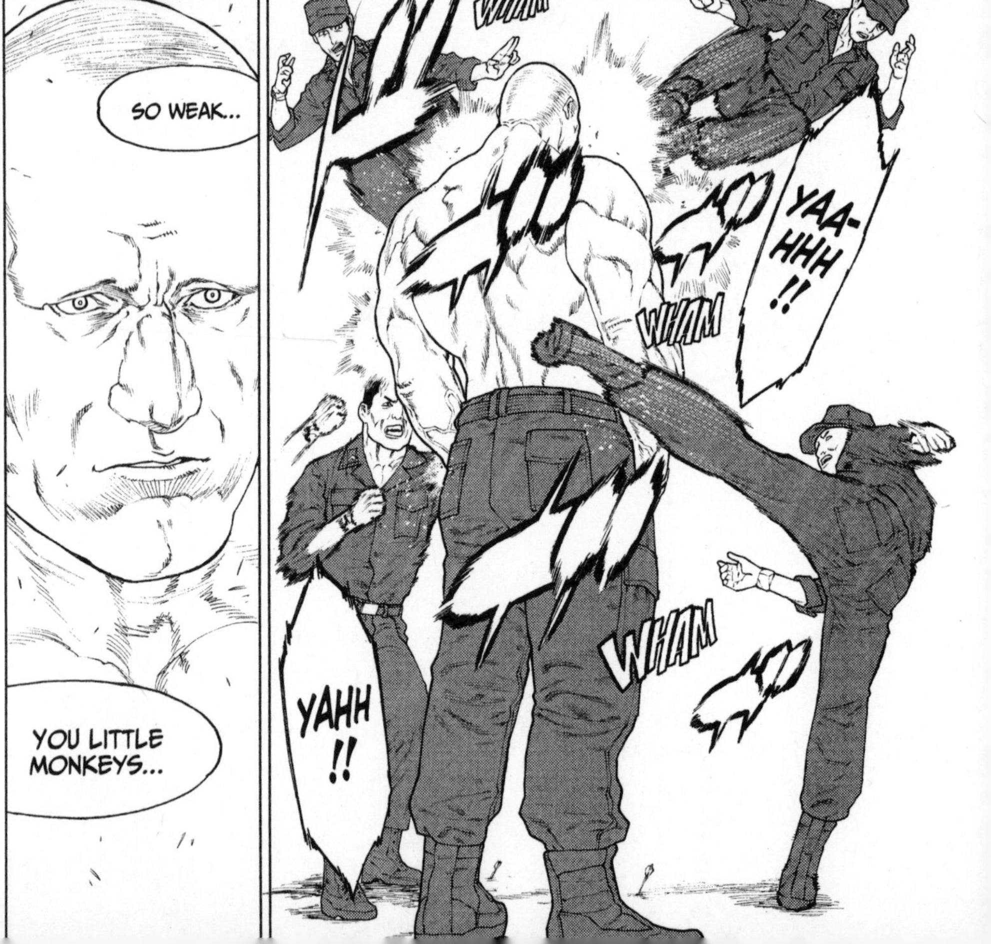
WHAM
YAA-HHH !!
WHAM
WHAM
YAHH !!
SO WEAK...
YOU LITTLE MONKEYS...

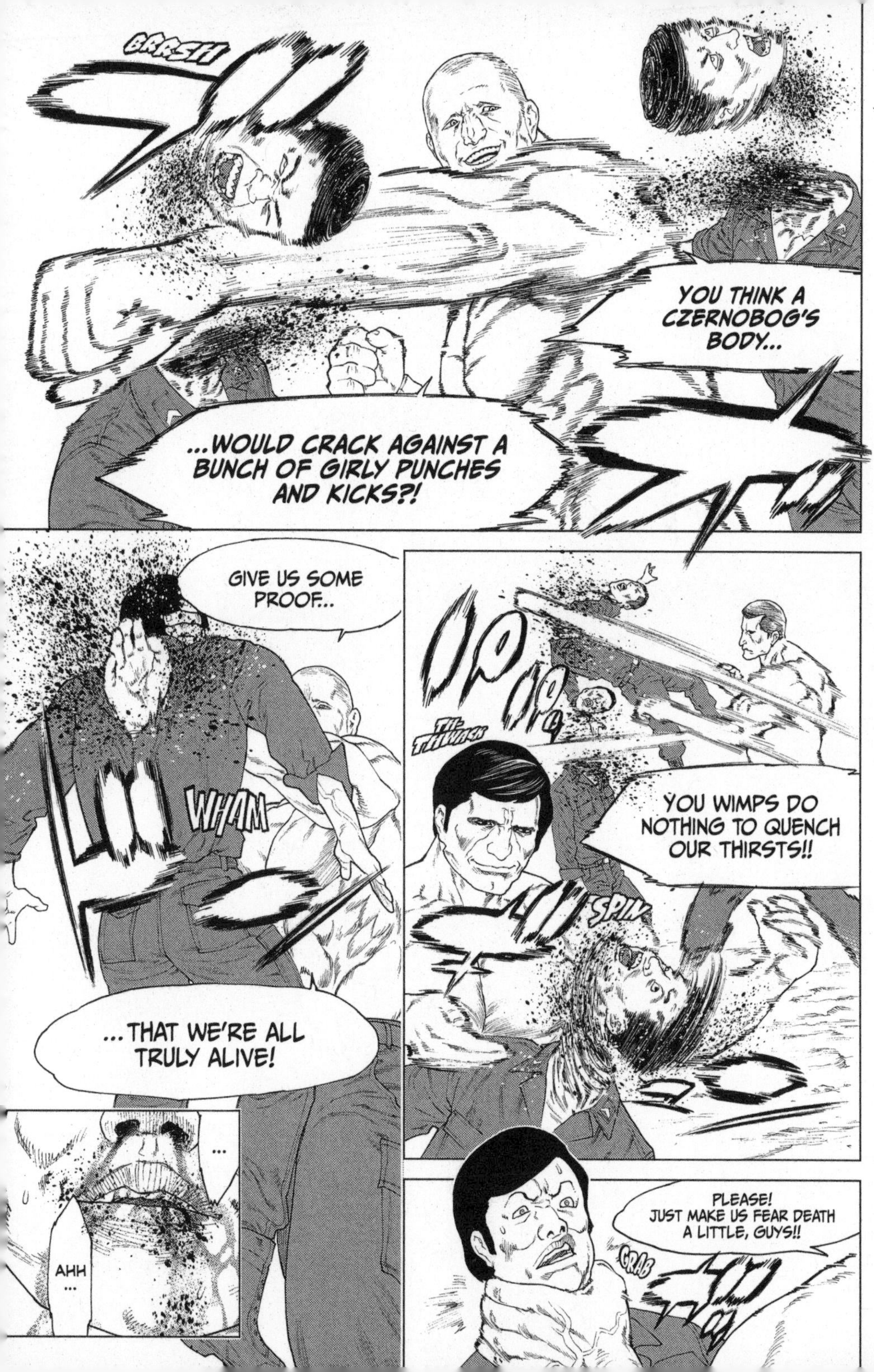
GRRSH
YOU THINK A CZERNOBOG'S BODY...
...WOULD CRACK AGAINST A BUNCH OF GIRLY PUNCHES AND KICKS?!
TH-THWACK
YOU WIMPS DO NOTHING TO QUENCH OUR THIRSTS!!
SPIN
GIVE US SOME PROOF...
WHAM
...THAT WE'RE ALL TRULY ALIVE!
PLEASE! JUST MAKE US FEAR DEATH A LITTLE, GUYS!!
GRAB
...
AHH ...

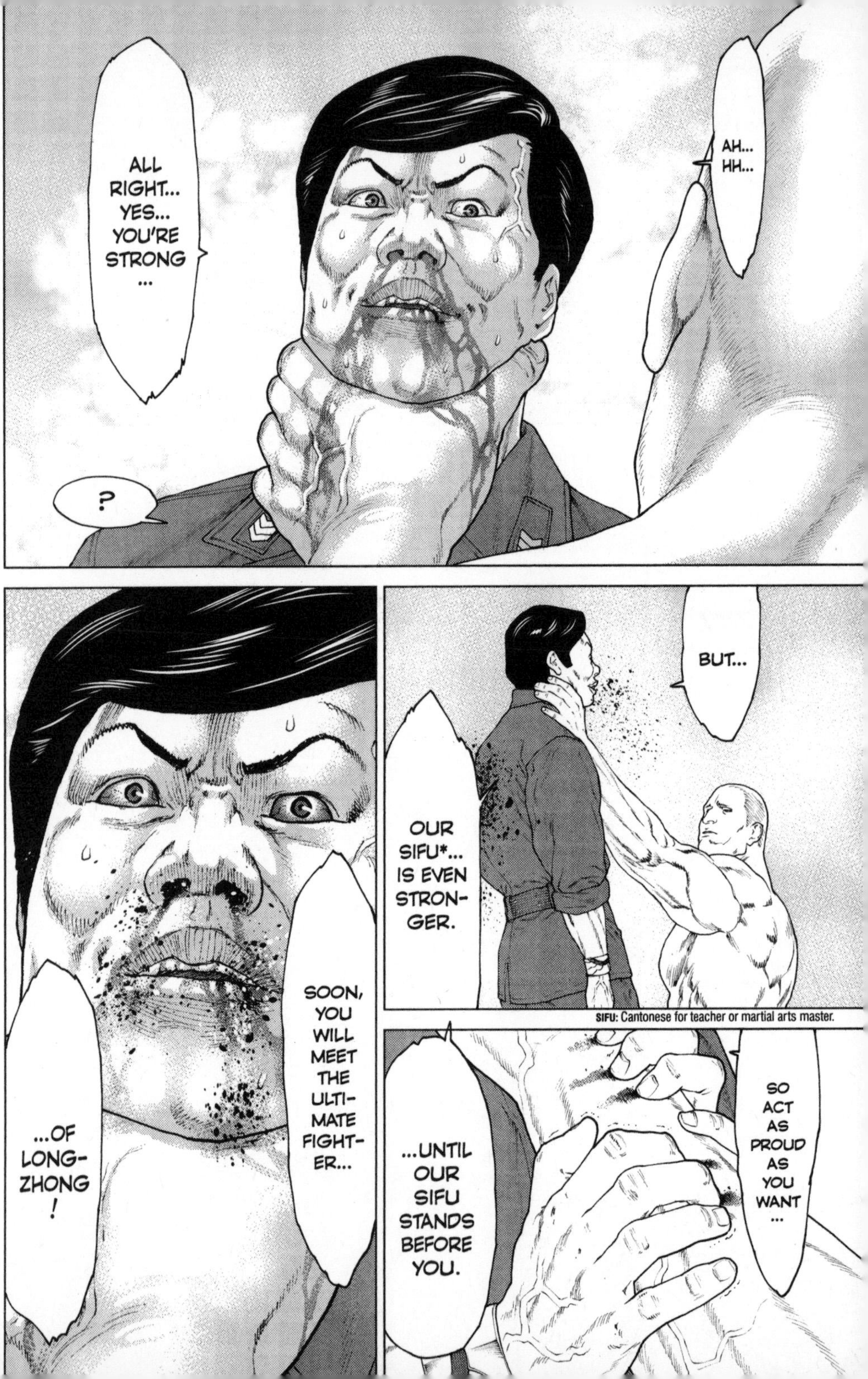
AH... HH...
ALL RIGHT... YES... YOU'RE STRONG ...
?
BUT...
OUR SIFU*... IS EVEN STRONGER.
SO ACT AS PROUD AS YOU WANT ...
...UNTIL OUR SIFU STANDS BEFORE YOU.
SOON, YOU WILL MEET THE ULTIMATE FIGHTER...
...OF LONG-ZHONG!
SIFU: Cantonese for teacher or martial arts master.

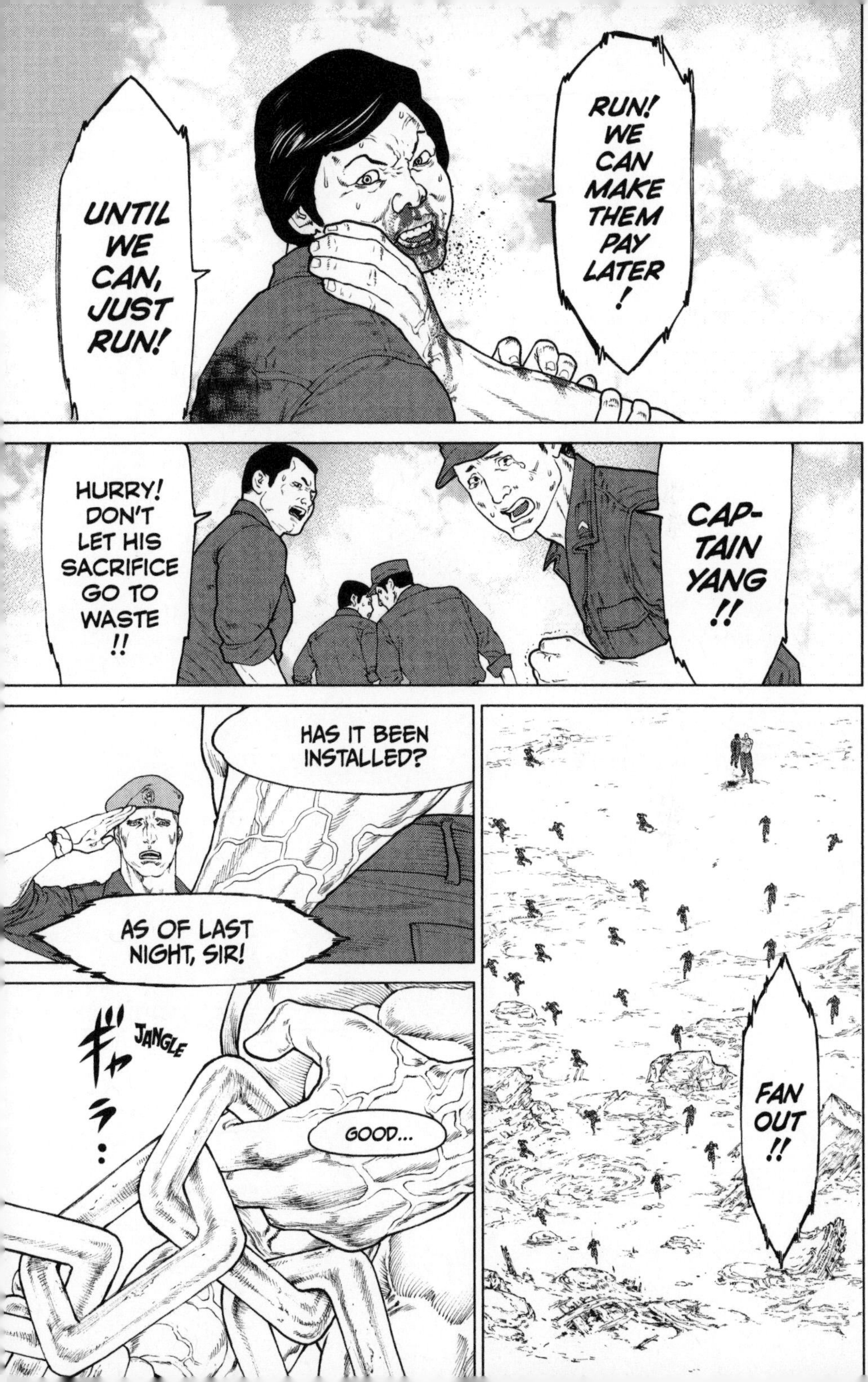
RUN! WE CAN MAKE THEM PAY LATER!
UNTIL WE CAN, JUST RUN!
CAPTAIN YANG!!
HURRY! DON'T LET HIS SACRIFICE GO TO WASTE!!
FAN OUT!!
HAS IT BEEN INSTALLED?
AS OF LAST NIGHT, SIR!
ギャラ…
JANGLE
GOOD...

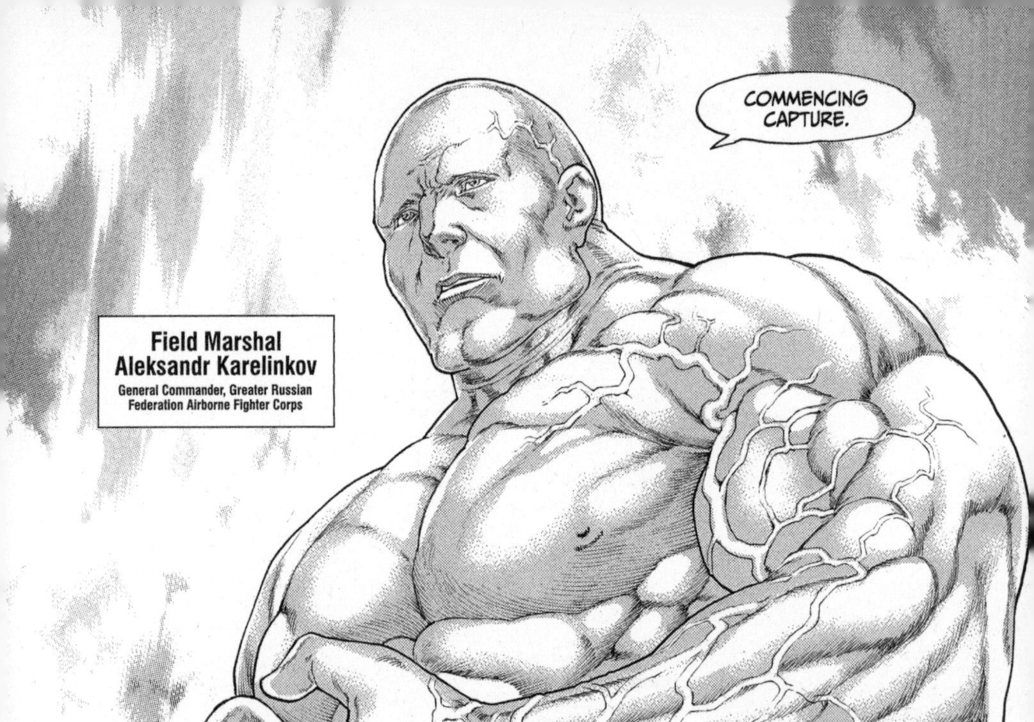
COMMENCING CAPTURE.
Field Marshal Aleksandr Karelinkov
General Commander, Greater Russian Federation Airborne Fighter Corps
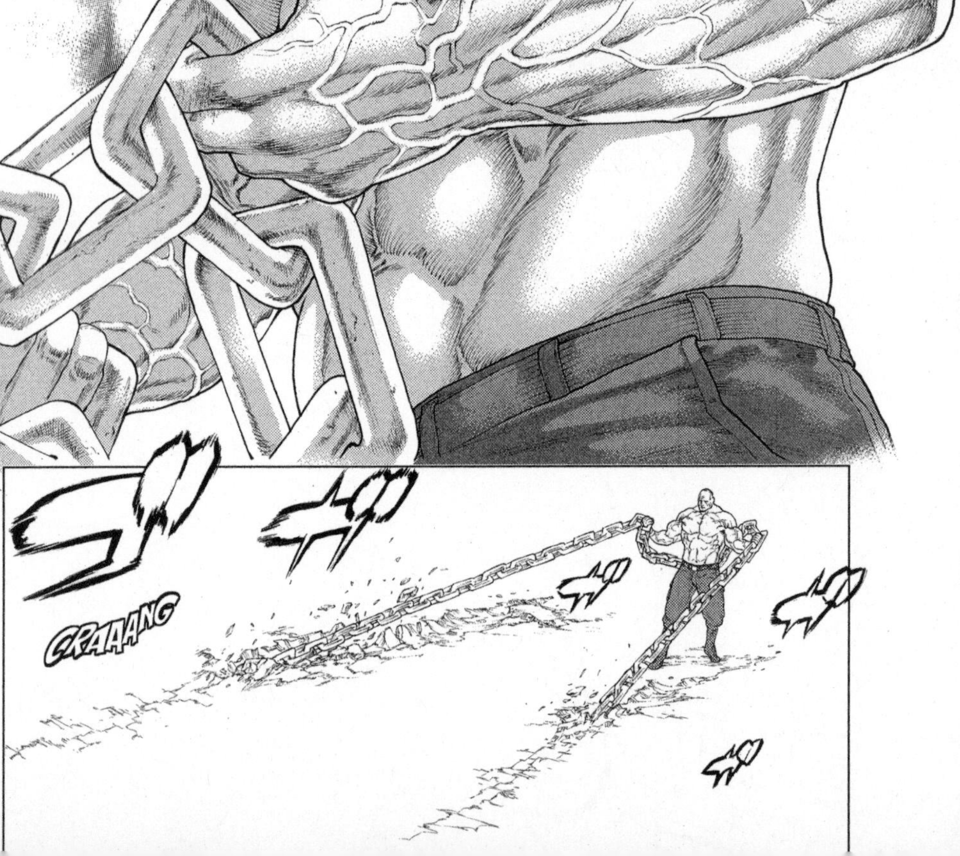
CRAAANG

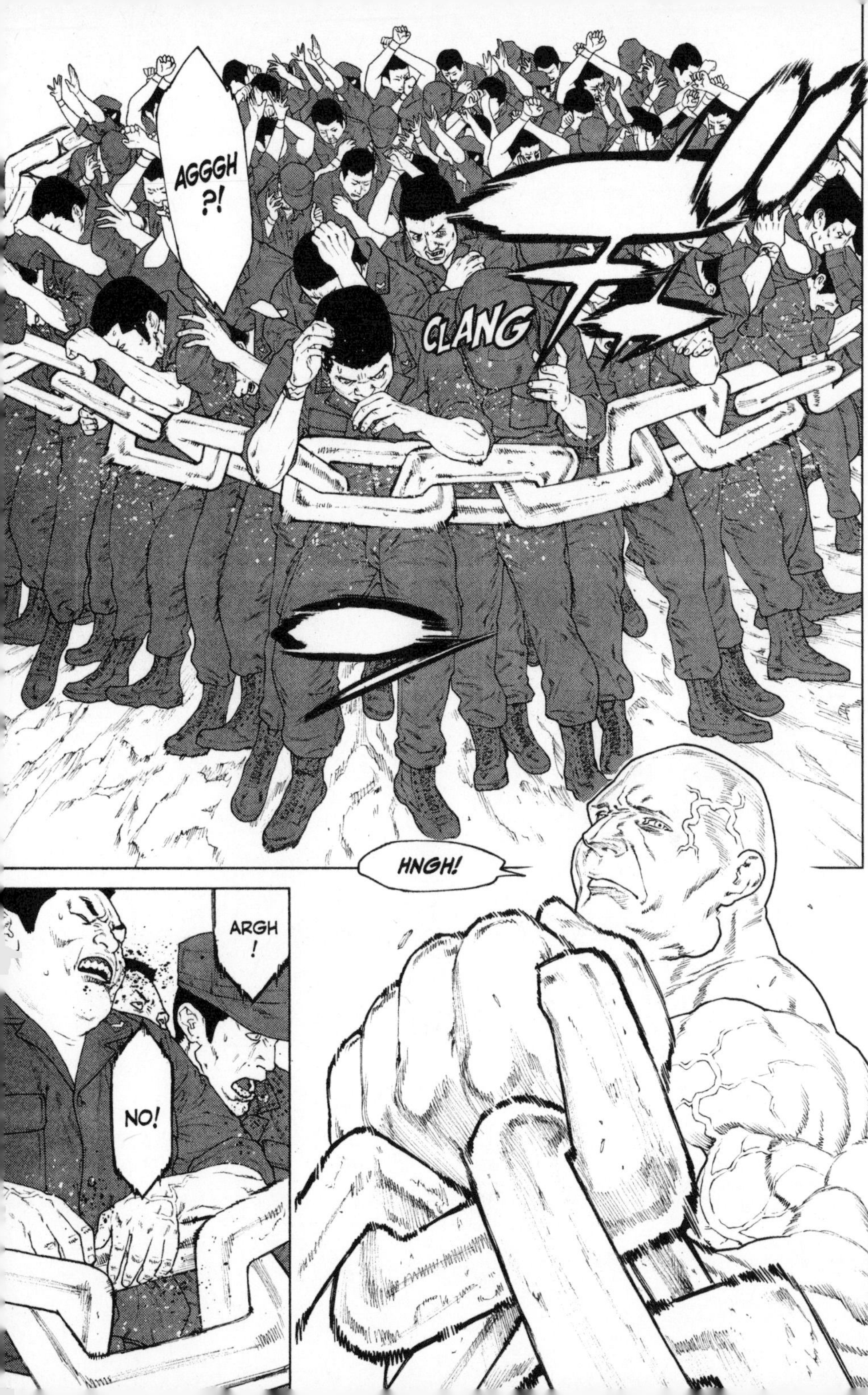
AGGGH ?!
CLANG
HNGH!
ARGH!
NO!

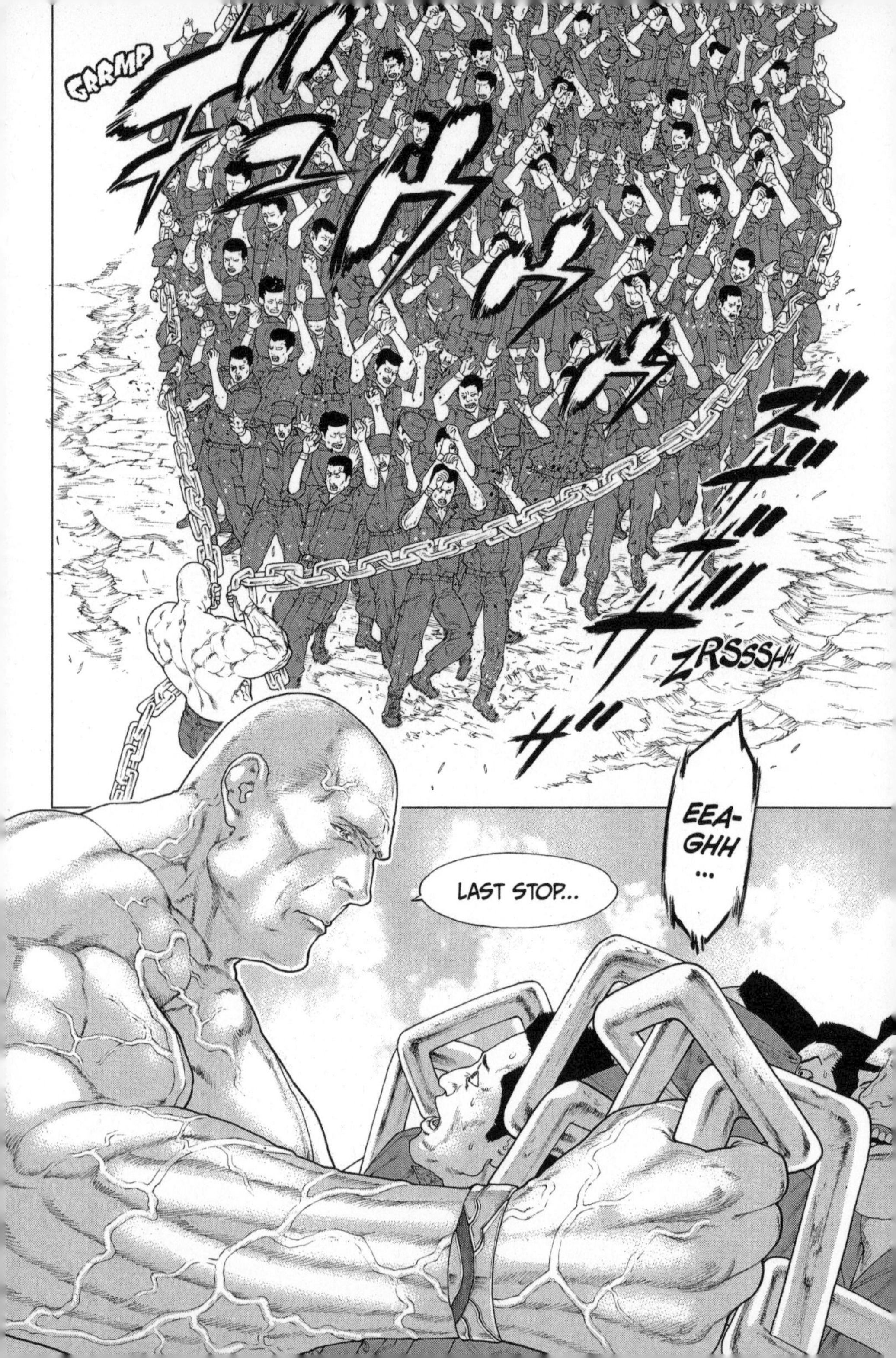
GRRMP
ZRSSSHH
EEA-GHH...
LAST STOP...

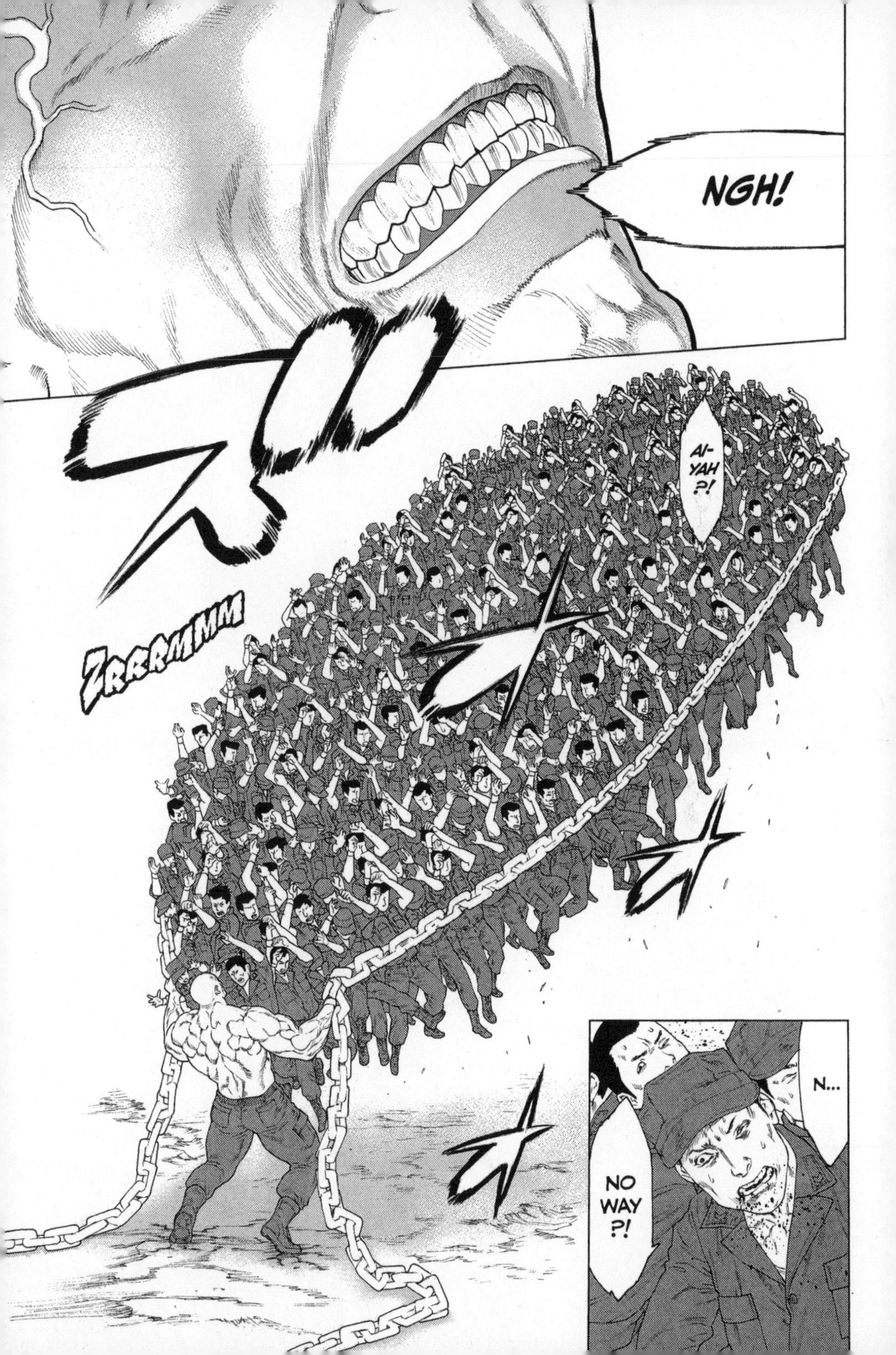
NGH!
AI-YAH ?!
ZRRRMMM
N...
NO WAY ?!

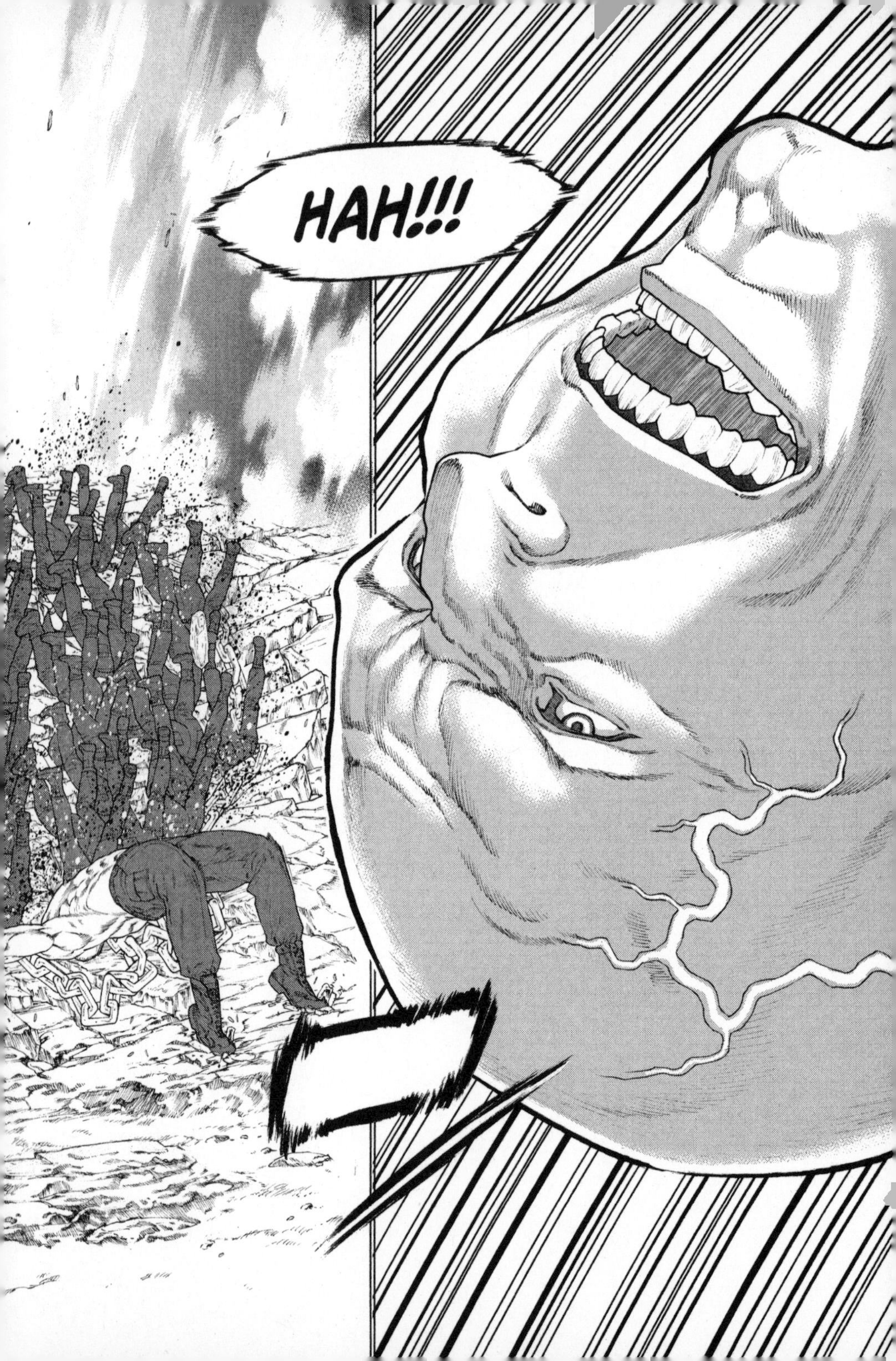
HAH!!!

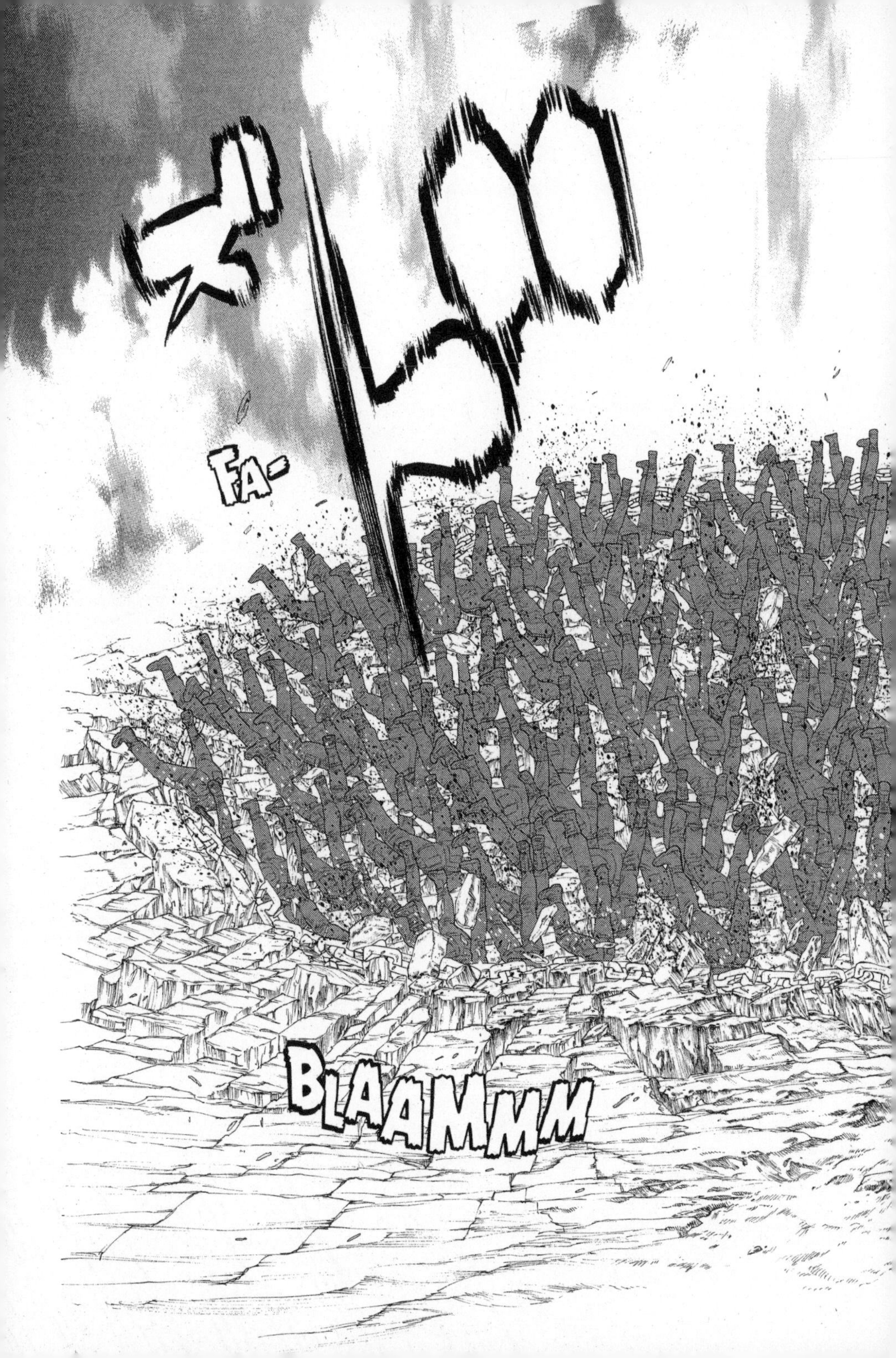
FA-
BLAAMMM

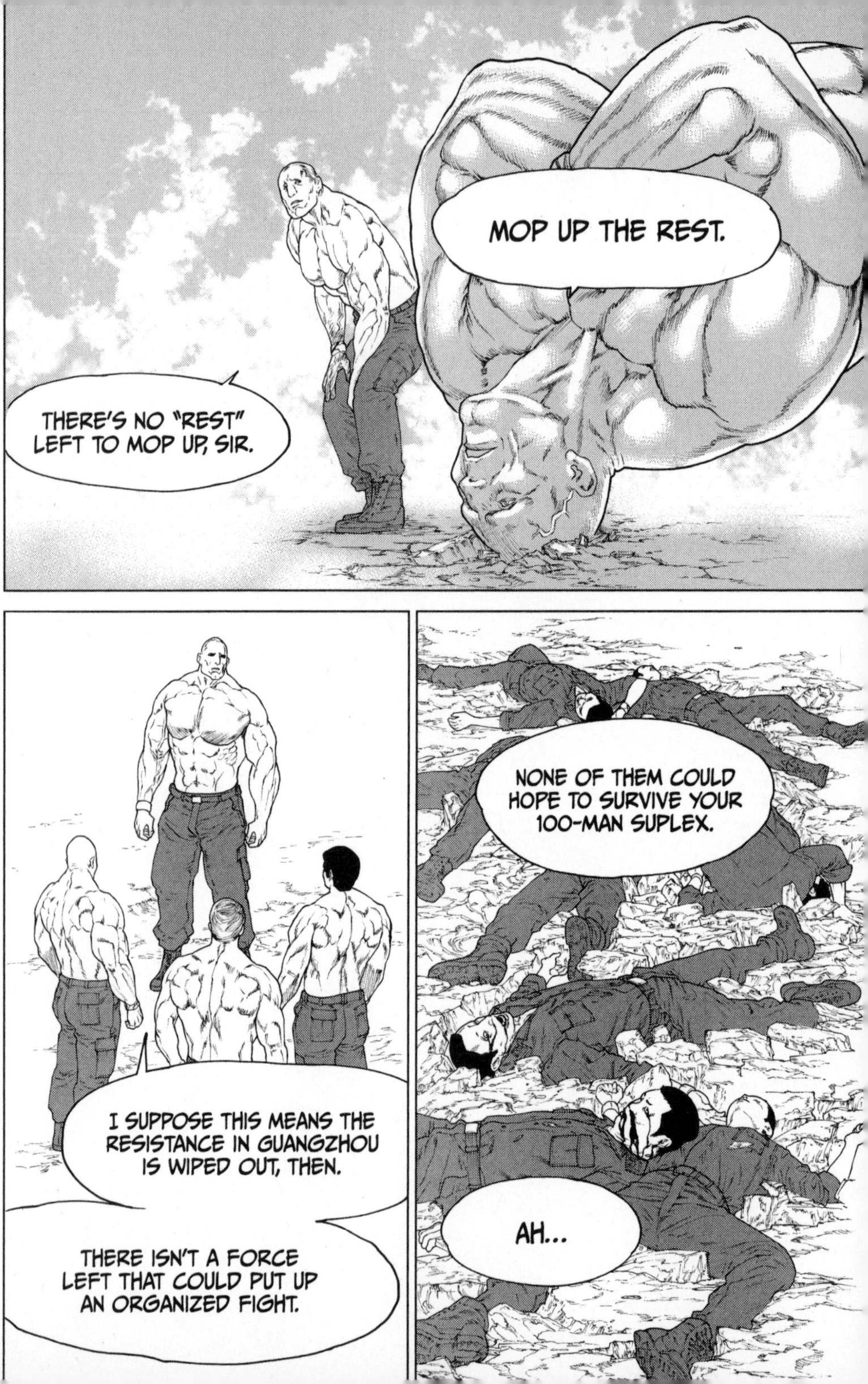
MOP UP THE REST.
THERE'S NO "REST" LEFT TO MOP UP, SIR.
NONE OF THEM COULD HOPE TO SURVIVE YOUR 100-MAN SUPLEX.
AH...
I SUPPOSE THIS MEANS THE RESISTANCE IN GUANGZHOU IS WIPED OUT, THEN.
THERE ISN'T A FORCE LEFT THAT COULD PUT UP AN ORGANIZED FIGHT.

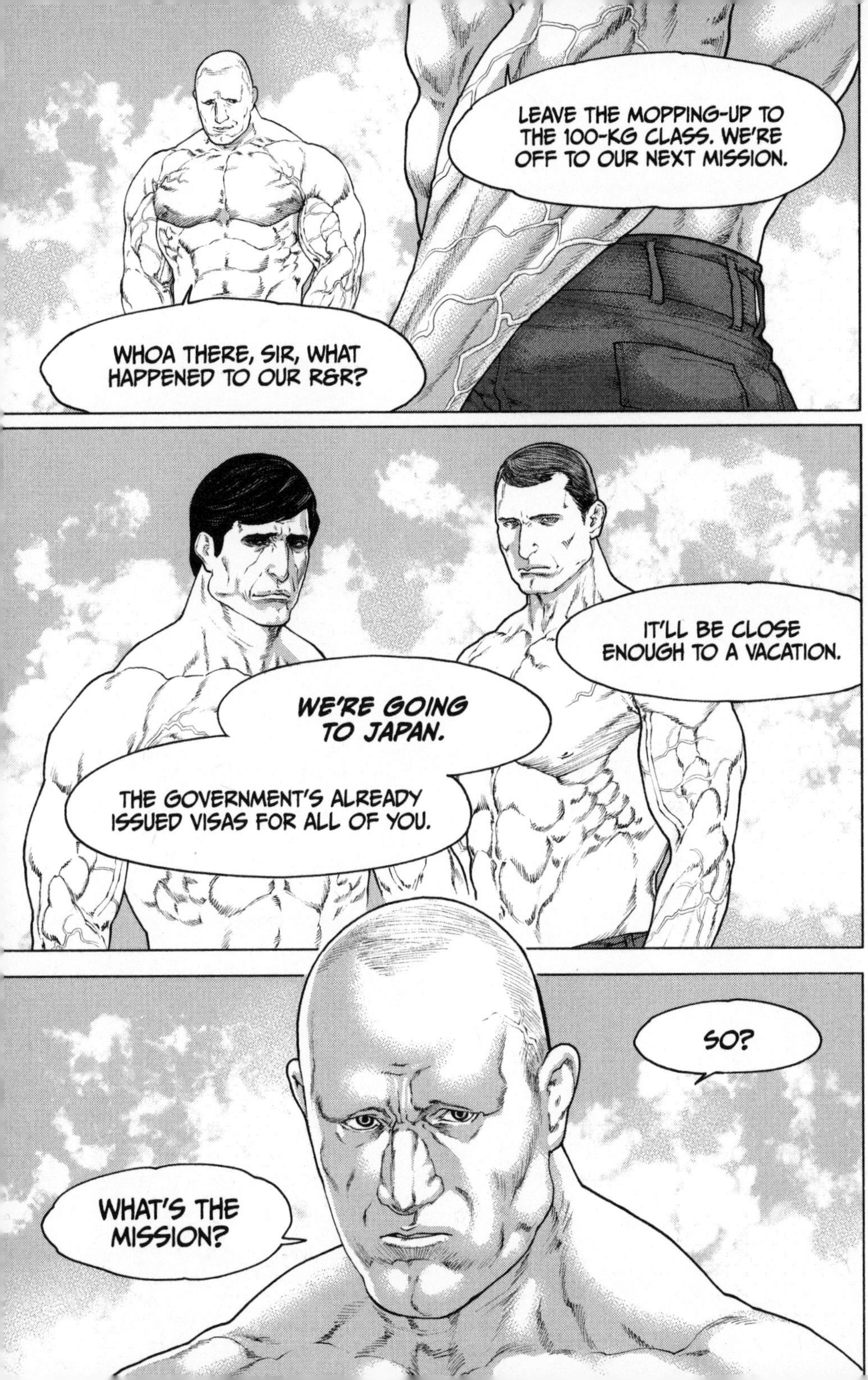
LEAVE THE MOPPING-UP TO THE 100-KG CLASS. WE'RE OFF TO OUR NEXT MISSION.
WHOA THERE, SIR, WHAT HAPPENED TO OUR R&R?
IT'LL BE CLOSE ENOUGH TO A VACATION.
WE'RE GOING TO JAPAN.
THE GOVERNMENT'S ALREADY ISSUED VISAS FOR ALL OF YOU.
SO?
WHAT'S THE MISSION?

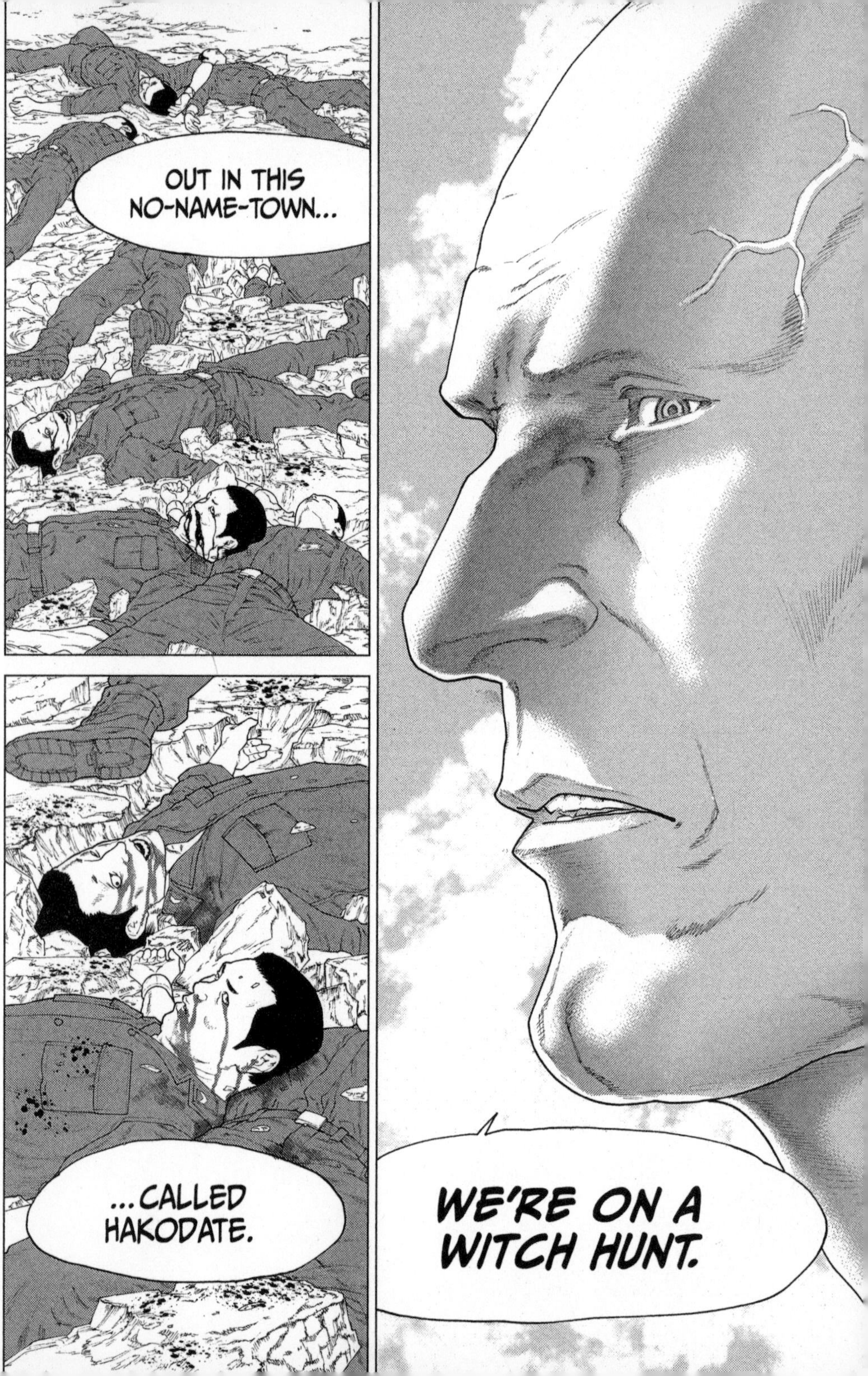
WE'RE ON A WITCH HUNT.
OUT IN THIS NO-NAME-TOWN...
...CALLED HAKODATE.

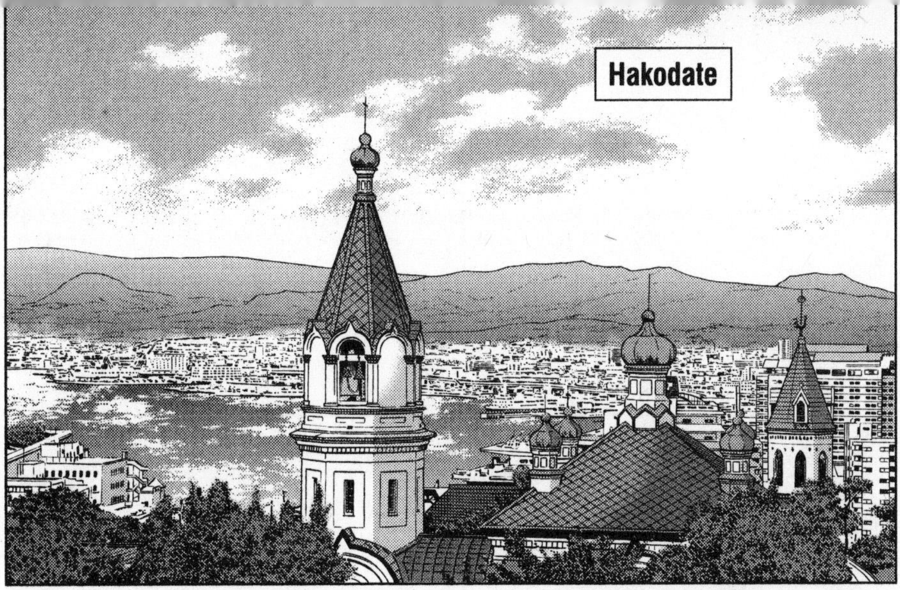
Hakodate

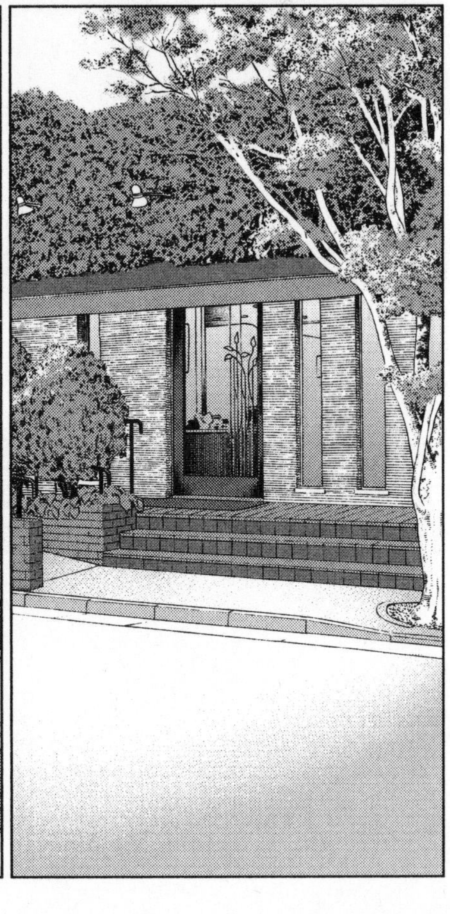

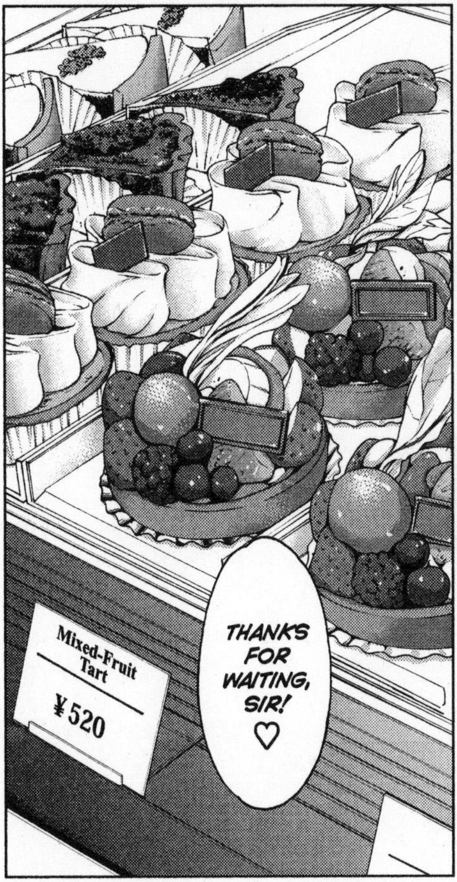
Mixed-Fruit Tart
¥520
THANKS FOR WAITING, SIR! ♡

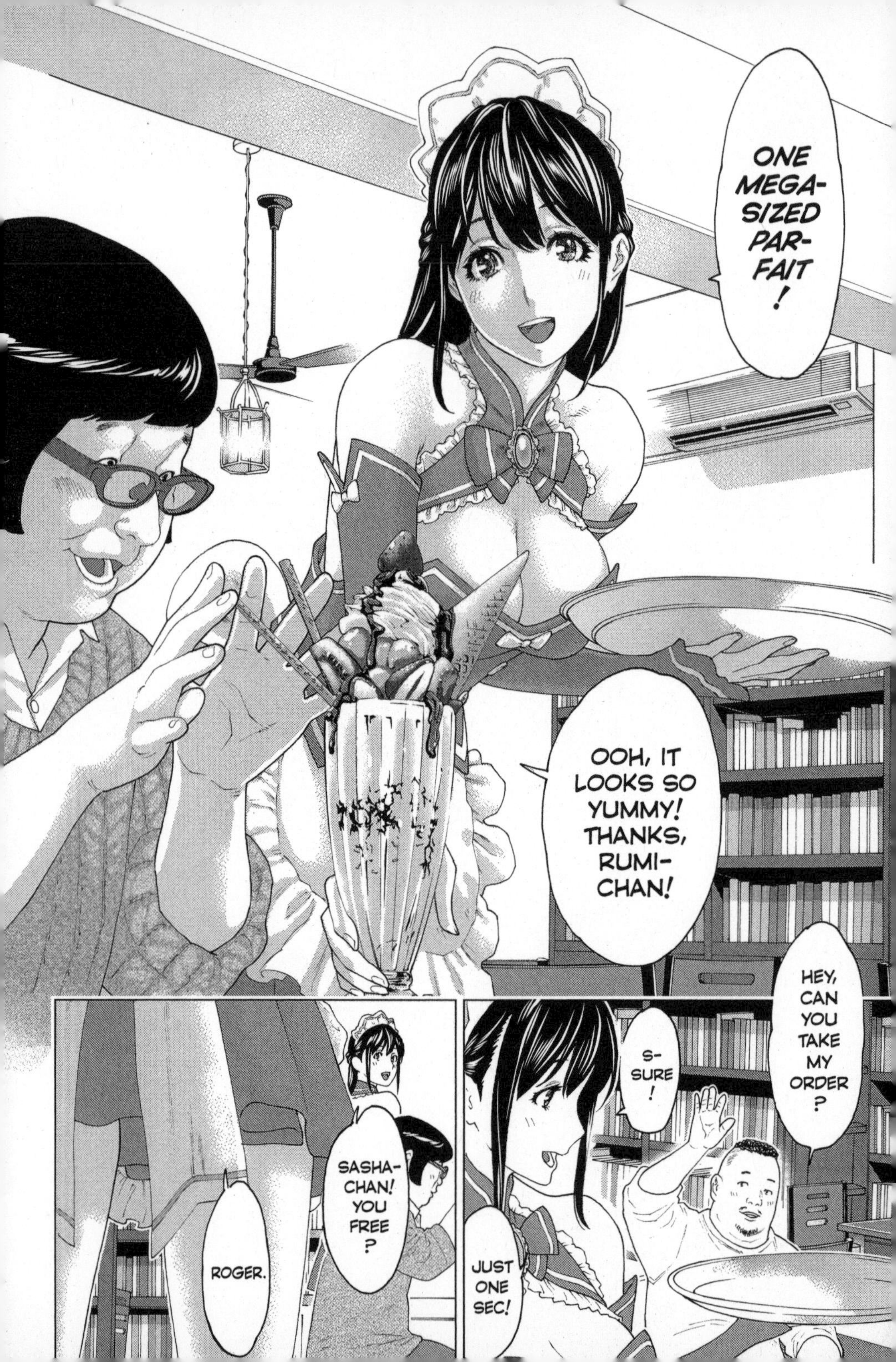
ONE MEGA-SIZED PAR-FAIT!
OOH, IT LOOKS SO YUMMY! THANKS, RUMI-CHAN!
HEY, CAN YOU TAKE MY ORDER?
S-SURE!
JUST ONE SEC!
SASHA-CHAN! YOU FREE?
ROGER.

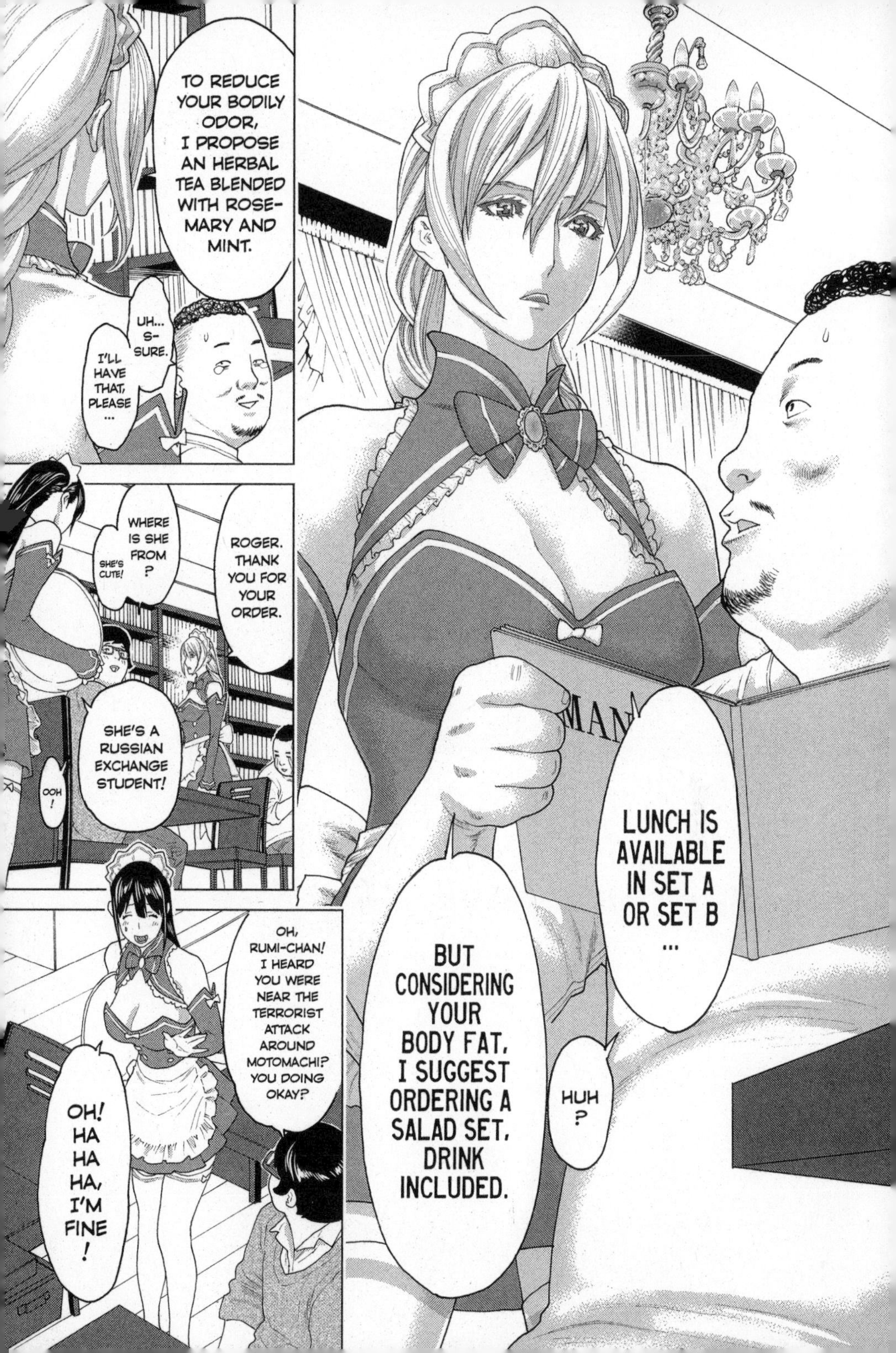
LUNCH IS AVAILABLE IN SET A OR SET B ...
HUH?
BUT CONSIDERING YOUR BODY FAT, I SUGGEST ORDERING A SALAD SET, DRINK INCLUDED.
TO REDUCE YOUR BODILY ODOR, I PROPOSE AN HERBAL TEA BLENDED WITH ROSE-MARY AND MINT.
UH... S-SURE.
I'LL HAVE THAT, PLEASE ...
ROGER. THANK YOU FOR YOUR ORDER.
WHERE IS SHE FROM ?
SHE'S CUTE!
SHE'S A RUSSIAN EXCHANGE STUDENT!
OOH !
OH, RUMI-CHAN! I HEARD YOU WERE NEAR THE TERRORIST ATTACK AROUND MOTOMACHI? YOU DOING OKAY?
OH! HA HA HA, I'M FINE !

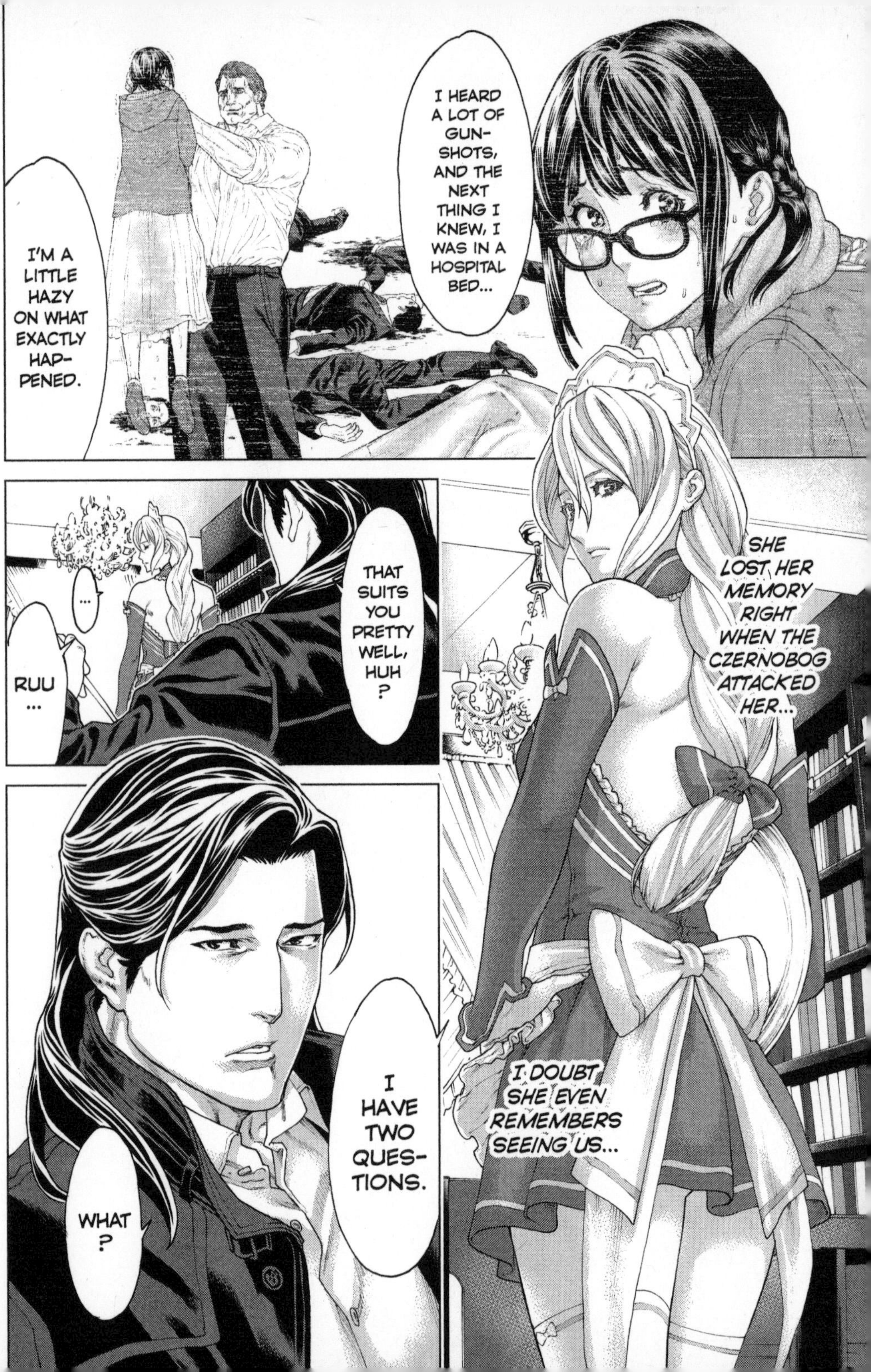
I HEARD A LOT OF GUN-SHOTS, AND THE NEXT THING I KNEW, I WAS IN A HOSPITAL BED...
I'M A LITTLE HAZY ON WHAT EXACTLY HAP-PENED.
SHE LOST HER MEMORY RIGHT WHEN THE CZERNOBOG ATTACKED HER...
I DOUBT SHE EVEN REMEMBERS SEEING US...
THAT SUITS YOU PRETTY WELL, HUH?
...
RUU...
I HAVE TWO QUES-TIONS.
WHAT?

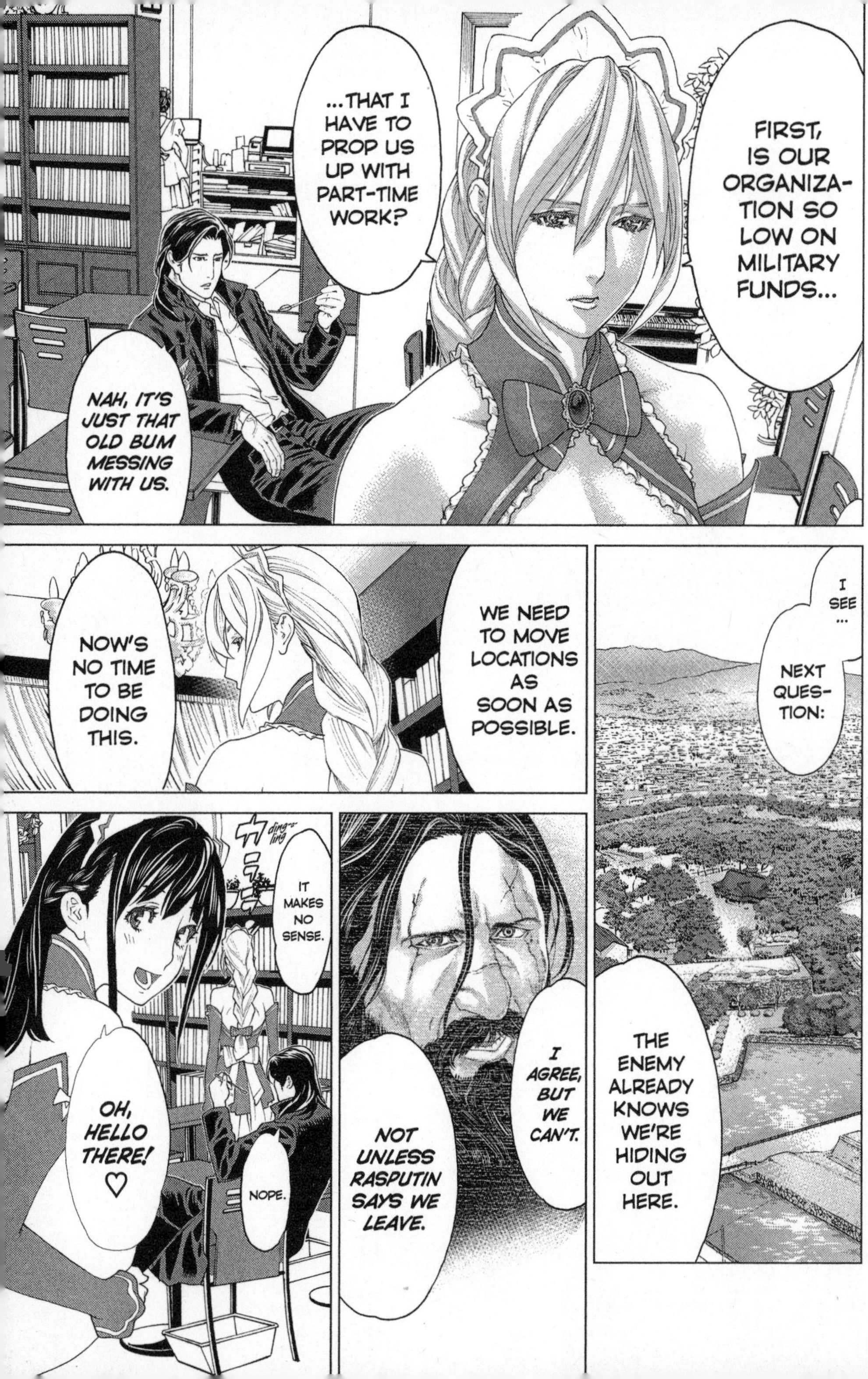
FIRST, IS OUR ORGANIZATION SO LOW ON MILITARY FUNDS...
...THAT I HAVE TO PROP US UP WITH PART-TIME WORK?
NAH, IT'S JUST THAT OLD BUM MESSING WITH US.
I SEE...
NEXT QUESTION:
THE ENEMY ALREADY KNOWS WE'RE HIDING OUT HERE.
WE NEED TO MOVE LOCATIONS AS SOON AS POSSIBLE.
NOW'S NO TIME TO BE DOING THIS.
I AGREE, BUT WE CAN'T.
NOT UNLESS RASPUTIN SAYS WE LEAVE.
ding-a-ling
IT MAKES NO SENSE.
OH, HELLO THERE! ♡
NOPE.

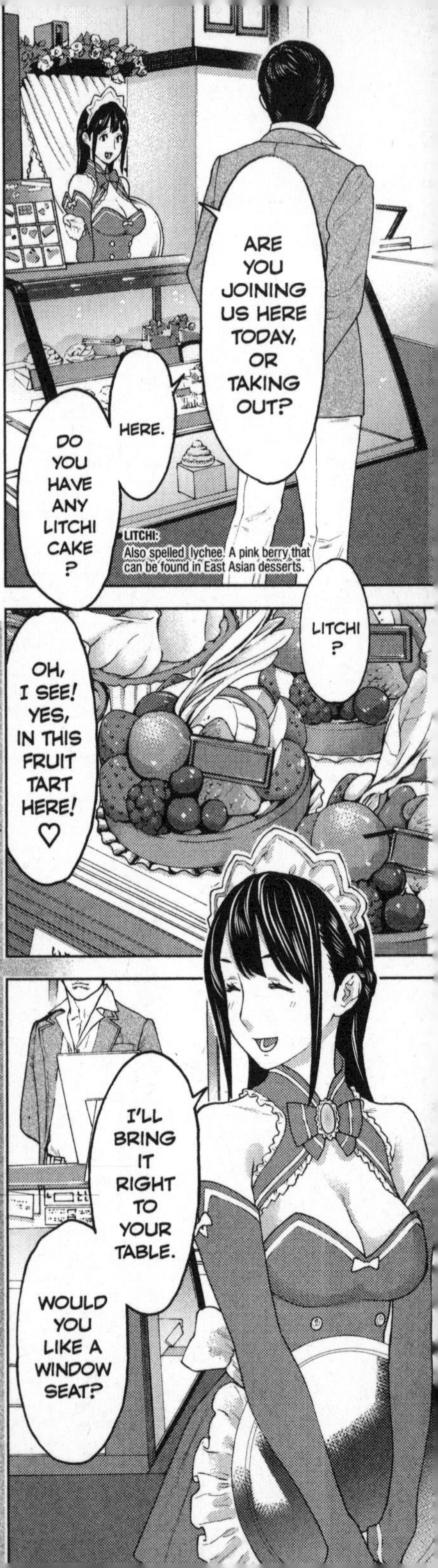
ARE YOU JOINING US HERE TODAY, OR TAKING OUT?
HERE.
DO YOU HAVE ANY LITCHI CAKE?
LITCHI:
Also spelled lychee. A pink berry that can be found in East Asian desserts.
LITCHI?
OH, I SEE! YES, IN THIS FRUIT TART HERE! ♡
I'LL BRING IT RIGHT TO YOUR TABLE.
WOULD YOU LIKE A WINDOW SEAT?

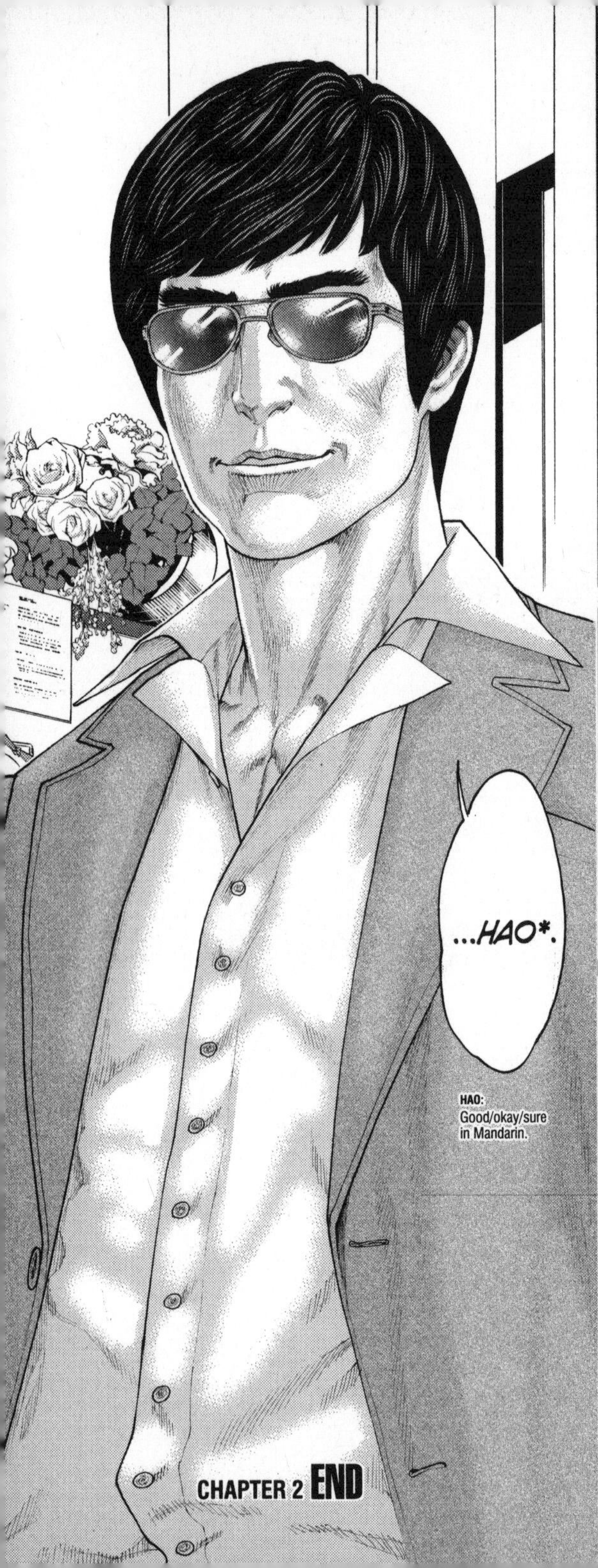
...HAO*.
HAO:
Good/okay/sure in Mandarin.
CHAPTER 2 END

GOLOSSEUM

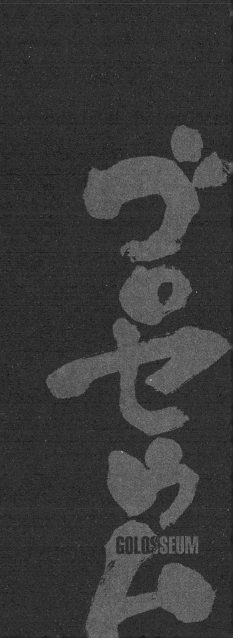

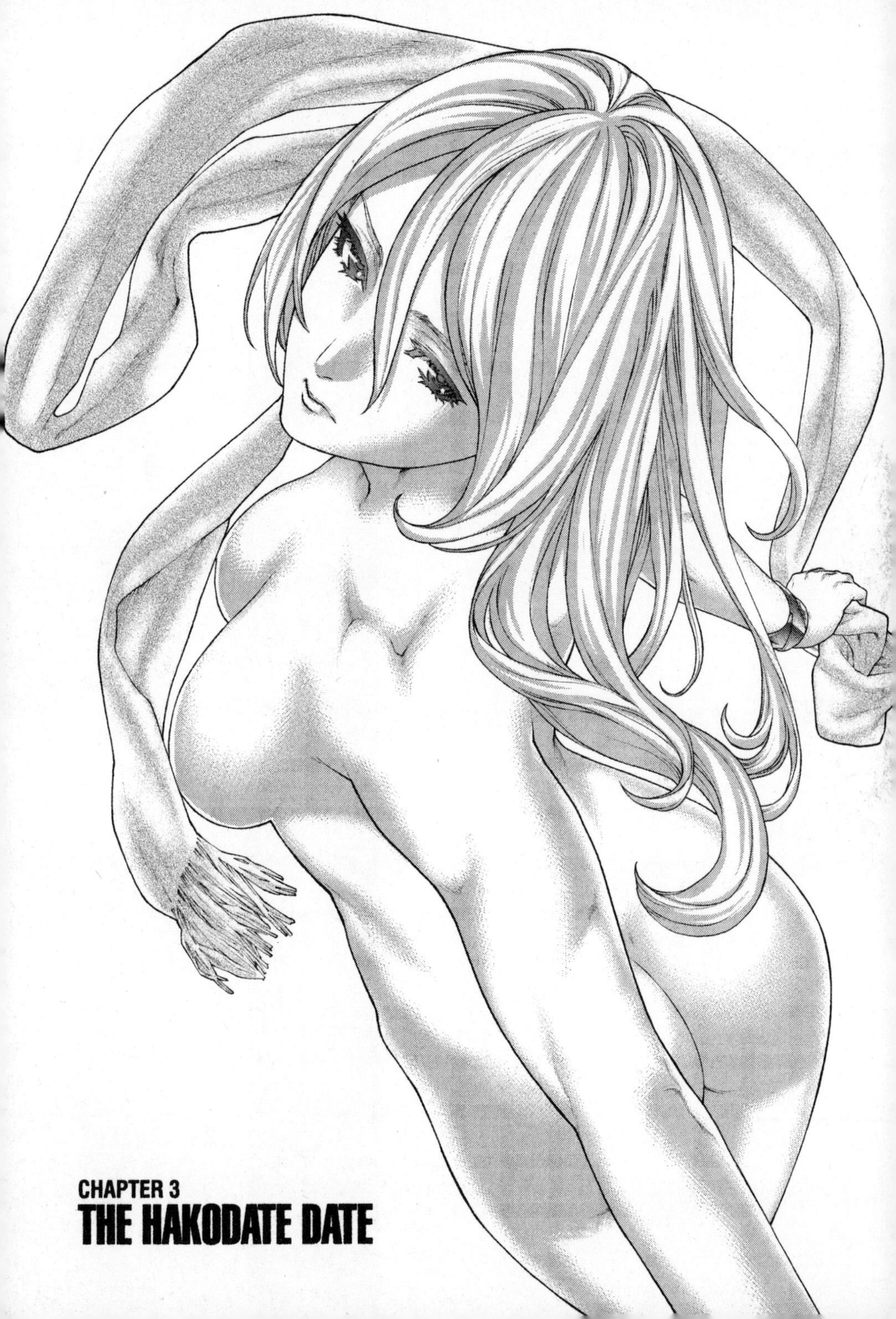

CHAPTER 3

THE HAKODATE DATE

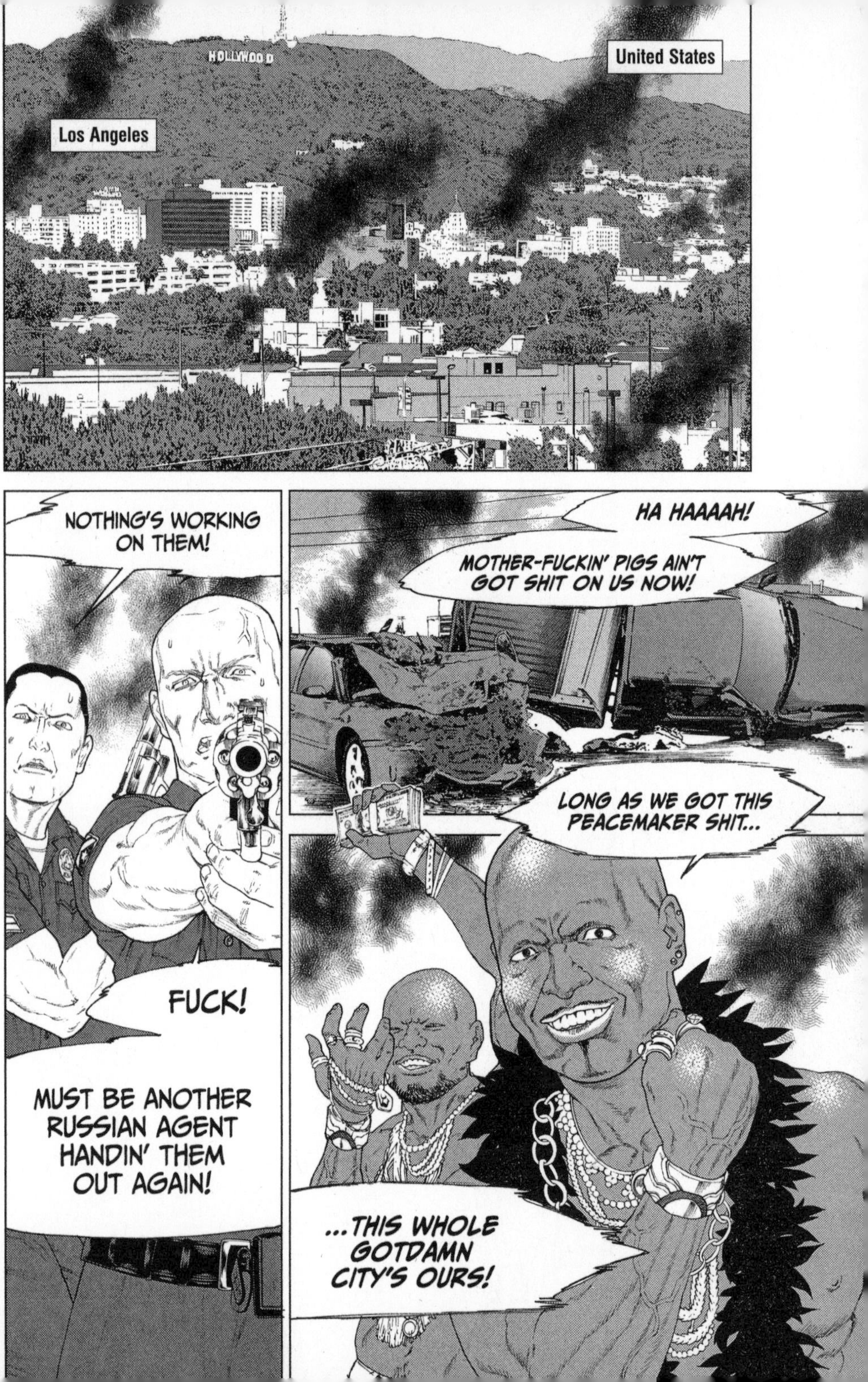
United States
HOLLYWOOD
Los Angeles
HA HAAAAH!
MOTHER-FUCKIN' PIGS AIN'T GOT SHIT ON US NOW!
LONG AS WE GOT THIS PEACEMAKER SHIT...
...THIS WHOLE GOTDAMN CITY'S OURS!
NOTHING'S WORKING ON THEM!
FUCK!
MUST BE ANOTHER RUSSIAN AGENT HANDIN' THEM OUT AGAIN!

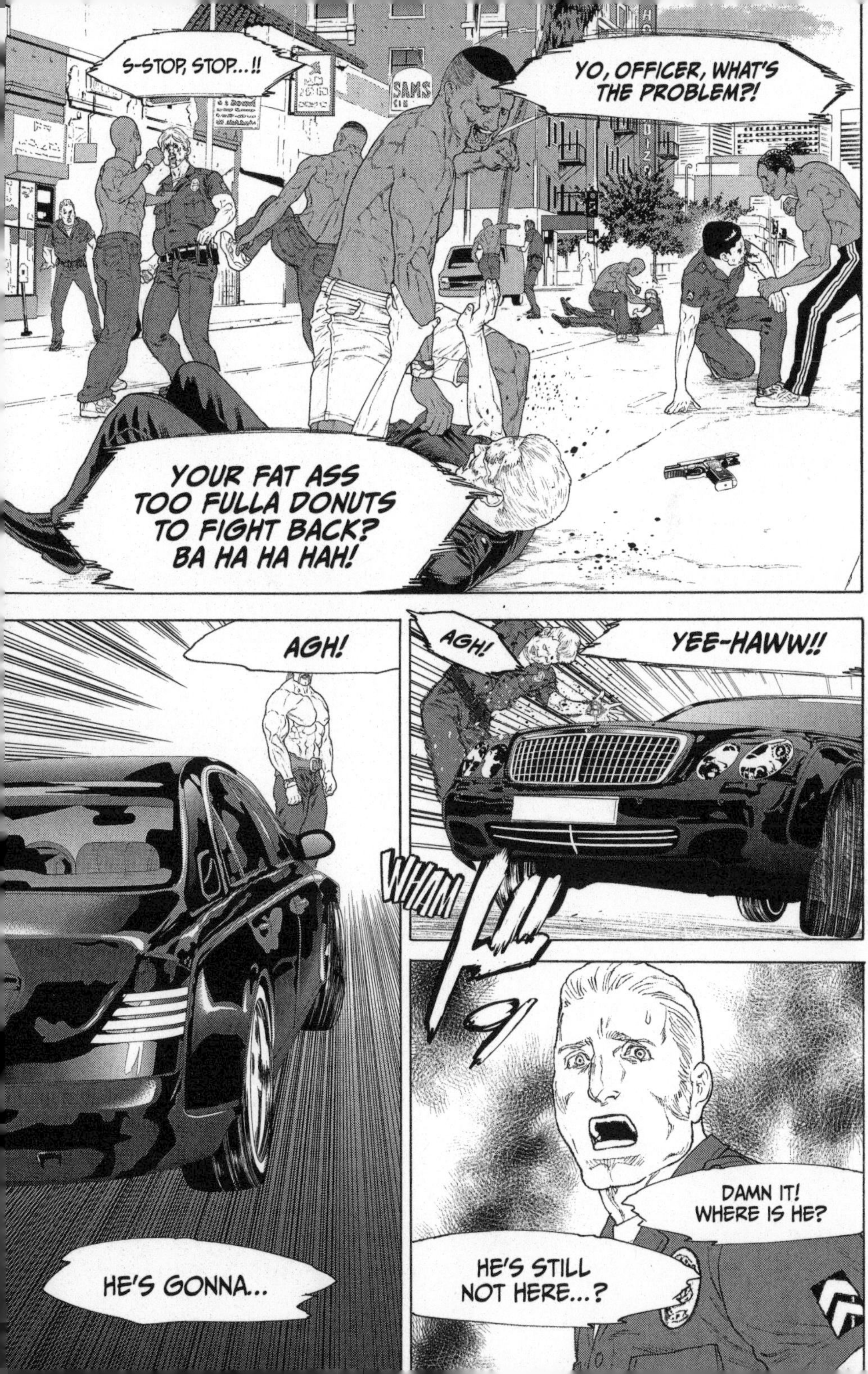
YO, OFFICER, WHAT'S THE PROBLEM?!
S-STOP, STOP...!!
YOUR FAT ASS TOO FULLA DONUTS TO FIGHT BACK? BA HA HA HAH!
YEE-HAWW!!
AGH!
WHAM
DAMN IT! WHERE IS HE?
HE'S STILL NOT HERE...?
AGH!
HE'S GONNA...

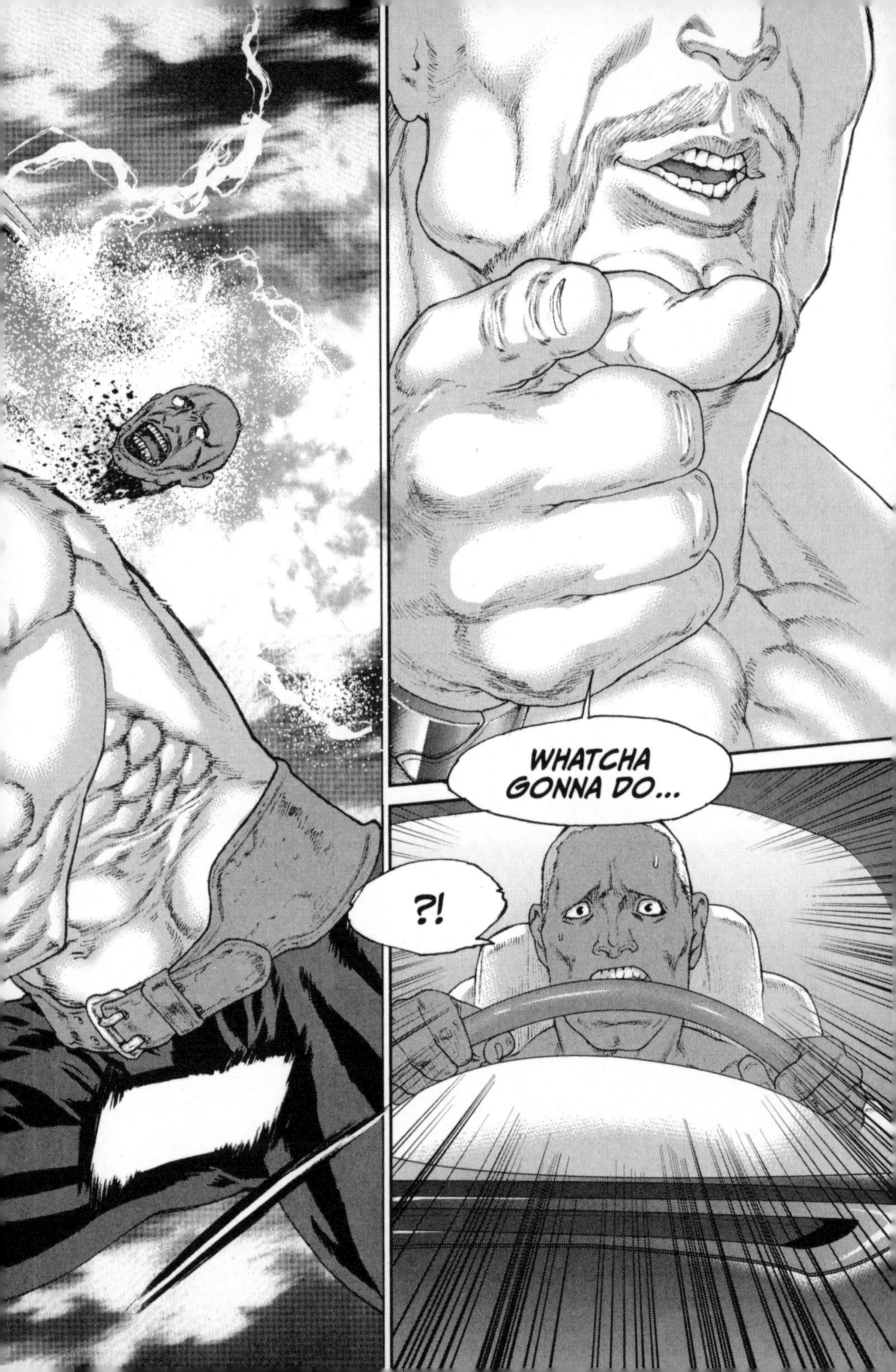
WHATCHA GONNA DO...
?!

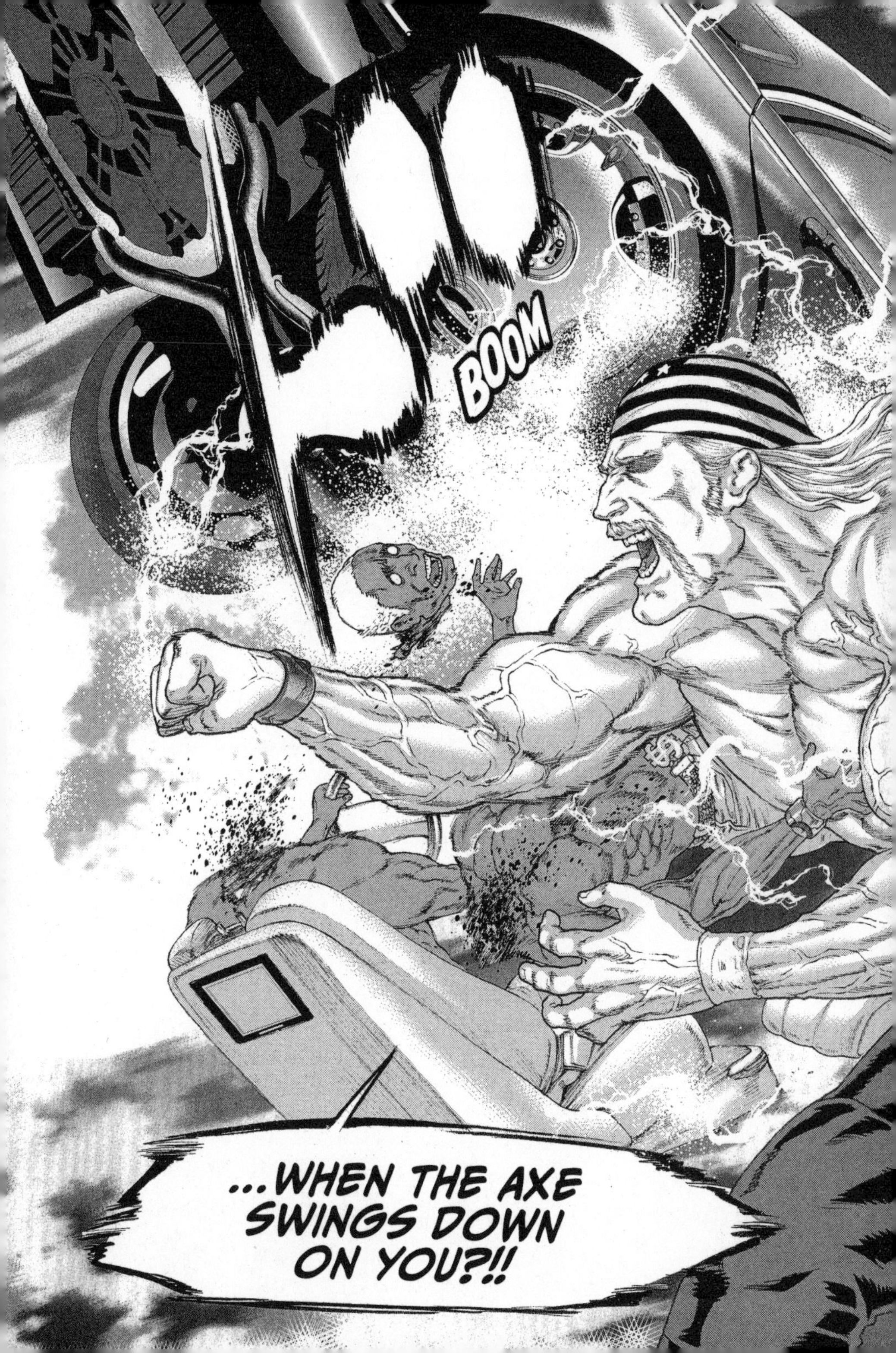
BOOM
...WHEN THE AXE
SWINGS DOWN
ON YOU?!!

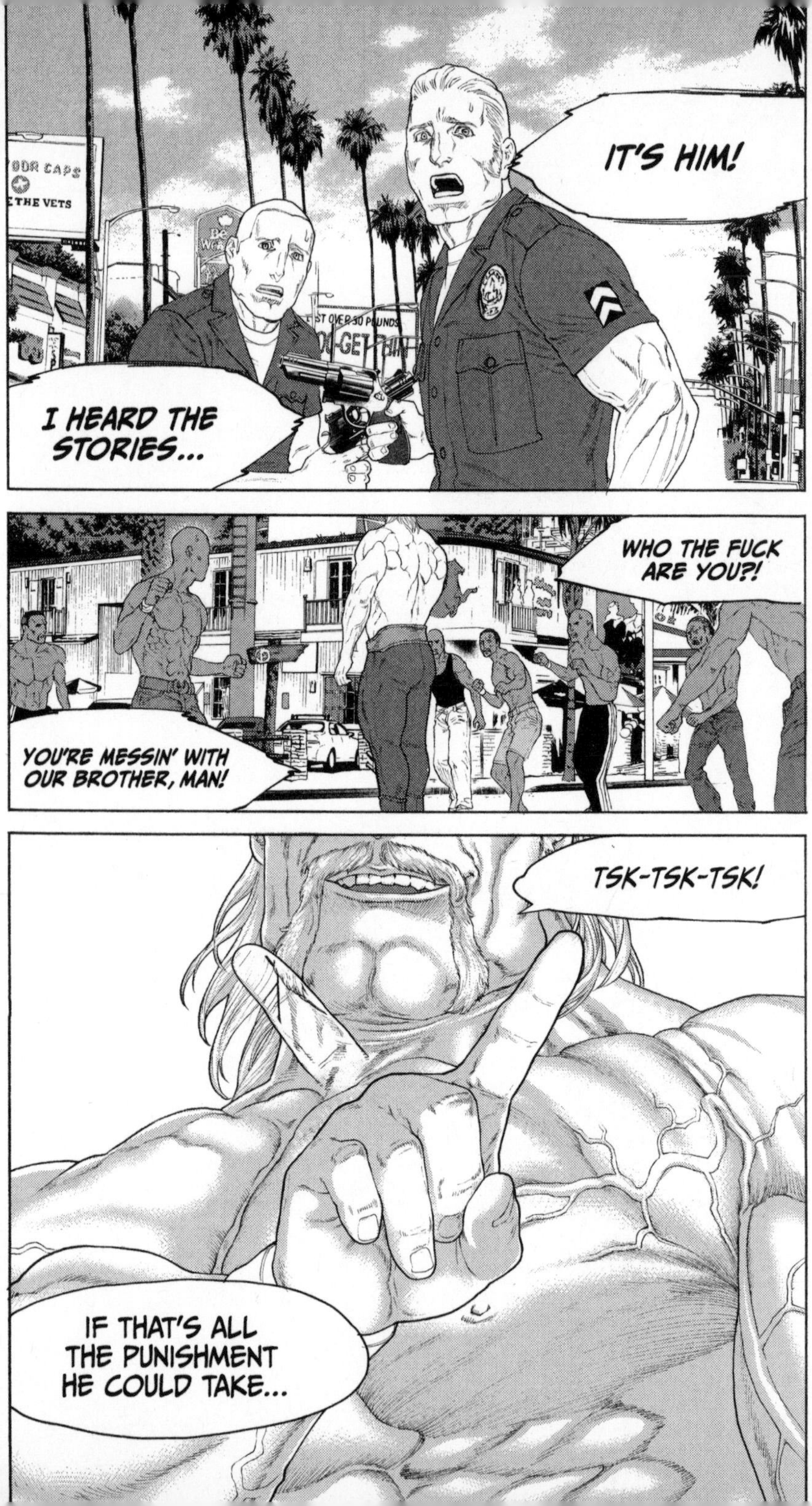
IT'S HIM!
I HEARD THE STORIES...
WHO THE FUCK ARE YOU?!
YOU'RE MESSIN' WITH OUR BROTHER, MAN!
TSK-TSK-TSK!
IF THAT'S ALL THE PUNISHMENT HE COULD TAKE...

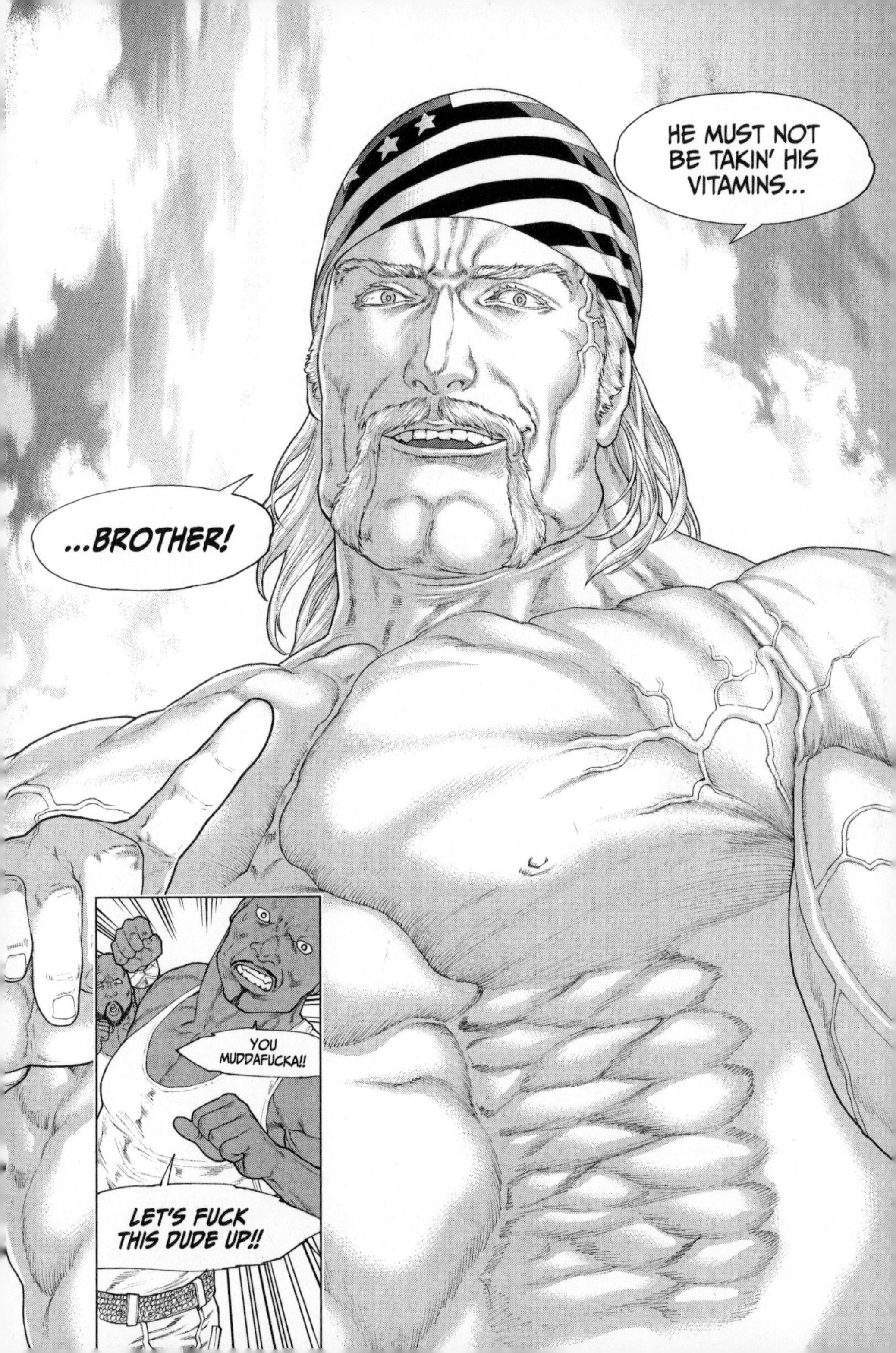
HE MUST NOT BE TAKIN' HIS VITAMINS...
...BROTHER!
YOU MUDDAFUCKA!!
LET'S FUCK THIS DUDE UP!!

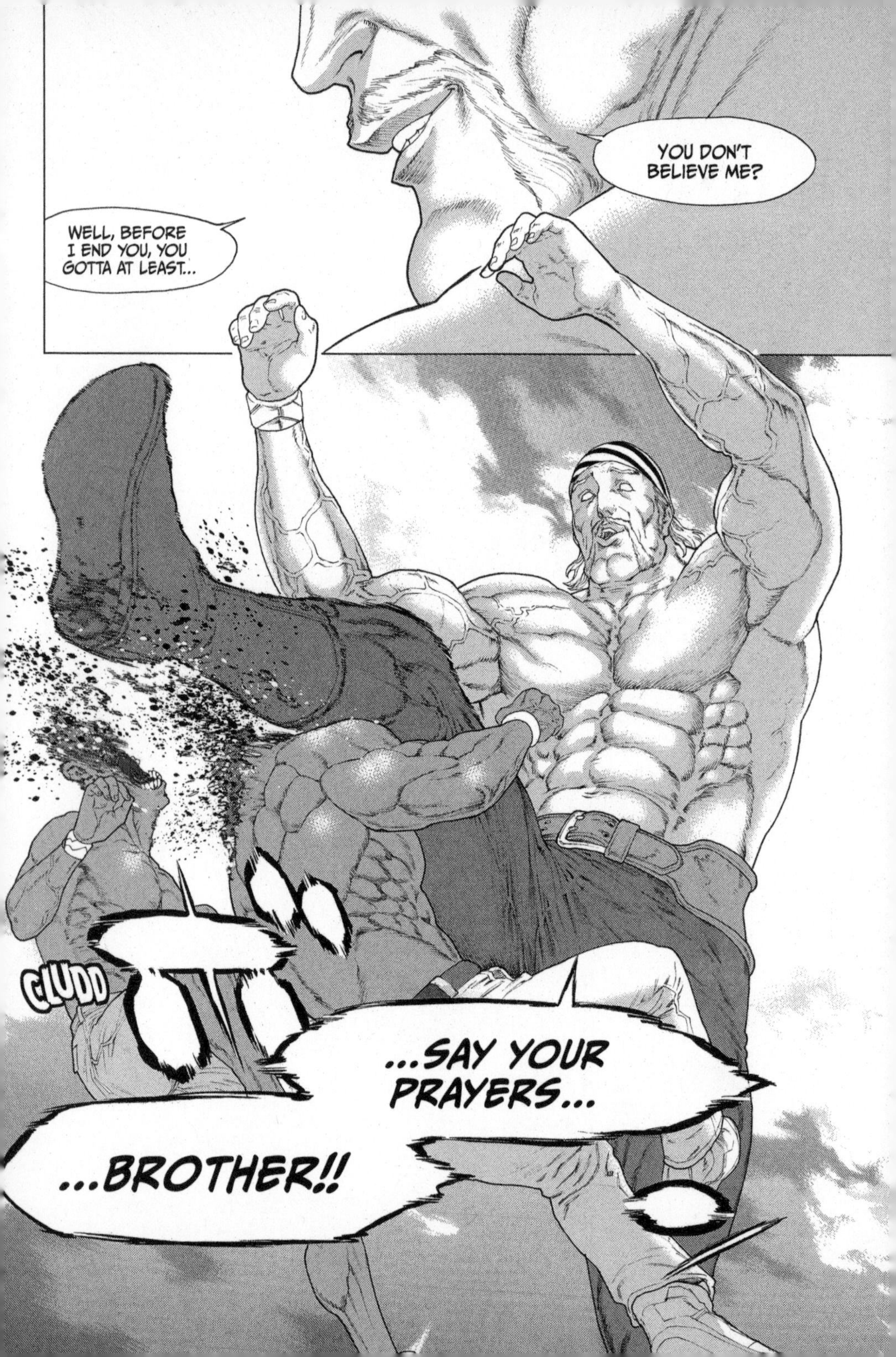
YOU DON'T BELIEVE ME?
WELL, BEFORE I END YOU, YOU GOTTA AT LEAST...
CLUDD
...SAY YOUR PRAYERS...
...BROTHER!!

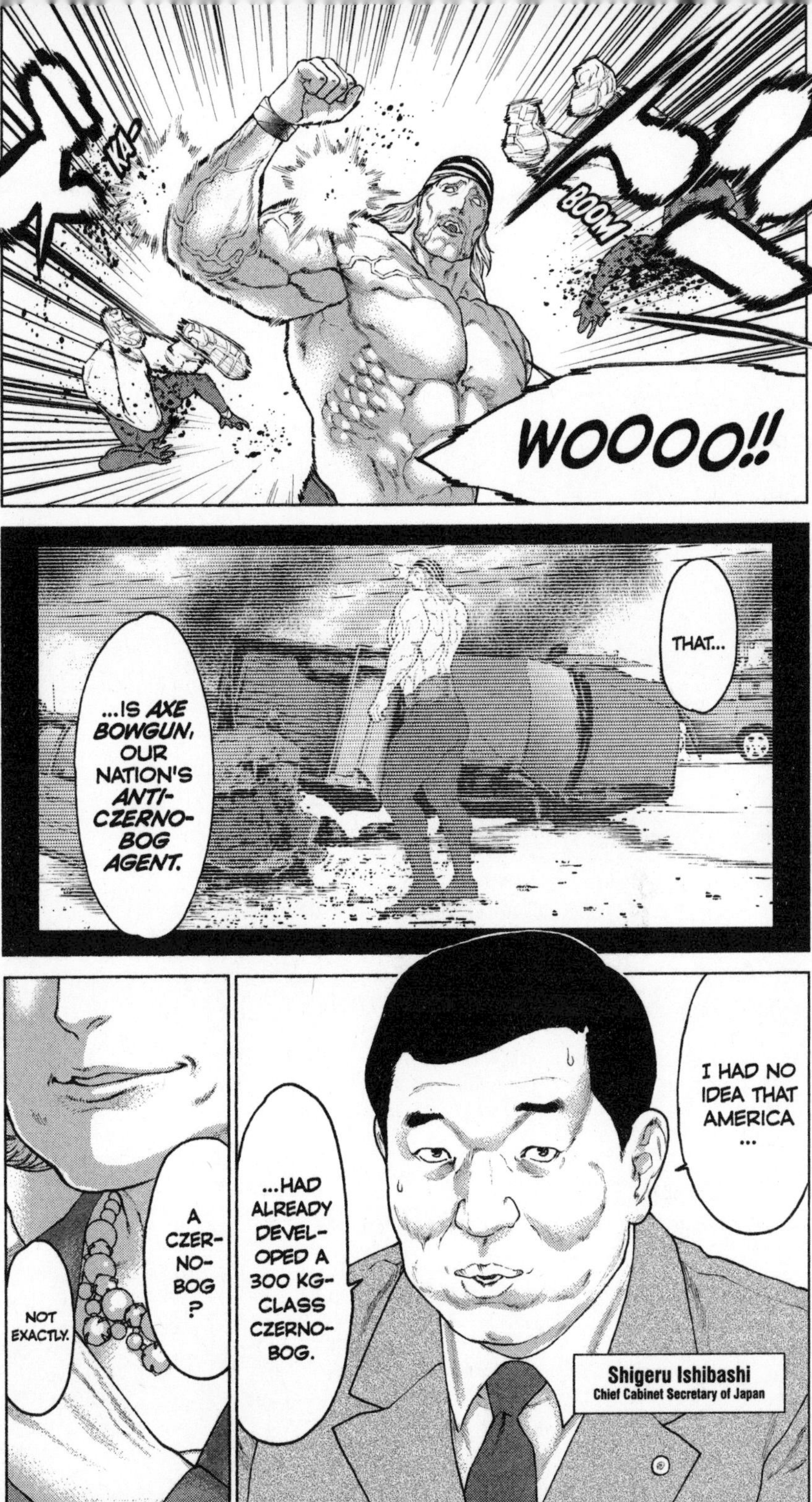
BOOM
KA-
WOOOO!!
THAT...
...IS AXE BOWGUN, OUR NATION'S ANTI-CZERNO-BOG AGENT.
I HAD NO IDEA THAT AMERICA ...
...HAD ALREADY DEVEL-OPED A 300 KG-CLASS CZERNO-BOG.
Shigeru Ishibashi
Chief Cabinet Secretary of Japan
A CZER-NO-BOG ?
NOT EXACTLY.

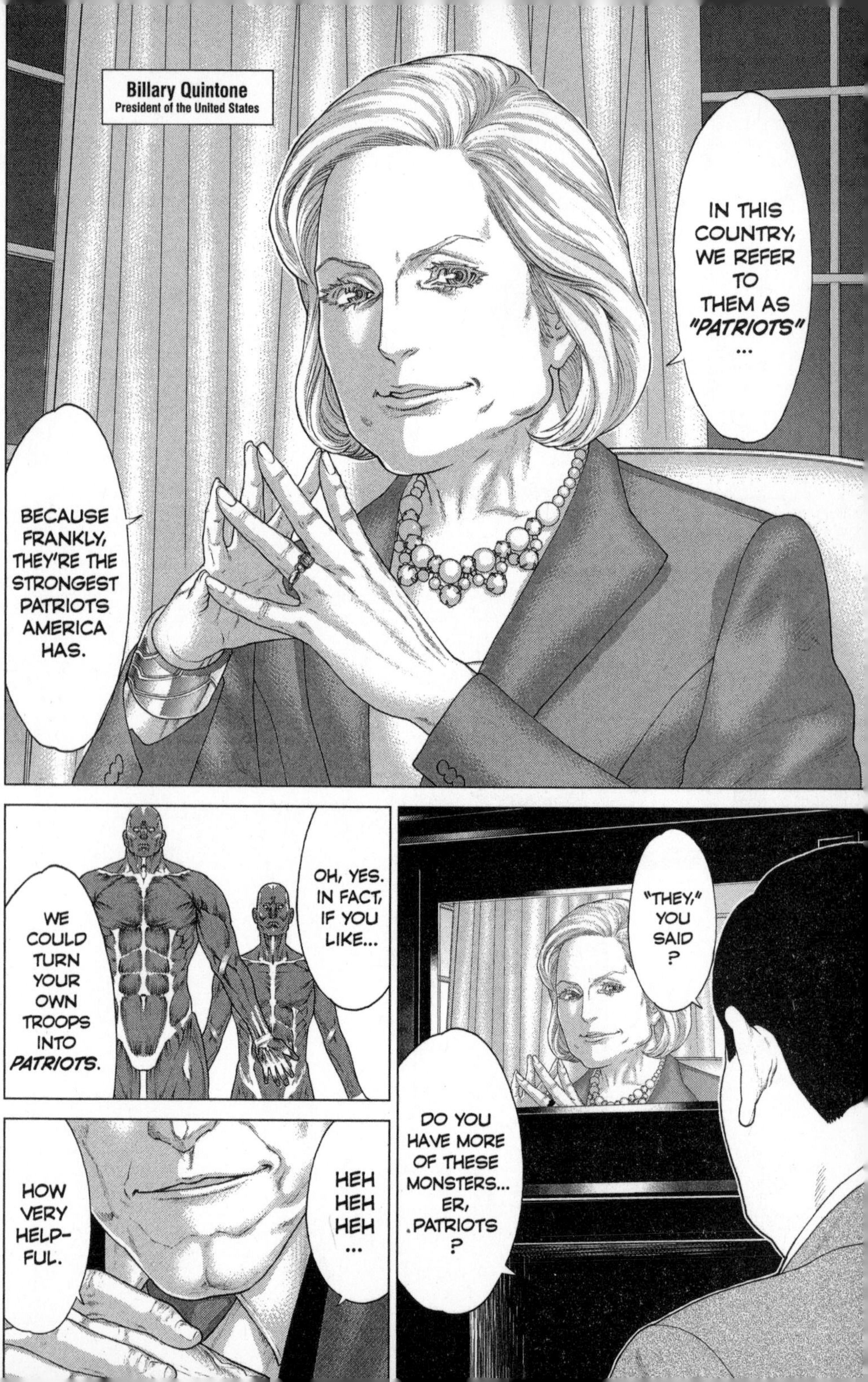
Billary Quintone
President of the United States
IN THIS COUNTRY, WE REFER TO THEM AS "PATRIOTS"...
BECAUSE FRANKLY, THEY'RE THE STRONGEST PATRIOTS AMERICA HAS.
"THEY," YOU SAID?
DO YOU HAVE MORE OF THESE MONSTERS... ER, PATRIOTS?
OH, YES. IN FACT, IF YOU LIKE...
WE COULD TURN YOUR OWN TROOPS INTO PATRIOTS.
HEH HEH HEH...
HOW VERY HELP-FUL.

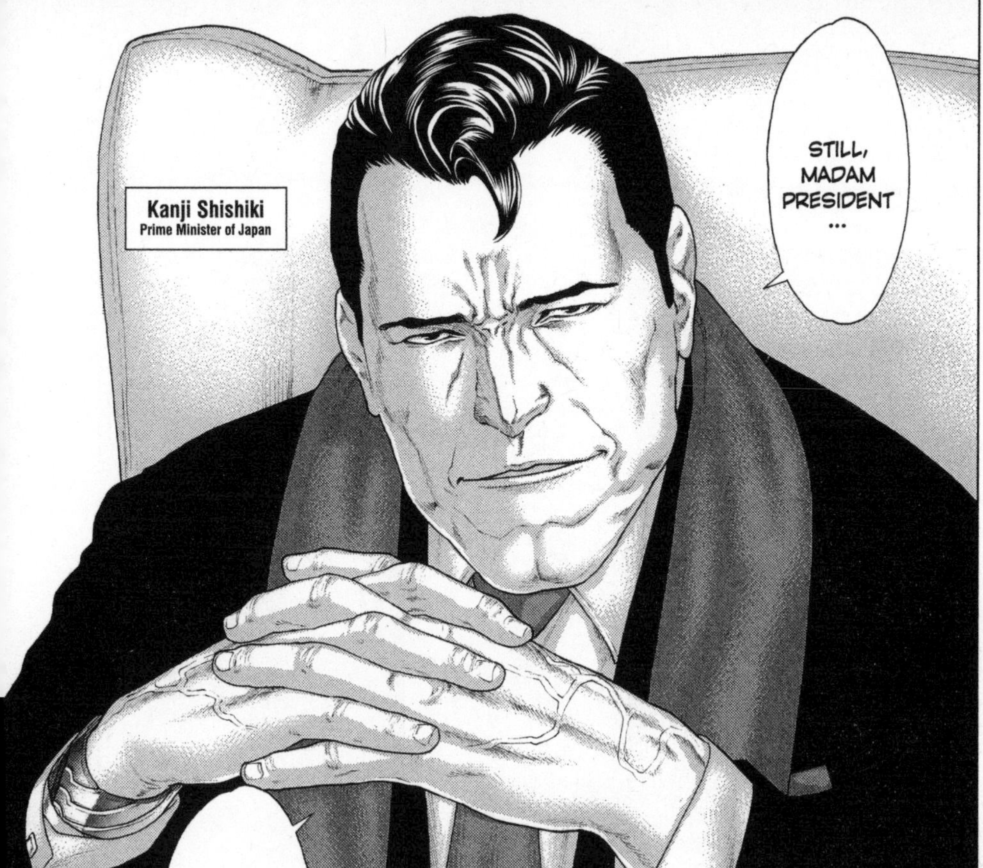
STILL, MADAM PRESIDENT ...
Kanji Shishiki
Prime Minister of Japan
I MUST SAY, YOU LOOK YOUNGER THAN EVER TODAY.
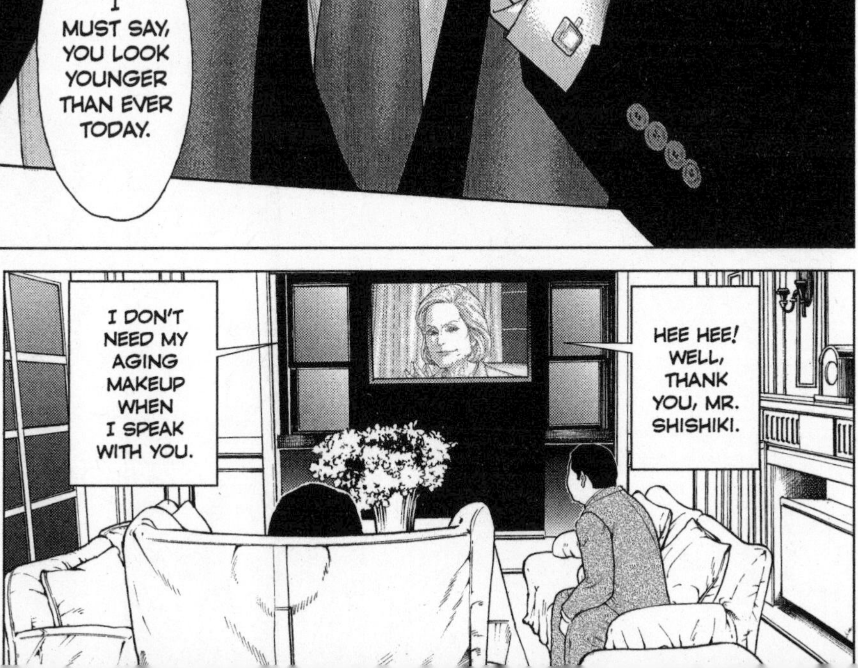
HEE HEE! WELL, THANK YOU, MR. SHISHIKI.
I DON'T NEED MY AGING MAKEUP WHEN I SPEAK WITH YOU.

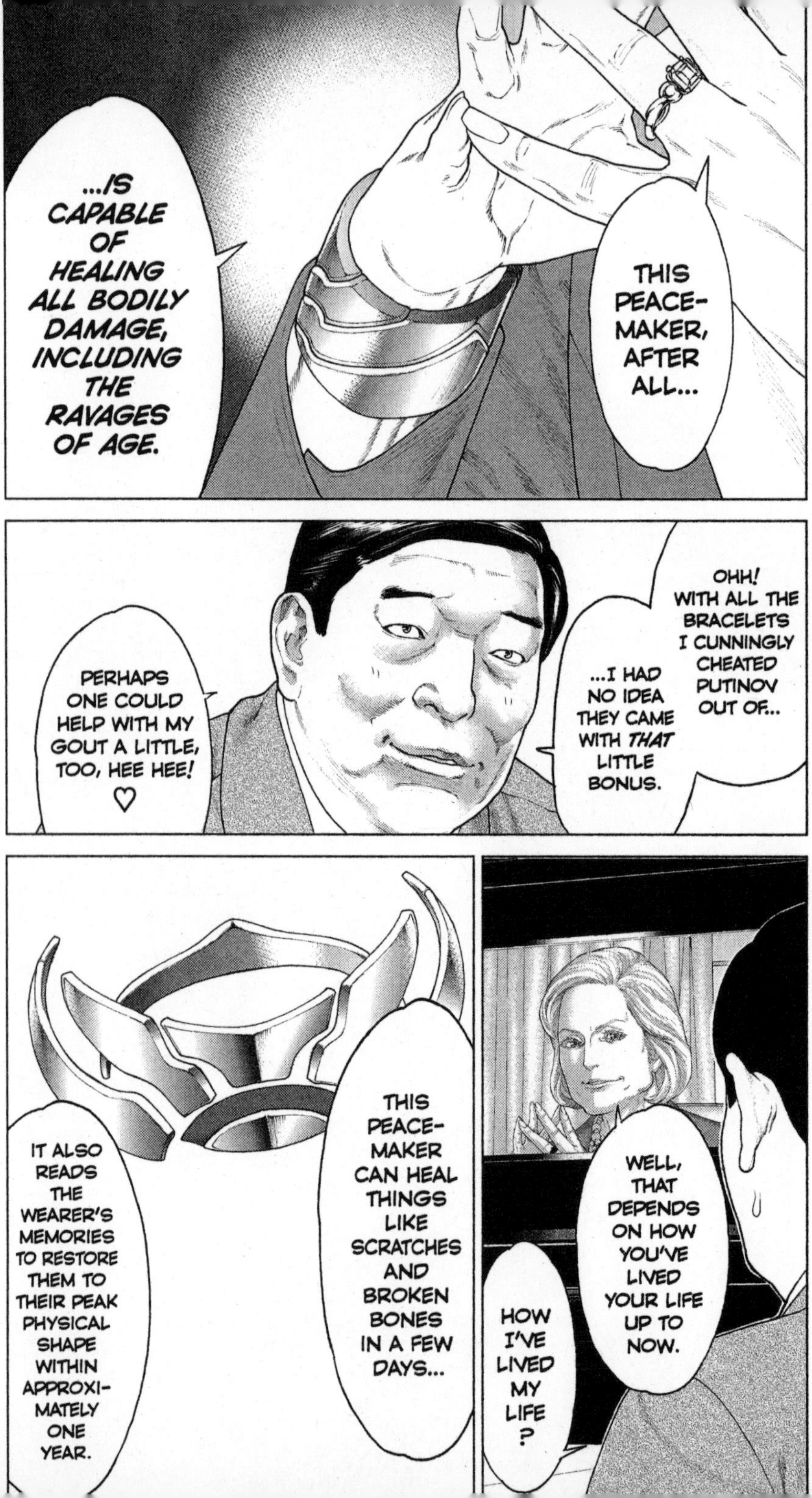
THIS PEACE-MAKER, AFTER ALL...
...IS CAPABLE OF HEALING ALL BODILY DAMAGE, INCLUDING THE RAVAGES OF AGE.
OHH! WITH ALL THE BRACELETS I CUNNINGLY CHEATED PUTINOV OUT OF...
...I HAD NO IDEA THEY CAME WITH THAT LITTLE BONUS.
PERHAPS ONE COULD HELP WITH MY GOUT A LITTLE, TOO, HEE HEE! ♡
WELL, THAT DEPENDS ON HOW YOU'VE LIVED YOUR LIFE UP TO NOW.
HOW I'VE LIVED MY LIFE?
THIS PEACE-MAKER CAN HEAL THINGS LIKE SCRATCHES AND BROKEN BONES IN A FEW DAYS...
IT ALSO READS THE WEARER'S MEMORIES TO RESTORE THEM TO THEIR PEAK PHYSICAL SHAPE WITHIN APPROXIMATELY ONE YEAR.

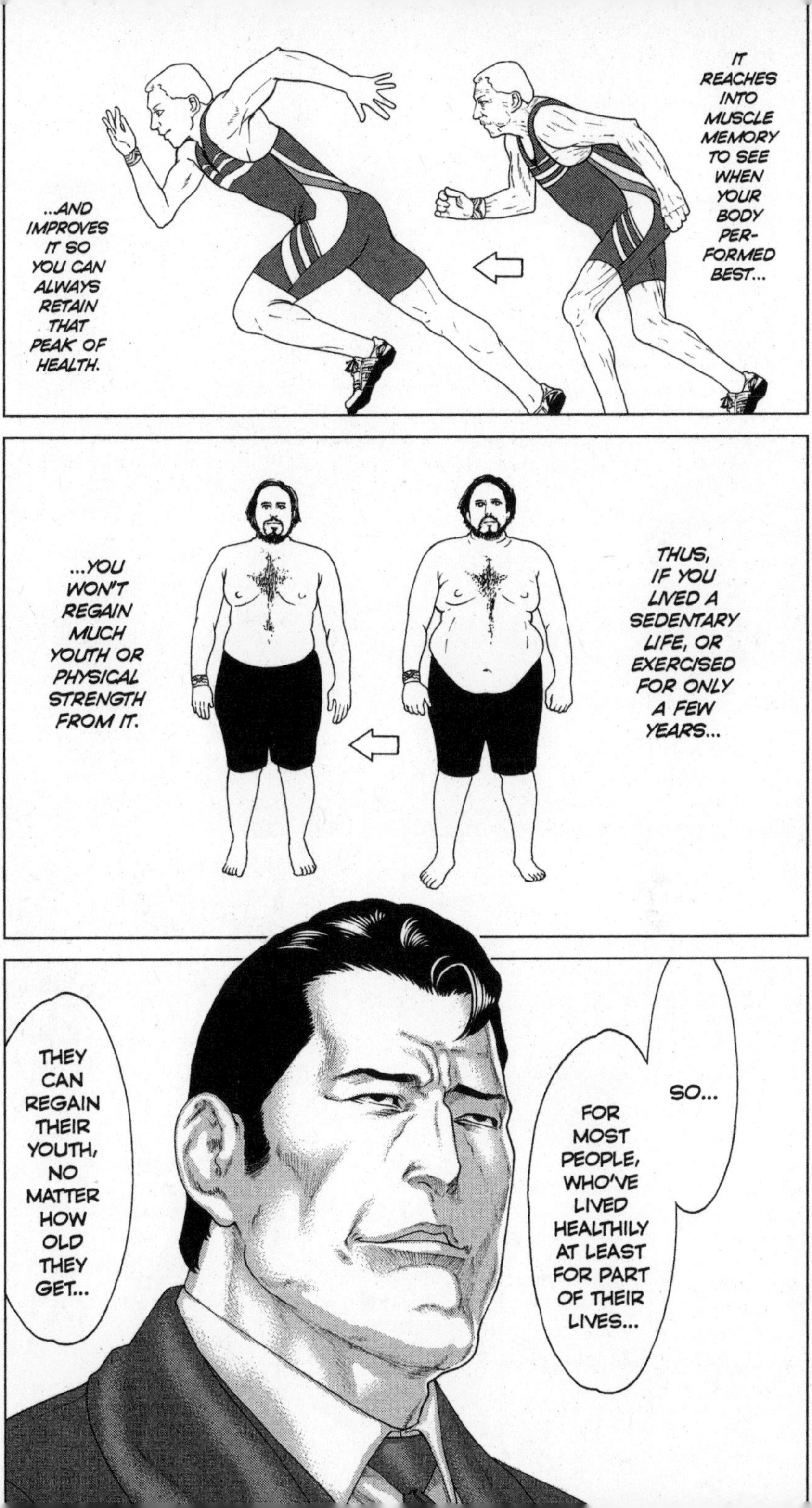
IT REACHES INTO MUSCLE MEMORY TO SEE WHEN YOUR BODY PER-FORMED BEST...
...AND IMPROVES IT SO YOU CAN ALWAYS RETAIN THAT PEAK OF HEALTH.
THUS, IF YOU LIVED A SEDENTARY LIFE, OR EXERCISED FOR ONLY A FEW YEARS...
...YOU WON'T REGAIN MUCH YOUTH OR PHYSICAL STRENGTH FROM IT.
SO...
FOR MOST PEOPLE, WHO'VE LIVED HEALTHILY AT LEAST FOR PART OF THEIR LIVES...
THEY CAN REGAIN THEIR YOUTH, NO MATTER HOW OLD THEY GET...

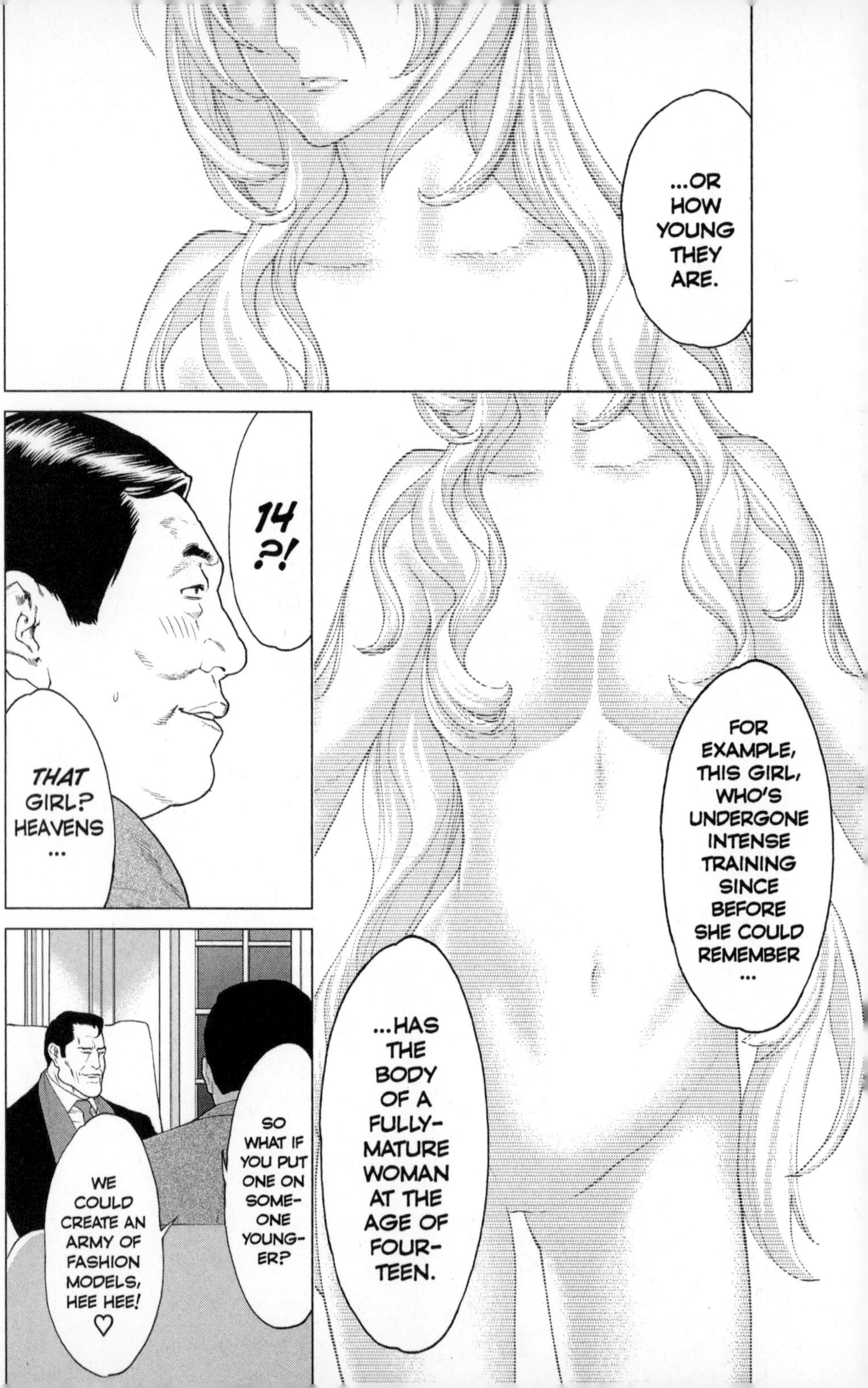
...OR HOW YOUNG THEY ARE.
FOR EXAMPLE, THIS GIRL, WHO'S UNDERGONE INTENSE TRAINING SINCE BEFORE SHE COULD REMEMBER...
...HAS THE BODY OF A FULLY-MATURE WOMAN AT THE AGE OF FOUR-TEEN.
14?!
THAT GIRL? HEAVENS...
SO WHAT IF YOU PUT ONE ON SOME-ONE YOUNG-ER?
WE COULD CREATE AN ARMY OF FASHION MODELS, HEE HEE! ♡

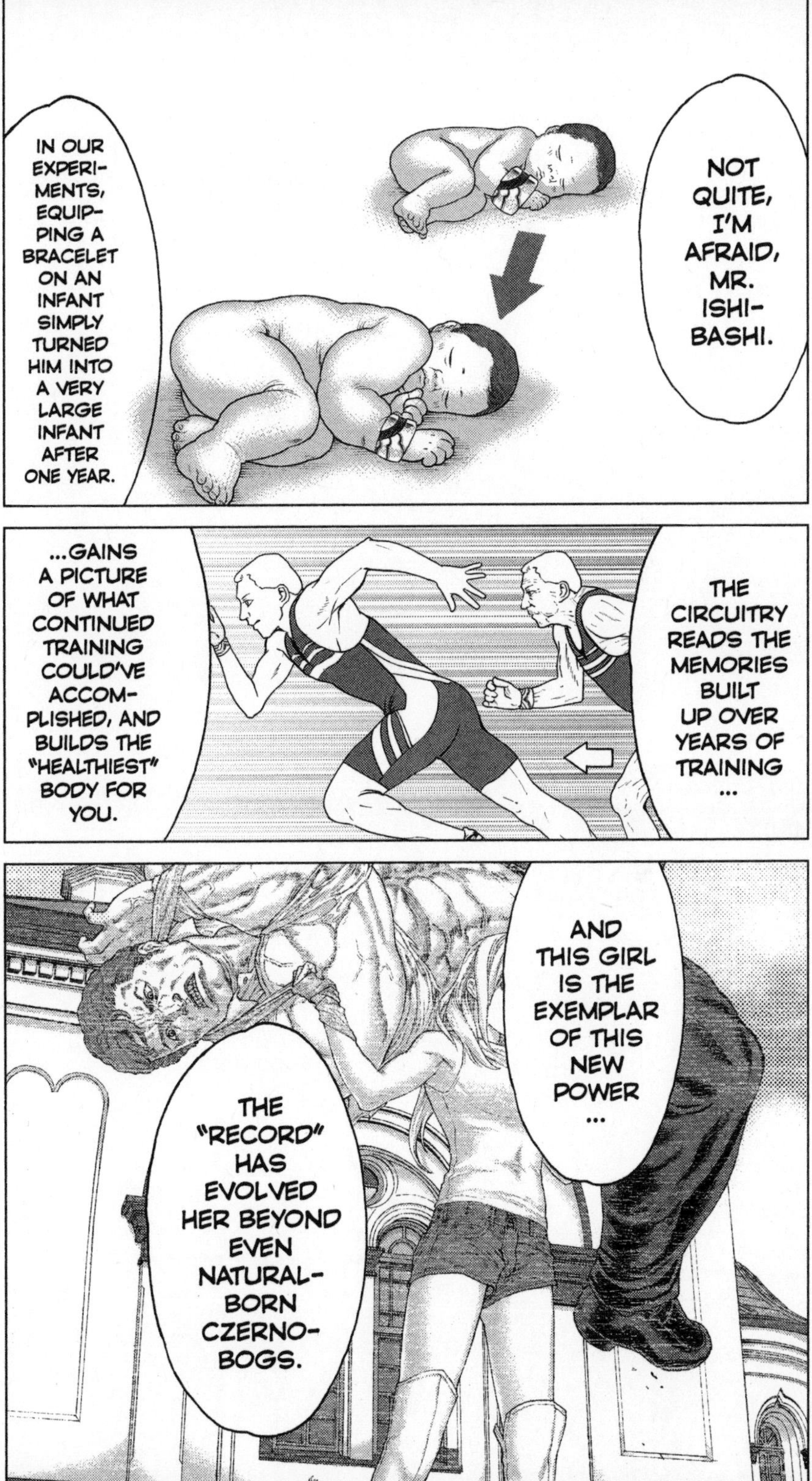
NOT QUITE, I'M AFRAID, MR. ISHI-BASHI.
IN OUR EXPERI-MENTS, EQUIP-PING A BRACELET ON AN INFANT SIMPLY TURNED HIM INTO A VERY LARGE INFANT AFTER ONE YEAR.
THE CIRCUITRY READS THE MEMORIES BUILT UP OVER YEARS OF TRAINING ...
...GAINS A PICTURE OF WHAT CONTINUED TRAINING COULD'VE ACCOM-PLISHED, AND BUILDS THE "HEALTHIEST" BODY FOR YOU.
AND THIS GIRL IS THE EXEMPLAR OF THIS NEW POWER ...
THE "RECORD" HAS EVOLVED HER BEYOND EVEN NATURAL-BORN CZERNO-BOGS.

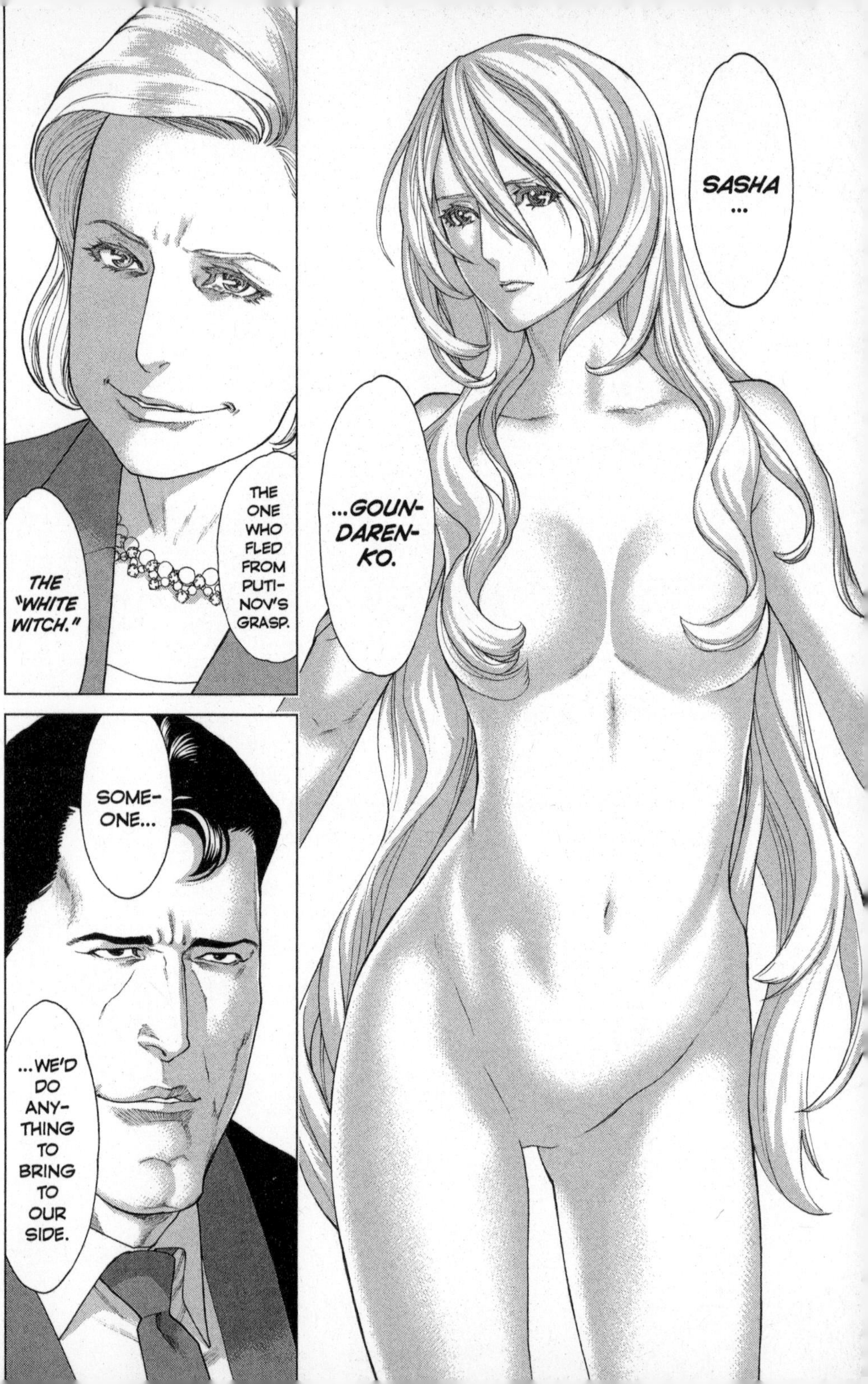
SASHA ...
...GOUN-DAREN-KO.
THE ONE WHO FLED FROM PUTI-NOV'S GRASP.
THE "WHITE WITCH."
SOME-ONE...
...WE'D DO ANY-THING TO BRING TO OUR SIDE.

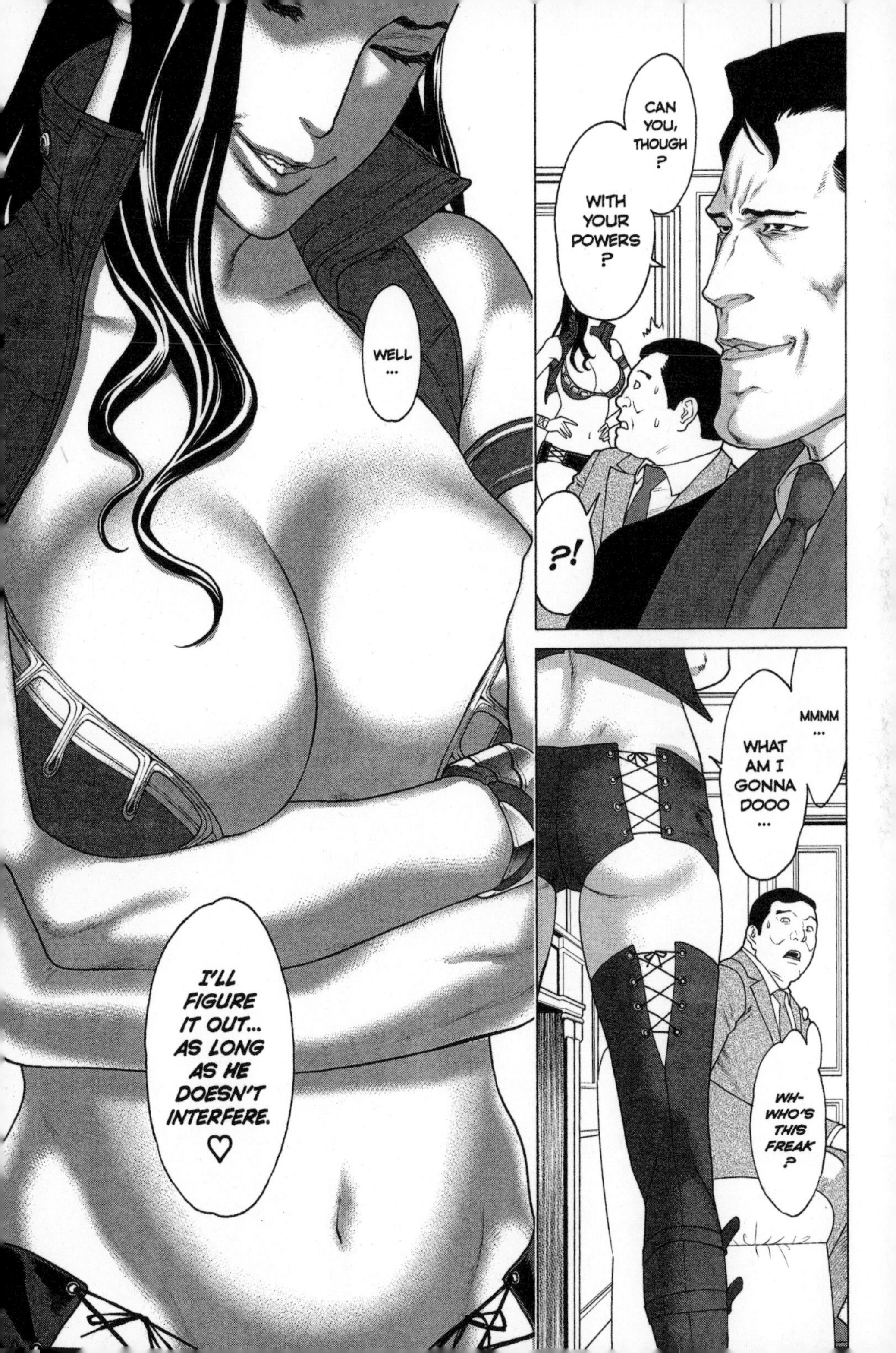
CAN YOU, THOUGH?
WITH YOUR POWERS?
?!
MMMM... WHAT AM I GONNA DOOO...
WH- WHO'S THIS FREAK?
WELL...
I'LL FIGURE IT OUT... AS LONG AS HE DOESN'T INTERFERE. ♡

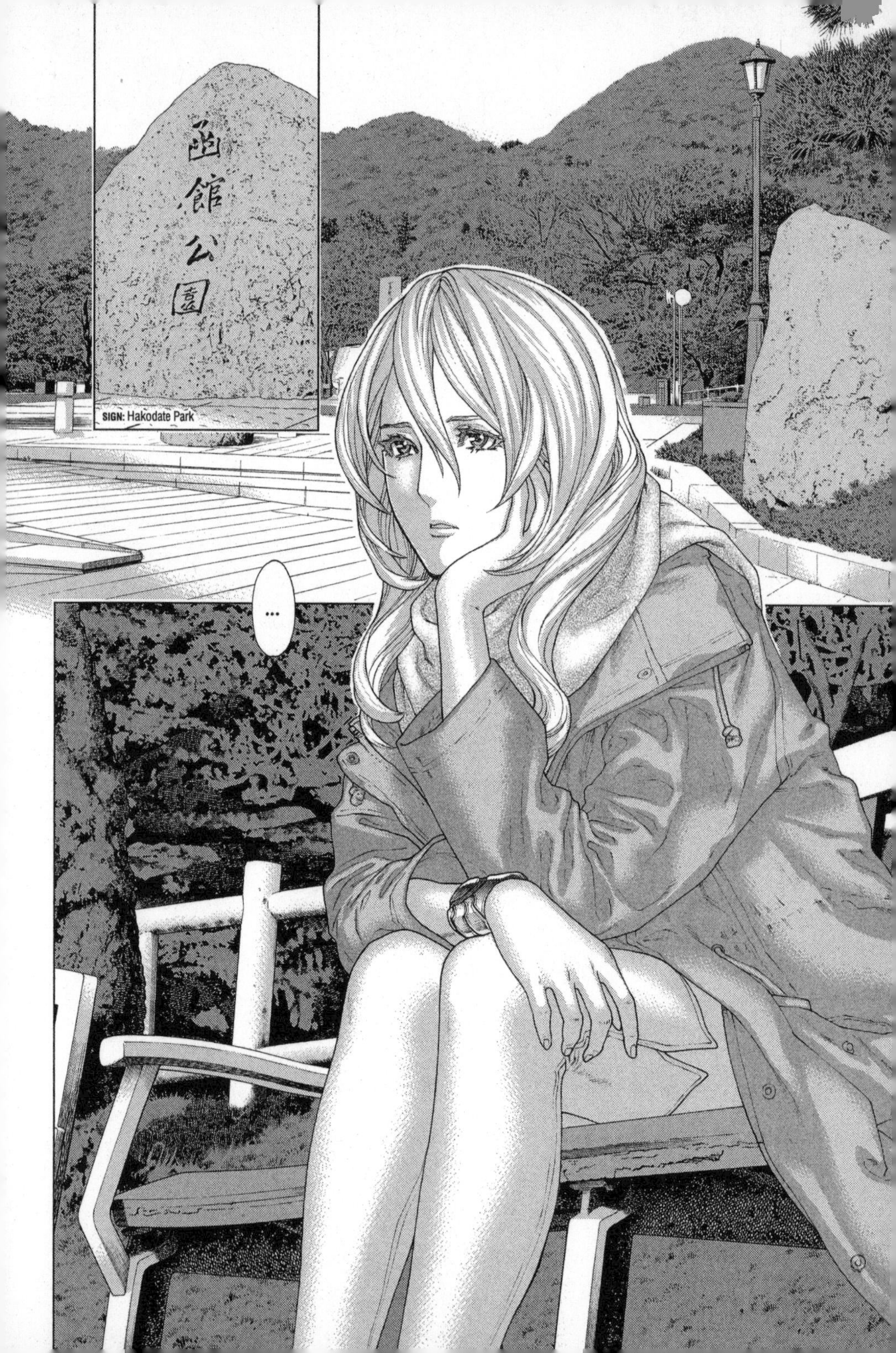
函館公園
SIGN: Hakodate Park
...

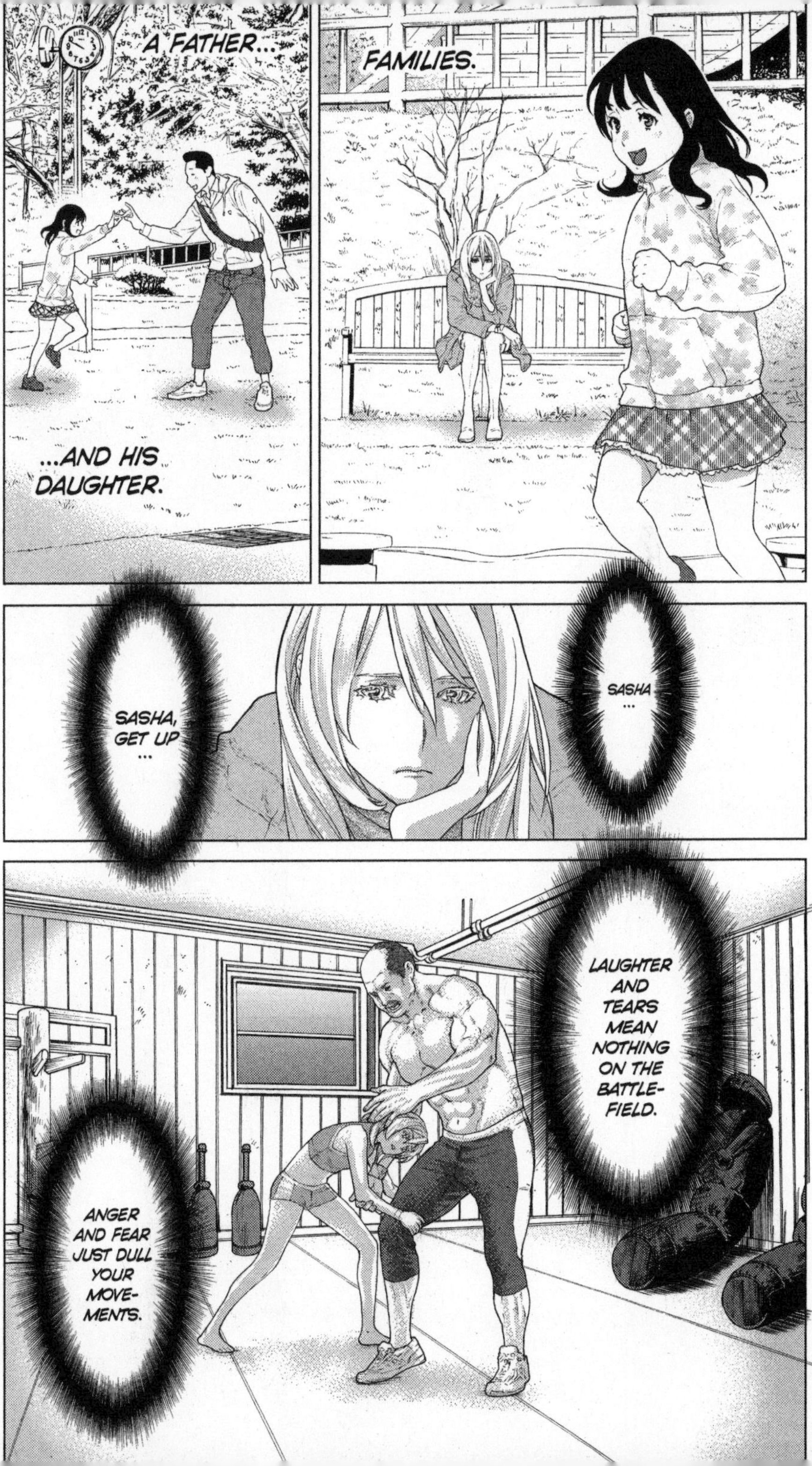
FAMILIES.
A FATHER...
...AND HIS DAUGHTER.
SASHA ...
SASHA, GET UP ...
LAUGHTER AND TEARS MEAN NOTHING ON THE BATTLE-FIELD.
ANGER AND FEAR JUST DULL YOUR MOVE-MENTS.

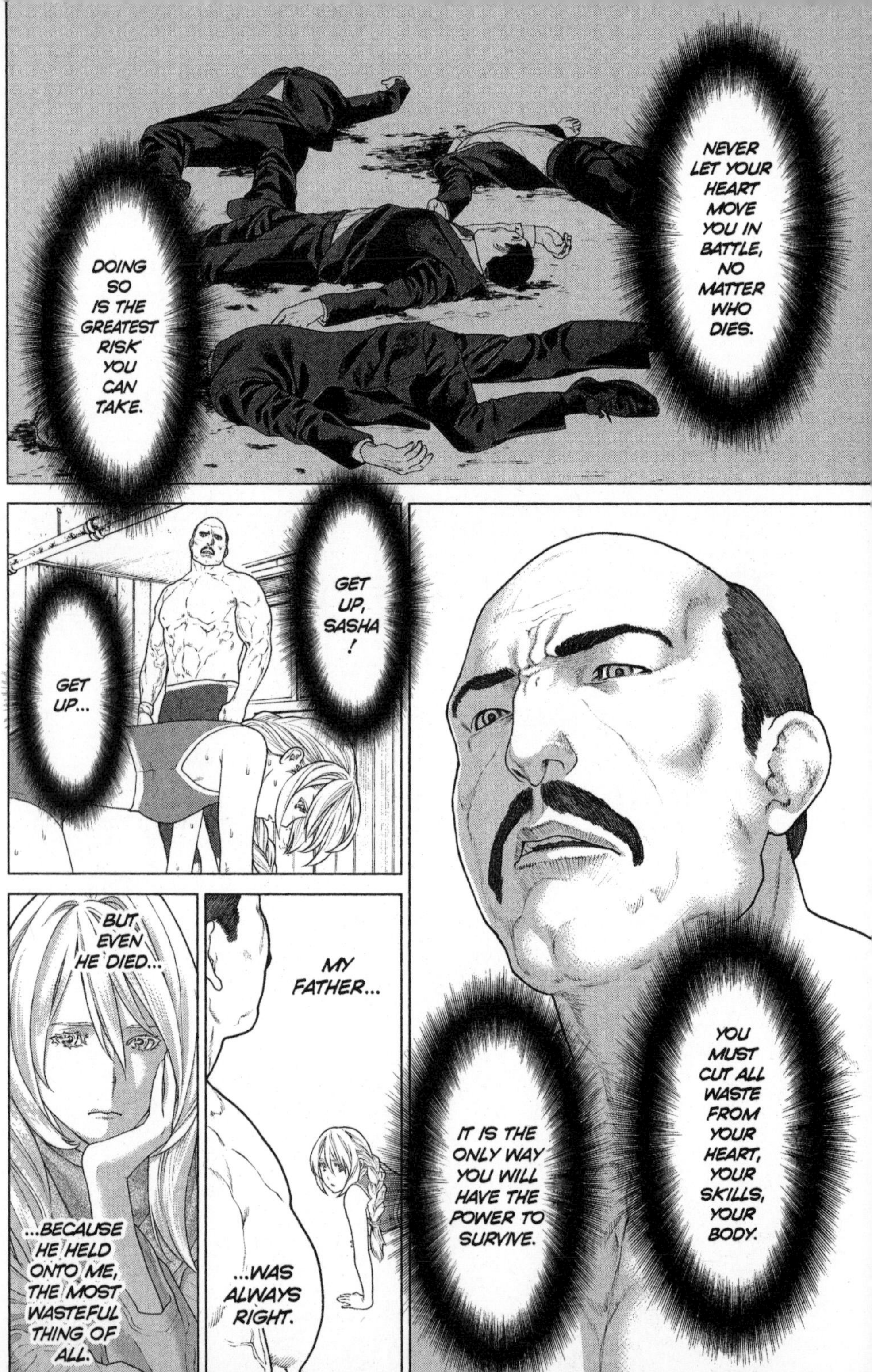
NEVER LET YOUR HEART MOVE YOU IN BATTLE, NO MATTER WHO DIES.
DOING SO IS THE GREATEST RISK YOU CAN TAKE.
YOU MUST CUT ALL WASTE FROM YOUR HEART, YOUR SKILLS, YOUR BODY.
IT IS THE ONLY WAY YOU WILL HAVE THE POWER TO SURVIVE.
GET UP, SASHA!
GET UP...
MY FATHER...
...WAS ALWAYS RIGHT.
BUT EVEN HE DIED...
...BECAUSE HE HELD ONTO ME, THE MOST WASTEFUL THING OF ALL.

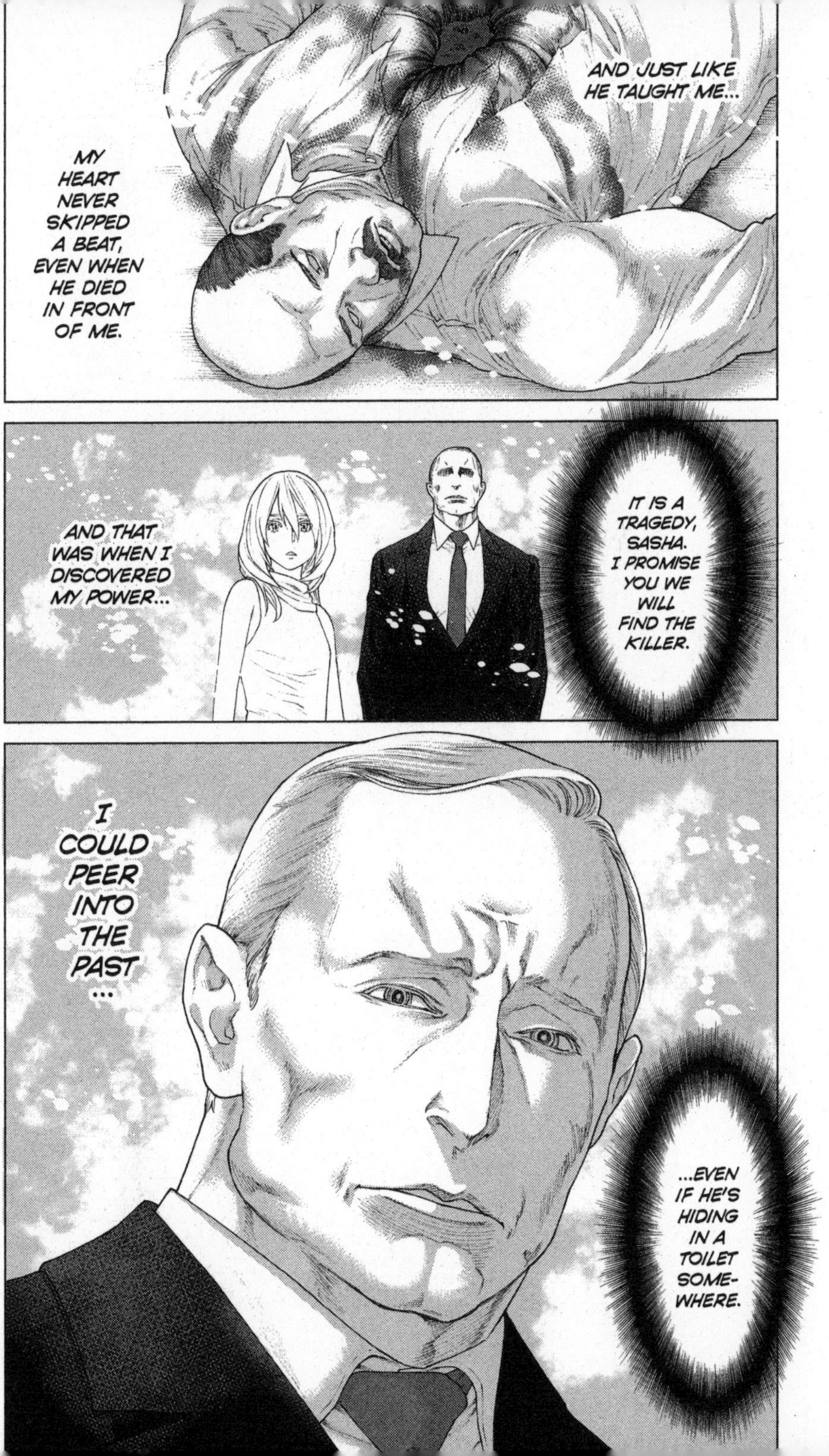
AND JUST LIKE HE TAUGHT ME...
MY HEART NEVER SKIPPED A BEAT, EVEN WHEN HE DIED IN FRONT OF ME.
IT IS A TRAGEDY, SASHA. I PROMISE YOU WE WILL FIND THE KILLER.
AND THAT WAS WHEN I DISCOVERED MY POWER...
I COULD PEER INTO THE PAST...
...EVEN IF HE'S HIDING IN A TOILET SOME-WHERE.

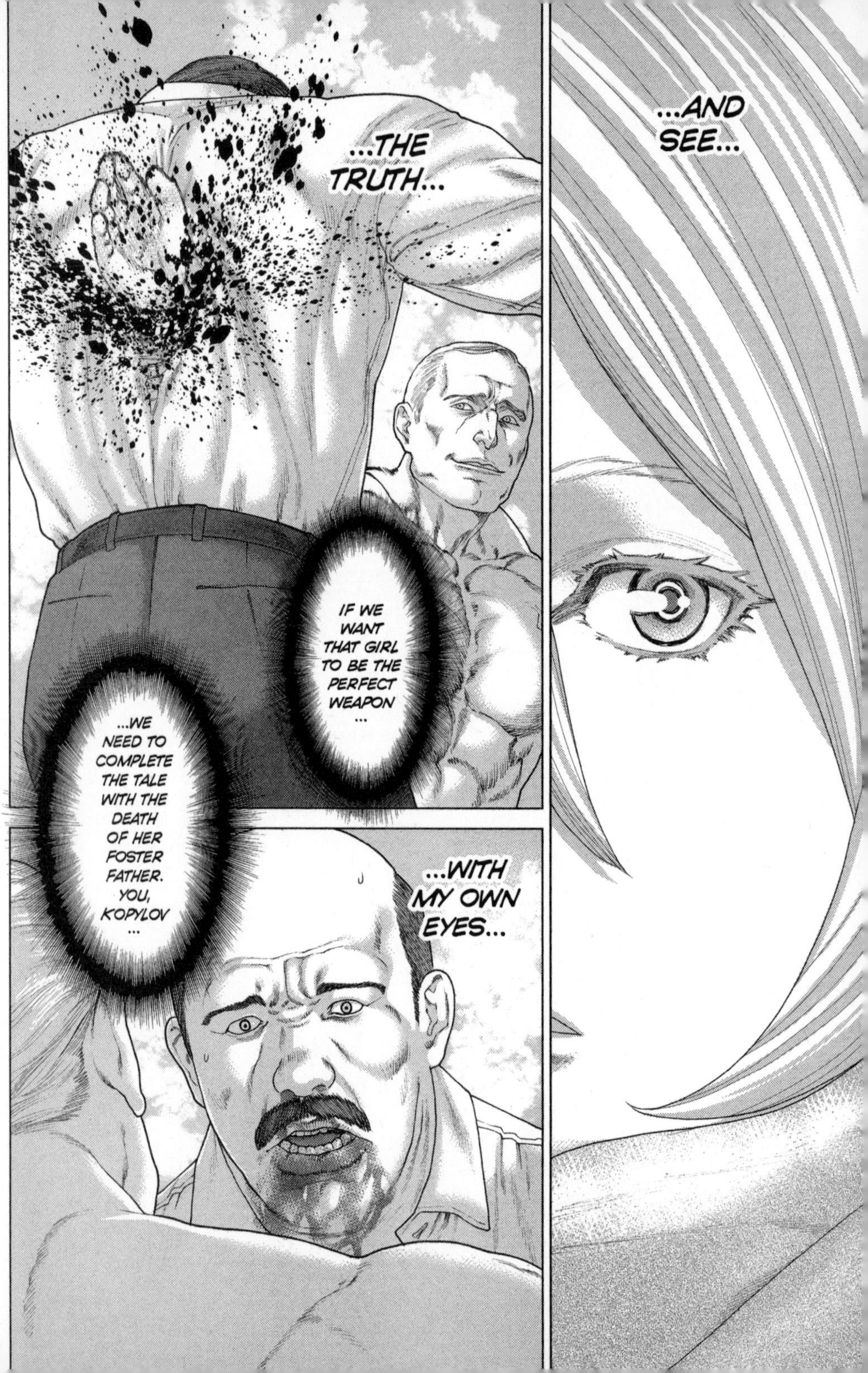
...AND SEE...
...THE TRUTH...
IF WE WANT THAT GIRL TO BE THE PERFECT WEAPON ...
...WE NEED TO COMPLETE THE TALE WITH THE DEATH OF HER FOSTER FATHER. YOU, KOPYLOV ...
...WITH MY OWN EYES...

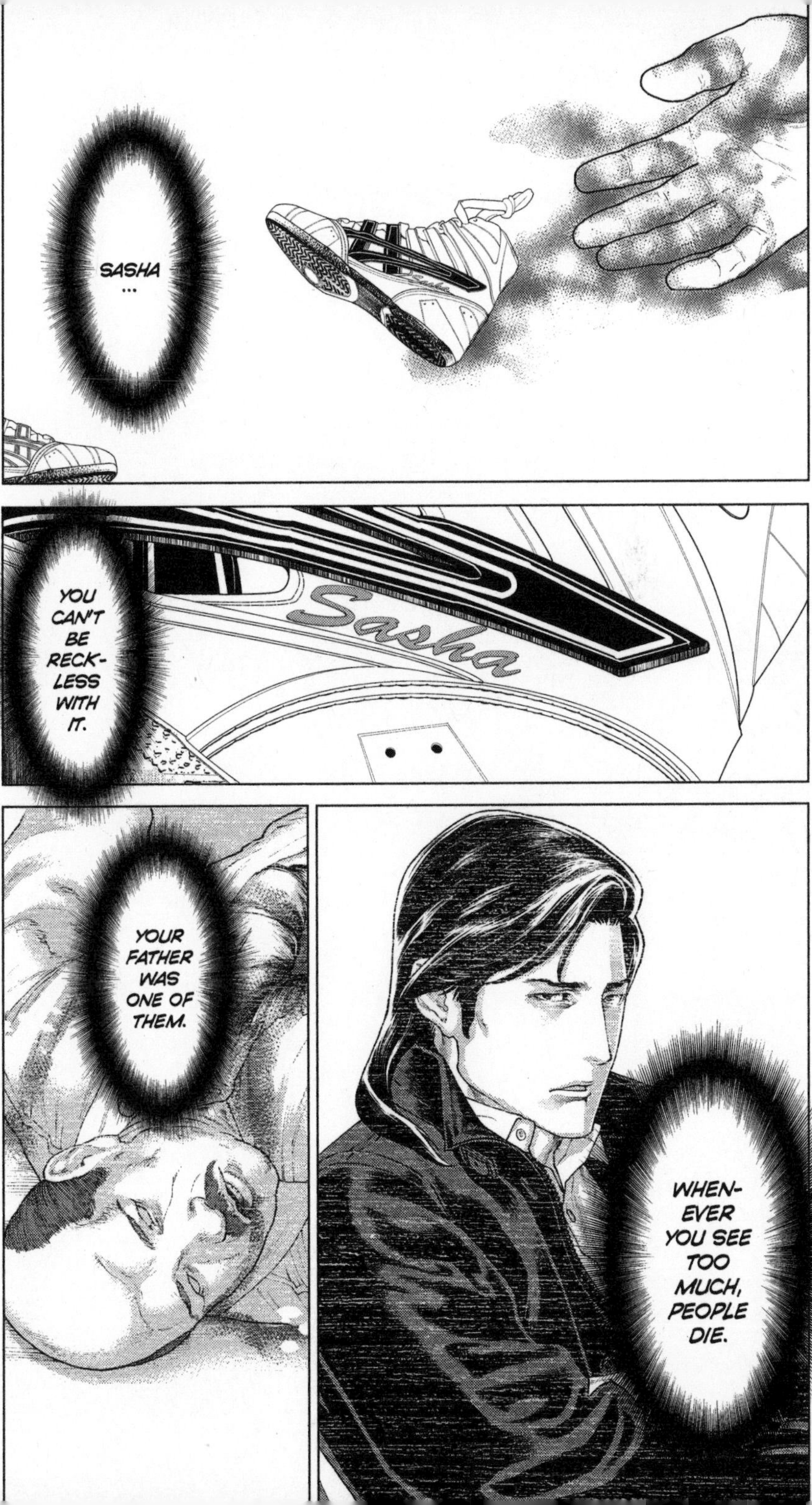
SASHA ...
Sasha
YOU CAN'T BE RECKLESS WITH IT.
WHENEVER YOU SEE TOO MUCH, PEOPLE DIE.
YOUR FATHER WAS ONE OF THEM.

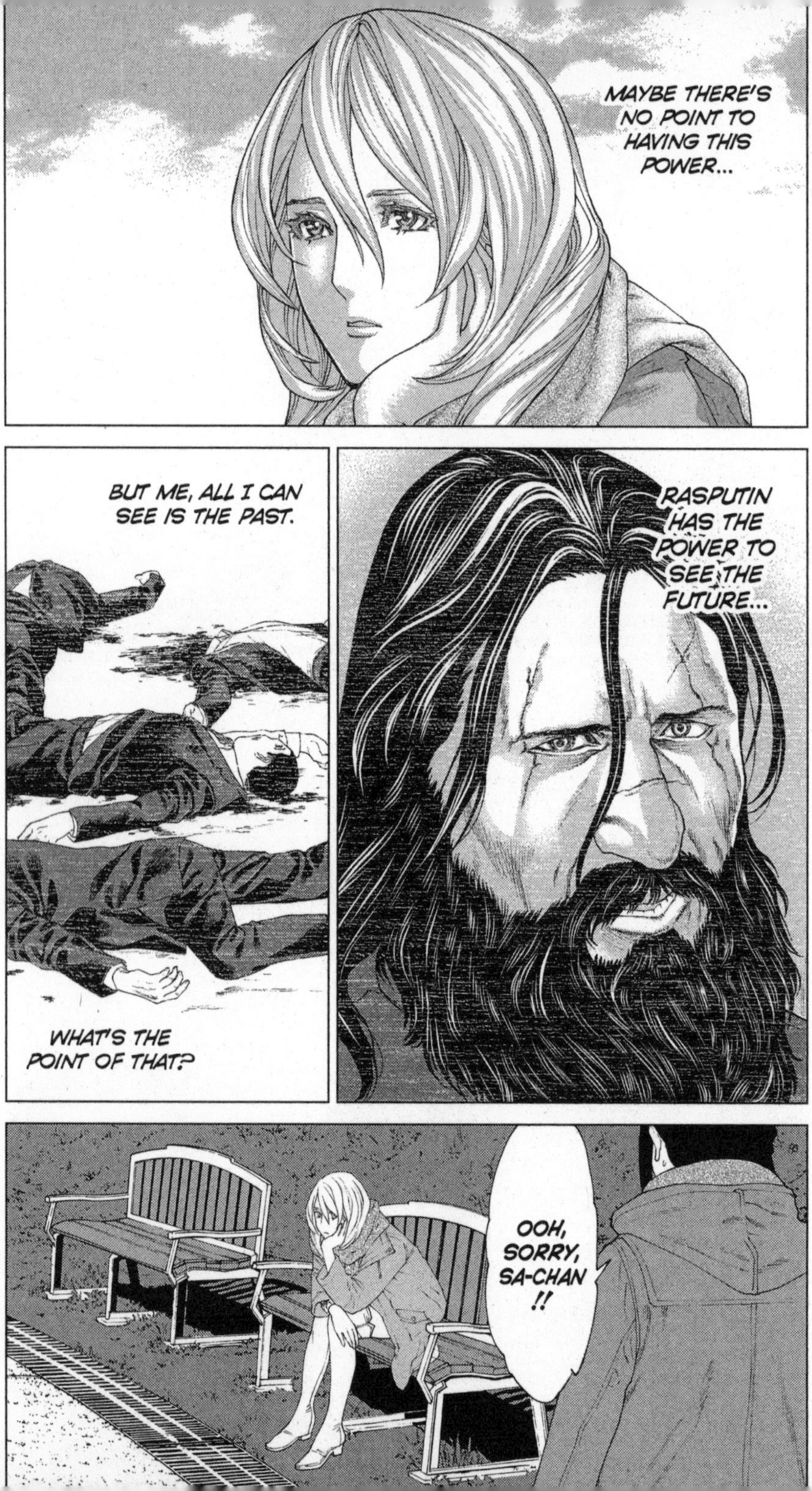
MAYBE THERE'S NO POINT TO HAVING THIS POWER...
RASPUTIN HAS THE POWER TO SEE THE FUTURE...
BUT ME, ALL I CAN SEE IS THE PAST.
WHAT'S THE POINT OF THAT?
OOH, SORRY, SA-CHAN!!

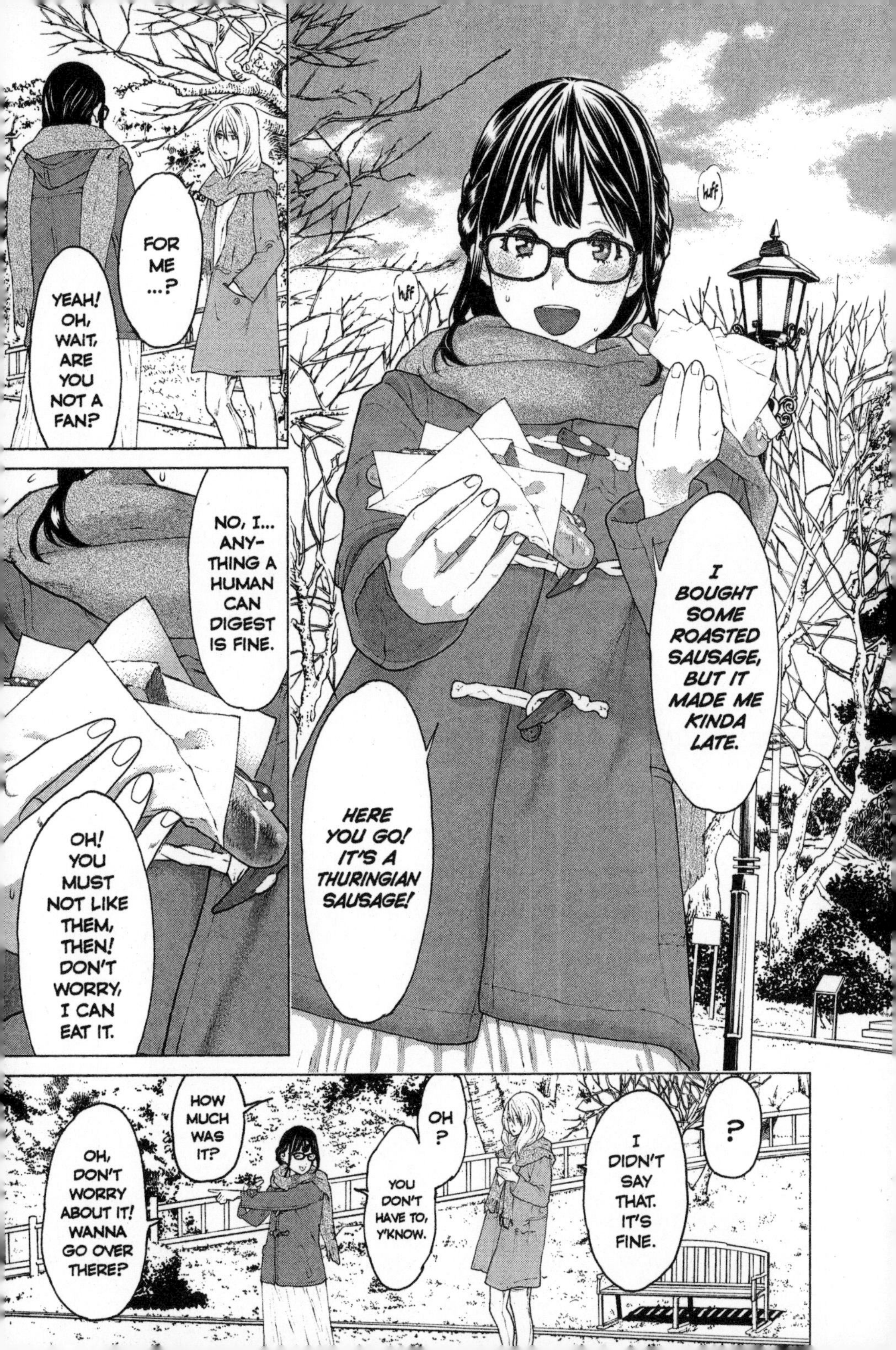
huff
huff
I BOUGHT SOME ROASTED SAUSAGE, BUT IT MADE ME KINDA LATE.
HERE YOU GO! IT'S A THURINGIAN SAUSAGE!
FOR ME ...?
YEAH! OH, WAIT, ARE YOU NOT A FAN?
NO, I... ANYTHING A HUMAN CAN DIGEST IS FINE.
OH! YOU MUST NOT LIKE THEM, THEN! DON'T WORRY, I CAN EAT IT.
?
I DIDN'T SAY THAT. IT'S FINE.
OH ?
YOU DON'T HAVE TO, Y'KNOW.
HOW MUCH WAS IT?
OH, DON'T WORRY ABOUT IT! WANNA GO OVER THERE?

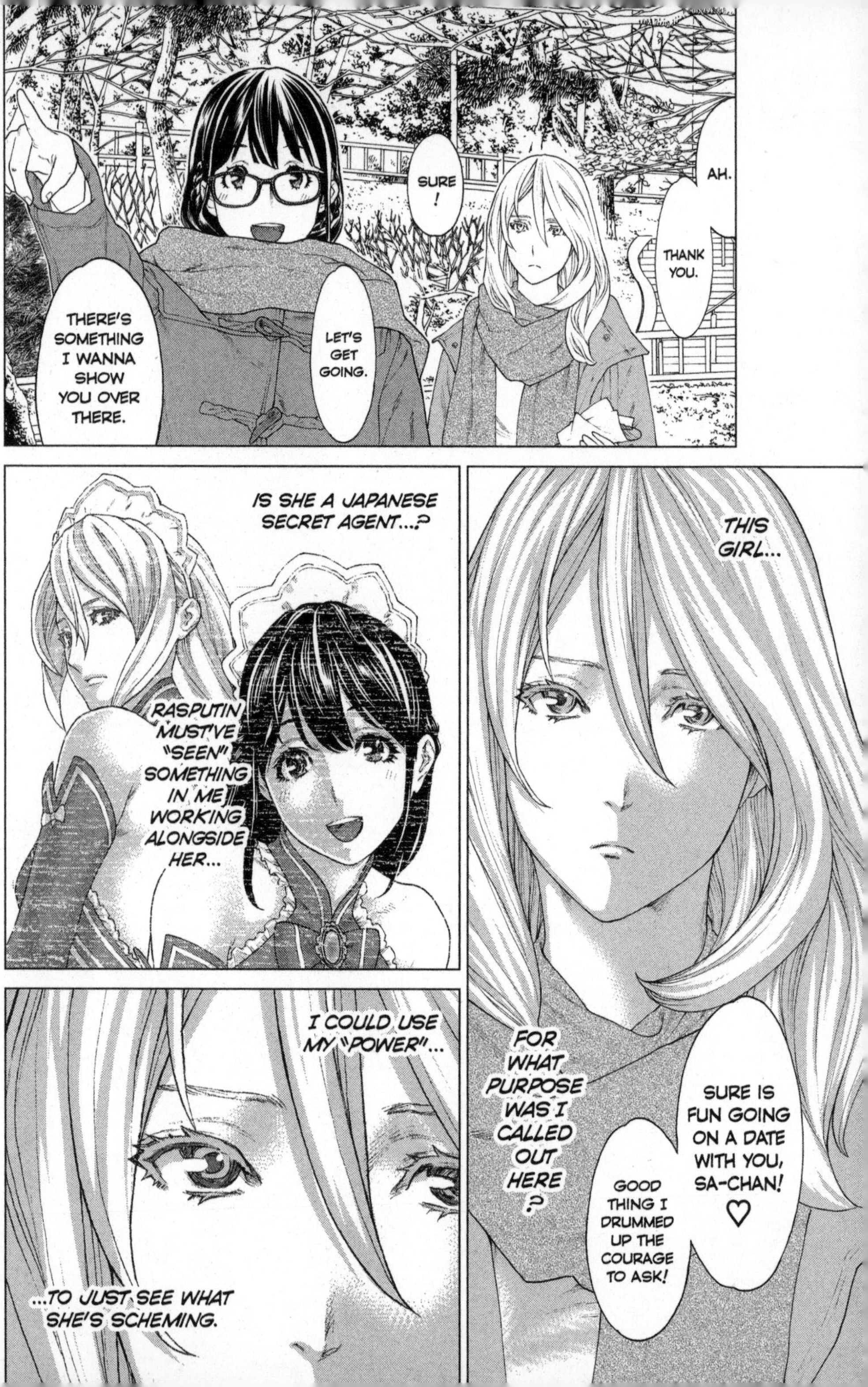
AH.
THANK YOU.
SURE!
LET'S GET GOING.
THERE'S SOMETHING I WANNA SHOW YOU OVER THERE.
THIS GIRL...
FOR WHAT PURPOSE WAS I CALLED OUT HERE?
SURE IS FUN GOING ON A DATE WITH YOU, SA-CHAN! ♡
GOOD THING I DRUMMED UP THE COURAGE TO ASK!
IS SHE A JAPANESE SECRET AGENT...?
RASPUTIN MUST'VE "SEEN" SOMETHING IN ME WORKING ALONGSIDE HER...
I COULD USE MY "POWER"...
...TO JUST SEE WHAT SHE'S SCHEMING.

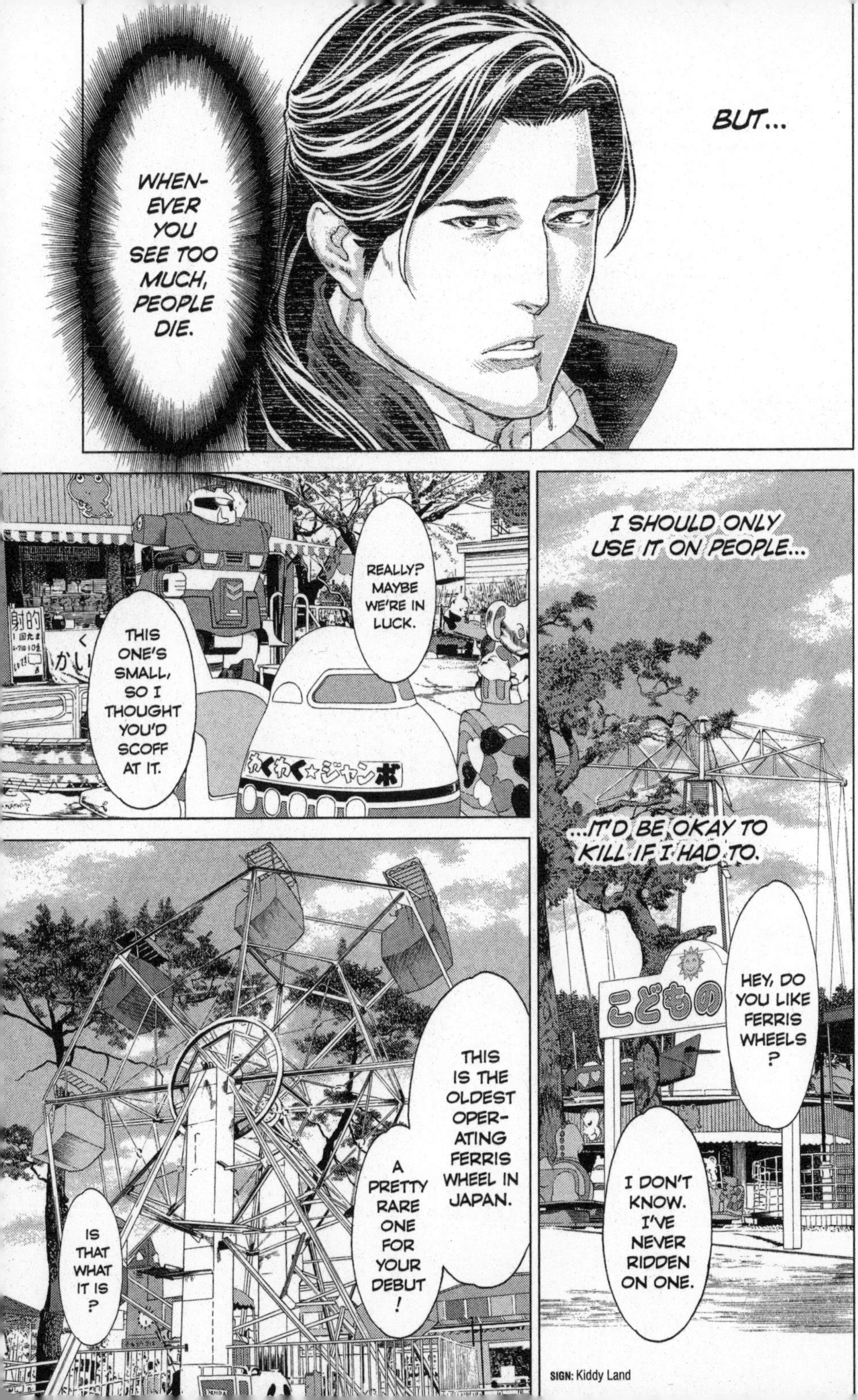
BUT...
WHEN-EVER YOU SEE TOO MUCH, PEOPLE DIE.
I SHOULD ONLY USE IT ON PEOPLE...
...IT'D BE OKAY TO KILL IF I HAD TO.
こどもの
HEY, DO YOU LIKE FERRIS WHEELS?
I DON'T KNOW. I'VE NEVER RIDDEN ON ONE.
REALLY? MAYBE WE'RE IN LUCK.
射的
THIS ONE'S SMALL, SO I THOUGHT YOU'D SCOFF AT IT.
わくわく☆ジャンボ
THIS IS THE OLDEST OPER-ATING FERRIS WHEEL IN JAPAN.
A PRETTY RARE ONE FOR YOUR DEBUT!
IS THAT WHAT IT IS?

SIGN: Kiddy Land

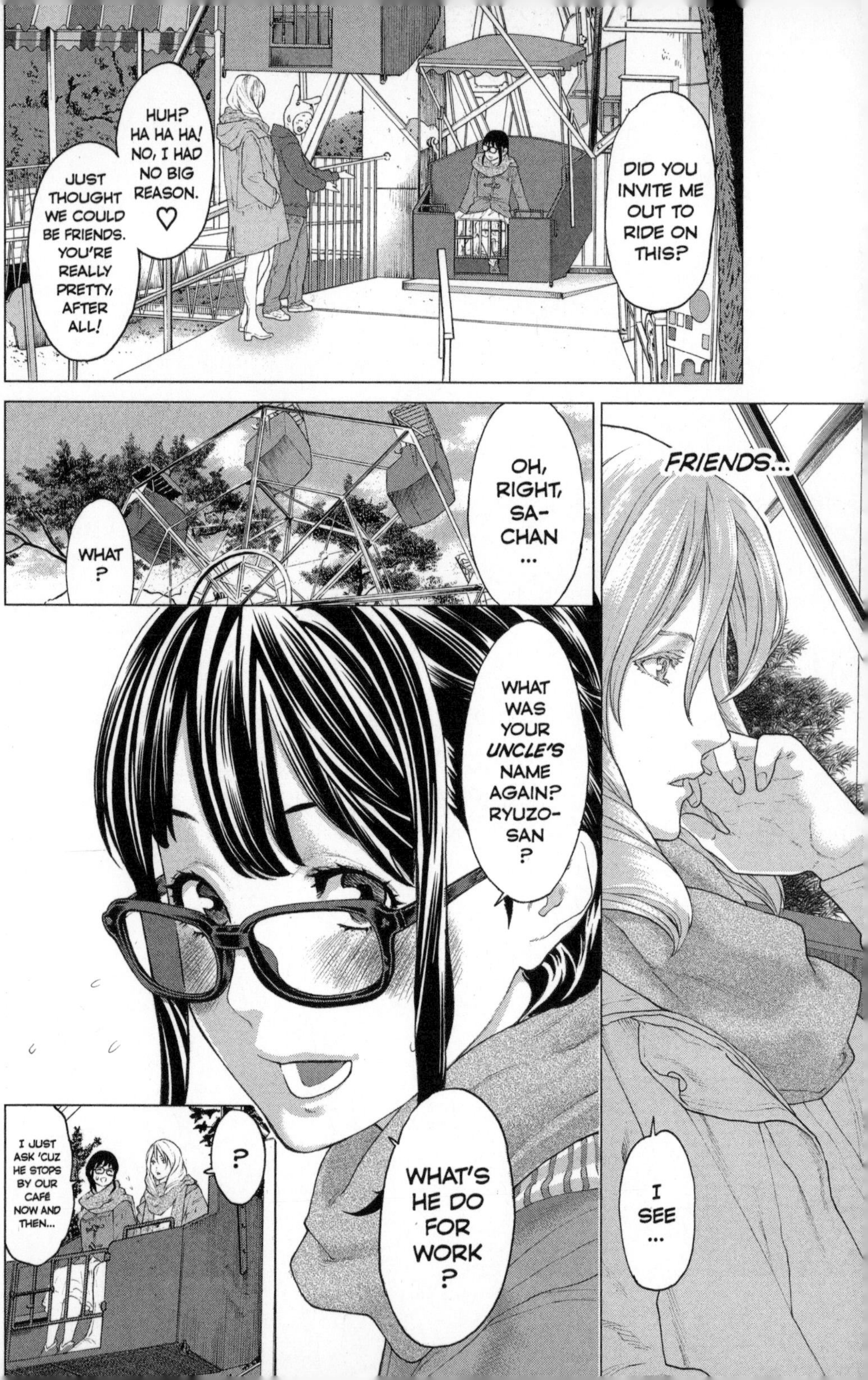
DID YOU INVITE ME OUT TO RIDE ON THIS?
HUH? HA HA HA! NO, I HAD NO BIG REASON. ♡
JUST THOUGHT WE COULD BE FRIENDS. YOU'RE REALLY PRETTY, AFTER ALL!
FRIENDS...
I SEE ...
OH, RIGHT, SA-CHAN ...
WHAT ?
WHAT WAS YOUR *UNCLE'S* NAME AGAIN? RYUZO-SAN ?
WHAT'S HE DO FOR WORK ?
?
I JUST ASK 'CUZ HE STOPS BY OUR CAFÉ NOW AND THEN...

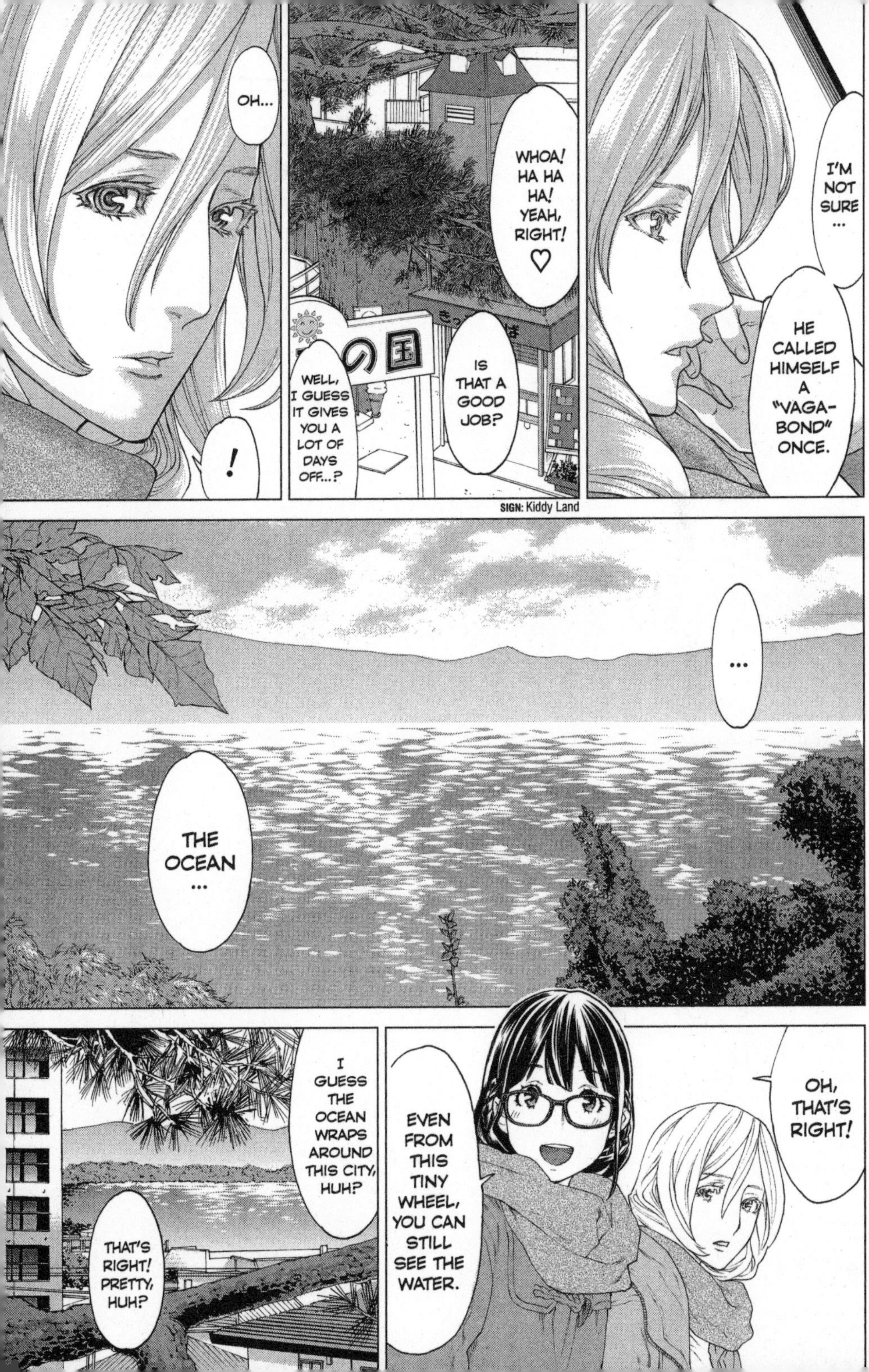
I'M NOT SURE ...
HE CALLED HIMSELF A "VAGA-BOND" ONCE.
WHOA! HA HA HA! YEAH, RIGHT! ♡
IS THAT A GOOD JOB?
WELL, I GUESS IT GIVES YOU A LOT OF DAYS OFF...?
OH...
!
...
THE OCEAN ...
OH, THAT'S RIGHT!
EVEN FROM THIS TINY WHEEL, YOU CAN STILL SEE THE WATER.
I GUESS THE OCEAN WRAPS AROUND THIS CITY, HUH?
THAT'S RIGHT! PRETTY, HUH?
SIGN: Kiddy Land

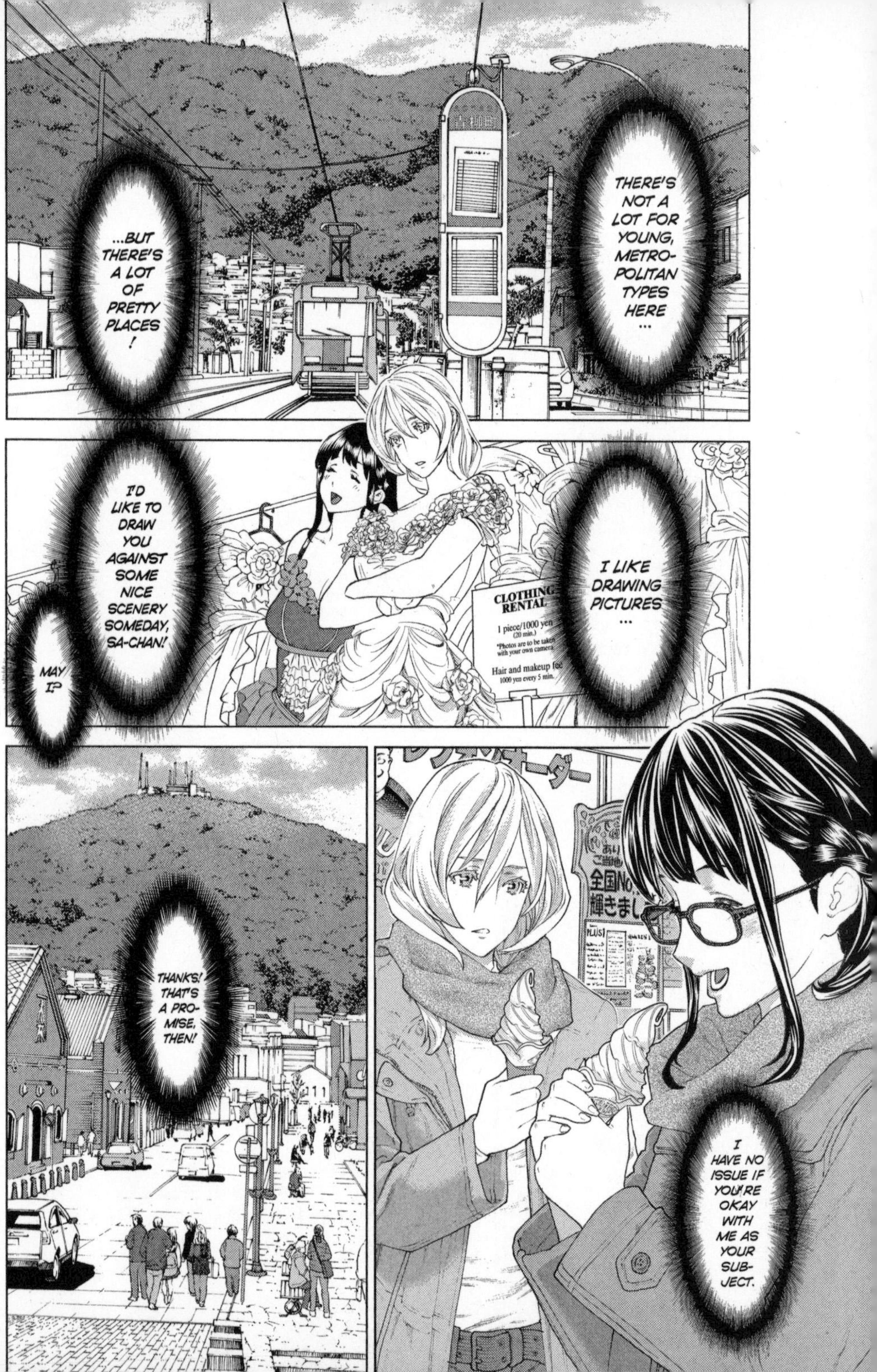
THERE'S NOT A LOT FOR YOUNG, METRO-POLITAN TYPES HERE ...
...BUT THERE'S A LOT OF PRETTY PLACES!
I LIKE DRAWING PICTURES ...
CLOTHING RENTAL
1 piece/1000 yen (20 min.)
*Photos are to be taken with your own camera.
Hair and makeup fee 1000 yen every 5 min.
I'D LIKE TO DRAW YOU AGAINST SOME NICE SCENERY SOMEDAY, SA-CHAN!
MAY I?
I HAVE NO ISSUE IF YOU'RE OKAY WITH ME AS YOUR SUB-JECT.
THANKS! THAT'S A PRO-MISE, THEN!

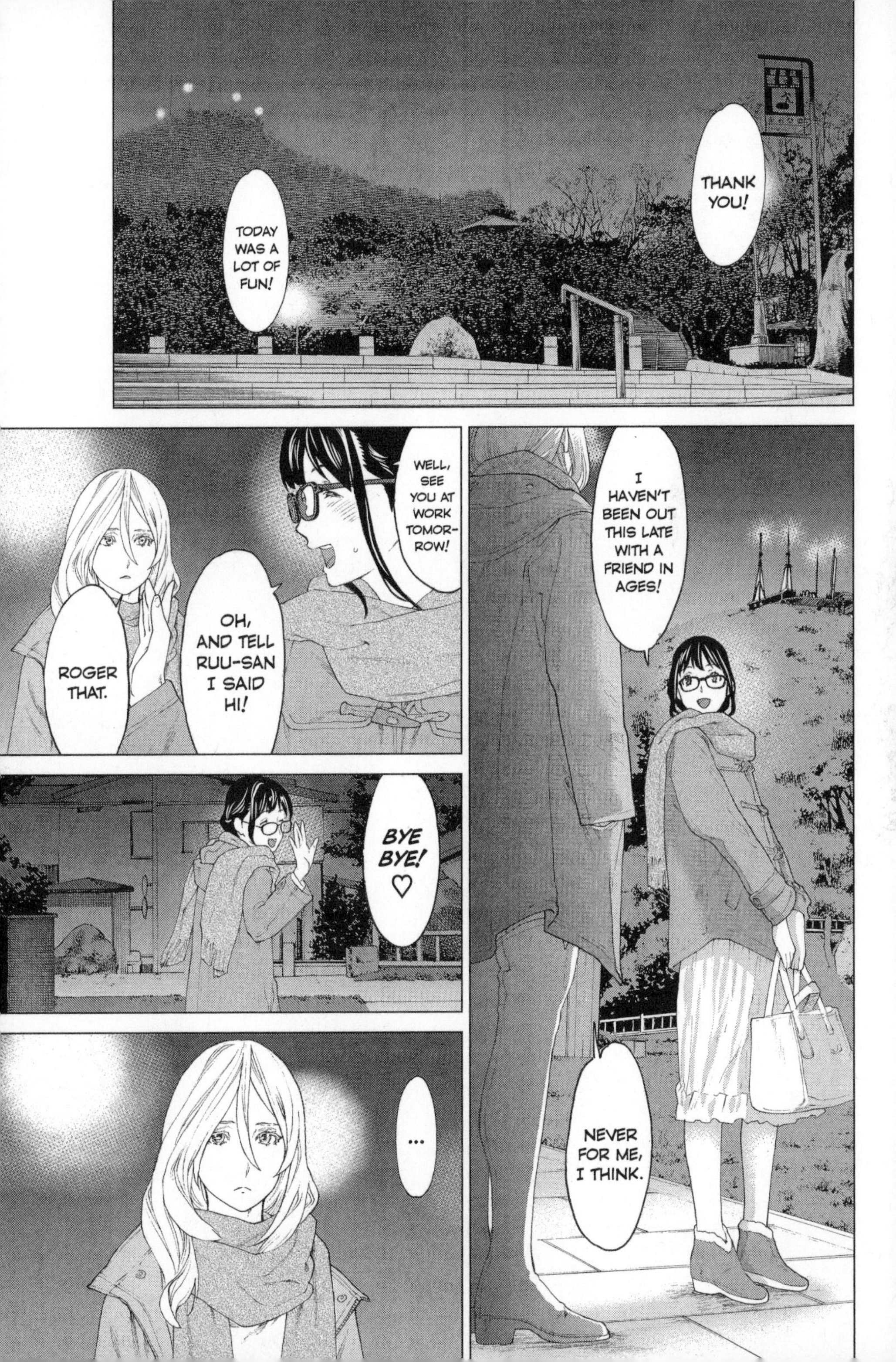
THANK YOU!
TODAY WAS A LOT OF FUN!
I HAVEN'T BEEN OUT THIS LATE WITH A FRIEND IN AGES!
NEVER FOR ME, I THINK.
WELL, SEE YOU AT WORK TOMORROW!
OH, AND TELL RUU-SAN I SAID HI!
ROGER THAT.
BYE BYE! ♡
...

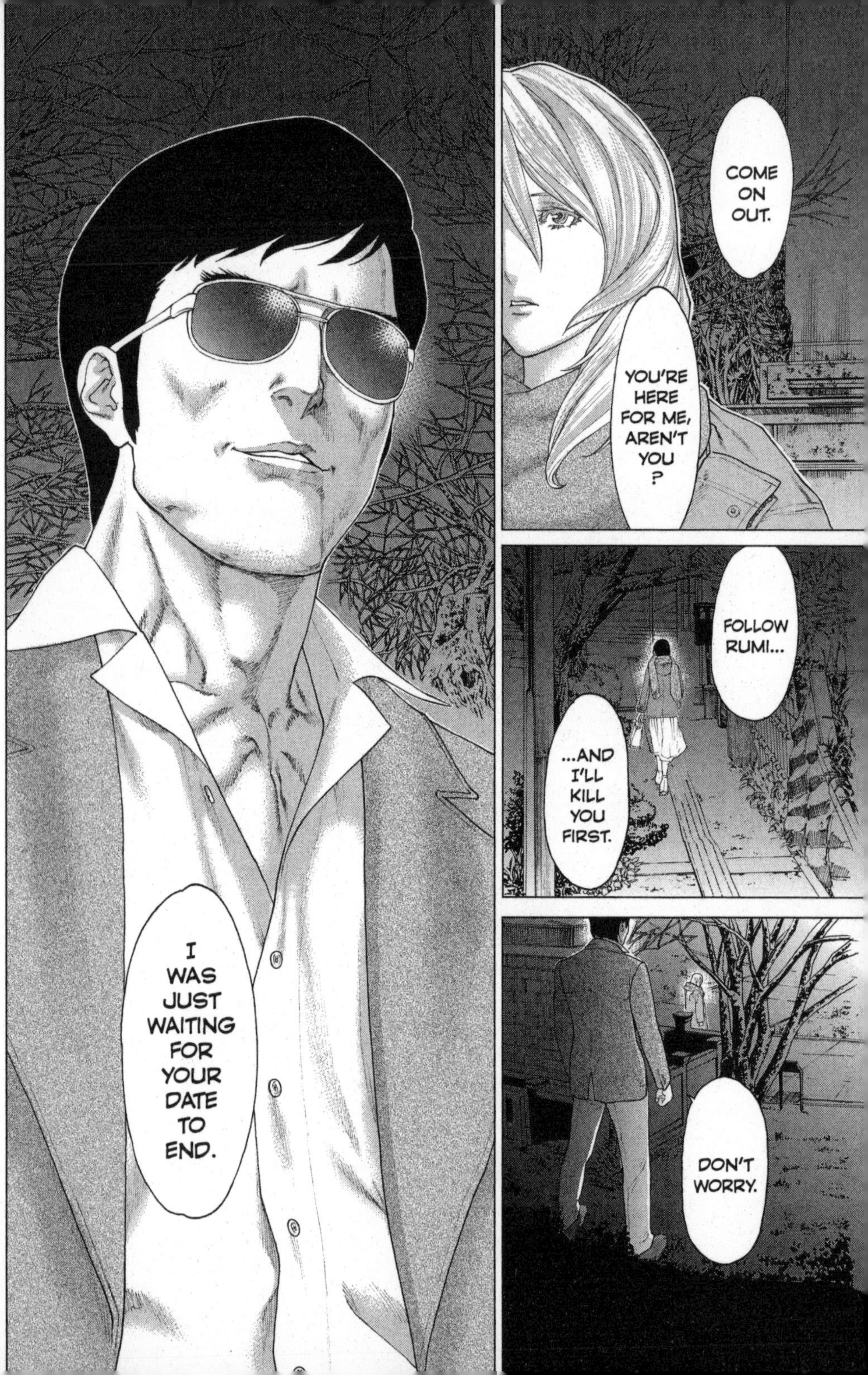
COME ON OUT.
YOU'RE HERE FOR ME, AREN'T YOU ?
FOLLOW RUMI...
...AND I'LL KILL YOU FIRST.
DON'T WORRY.
I WAS JUST WAITING FOR YOUR DATE TO END.

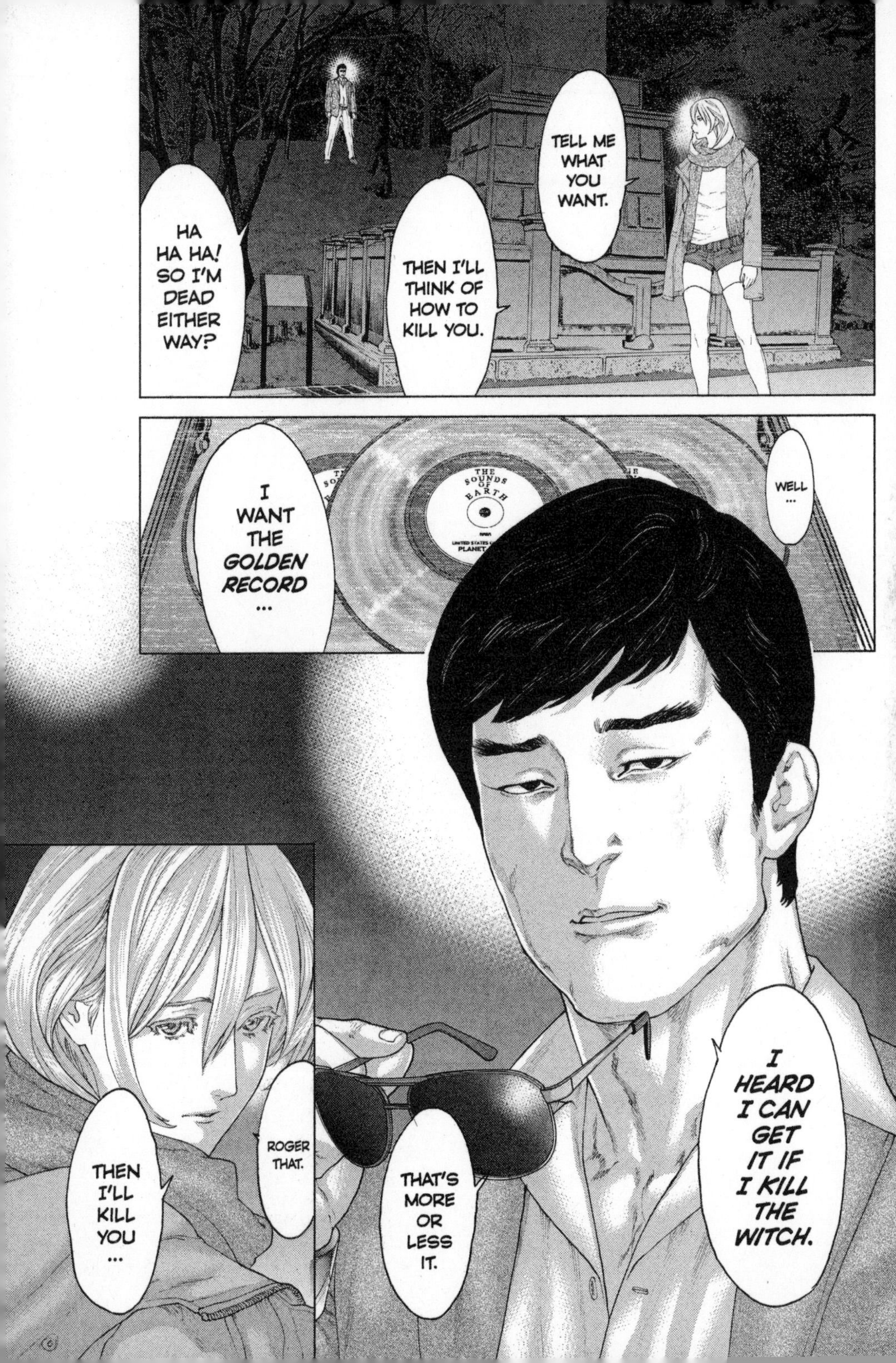
TELL ME WHAT YOU WANT.
THEN I'LL THINK OF HOW TO KILL YOU.
HA HA HA! SO I'M DEAD EITHER WAY?
WELL ...
I WANT THE *GOLDEN RECORD* ...
THE SOUNDS OF EARTH
I HEARD I CAN GET IT IF I KILL THE WITCH.
THAT'S MORE OR LESS IT.
ROGER THAT.
THEN I'LL KILL YOU ...

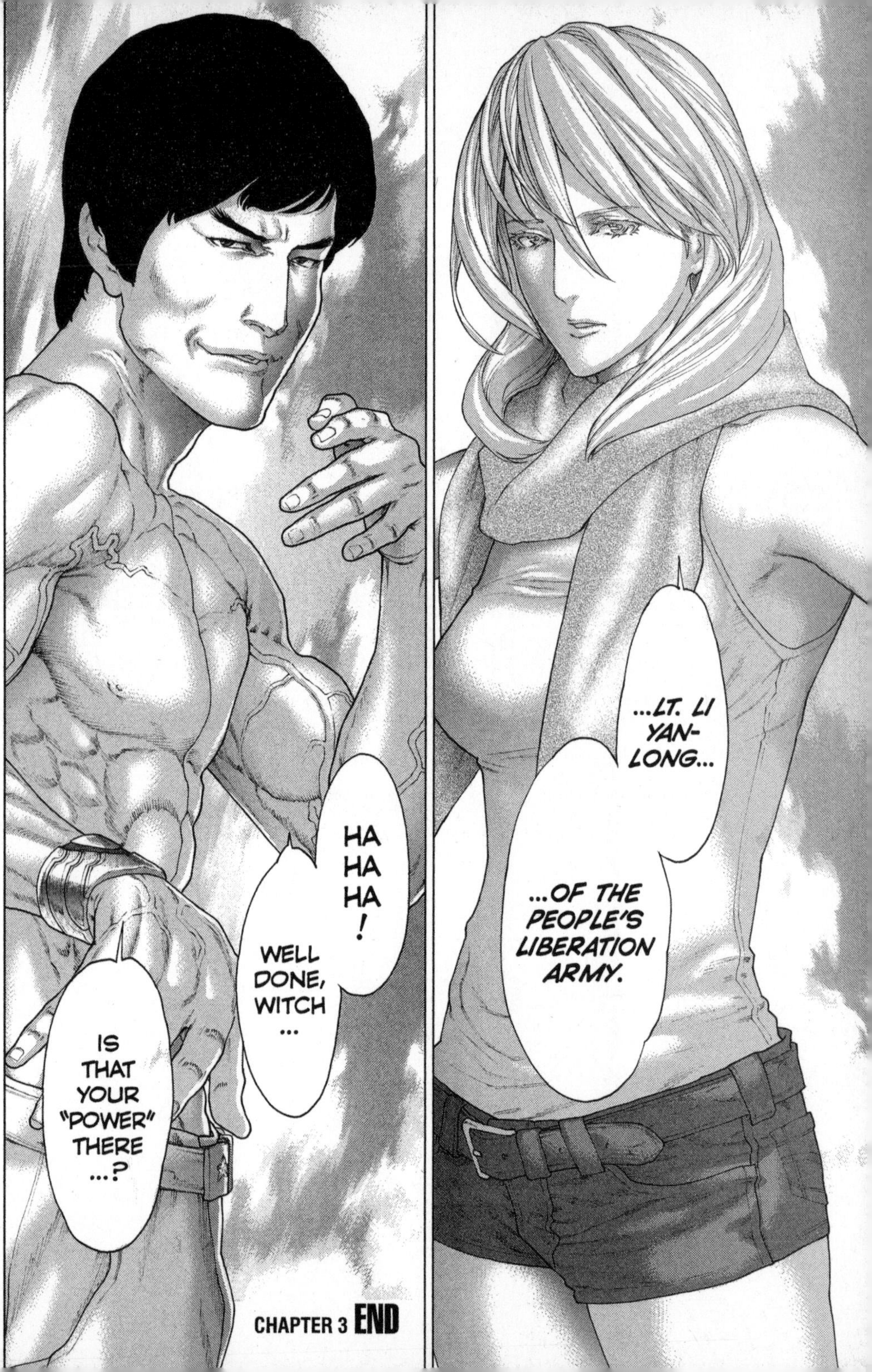
...LT. LI YAN-LONG...
...OF THE PEOPLE'S LIBERATION ARMY.
HA HA HA!
WELL DONE, WITCH...
IS THAT YOUR "POWER" THERE...?
CHAPTER 3 END

GOLOSSEUM

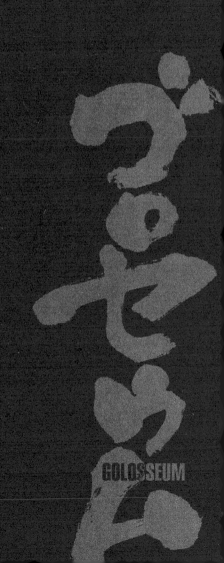

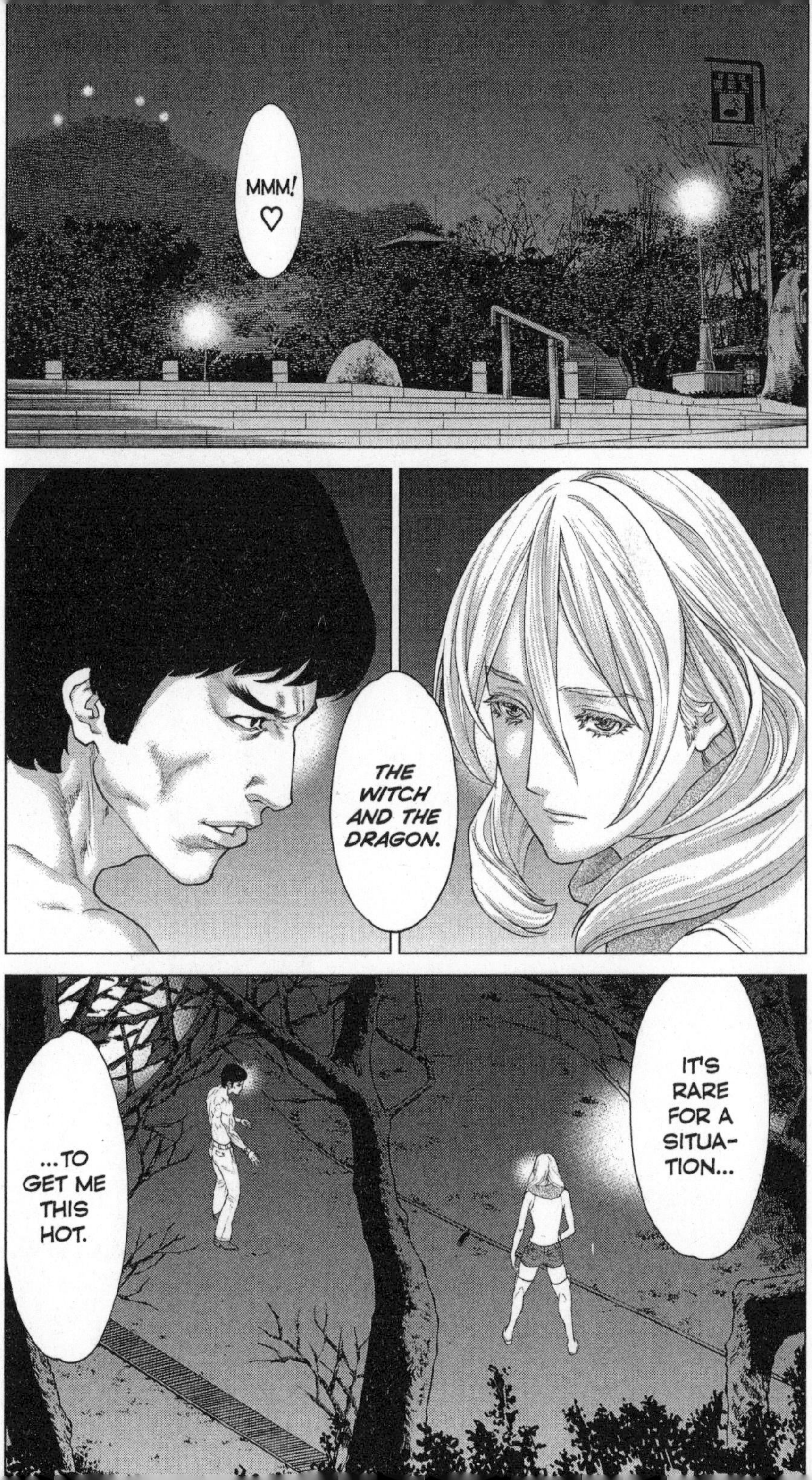
MMM! ♡
THE WITCH AND THE DRAGON.
IT'S RARE FOR A SITUA-TION...
...TO GET ME THIS HOT.

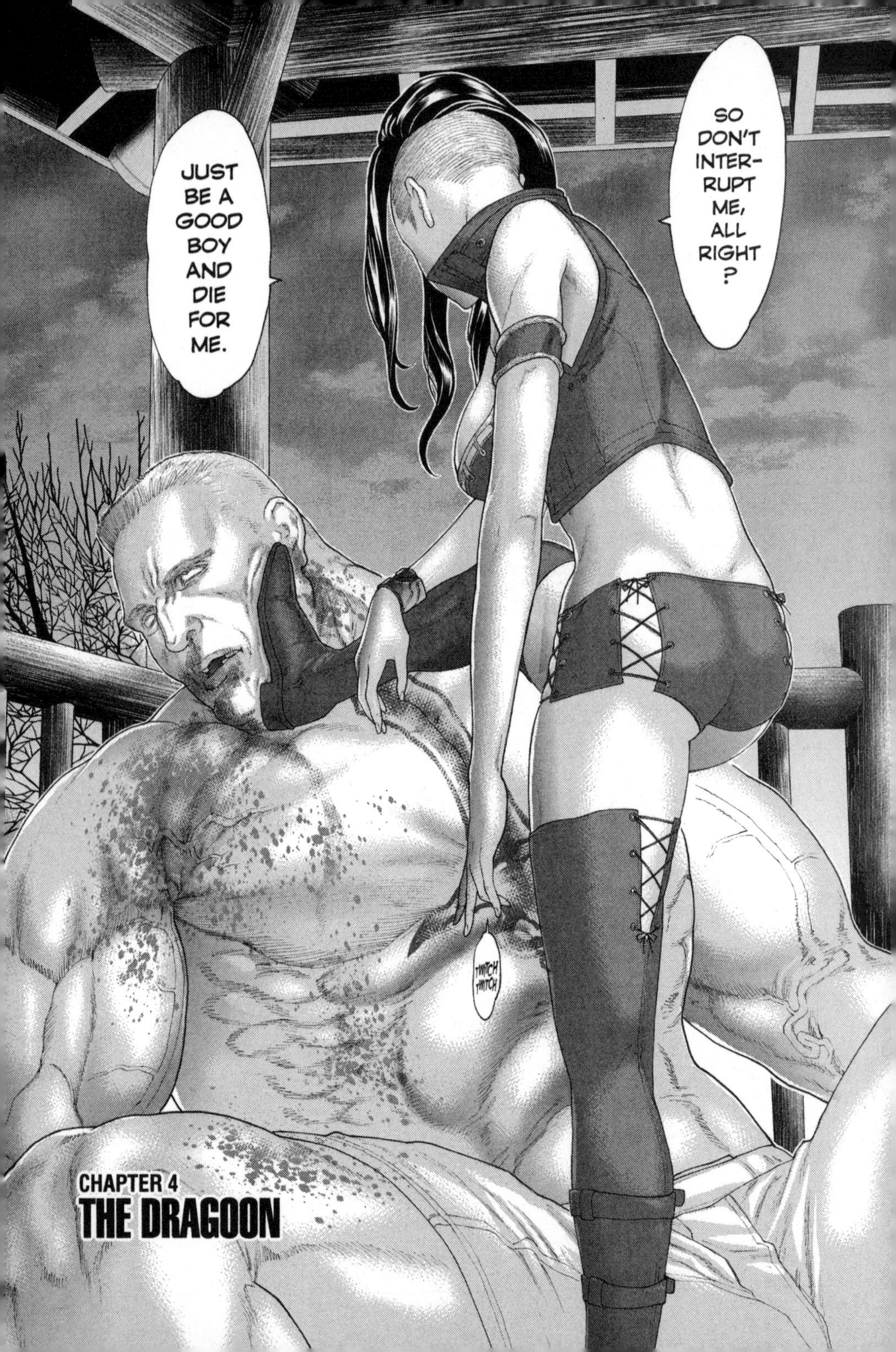
SO DON'T INTER-RUPT ME, ALL RIGHT?
JUST BE A GOOD BOY AND DIE FOR ME.
TWITCH TWITCH

CHAPTER 4
THE DRAGOON

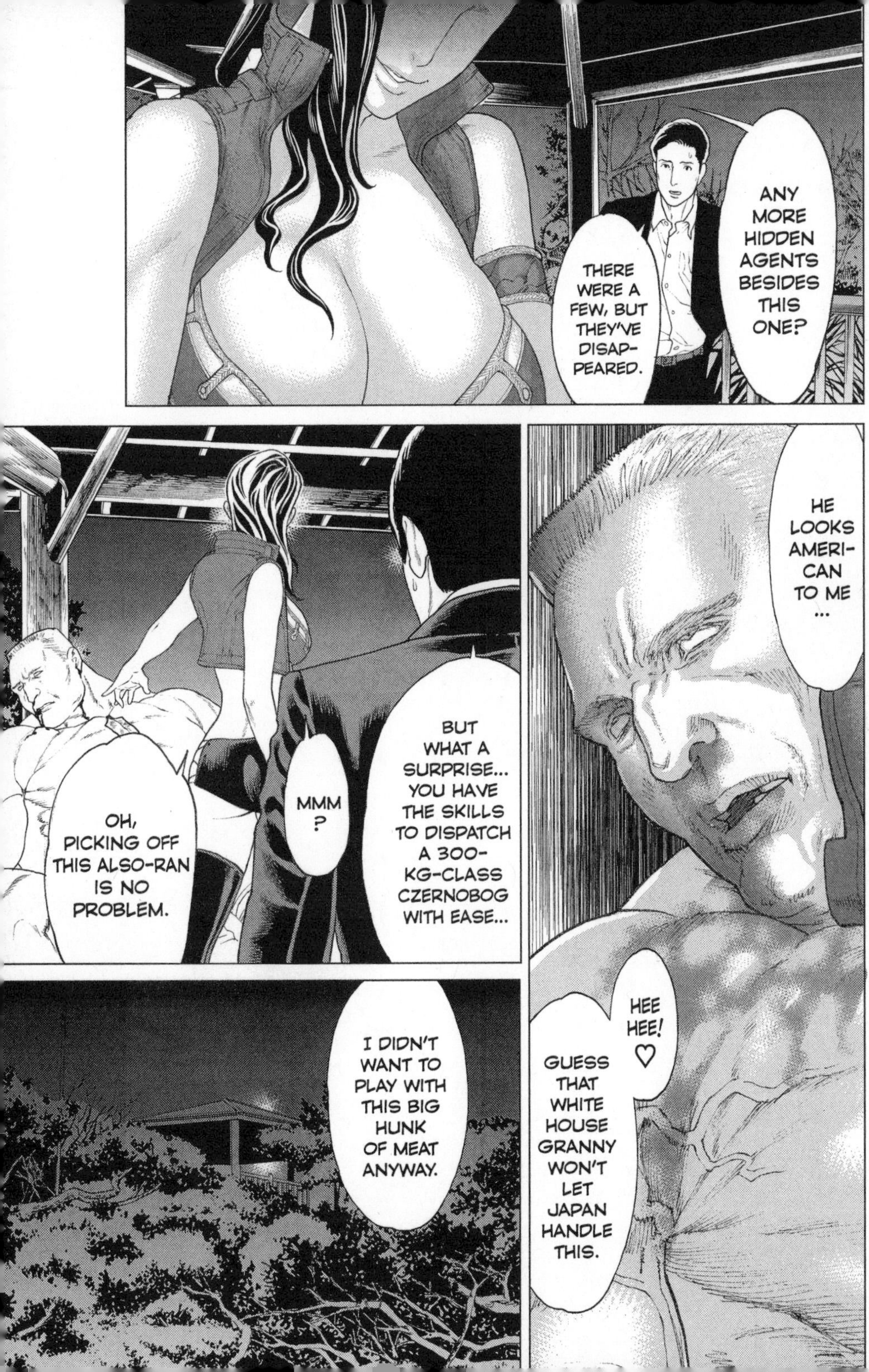
ANY MORE HIDDEN AGENTS BESIDES THIS ONE?
THERE WERE A FEW, BUT THEY'VE DISAP-PEARED.
HE LOOKS AMERI-CAN TO ME ...
HEE HEE! ♡
GUESS THAT WHITE HOUSE GRANNY WON'T LET JAPAN HANDLE THIS.
BUT WHAT A SURPRISE... YOU HAVE THE SKILLS TO DISPATCH A 300-KG-CLASS CZERNOBOG WITH EASE...
MMM ?
OH, PICKING OFF THIS ALSO-RAN IS NO PROBLEM.
I DIDN'T WANT TO PLAY WITH THIS BIG HUNK OF MEAT ANYWAY.

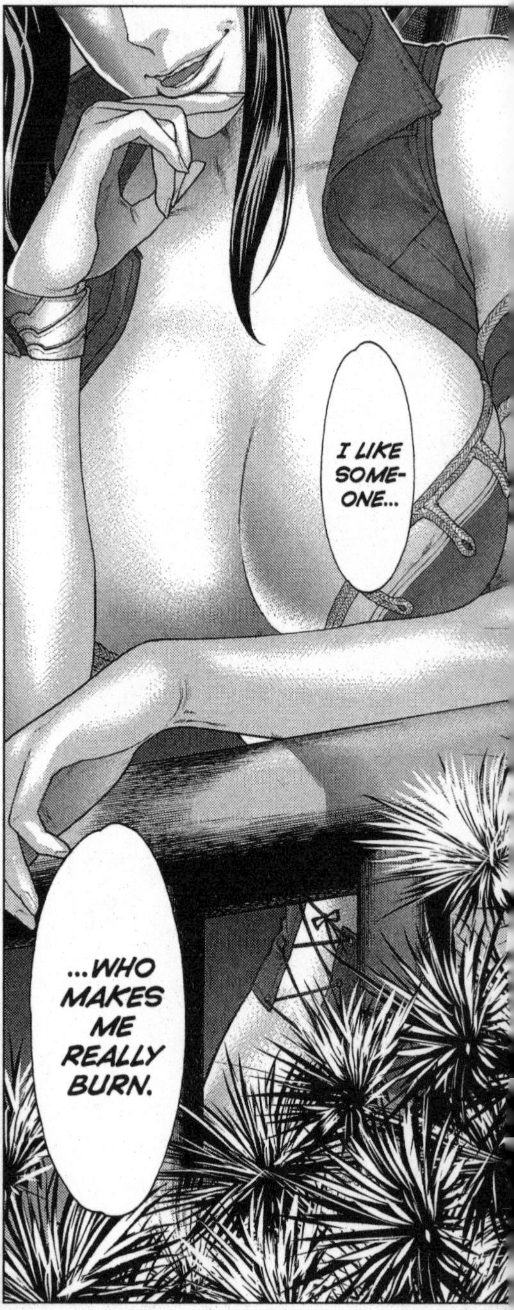
I LIKE SOME-ONE...
...WHO MAKES ME REALLY BURN.
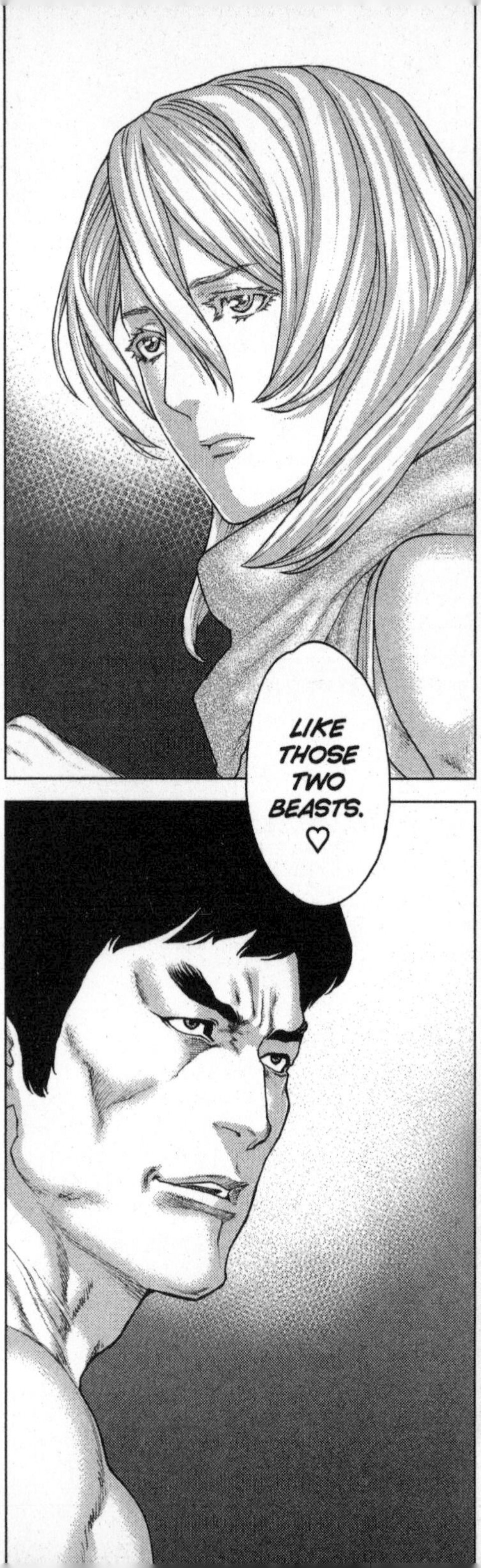
LIKE THOSE TWO BEASTS. ♡

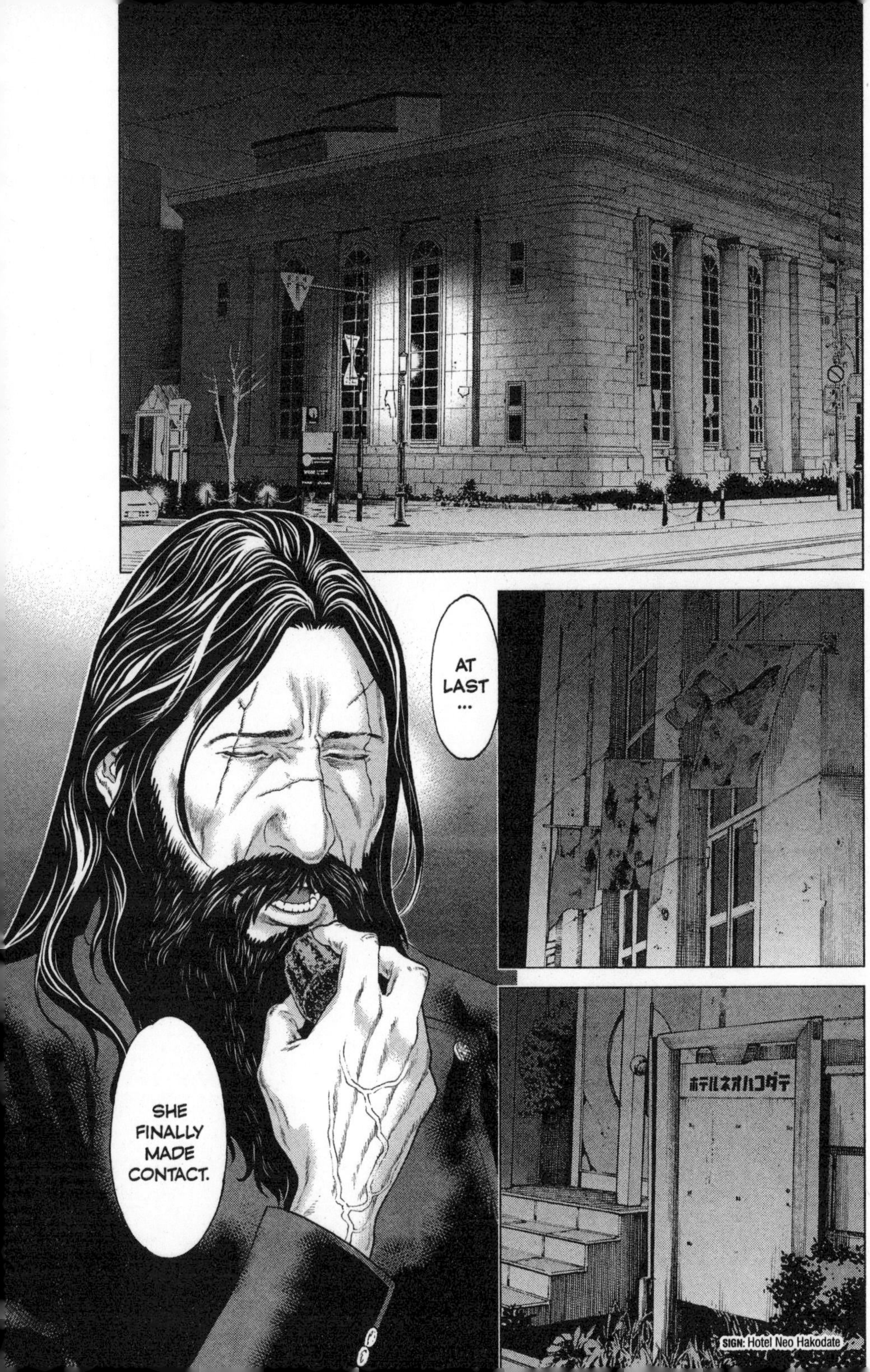
ホテルネオハコダテ
SIGN: Hotel Neo Hakodate
AT LAST...
SHE FINALLY MADE CONTACT.

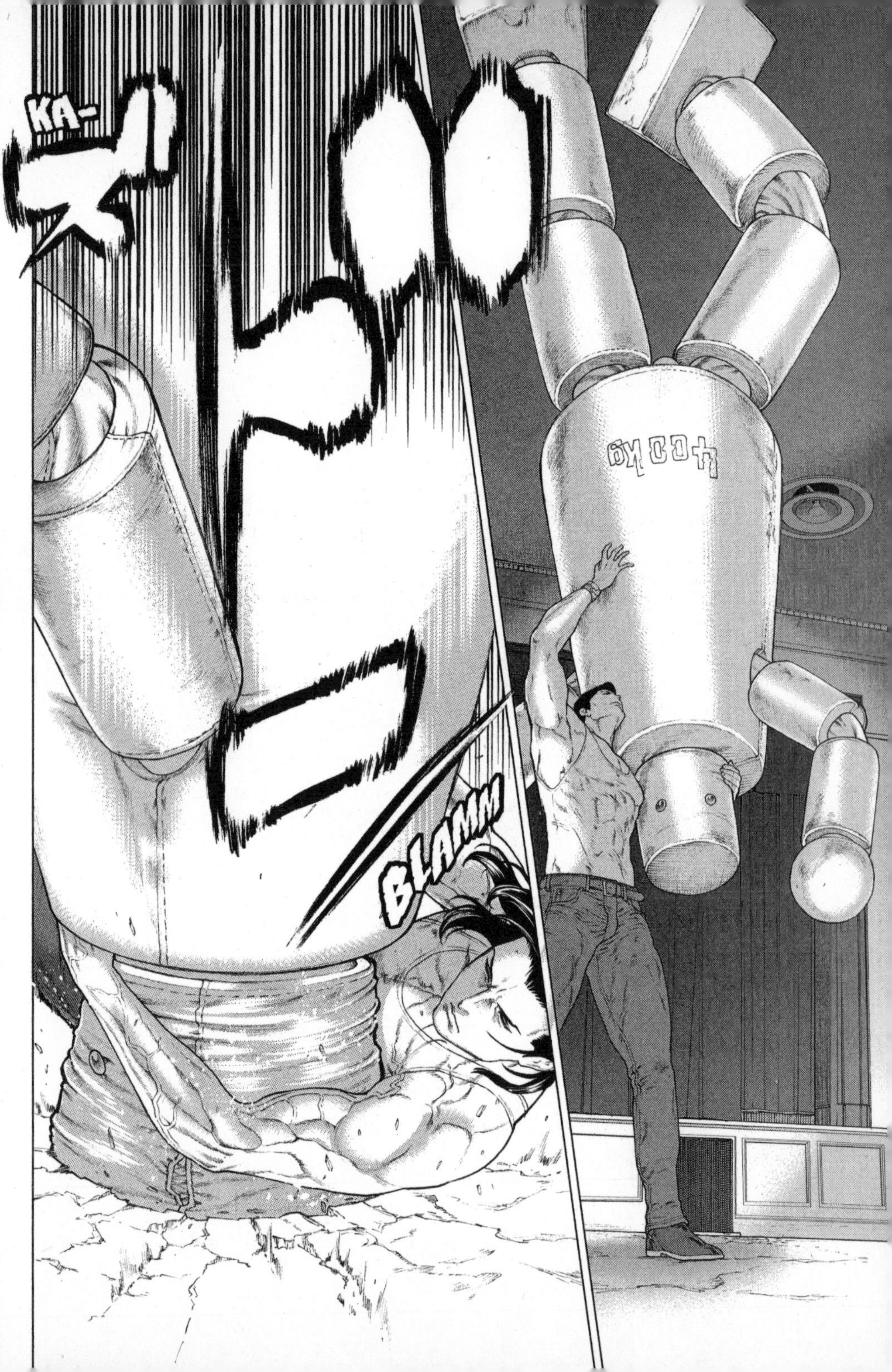
400kg
KA-
BLAMM

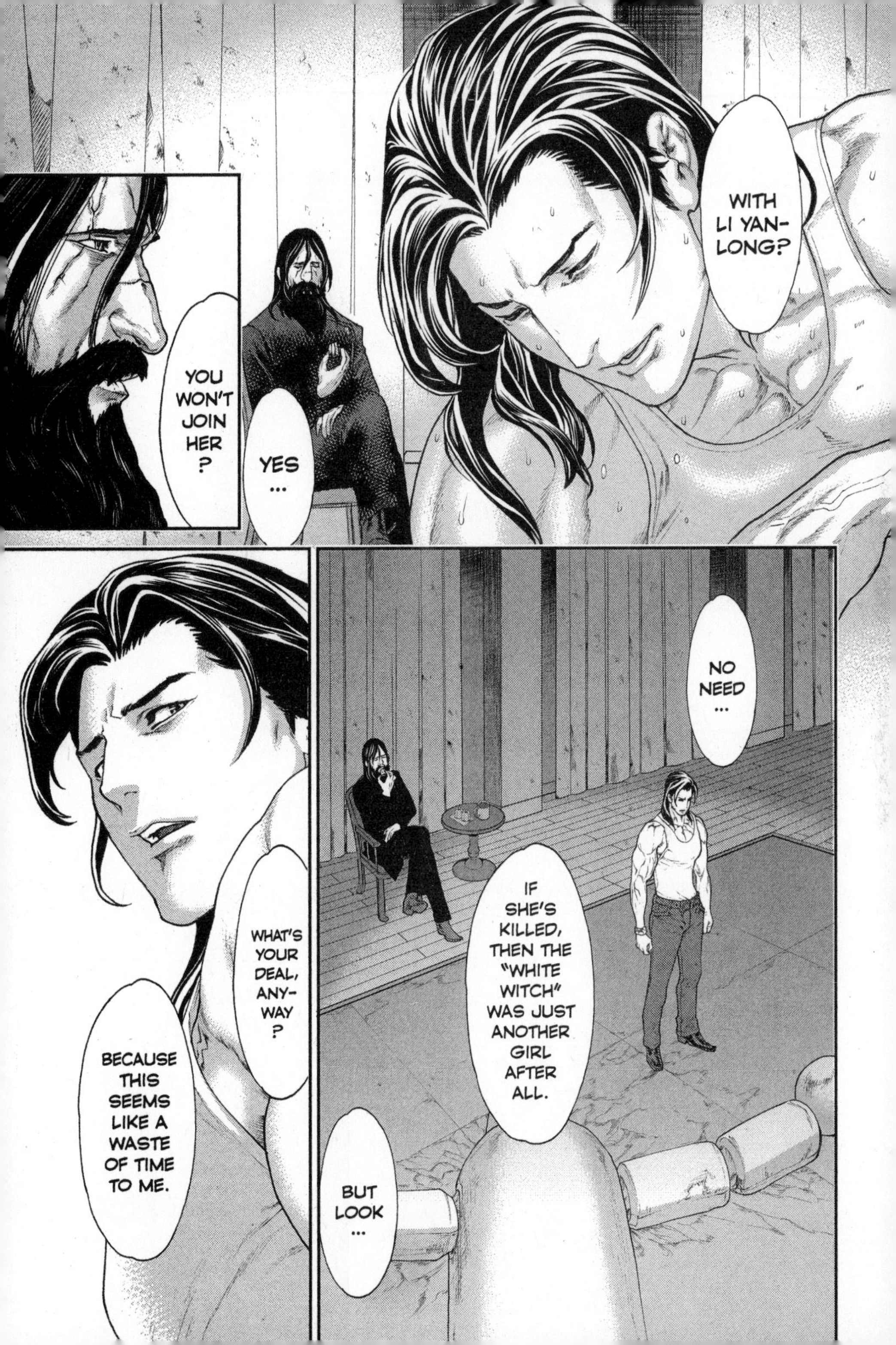
WITH LI YAN-LONG?
YOU WON'T JOIN HER?
YES...
NO NEED...
IF SHE'S KILLED, THEN THE "WHITE WITCH" WAS JUST ANOTHER GIRL AFTER ALL.
BUT LOOK...
WHAT'S YOUR DEAL, ANYWAY?
BECAUSE THIS SEEMS LIKE A WASTE OF TIME TO ME.

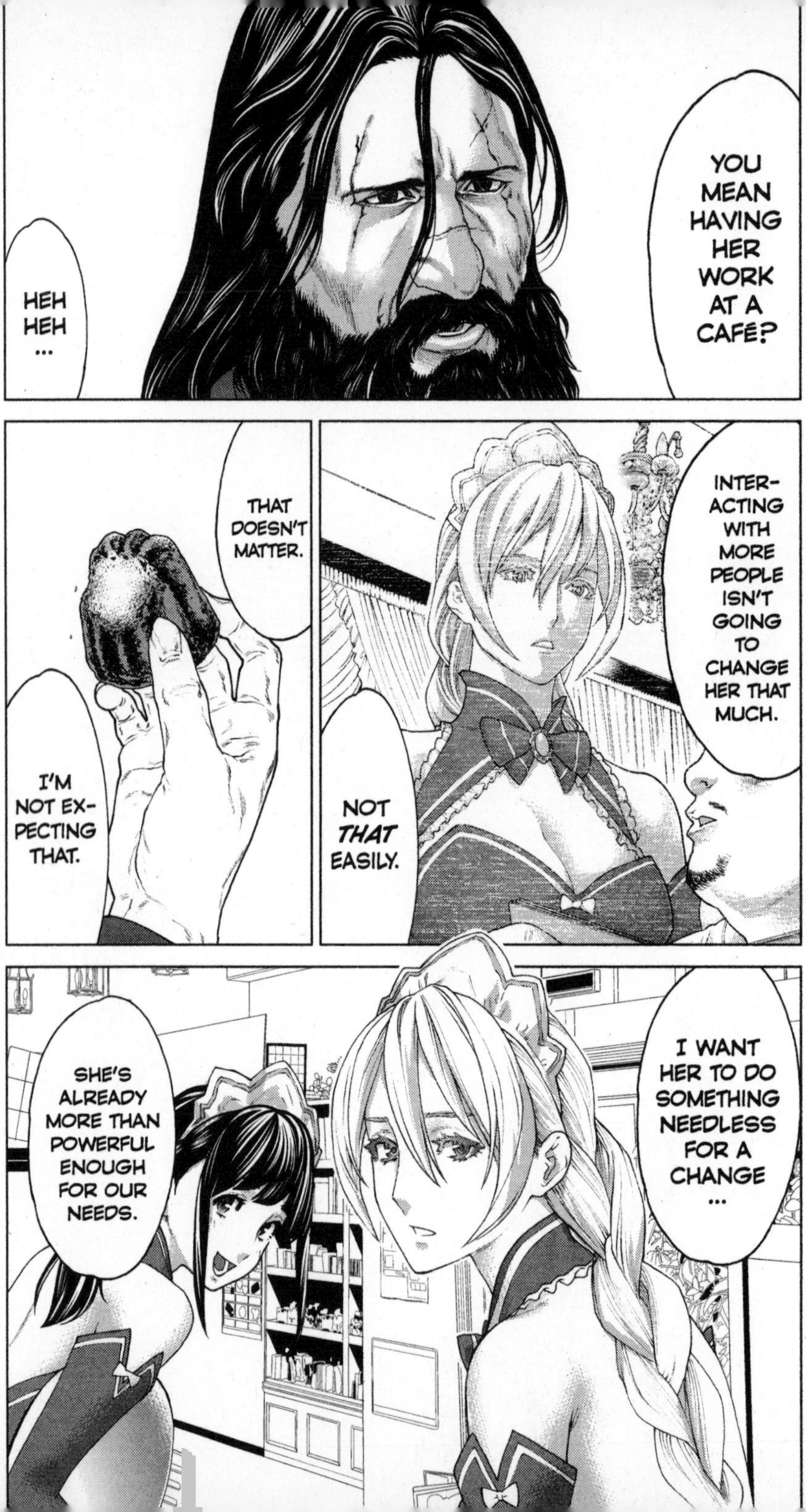
YOU MEAN HAVING HER WORK AT A CAFÉ?
HEH HEH ...
INTER-ACTING WITH MORE PEOPLE ISN'T GOING TO CHANGE HER THAT MUCH.
NOT *THAT* EASILY.
THAT DOESN'T MATTER.
I'M NOT EX-PECTING THAT.
I WANT HER TO DO SOMETHING NEEDLESS FOR A CHANGE ...
SHE'S ALREADY MORE THAN POWERFUL ENOUGH FOR OUR NEEDS.

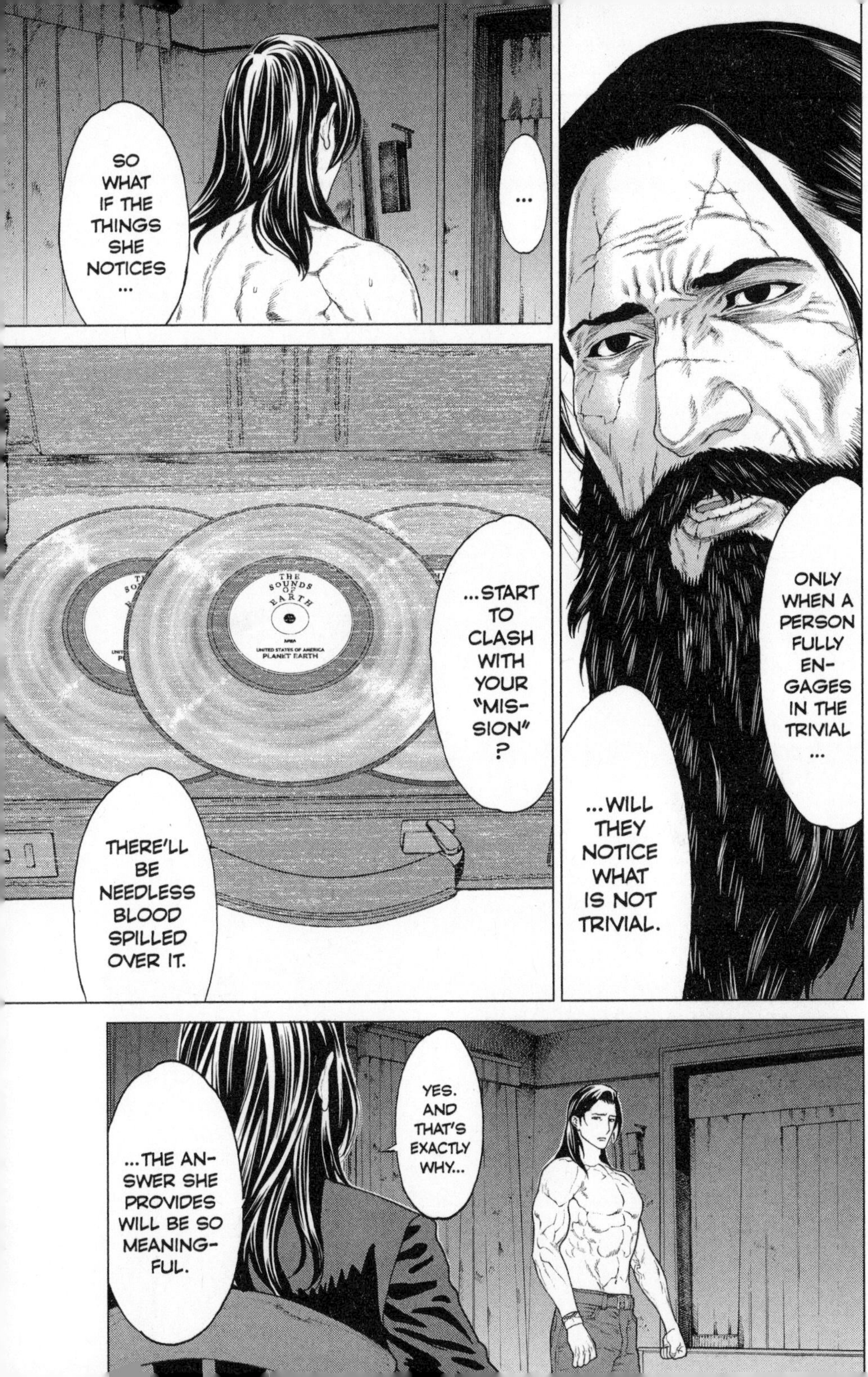
ONLY WHEN A PERSON FULLY EN-GAGES IN THE TRIVIAL ...
...WILL THEY NOTICE WHAT IS NOT TRIVIAL.
...
SO WHAT IF THE THINGS SHE NOTICES ...
THE SOUNDS OF EARTH
UNITED STATES OF AMERICA
PLANET EARTH
...START TO CLASH WITH YOUR "MIS-SION" ?
THERE'LL BE NEEDLESS BLOOD SPILLED OVER IT.
YES. AND THAT'S EXACTLY WHY...
...THE AN-SWER SHE PROVIDES WILL BE SO MEANING-FUL.

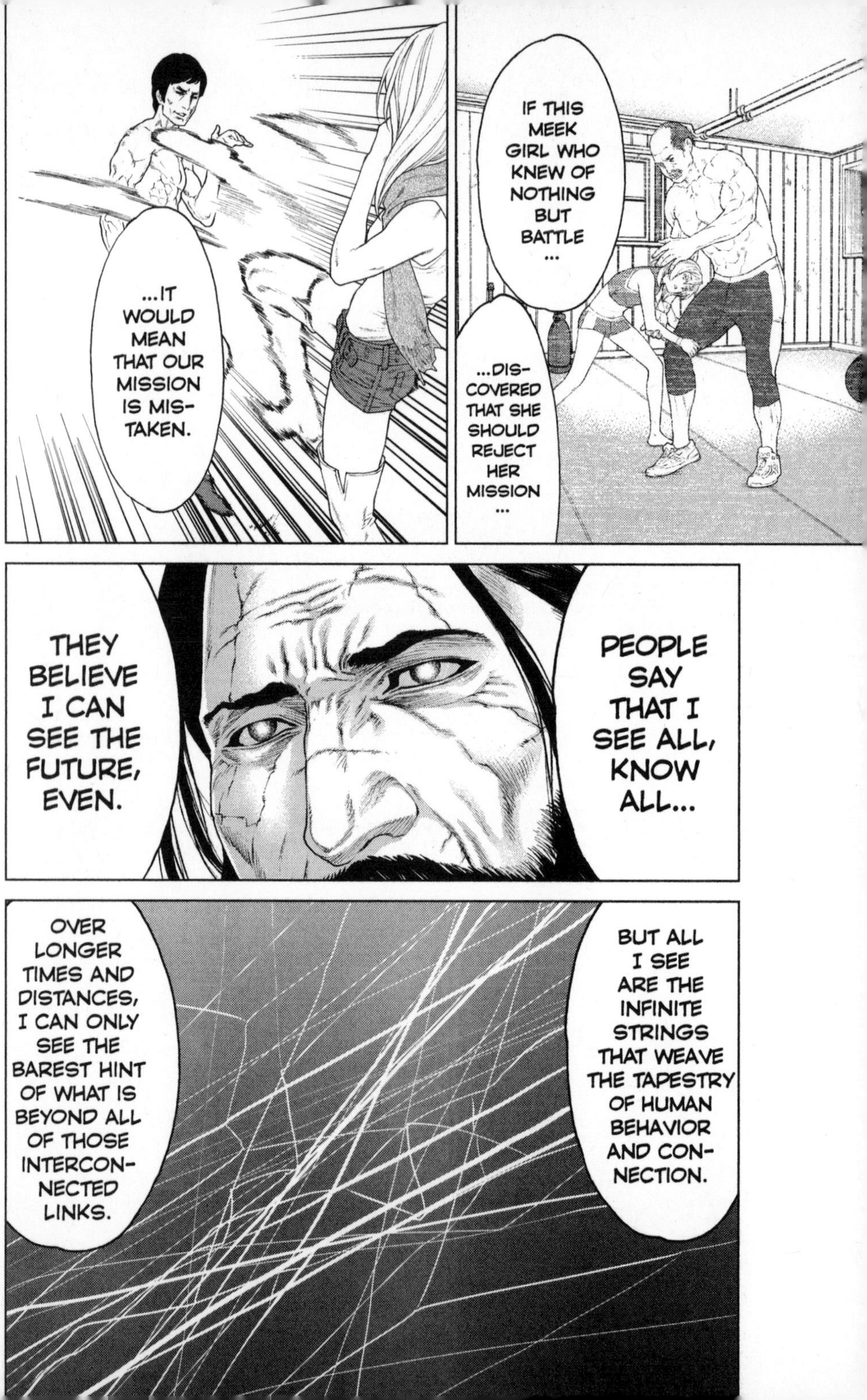
IF THIS MEEK GIRL WHO KNEW OF NOTHING BUT BATTLE ...
...DIS-COVERED THAT SHE SHOULD REJECT HER MISSION ...
...IT WOULD MEAN THAT OUR MISSION IS MIS-TAKEN.
PEOPLE SAY THAT I SEE ALL, KNOW ALL...
THEY BELIEVE I CAN SEE THE FUTURE, EVEN.
BUT ALL I SEE ARE THE INFINITE STRINGS THAT WEAVE THE TAPESTRY OF HUMAN BEHAVIOR AND CON-NECTION.
OVER LONGER TIMES AND DISTANCES, I CAN ONLY SEE THE BAREST HINT OF WHAT IS BEYOND ALL OF THOSE INTERCON-NECTED LINKS.

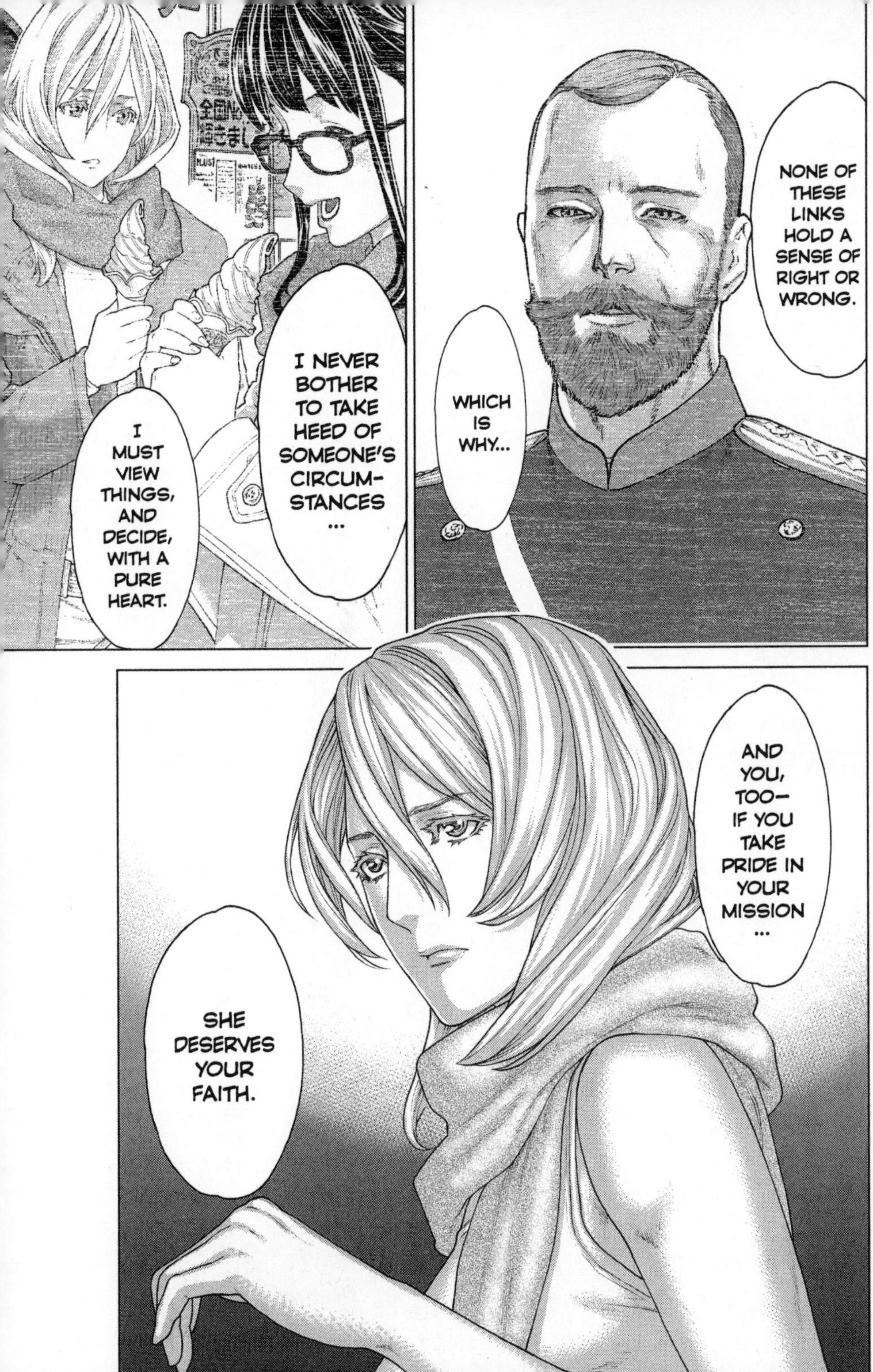
NONE OF THESE LINKS HOLD A SENSE OF RIGHT OR WRONG.
WHICH IS WHY...
I NEVER BOTHER TO TAKE HEED OF SOMEONE'S CIRCUM-STANCES...
I MUST VIEW THINGS, AND DECIDE, WITH A PURE HEART.
AND YOU, TOO— IF YOU TAKE PRIDE IN YOUR MISSION...
SHE DESERVES YOUR FAITH.

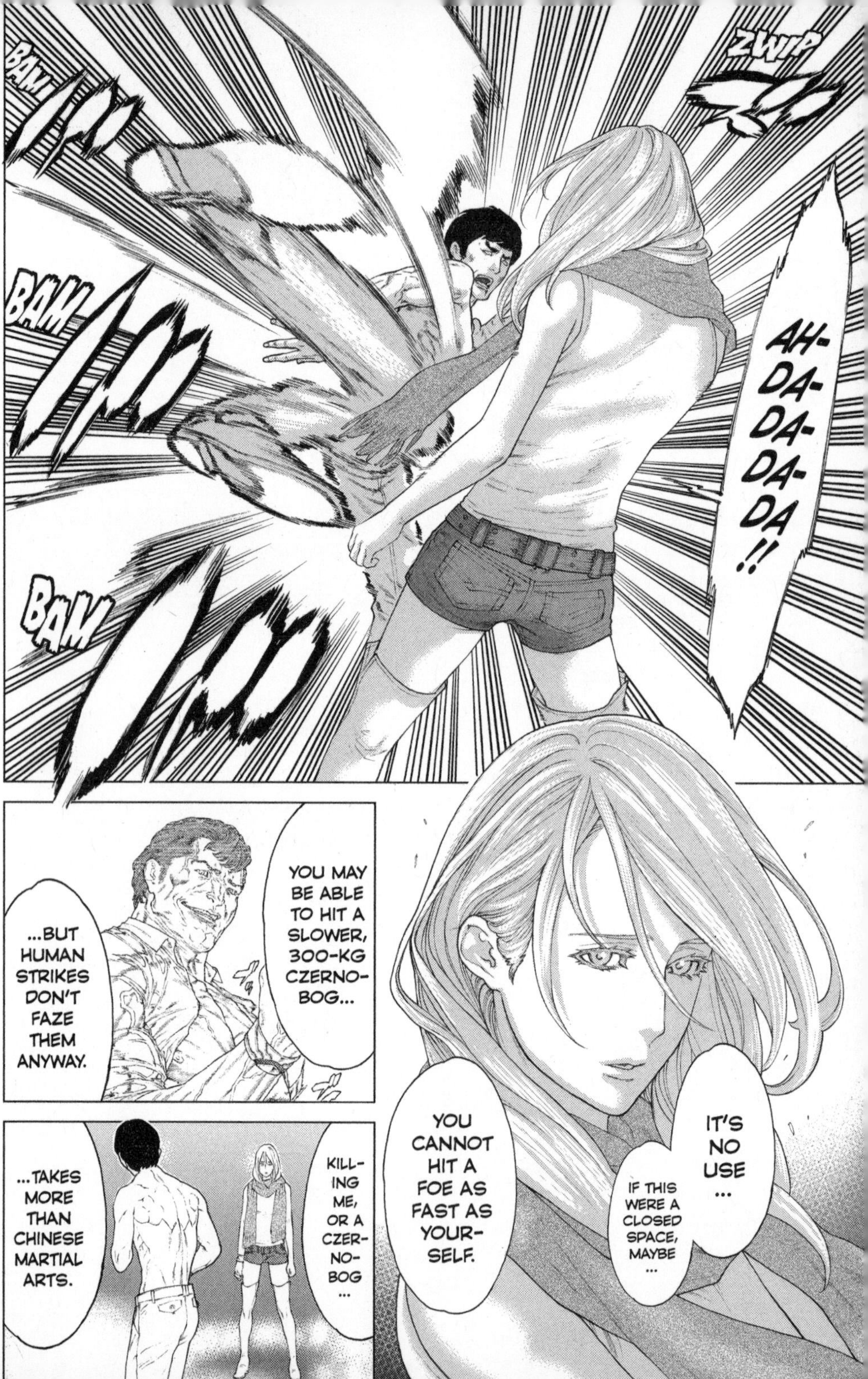
ZWIP
AH-DA-DA-DA-DA-DA!!
BAM
BAM
BAM
IT'S NO USE ...
IF THIS WERE A CLOSED SPACE, MAYBE ...
YOU CANNOT HIT A FOE AS FAST AS YOURSELF.
YOU MAY BE ABLE TO HIT A SLOWER, 300-KG CZERNOBOG...
...BUT HUMAN STRIKES DON'T FAZE THEM ANYWAY.
KILLING ME, OR A CZERNOBOG ...
...TAKES MORE THAN CHINESE MARTIAL ARTS.

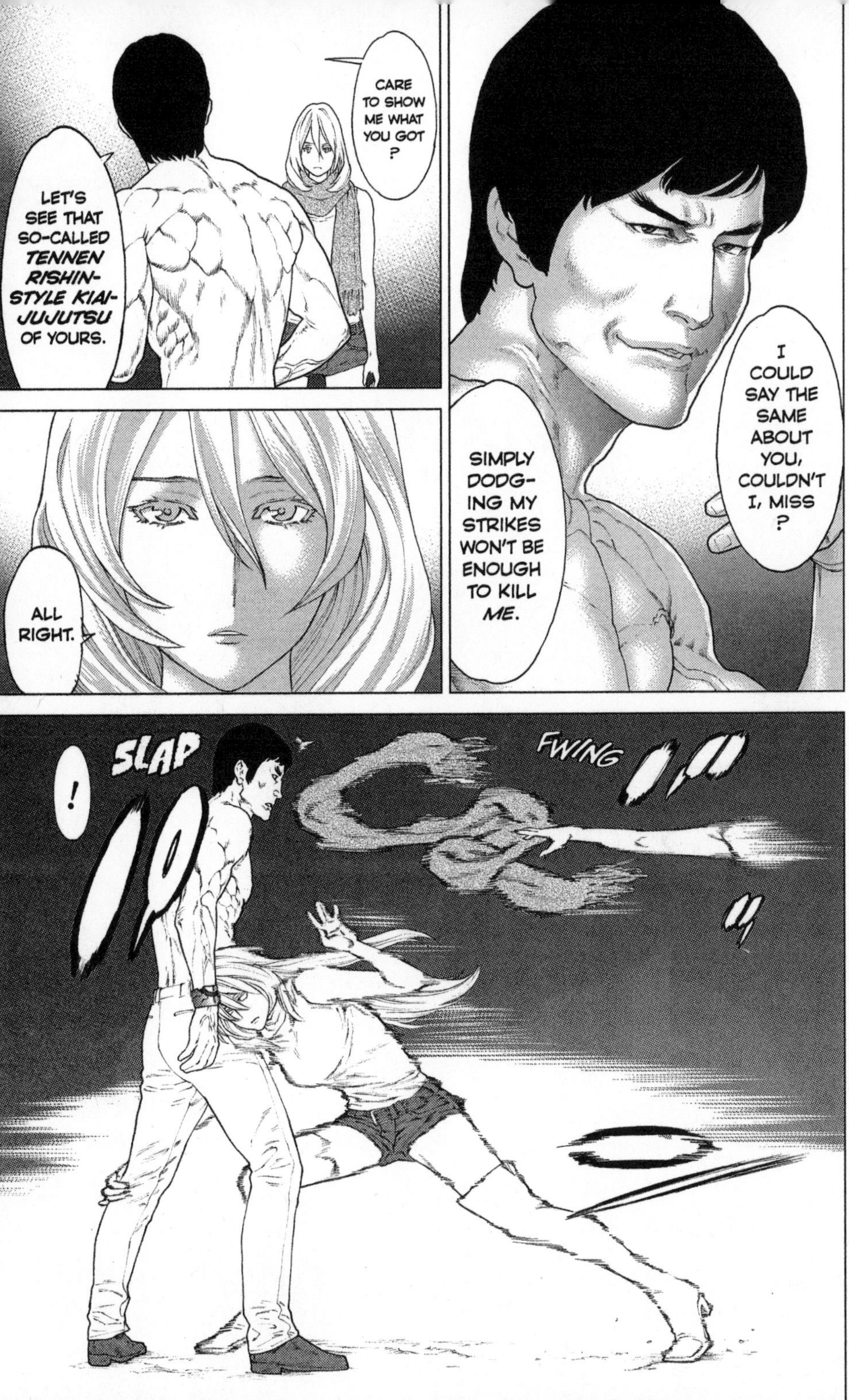
I COULD SAY THE SAME ABOUT YOU, COULDN'T I, MISS?
SIMPLY DODGING MY STRIKES WON'T BE ENOUGH TO KILL ME.
CARE TO SHOW ME WHAT YOU GOT?
LET'S SEE THAT SO-CALLED TENNEN RISHIN-STYLE KIAI-JUJUTSU OF YOURS.
ALL RIGHT.
FWING
SLAP
!

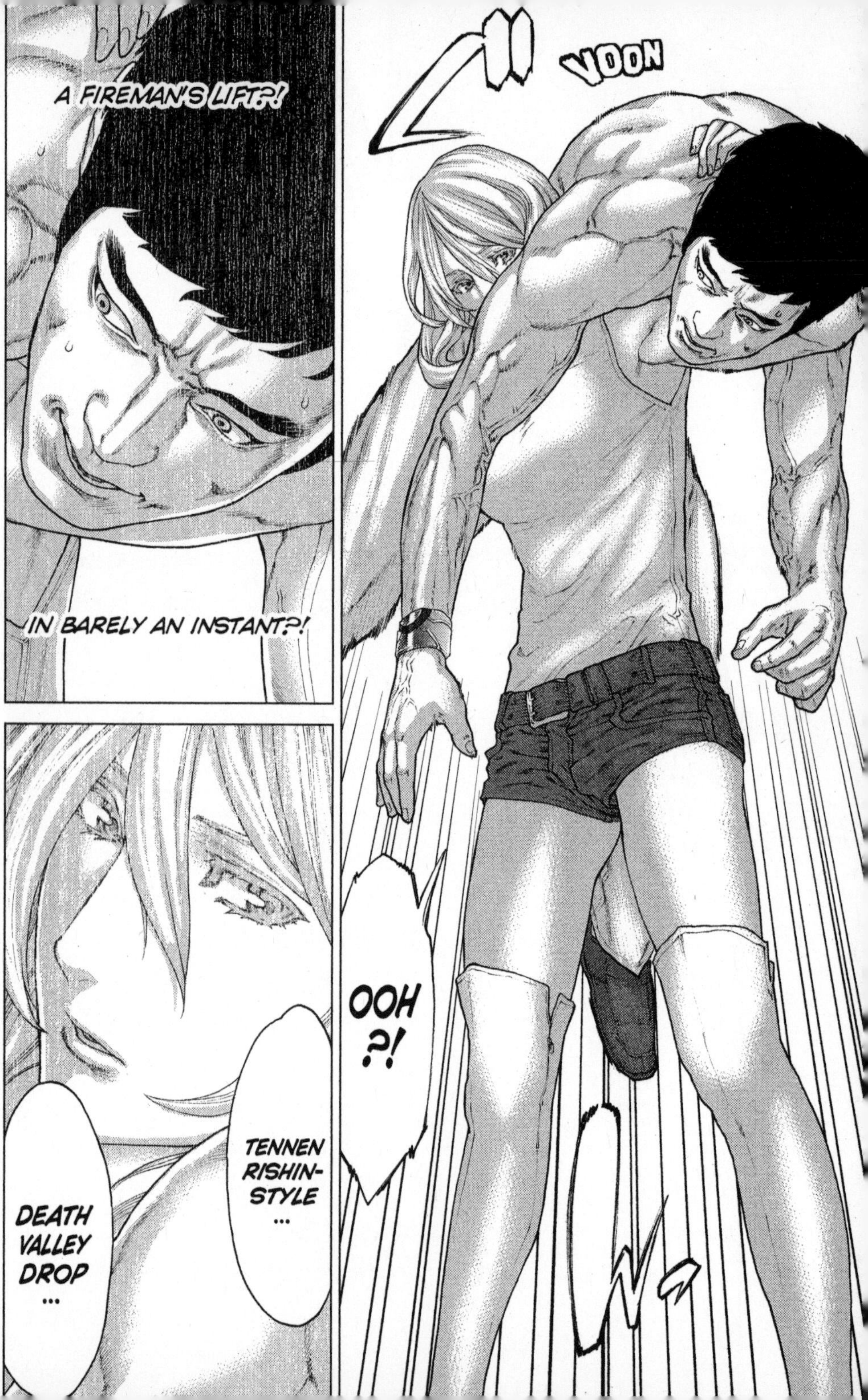
VOON
OOH ?!
A FIREMAN'S LIFT?!
IN BARELY AN INSTANT?!
TENNEN RISHIN-STYLE ...
DEATH VALLEY DROP ...

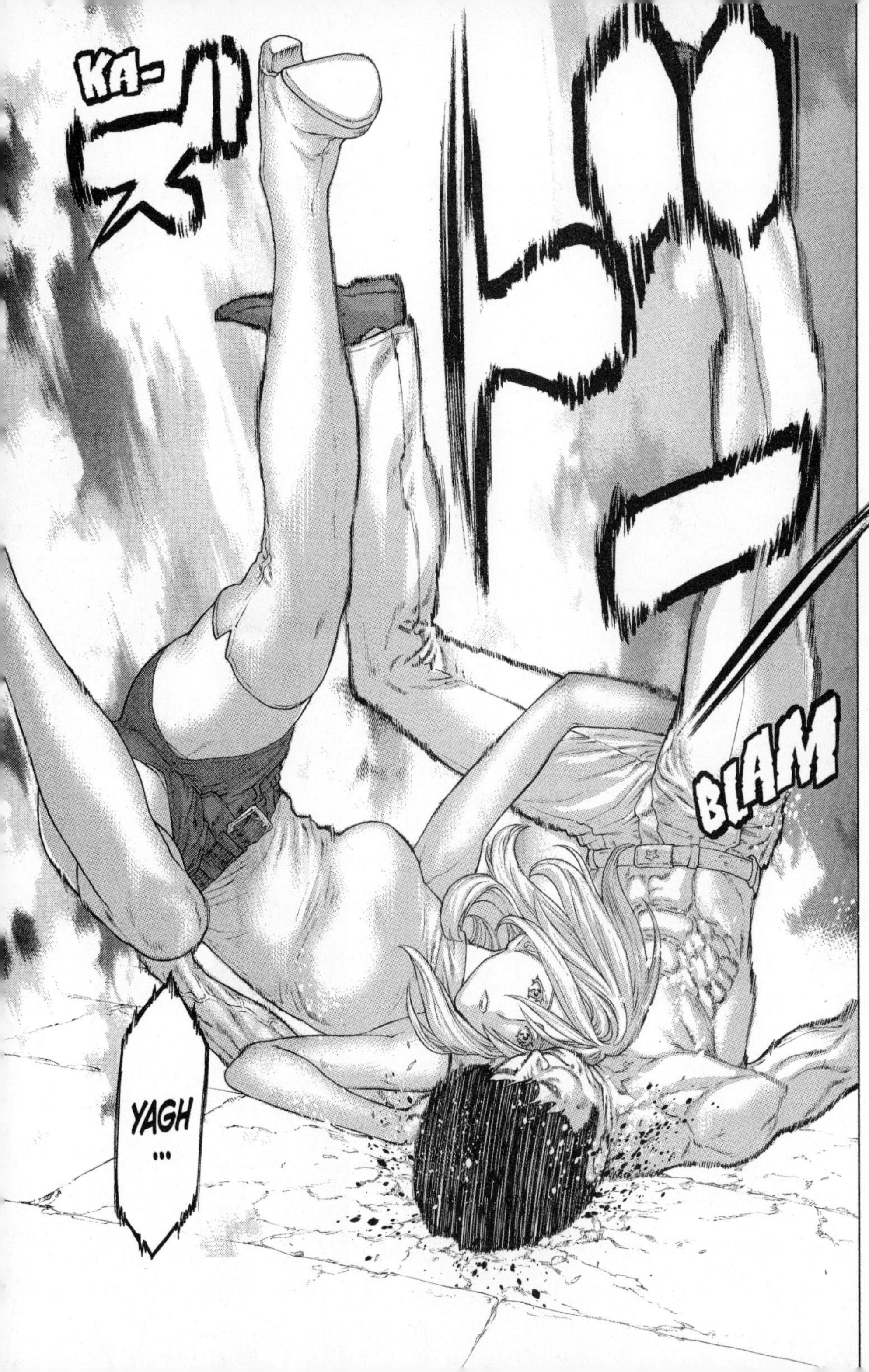
KA-
BLAM
YAGH ...

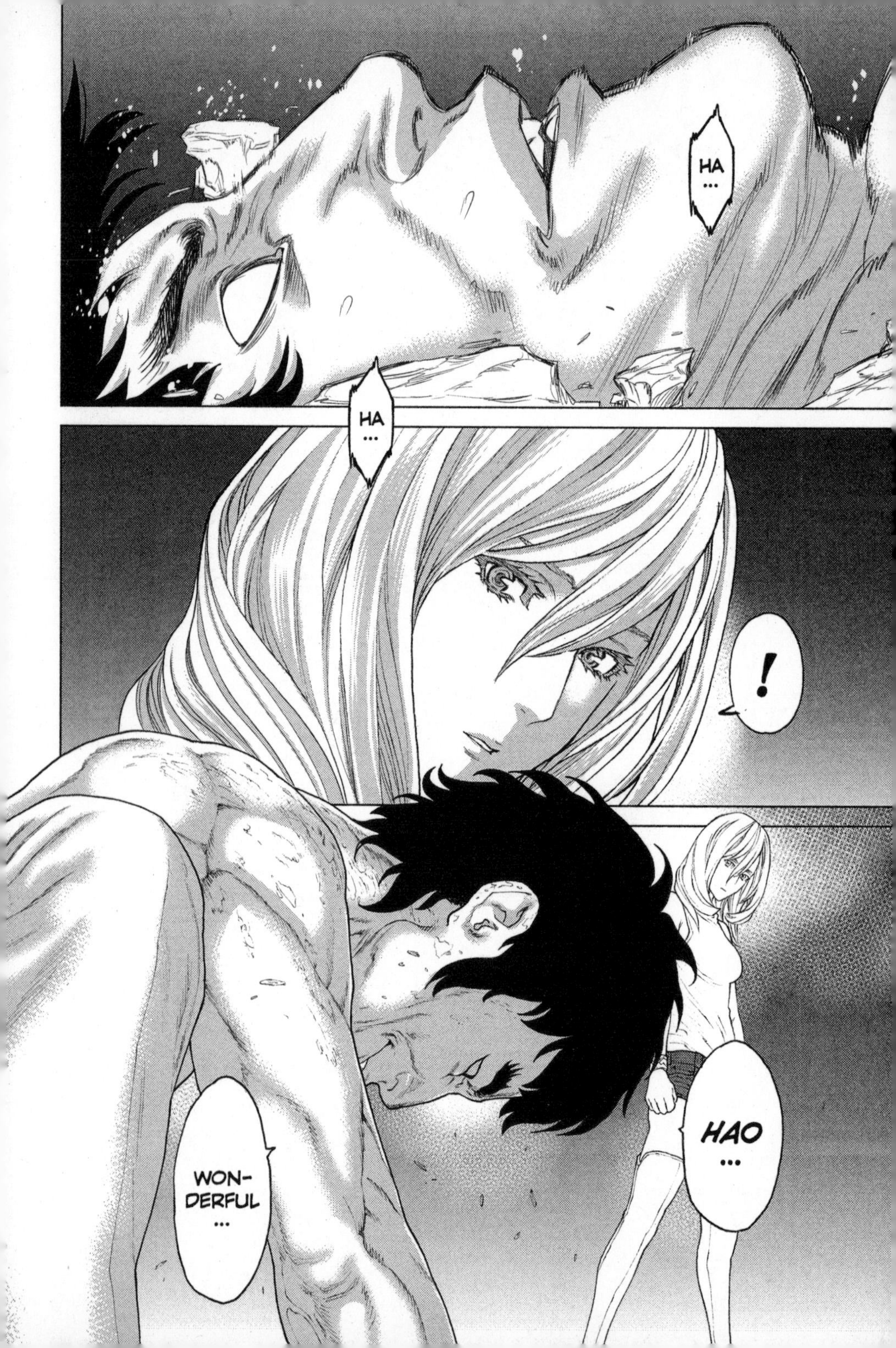
HA...
HA...
!
HAO...
WON-DERFUL...

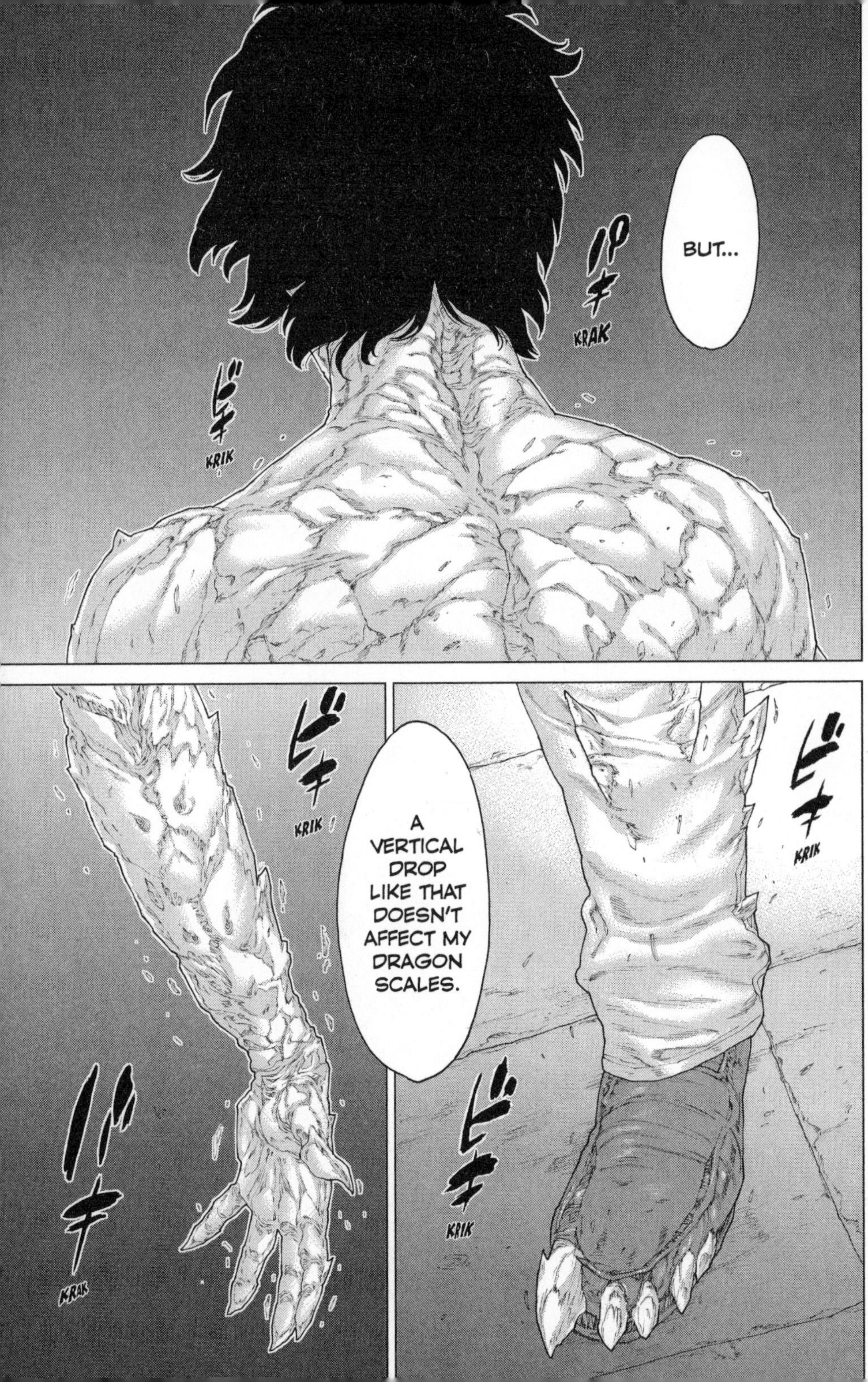
BUT...
パキ
KRAK
ビキ
KRIK
ビキ
KRIK
A VERTICAL DROP LIKE THAT DOESN'T AFFECT MY DRAGON SCALES.
ビキ
KRIK
ビキ
KRIK
バキ
KRAK

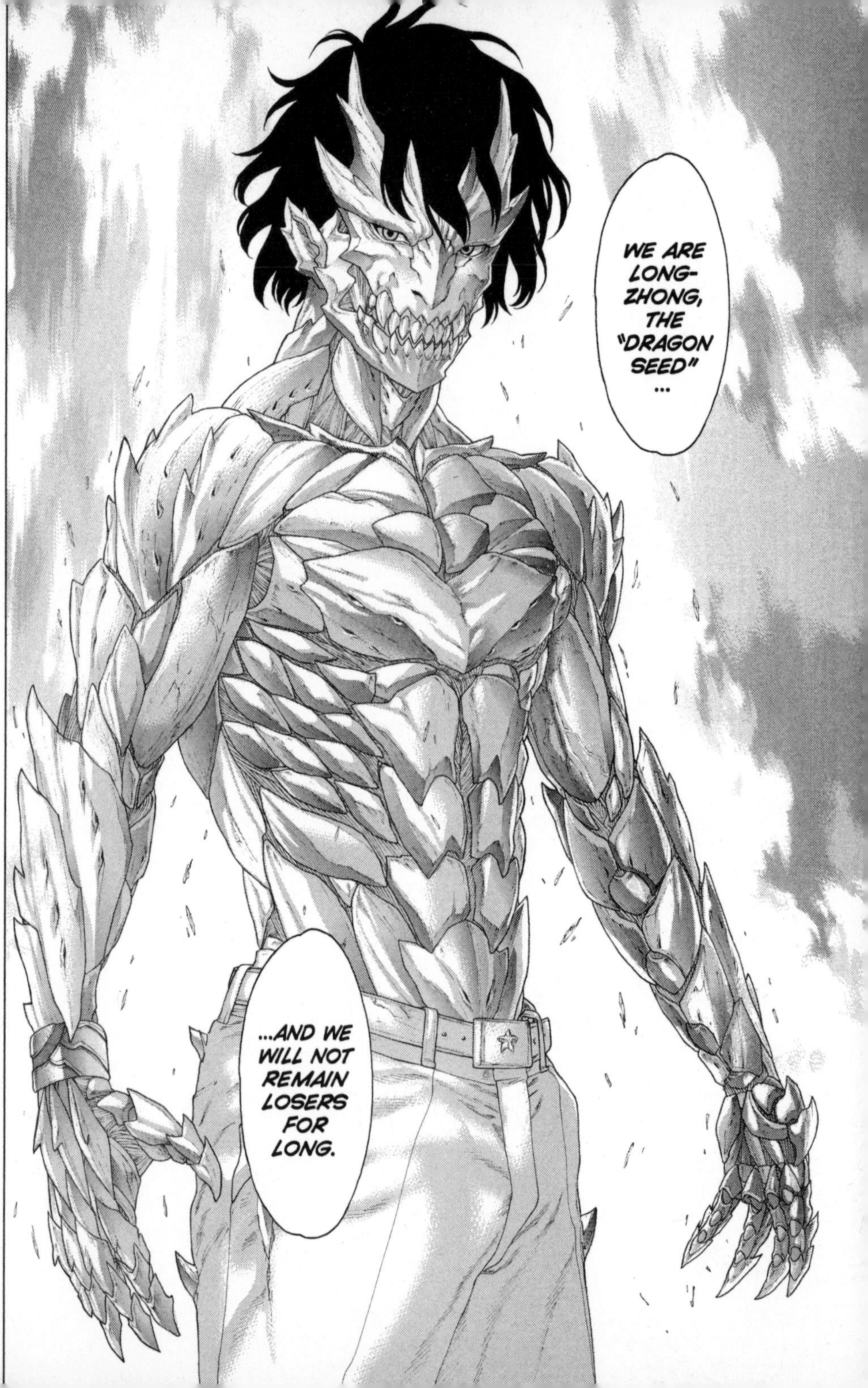
WE ARE LONG-ZHONG, THE "DRAGON SEED"...
...AND WE WILL NOT REMAIN LOSERS FOR LONG.

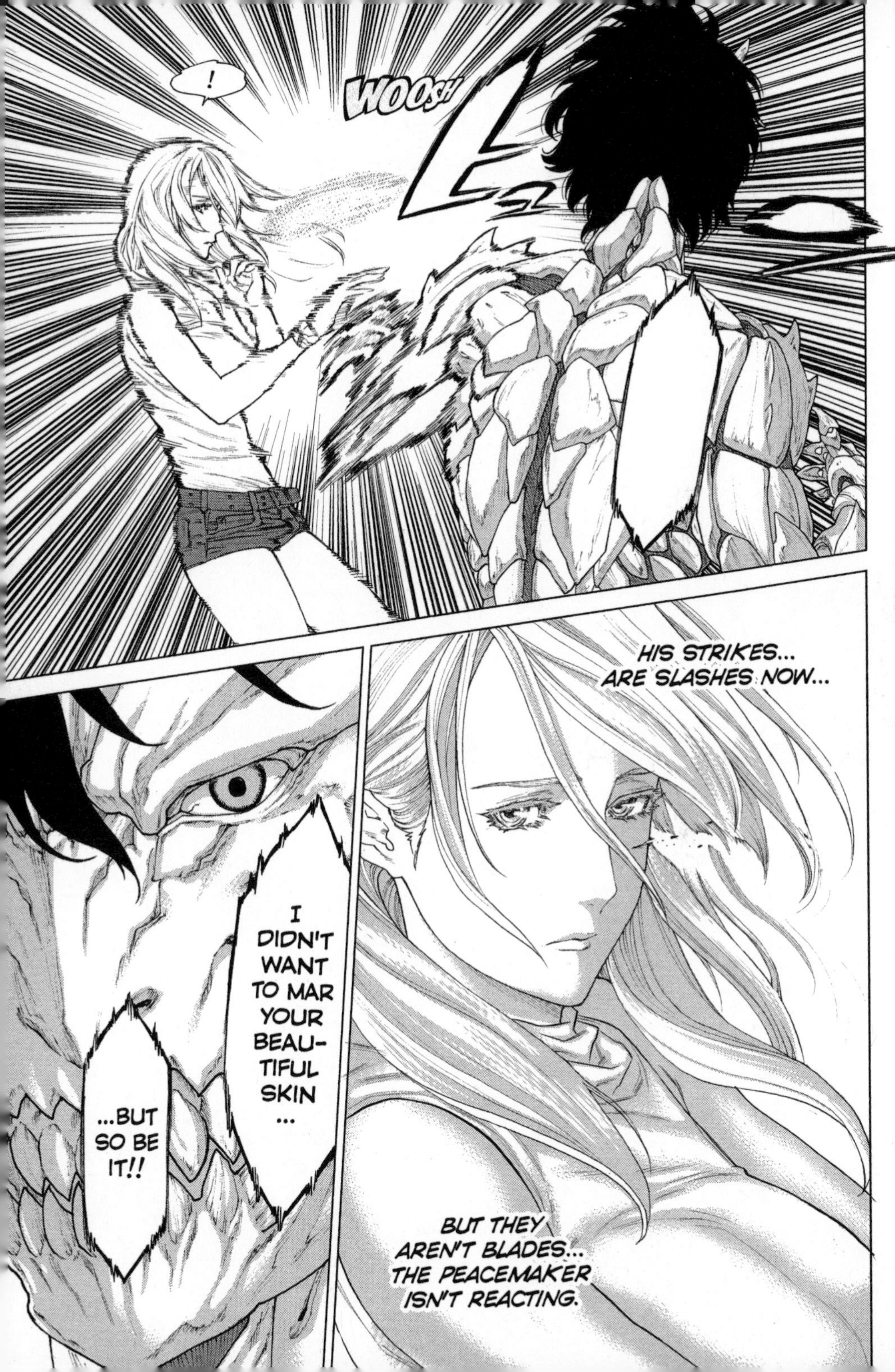
WOOSH
!
HIS STRIKES... ARE SLASHES NOW...
BUT THEY AREN'T BLADES... THE PEACEMAKER ISN'T REACTING.
I DIDN'T WANT TO MAR YOUR BEAU-TIFUL SKIN ...
...BUT SO BE IT!!

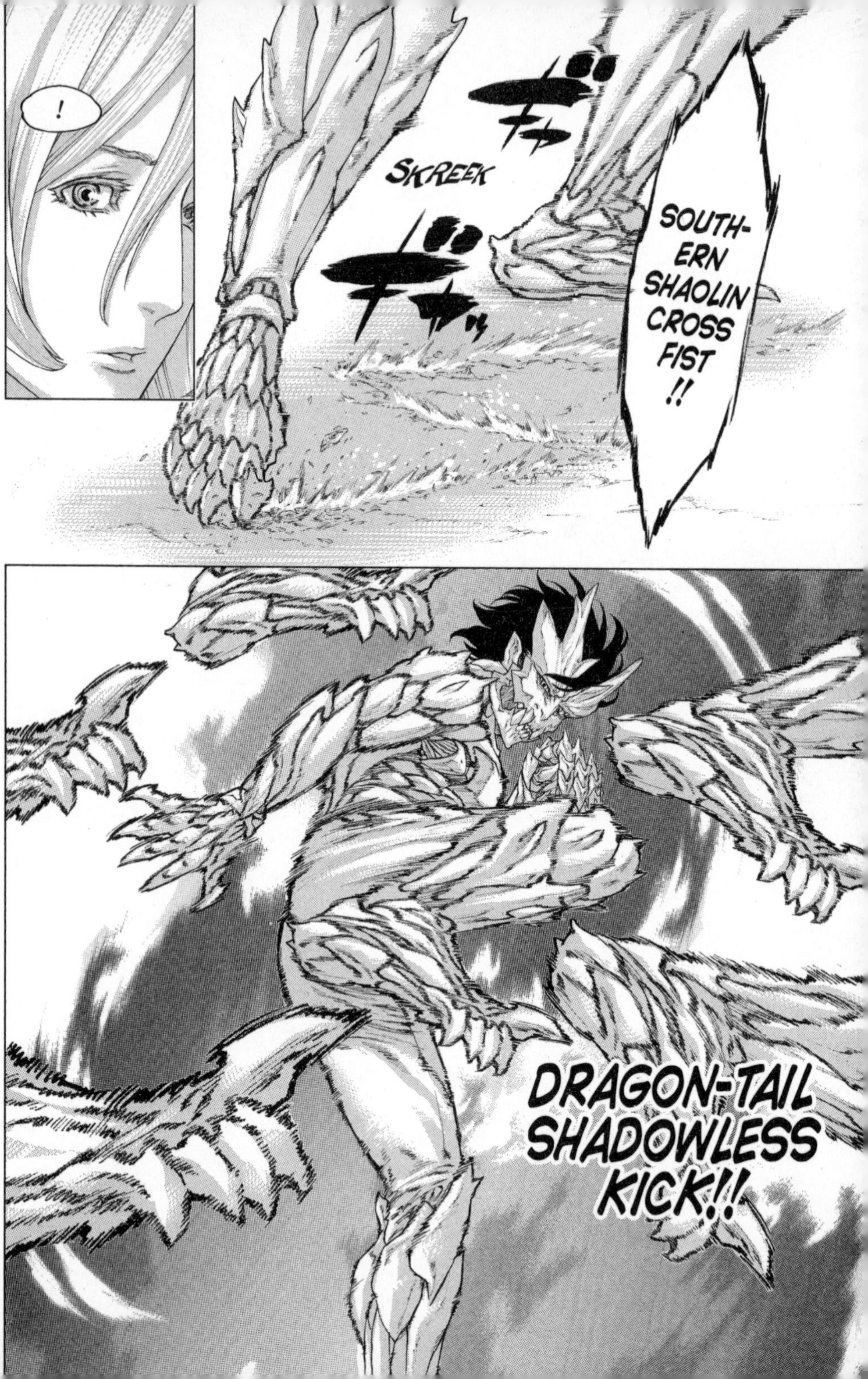
SOUTH-ERN SHAOLIN CROSS FIST!!
SKREEK
!
DRAGON-TAIL SHADOWLESS KICK!!

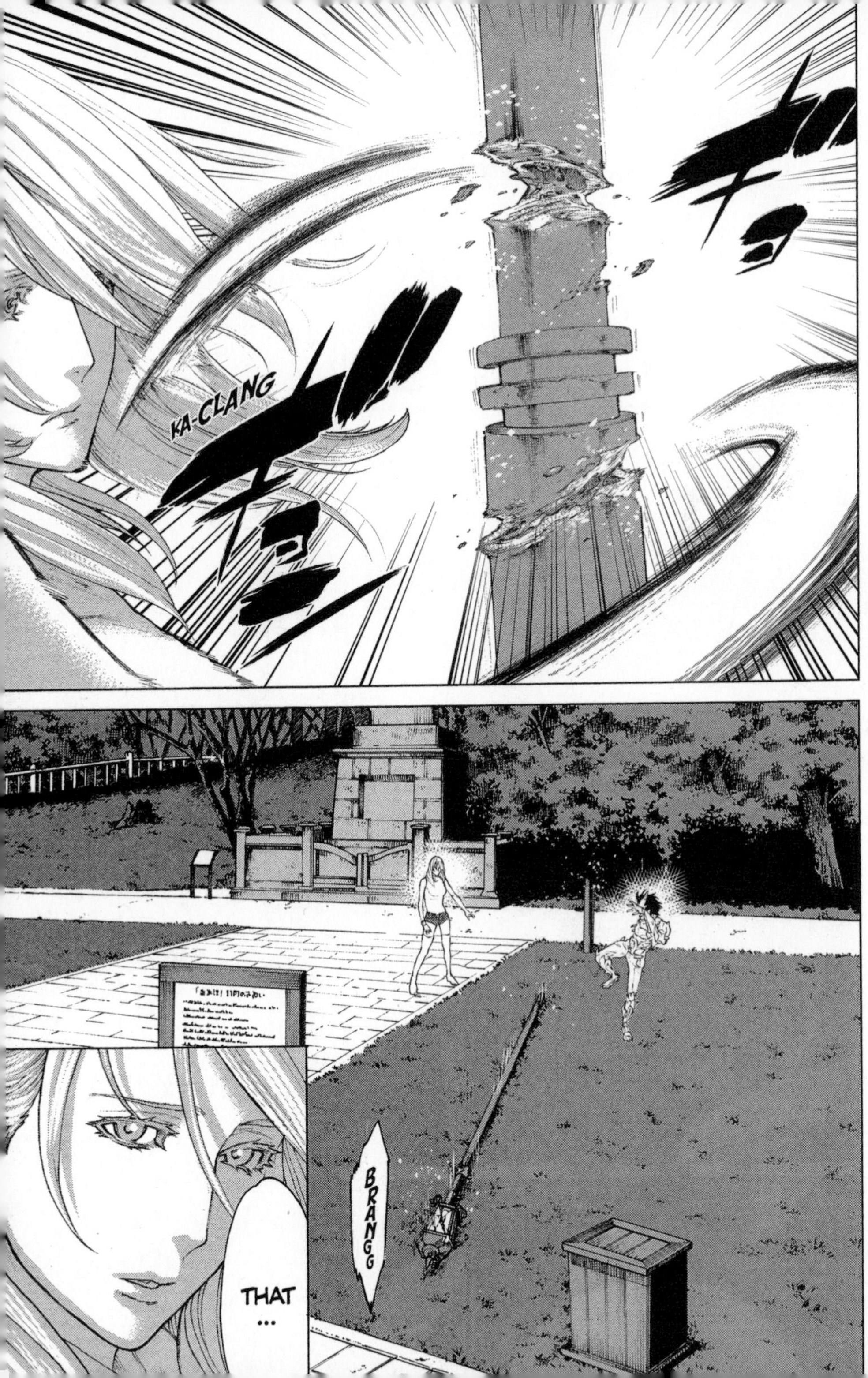
KA-CLANG
BRANGG
THAT
...

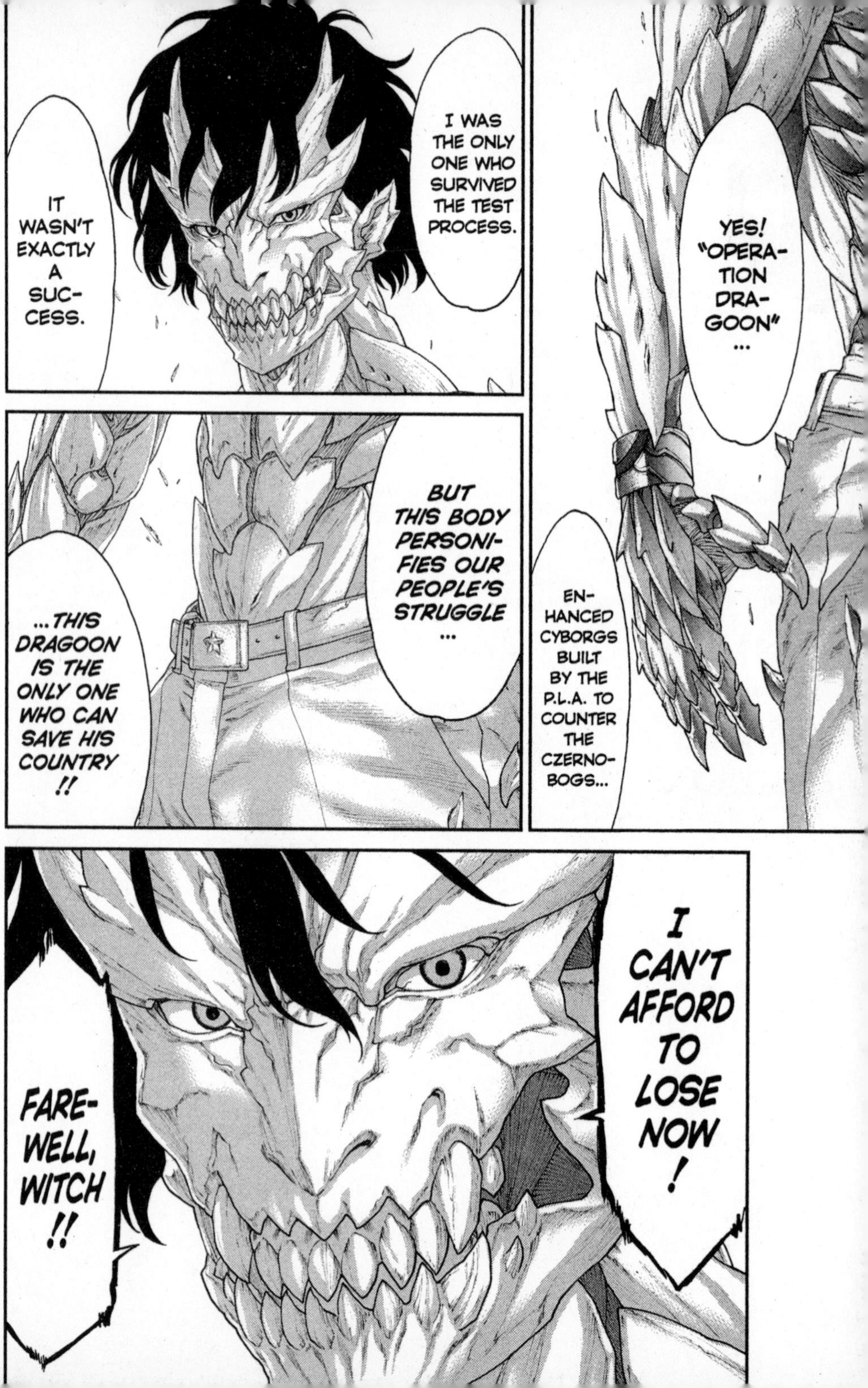
YES! "OPERATION DRAGOON"...
ENHANCED CYBORGS BUILT BY THE P.L.A. TO COUNTER THE CZERNOBOGS...
I WAS THE ONLY ONE WHO SURVIVED THE TEST PROCESS.
IT WASN'T EXACTLY A SUCCESS.
BUT THIS BODY PERSONIFIES OUR PEOPLE'S STRUGGLE...
...THIS DRAGOON IS THE ONLY ONE WHO CAN SAVE HIS COUNTRY!!
I CAN'T AFFORD TO LOSE NOW!
FAREWELL, WITCH!!

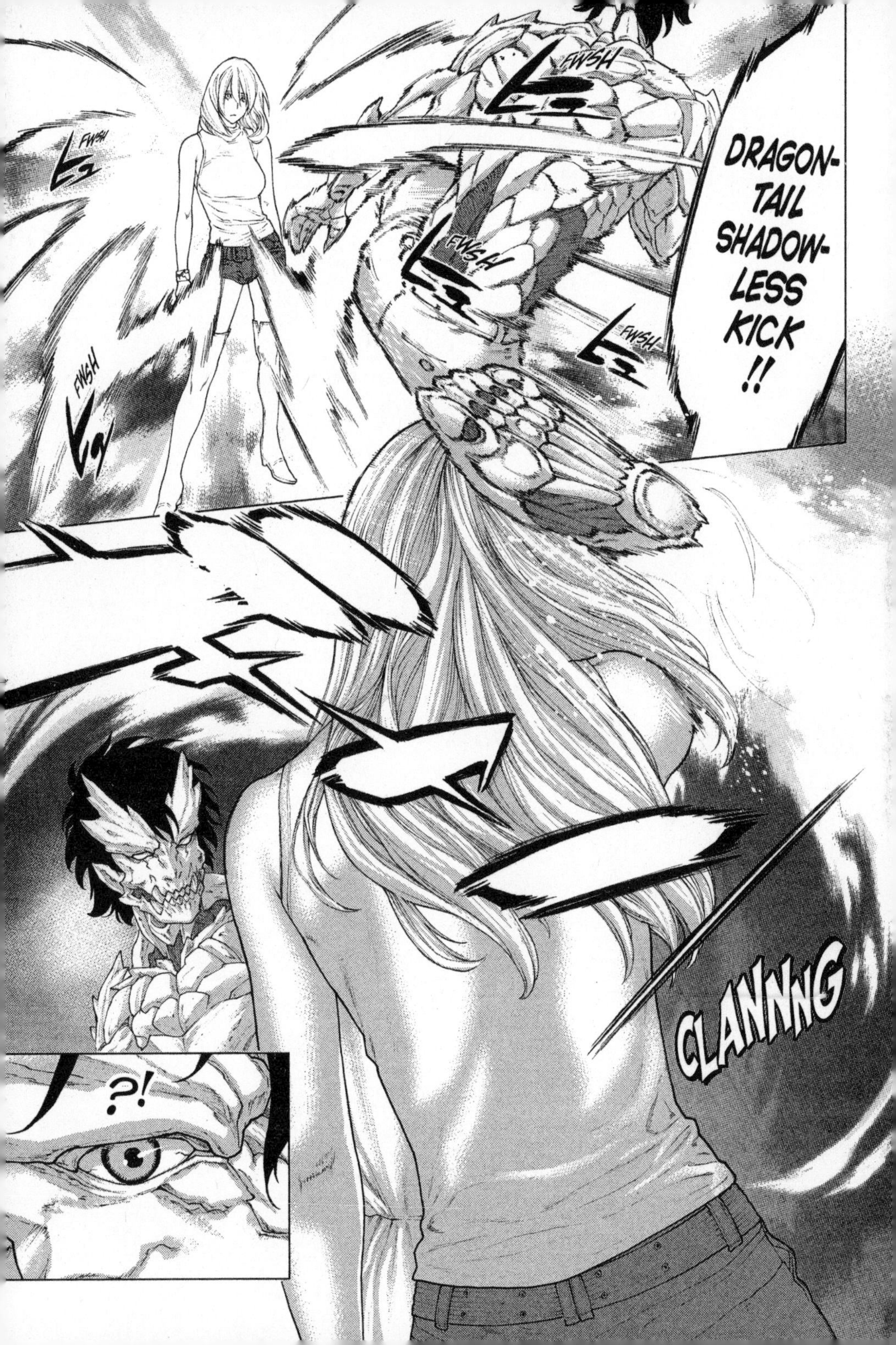
DRAGON-TAIL SHADOWLESS KICK !!
FWSH
FWSH
FWSH
FWSH
FWSH
CLANNNG
?!

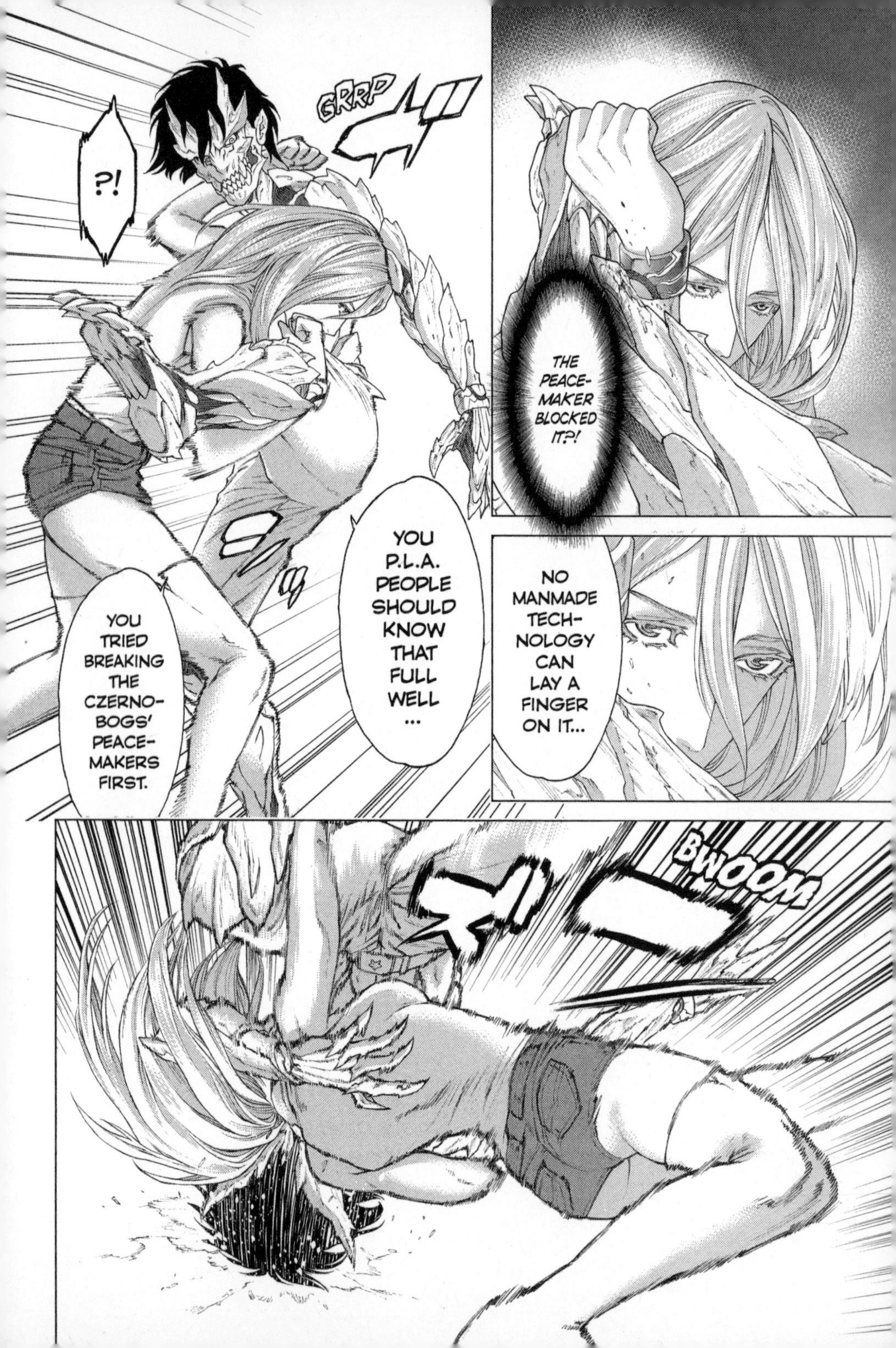
THE PEACE-MAKER BLOCKED IT?!
NO MANMADE TECH-NOLOGY CAN LAY A FINGER ON IT...
GRRP
?!
YOU P.L.A. PEOPLE SHOULD KNOW THAT FULL WELL ...
YOU TRIED BREAKING THE CZERNO-BOGS' PEACE-MAKERS FIRST.
BWOOM

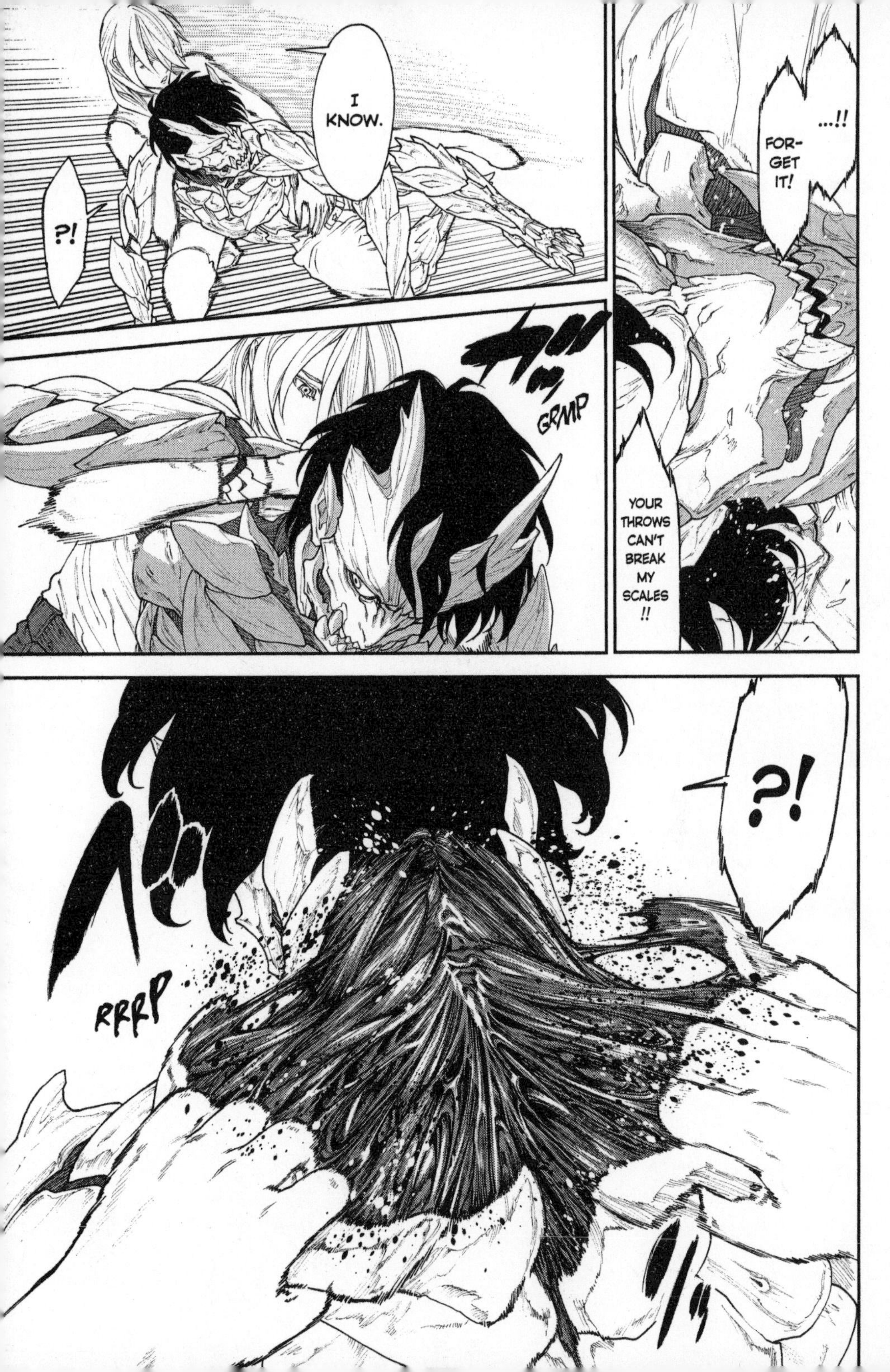
...!!
FOR-GET IT!
YOUR THROWS CAN'T BREAK MY SCALES !!
I KNOW.
?!
GRMP
?!
RRRP

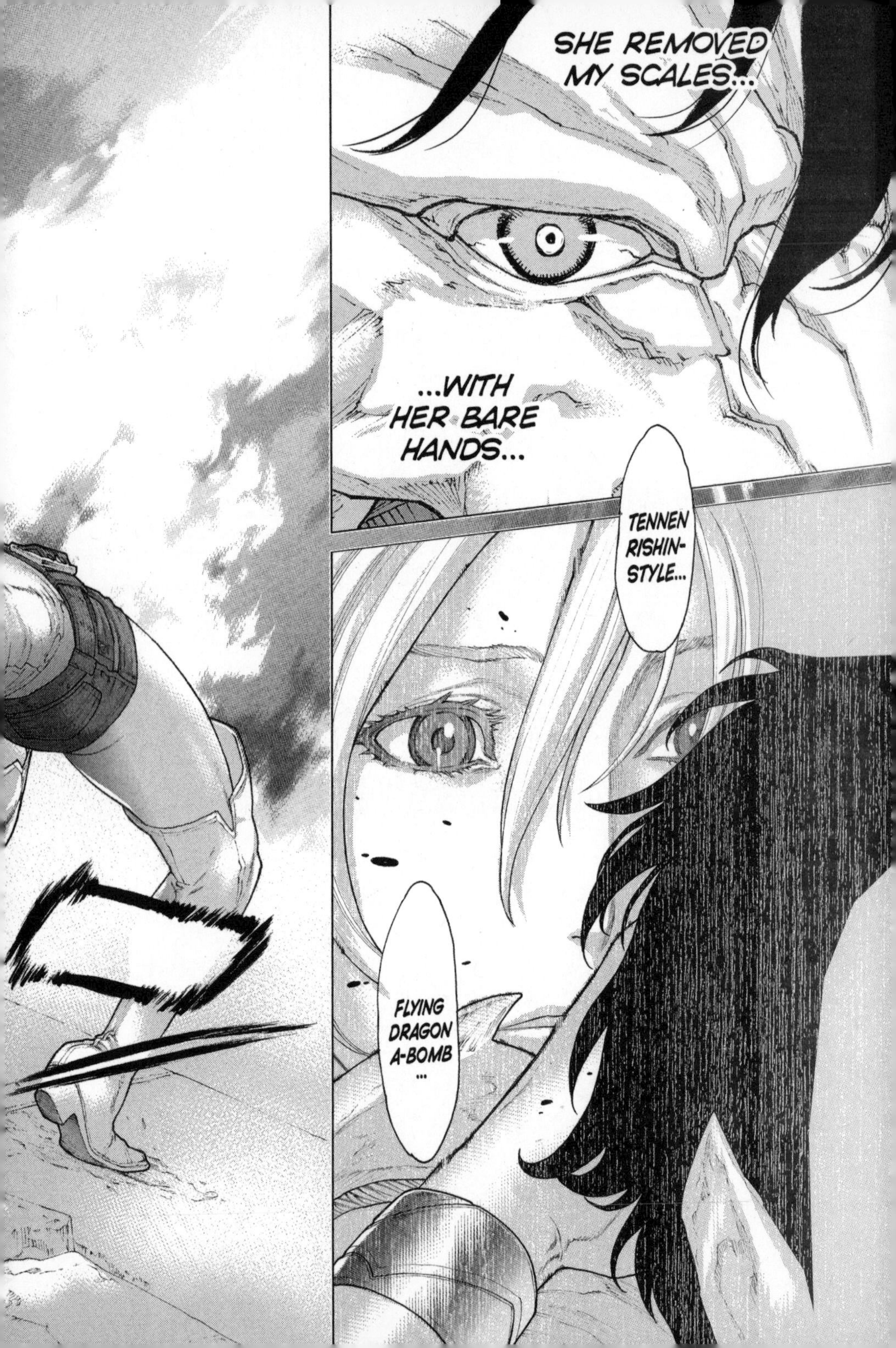
SHE REMOVED MY SCALES...
...WITH HER BARE HANDS...
TENNEN RISHIN-STYLE...
FLYING DRAGON A-BOMB ...

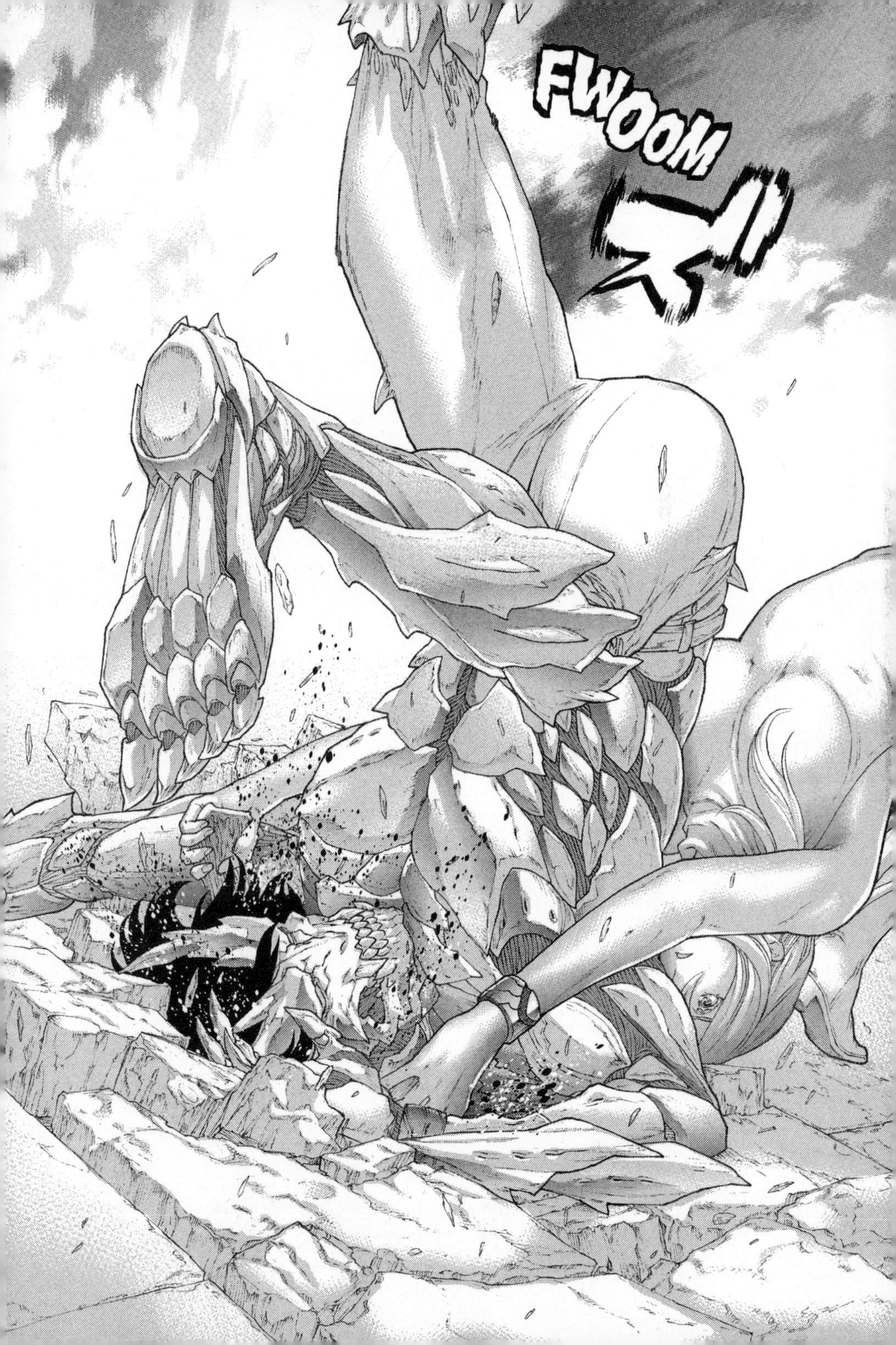
FWOOM

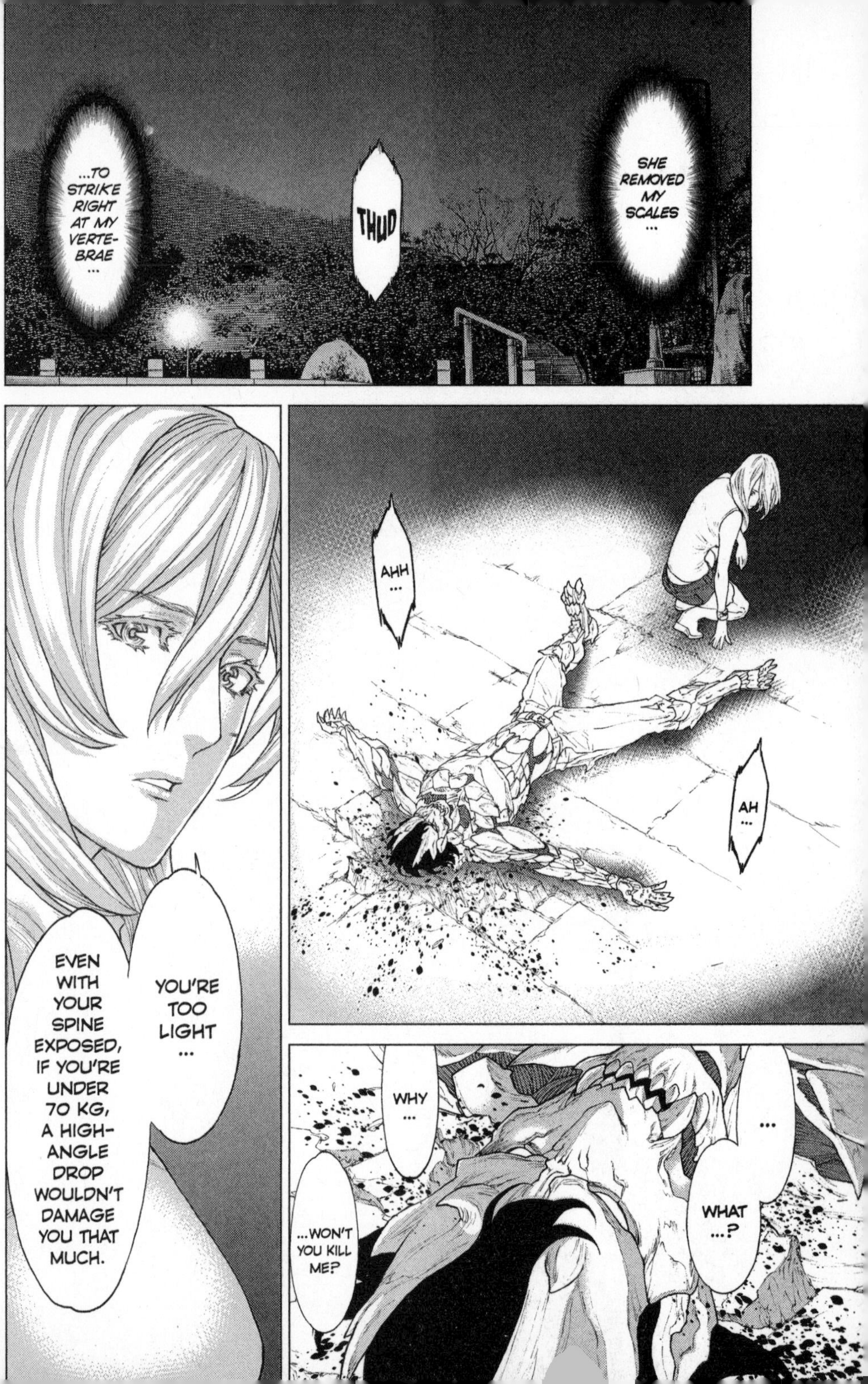
SHE REMOVED MY SCALES ...
THUD
...TO STRIKE RIGHT AT MY VERTEBRAE ...
AHH ...
AH ...
...
WHAT ...?
WHY ...
...WON'T YOU KILL ME?
YOU'RE TOO LIGHT ...
EVEN WITH YOUR SPINE EXPOSED, IF YOU'RE UNDER 70 KG, A HIGH-ANGLE DROP WOULDN'T DAMAGE YOU THAT MUCH.

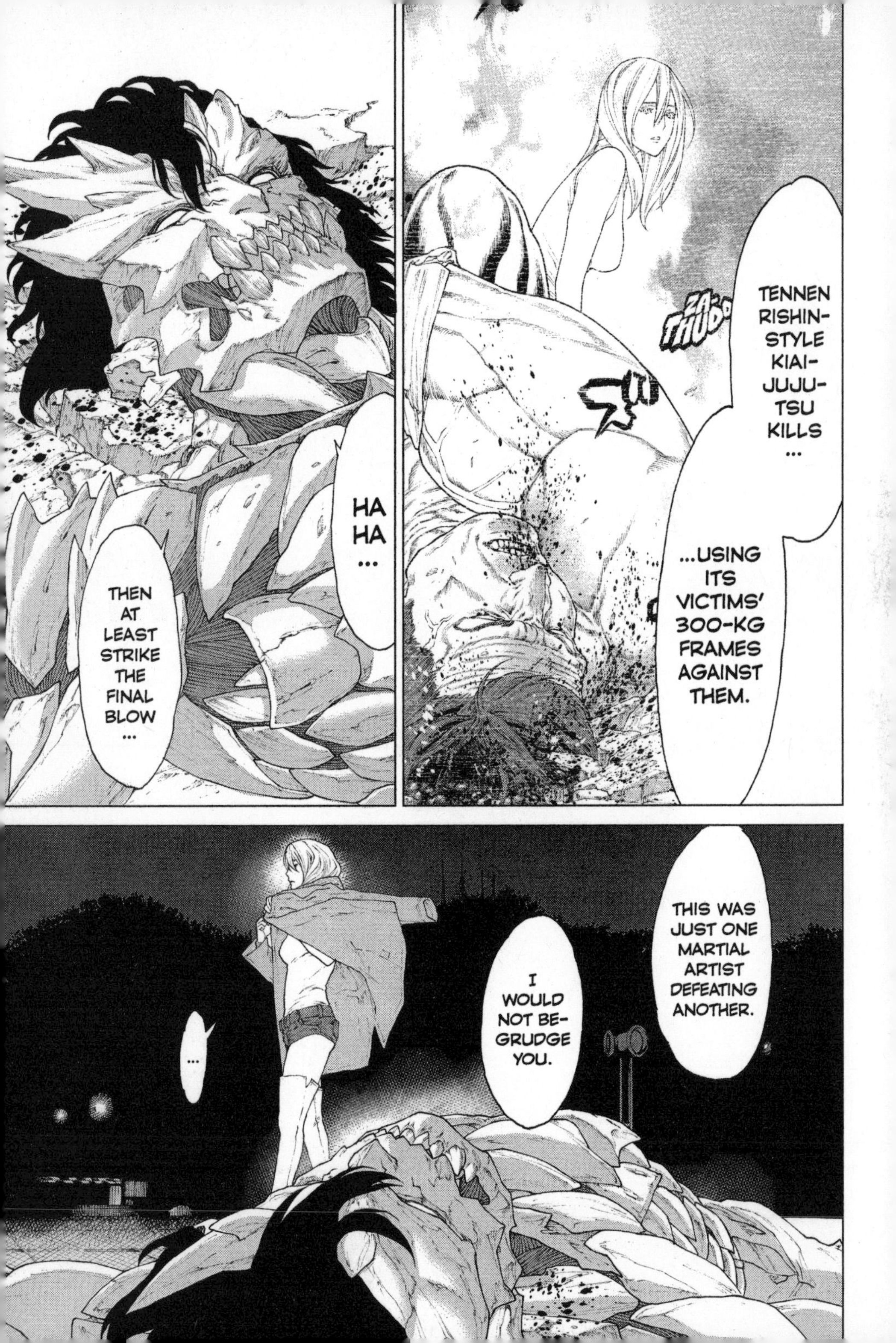
ZA-THUD
TENNEN RISHIN-STYLE KIAI-JUJUTSU KILLS...
...USING ITS VICTIMS' 300-KG FRAMES AGAINST THEM.
HA HA...
THEN AT LEAST STRIKE THE FINAL BLOW...
THIS WAS JUST ONE MARTIAL ARTIST DEFEATING ANOTHER.
I WOULD NOT BE-GRUDGE YOU.
...

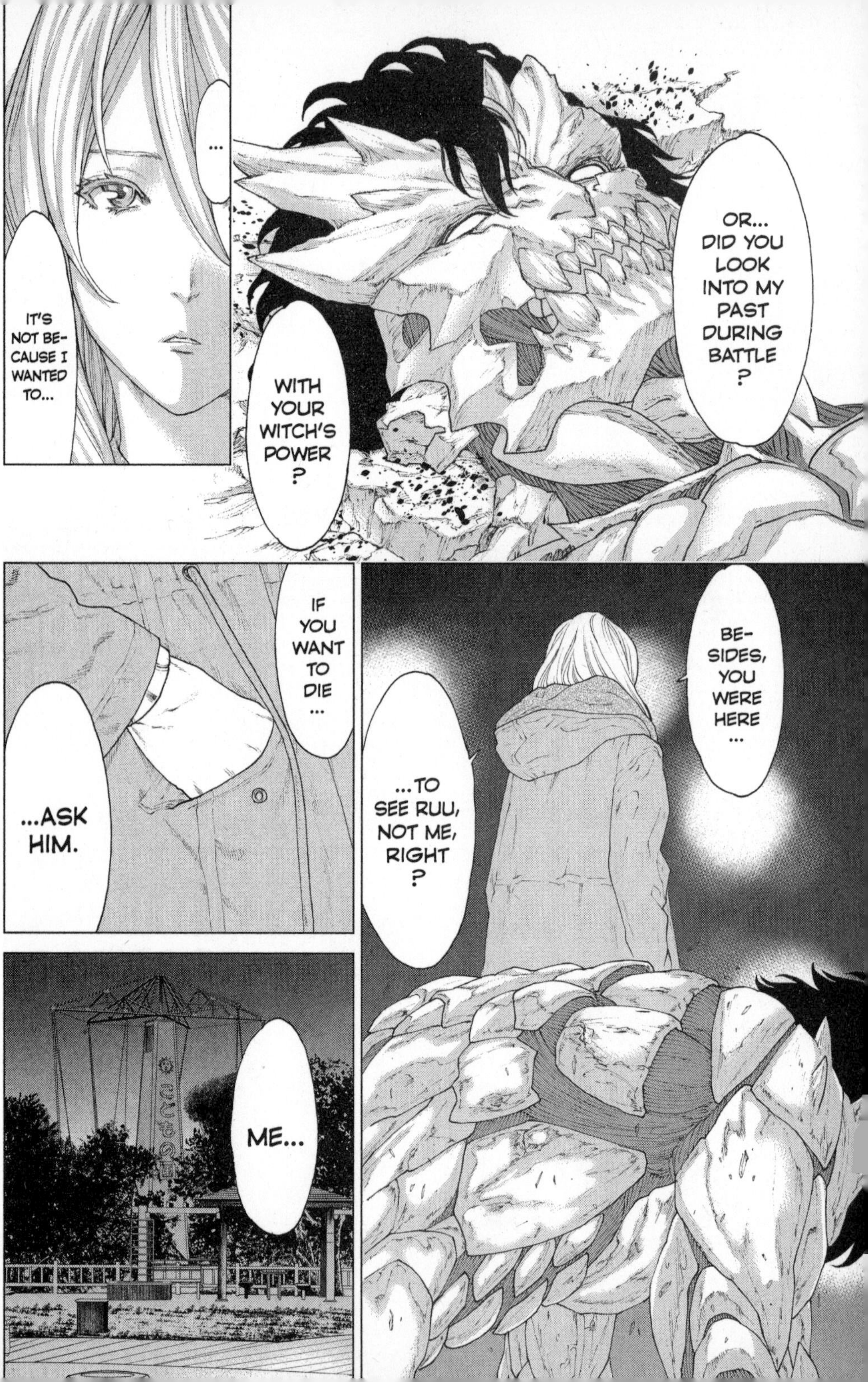
OR... DID YOU LOOK INTO MY PAST DURING BATTLE?
WITH YOUR WITCH'S POWER?
...
IT'S NOT BE-CAUSE I WANTED TO...
BE-SIDES, YOU WERE HERE...
...TO SEE RUU, NOT ME, RIGHT?
IF YOU WANT TO DIE...
...ASK HIM.
ME...

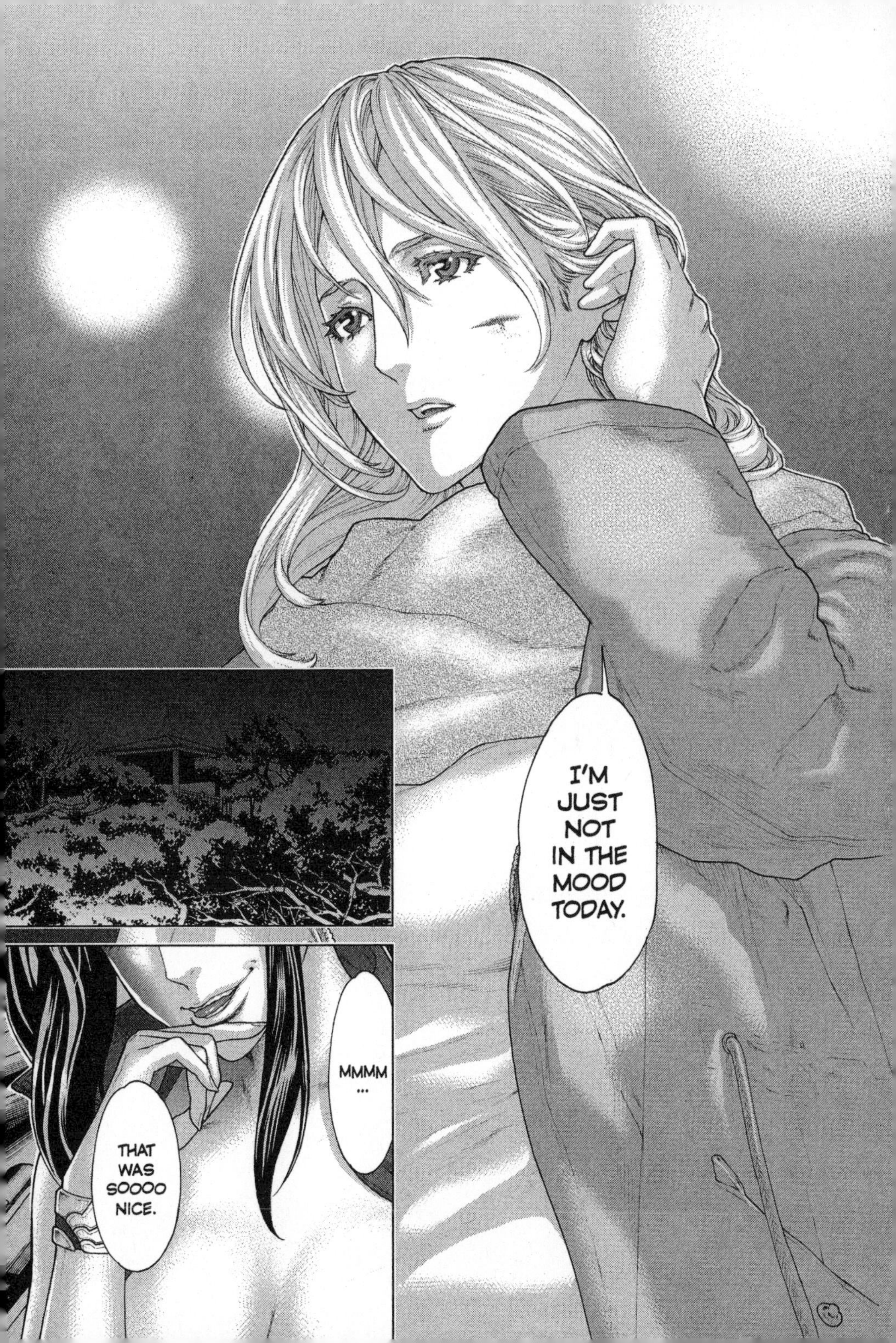
I'M JUST NOT IN THE MOOD TODAY.
MMMM...
THAT WAS SOOOO NICE.

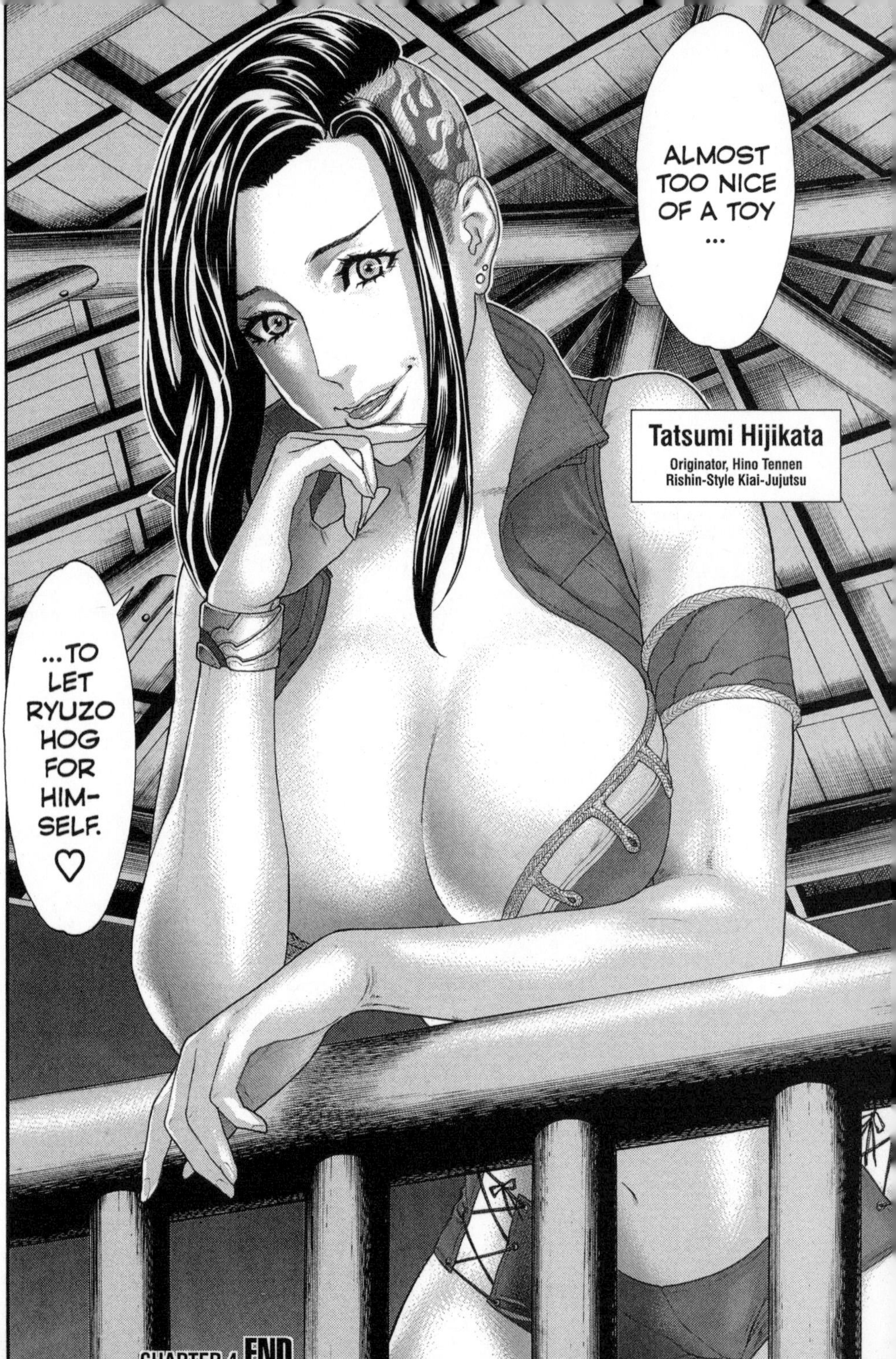
ALMOST TOO NICE OF A TOY ...
Tatsumi Hijikata
Originator, Hino Tennen Rishin-Style Kiai-Jujutsu
...TO LET RYUZO HOG FOR HIM-SELF. ♡
CHAPTER 4 END

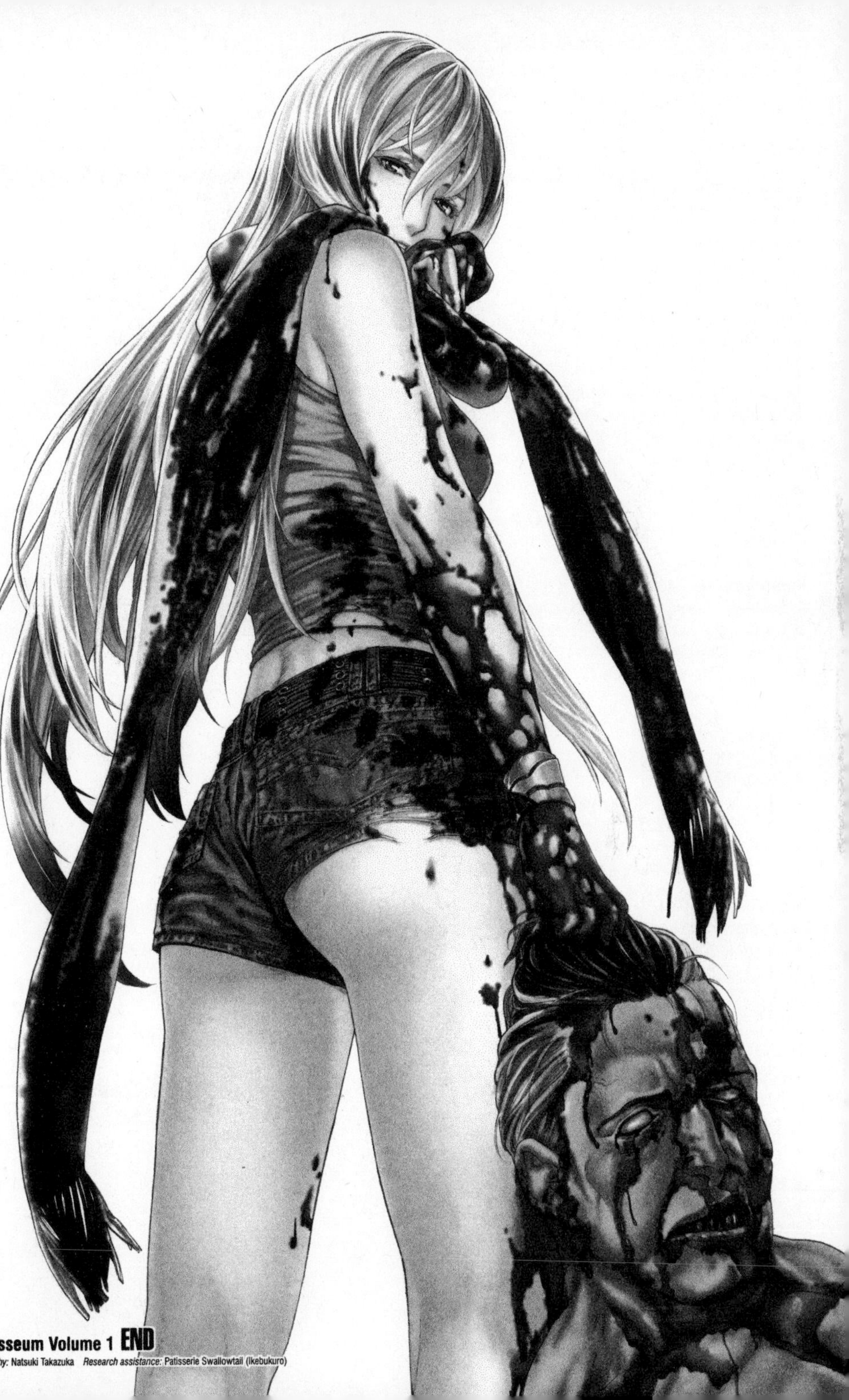

Golosseum Volume 1 **END**

Calligraphy: Natsuki Takazuka *Research assistance:* Patisserie Swallowtail (Ikebukuro)

PEACEMAKERS

A mysterious material that has brought new order—and new chaos—to the world. Said to be developed by the Greater Russian Federation, they take the form of a protective brace-let which can be worn in "normal" mode on the right hand or "extreme" mode on the left. Normal-mode bracelets (mainly worn by Czernobogs, martial artists, and important figures) teleport any bullets, blades, or other objects that damage the human body into another dimension. The effect works solely upon the wearer, and there are no time limits on its effective-ness. Extreme-mode Peacemakers (mainly worn by fighter pilots, mechanized forces, or the security forces of vital facilities) can neutralize any nuclear, biological, or chemical weapon within 100 meters of the wearer. A "human shield" of several Peacemaker wearers positioned in 100-meter inter-vals can neutralize almost any large-scale weapon. However, constant usage for over three seconds requires a subsequent cool-down period of approximately one second. The wearer can change modes by placing the insides of both wrists together, causing the bracelet to automatically switch hands.

ATTACHMENT AND REMOVAL
A Peacemaker cannot be removed from a wearer's wrist until their heart has stopped (cardio-pulmonary arrest).

NON-DEFENDABLE ATTACKS
Strikes made by bare hands. Kicks and locking techniques. Throws and choke holds executed by grasping clothing. Weapons made from human corpses or parts, such as frozen fingers. However, such weapons, when traveling at over 100 m/s, have been observed to be treated like bullets and teleported away. If clothing, shoes, or other equipment is not made or en-hanced with human skin or hair, it will be teleported into another dimension. Metal can make contact if treated with powdered bone, but the circuitry will respond to any strikes that are fast enough to cause injury.

HEALING ABILITY
External injuries like lacerations and burns, along with internal or infectious diseases, poison-ing, and more are healed within several hours to several days. However, healing in cases such as heart stoppage, cerebral contusion, organ rupture, or other situations requiring immediate surgical attention will not complete in time to save the patient.

BODY ENHANCEMENT
The Peacemaker can restore the wearer to the age and state at which their physical form was at its healthiest. It performs the necessary bodily rebuilding in approximately one year. Some younger wearers have been observed to reach maturity instead.

DEVELOPMENT PERIOD
Unknown. Images of President Putinov wearing a Peacemaker 15 years ago have been confirmed, with more found world-wide before Greater Russia began its "Peaceful War" invasion five years ago.

IMPACT ON LAW AND ORDER
Greater Russian spies are suspected of actively providing Peacemakers to criminal organizations in Japan and other nations. The creation of Peacemaker-wearing security teams of martial artists and fighters is an urgent priority.

Next volume: Our report on Czernobogs.

THE WORLD OF GOLOSSEUM
KEYWORDS & DOSSIERS ON KEY FIGURES

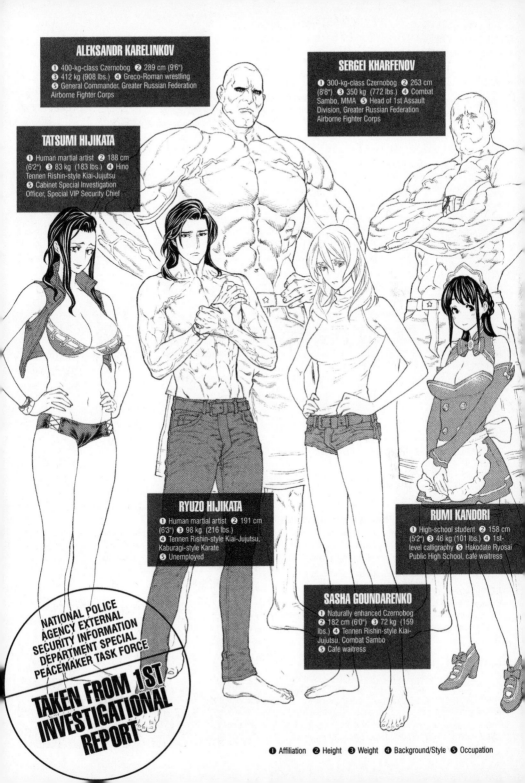

ALEKSANDR KARELINKOV
❶ 400-kg-class Czernobog ❷ 289 cm (9'6")
❸ 412 kg (908 lbs.) ❹ Greco-Roman wrestling
❺ General Commander, Greater Russian Federation Airborne Fighter Corps

SERGEI KHARFENOV
❶ 300-kg-class Czernobog ❷ 263 cm (8'8") ❸ 350 kg (772 lbs.) ❹ Combat Sambo, MMA ❺ Head of 1st Assault Division, Greater Russian Federation Airborne Fighter Corps

TATSUMI HIJIKATA
❶ Human martial artist ❷ 188 cm (6'2") ❸ 83 kg (183 lbs.) ❹ Hino Tennen Rishin-style Kiai-Jujutsu ❺ Cabinet Special Investigation Officer, Special VIP Security Chief

RYUZO HIJIKATA
❶ Human martial artist ❷ 191 cm (6'3") ❸ 98 kg (216 lbs.) ❹ Tennen Rishin-style Kiai-Jujutsu, Kaburagi-style Karate ❺ Unemployed

RUMI KANDORI
❶ High-school student ❷ 158 cm (5'2") ❸ 46 kg (101 lbs.) ❹ 1st-level calligraphy ❺ Hakodate Ryosai Public High School, café waitress

SASHA GOUNDARENKO
❶ Naturally enhanced Czernobog ❷ 182 cm (6'0") ❸ 72 kg (159 lbs.) ❹ Tennen Rishin-style Kiai-Jujutsu, Combat Sambo ❺ Café waitress

NATIONAL POLICE AGENCY EXTERNAL SECURITY INFORMATION DEPARTMENT SPECIAL PEACEMAKER TASK FORCE

TAKEN FROM 1ST INVESTIGATIONAL REPORT

❶ Affiliation ❷ Height ❸ Weight ❹ Background/Style ❺ Occupation

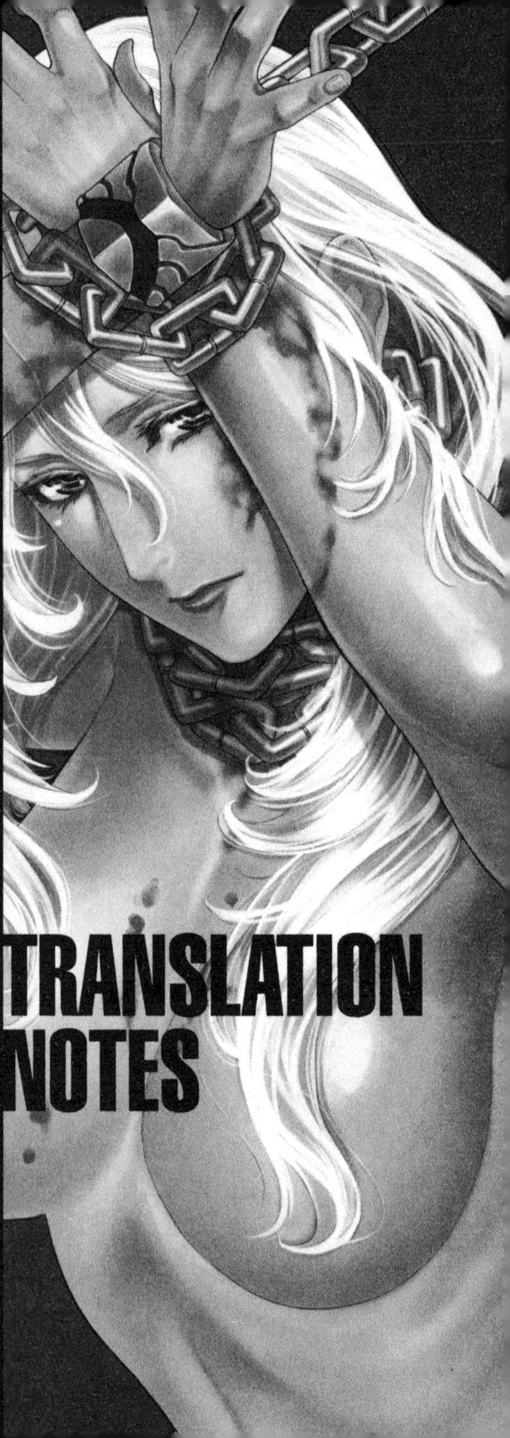

TRANSLATION NOTES

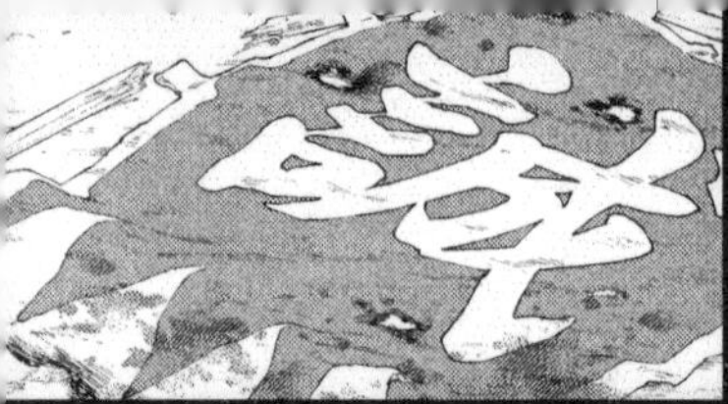

MAKOTO

The kanji for "sincerity/faithfulness" is associated with several historical groups in Japan, most notably the forty-seven ronin who, according to a well-known story told often in kabuki plays, gave their lives to defend their master in the 18th century. It is also heavily associated with the Shinsengumi, a group of samurai based in Kyoto who fought against anti-shogunate ronin in the 1860s. Toshizo Hijikata, a Shinsengumi leader, was later a military general fighting against the newly built Empire of Japan; he died in battle in 1869.

PAGE 5

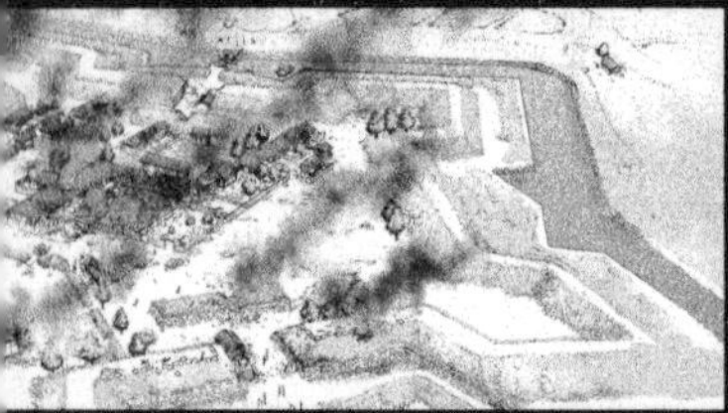

THE BATTLE OF HAKODATE

The Battle of Hakodate (1868-1869) was fought between the then-new Japanese imperial government and the final remnants of the collapsing Tokugawa shogunate, which had taken refuge on the island of Hokkaido and declared it to be an independent state, the Ezo Republic. The imperialists won, bringing a formal end to Japan's feudal era and all armed resistance to the Meiji Restoration.

Golosseum 1 is a work of fiction. Names, characters, places, and incidents are the products of the author's imagination or are used fictitiously. Any resemblance to actual events, locales, or persons, living or dead, is entirely coincidental.

A Kodansha Comics Trade Paperback Original

Published in the United States by Kodansha Comics, an imprint of Kodansha USA Publishing, LLC, New York.

Publication rights for this English edition arranged through Kodansha Ltd, Tokyo.

ISBN 978-1-63236-6-955

Original cover design by Takashi Shimoyama (Red Rooster)

Printed in the United States of America.

www.kodanshacomics.com

9 8 7 6 5 4 3 2 1
Translation: Kevin Gifford
Lettering: Evan Hayden
Editing: Ajani Oloye
Kodansha Comics edition cover design by Phil Balsman

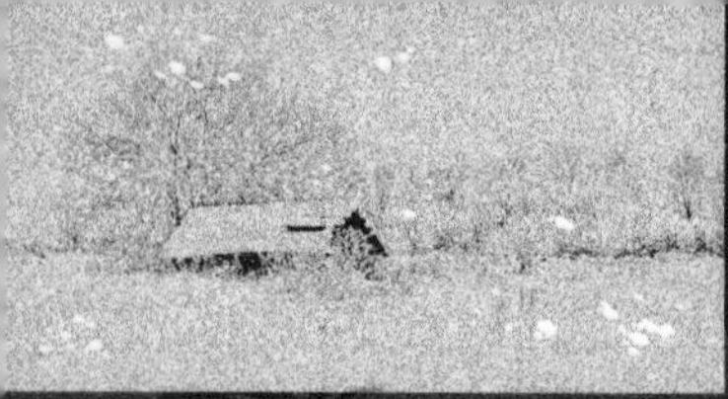

JAPANESE MILITARY STATION

Beginning in 1918, Japan dispatched their military to the Siberian province of Primorsky Krai, part of a multi-nation effort to support the White Russian forces fighting against the Bol-shevik Red Army during the Russian Civil War. The force eventually numbered 70,000 troops, bringing with them 50,000 civilians and a large Japanese cultural presence in Vladivostok and other parts of east Russia. The interven-tion, however, grew highly unpopular in Japan due to its massive cost, and the government withdrew most of its troops from the region in 1922.

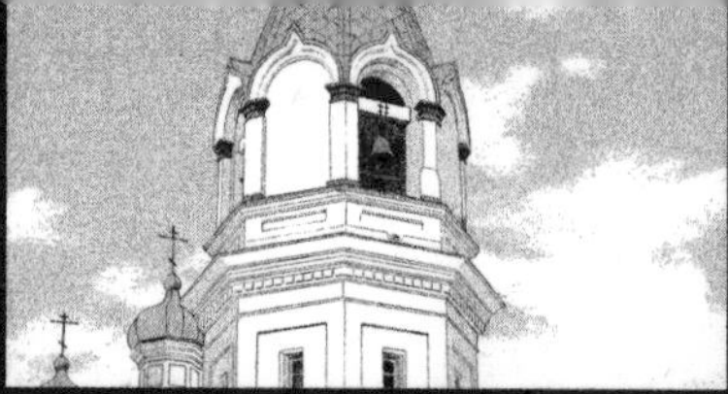

HAKODATE RUSSIAN ORTHODOX CHURCH

The building featured on this page is the Hakodate Russian Orthodox Church, first built in 1859 after the Russian Empire opened a consulate in Hakodate—just five years after Japan unlocked its borders to foreign nations. It is a popular landmark and still operates as a church today.

PAGE 129

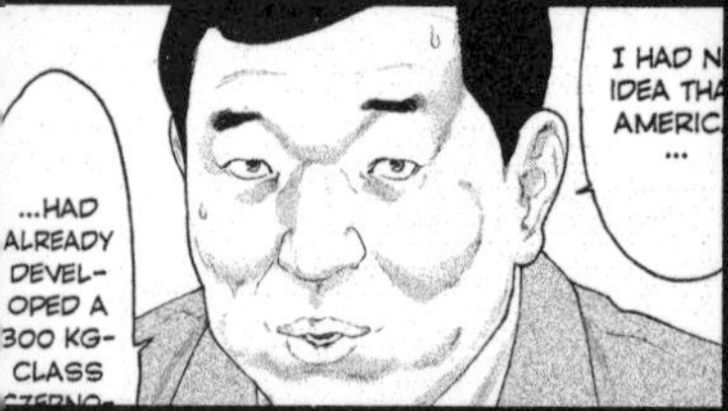
I HAD N IDEA THA AMERIC ...
...HAD ALREADY DEVEL-OPED A 300 KG-CLASS

CHIEF CABINET SECRETARY OF JAPAN

The Chief Cabinet Secretary of Japan is an ap-pointed official charged with coordinating the policies of Japan's assorted executive-branch ministries, as well as serving as the Prime Minister's press secretary. Like the Vice-President of the United States, the position is often considered a stepping stone to becoming Prime Minister, and if the PM dies or is inca-pacitated, the Chief Cabinet Secretary serves as acting PM until a new one is appointed.

PAGES 124-125

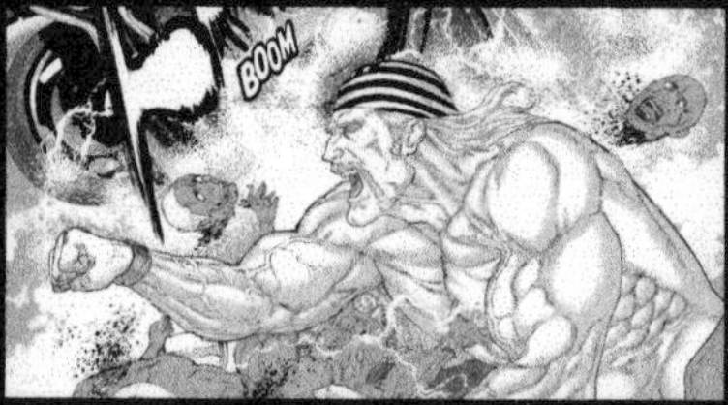
BOOM

"WHATCHA GONNA DO WHEN THE AXE SWINGS DOWN ON YOU?!!"

To many Americans, it should be obvious who Axe Bowgun takes his influence from, but Japanese pro-wrestling fans would also be aware of his influence because the personality whom Axe Bowgun is based on sometimes did matches and tours in Japan. To a Japanese fan, he is known for saying that he is "ichi-ban" (number one), which with his American accent, probably sounded like "itchy-barn" to the amusement of Japanese fans. In the Japanese edition of this manga, this scene had Axe saying "YOU!!! ICHIBURRRN!!" in English, but because it wouldn't make much sense, it was changed to something that would be more recognizable to American pro-wrestling fans.